Enlightenment and Catholicism in Europe

Enlightenment *and* Catholicism *in* Europe

A Transnational History

edited by

Jeffrey D. Burson *and* Ulrich L. Lehner

University of Notre Dame Press
Notre Dame, Indiana

Copyright © 2014 by University of Notre Dame Press
Notre Dame, Indiana 46556
www.undpress.nd.edu
All Rights Reserved

Manufactured in the United States of America

Chapter 19 is an abridged and revised version of Mark Goldie, "Alexander Geddes at the Limits of the Catholic Enlightenment," *Historical Journal* 53, no. 1 (2010): 61–86. © Cambridge University Press, reproduced with permission.

Library of Congress Cataloging-in-Publication Data

Enlightenment and Catholicism in Europe : a transnational history /
edited by Jeffrey D. Burson and Ulrich L. Lehner.
pages cm
Includes bibliographical references and index.
ISBN-13: 978-0-268-02240-2 (pbk. : alk. paper)
ISBN-10: 0-268-02240-2 (pbk. : alk. paper)
1. Catholic Church—Europe—History—18th century.
2. Enlightenment—Europe. 3. Europe—Church history—18th century.
4. Europe—Intellectual life—18th century.   I. Burson, Jeffrey D., editor of compilation.
BX1361.E55   2014
282'.409033—dc23
2013044487

∞ *The paper in this book meets the guidelines for permanence and durability of the Committee on Production Guidelines for Book Longevity of the Council on Library Resources.*

The editors of this volume wish to dedicate it to

Emmet Kennedy, Dale K. Van Kley, and David Sorkin.

Eminent among eighteenth-century scholars of their generation.

Generous and cherished mentors to us and to so many.

Contents

Introduction: Catholicism and Enlightenment,   1
Past, Present, and Future
JEFFREY D. BURSON

PART 1
Catholic Enlightenment and the Papacy

1   Pope Benedict XIV (1740–1758): The Ambivalent   41
Enlightener
MARIO ROSA

PART 2
Catholicism and the Siècle des Lumières in France and Savoy

2   Nicolas-Sylvestre Bergier (1718–1790): An Enlightened   63
Anti-*Philosophe*
JEFFREY D. BURSON

3   Giacinto Sigismondo Cardinal Gerdil (1718–1802):   89
Enlightenment as Cultural and Religious Achievement
DRIES VANYSACKER

4   Adrien Lamourette (1742–1794): The Unconventional   107
Revolutionary and Reformer
CAROLINE CHOPELIN-BLANC

5 Joseph de Maistre (1753–1821): Heir of the Enlightenment, 125
   Enemy of Revolutions, and Spiritual Progressivist
   CAROLINA ARMENTEROS

6 Hugues-Félicité Robert de Lamennais (1782–1854): 145
   Lost Sheep of the Religious Enlightenment
   CAROLINA ARMENTEROS

PART 3
Catholic Enlightenment in the Holy Roman Empire

7 Benedict Stattler (1728–1797): The Reinvention of 167
   Catholic Theology with the Help of Wolffian Metaphysics
   ULRICH L. LEHNER

8 Beda Mayr (1742–1794): Ecumenism and Dialogue with 191
   Modern Thought
   ULRICH L. LEHNER

PART 4
Catholicism, Enlightenment, and Habsburg Europe

9 Franz Stephan Rautenstrauch (1734–1785): Church 209
   Reform for the Sake of the State
   THOMAS WALLNIG

10 Johann Pezzl (1756–1823): Enlightenment in the 227
   Satirical Mode
   RITCHIE ROBERTSON

PART 5
Varieties of Italian Catholic Enlightenment

11 Lodovico Antonio Muratori (1672–1750): Enlightenment 249
   in a Tridentine Mode
   PAOLA VISMARA

12   Antonio Genovesi (1713–1769): Reform through   269
Commerce and Renewed Natural Law
NICCOLÒ GUASTI

13   Maria Gaetana Agnesi (1718–1799): Science and Mysticism   289
MASSIMO MAZZOTTI

PART 6
Catholicism, Enlightenment, and the Iberian States

14   Benito Jerónimo Feijoo y Montenegro (1676–1764):   309
Benedictine and Skeptic Enlightener
FRANCISCO SÁNCHEZ-BLANCO

15   Josep Climent i Avinent (1706–1781): Enlightened   327
Catholic, Civic Humanist, Seditionist
ANDREA J. SMIDT

PART 7
Transnational Trajectories: The Intersection of Irish, French, Italian, and Habsburg Developments

16   Ruggiero Boscovich (1711–1787): Jesuit Science in an   353
Enlightenment Context
JONATHAN A. WRIGHT

17   Luke Joseph Hooke (1714–1796): Theological Tolerance   371
in an Apologetic Mold
THOMAS O'CONNOR

PART 8
Catholicism in Protestant Territorial-Dynastic States: Scottish and English Enlightenment Variations

18   Andrew Michael Ramsay (1686–1743): Catholic   391
Freethinking and Enlightened Mysticism
GABRIEL GLICKMAN

19   Alexander Geddes (1737–1802): Biblical Criticism,   411
     Ecclesiastical Democracy, and Jacobinism
     MARK GOLDIE

PART 9
The Polish Catholic Enlightenment

20   Stanisław Konarski (1700–1772): A Polish Machiavelli?   433
     JERZY LUKOWSKI

21   Hugo Kołłątaj (1750–1812): The Revolutionary Priest   455
     ANNA ŁYSIAK-ŁĄTKOWSKA

List of Contributors   473

Index of Names   475

Introduction

Catholicism and Enlightenment, Past, Present, and Future

JEFFREY D. BURSON

The paradigm of "Catholic Enlightenment" originally derives from a milieu shaped by two events: German scholarly debates stimulated by the aftermath of the *Kulturkampf* in the German *Reich,* and much later, the interest in eighteenth-century reform Catholicism stimulated by Vatican II (1962–1965). Nevertheless, the future of the scholarship of Catholic Enlightenment or Enlightened Catholicism—interrelated concepts at the heart of this volume—reaches well beyond such history. What follows is an attempt to ignite broader interest in Catholic Enlightenment tendencies among mainstream historians, literary scholars, and historical theologians by further redefining the history of Enlightened Catholicism and integrating it into the dynamism now characteristic of eighteenth-century and Enlightenment studies as a whole. This volume represents the collaborative endeavor of nearly two dozen authors whose specializations range from history to historical theology, philosophy, and literature. All have studied Enlightened Catholicism among clergy and laity in France, the Iberian states and empires, Ireland, the United Kingdom, the Habsburg lands, Poland, the Italian states, and the Holy Roman Empire. Some of this research, while groundbreaking, has not been readily accessible in English to graduate students or more experienced researchers seeking to orient themselves to new developments within Catholic Enlightenment studies. Currently, no single publication exists for the purpose of introducing advanced undergraduates, graduate students, and young scholars to the complex phenomenon of Catholic Enlightenment thought. This volume will do just that by integrating the exciting interdisciplinary and multicultural research on various movements and personalities in the form of short biographies in context. We hope that future students and researchers will find this volume useful as an introduction to the field in transnational, comparative, and multidisciplinary perspective. The book is by no means definitive; instead it recommends a new beginning with all of the perils and promise that entails.

Catholic Enlightenment: The Etiology of a Concept

Only by charting a course through the history of Catholic Enlightenment scholarship to date will the outlines of a more transnational, more nuanced perspective on Catholicism and Enlightenment emerge. The notion of Catholic Enlightenment originally arose among academic historians of the early twentieth century, who traversed the course mapped out by Sebastian Merkle's 1909 work on the history of the eighteenth-century Catholic Church of the Holy Roman Empire. Merkle sought to rescue the Enlightenment from what was then the very common conservative charge that it had been responsible for the revolutionary era that crested in 1848. This prevalent Counter-Enlightenment Catholic perspective against which Merkle's scholarship reacted derived from the ultramontanist critique of Enlightenment. This critique had presumed that the skeptical and critical spirit of the eighteenth century had led ineluctably toward the modern atheism and anti-Catholicism against which the Catholic Church under the pontificates of Pius IX and Leo XIII joined battle. Merkle's

Catholic Enlightenment thereby commenced as a debate largely confined, at least at first, to early twentieth-century German Catholic historical and theological scholarship. The debate is relevant nonetheless to the broader historiography of the eighteenth century as a whole because Merkle's concept was quickly swept into early twentieth-century historical scholarship alongside increasingly politicized debates over the heterodoxy (or not) of the Enlightenment project relative to the understanding of the late nineteenth-century Catholic Church.

To a great extent, moreover, Merkle's early study of Catholic Enlightenment led to a rather more subdued continuation of the fractiousness engendered by the *Kulturkampf* in the new German Empire. In response to the revolutions of 1848, the later pontificate of Pius IX shaped an era of Catholic history that was inimical to "progress, liberalism, and modern civilization," all of which Pius soundly censured in the papal "Syllabus of Errors" (1854). Liberalism, modernism, and nationalism were additionally indicted in the aftermath of the First Vatican Council (1870), when the doctrine of papal infallibility was formally codified and promulgated. This newly stark counterrevolutionary tendency contrasted with the complex situation prevailing within the German Empire after 1871. The Roman Catholic Church still dominated the administration of education and marital laws throughout Catholic regions of the new empire, and German liberals grew ever more concerned by the impact of the church's reactionary trends on society.

Thus, many liberals sought to minimize the influence of ultramontane clergy on marriage and education. Chancellor Otto von Bismarck, generally no friend to German liberalism, nevertheless hoped to weld such interests to those of the conservative Protestant landlords, thereby insuring greater national unity among the elites (Sperber 1984, 207–8). In addition, Bismarck grew increasingly alarmed by the popularity of the Catholic Center Party, then well on its way toward uniting southern German Catholics with Rhenish workers and industrialists, disaffected Poles, and the recently annexed Francophile elements in Alsace-Lorraine. Alongside his German liberal nemeses, therefore, Bismarck opened an all-out war against the new ultramontane church, ostensibly in defense of "Old Catholics" who remained wary of the new formulation of papal infallibility and preferred a closer alliance of church and state. The Prussian minister of education, Adalbert Falk, aggressively attempted to regulate education, marriage, and church appointments, while popular violence and rioting escalated over open obstruction of *Kulturkampf* policies—violence that was often aided and abetted by local authorities. The result was, ironically, the strengthening and deepening of a populist ultramontane Catholicism for many Germans (Sperber 1984, 251). To the horror of embattled German Catholics, the new German state appeared to be protecting liberals whose anticlericalism, they believed, directly hailed from the Enlightenment. The Enlightenment was thereby further criticized by conservative German Catholics because the inevitable end of it was thought to be a repetition of the violence of the French Revolution and of 1848 (Sperber 1984, 216). For others, however, the *Kulturkampf* provided an impetus for pointing to the essential harmony between Catholicism on the one hand and social reformism and modernization on the other. After the *Kulturkampf*, some German Catholics sought a *juste milieu* between liberal positions deriving from the Enlightenment and respect for long-standing Catholic tradition and doctrine. In fact, it became easier for Bismarck to mend fences with moderates within the Catholic Center Party because the new pontificate of Leo XIII was itself ambivalent toward political Catholicism in Germany, and urged conciliation between French and German Catholics with their respective states (Kitchen 2006, 140–46, 192; Merriman 2010, 671; Sperber 1984, 207–52, 277–97).

The ideology of the *Kulturkampf* and the spirit of the "Syllabus of Errors" informed the leading luminaries of neo-scholastic German Catholic theologians, and often informed standard interpretations of the Enlightenment and revolutionary eras crafted by historians of the Catholic Church during the waning decades of the nineteenth century. That the Enlightenment listed indelibly toward atheism, materialism, and revolution, that eighteenth-century Catholic leaders in France and Austria, for example, had made foolhardy Faustian bargains by adapting to any of it, were all points that remained ensconced as the regnant interpretation of Church history before Sebastian Merkle. Instead, Merkle argued that the eighteenth century had in fact been an era of constructive reform within the Catholic Church—a veritable Catholic Enlightenment in fact—that had helped the Roman Catholic Church adapt to the modern world. Moreover, Merkle's Catholic Enlightenment was depicted in stark relief from secular and Protestant variants of *Aufklärung,* which, Merkle maintained, should not be made the measure of the contributions to the history of Modern Europe built by Catholic Enlightenment scholars (Merkle 1909; Lehner 2010, 3–4). Though Merkle's work was criticized at the time by many church historians in Germany, his concept slowly gained currency. Later scholars like Gustav Schnürer and Max Braubach each broached the thorny question of just where the center and periphery of Catholic Enlightenment ought to lie. Such issues arose because some Catholic reformers were censored or excommunicated by the church magisterium and yet continued to consider themselves Catholics. Schnürer maintained that Catholic Enlightenment should only comprise figures who adapted to the spirit of the age but did not reject the uniqueness of Catholic revelation, whereas Braubach believed a more critical definition was necessary to fairly capture the scope of those who self-identified as both Catholic and Enlightened (Lehner 2010, 4–5).

To a significant extent, however, the earliest decades of historical scholarship on the Catholic Enlightenment in Germany remained captive to nineteenth- and twentieth-century developments within the history of the Catholic Church. This observation is not meant to suggest that such debates are of no interest to historians. On the contrary, the cul-de-sacs in which German church historians have often found themselves in treating developments within eighteenth-century Catholicism have been replicated even well after the 1970s, as the Catholic Enlightenment ceased to be the exclusive purview of religious history and emerged into the consciousness of other eighteenth-century historians. In the decades after Merkle, more conservative scholars continued to criticize the Catholic Enlightenment for its cavalier compromises with "modern paganism" (Gay 1966, 3–27). On the other hand, advocates of Catholic Enlightenment often unintentionally reinforced the accepted historical metanarrative—that the *siècle des Lumières* was inherently and monolithically secular and anticlerical—by their continued insistence on the distinction between the secular mainstream and the Catholic Enlightenment, which they considered unique. Doubly inclined to reinforce the prevailing narrative about the inherent secularism of Enlightenment were those who would limit discussion of Catholic Enlightenment to only reformist clergy and writers never denounced as unorthodox. In large measure, many of these same debates have been inflected by nonchurch historians as well. For example, Anton Schindling's work on Catholic Reform and Enlightenment absolutism under Maria Theresa attempted to define the Catholic Enlightenment as a religious reform movement that made its peace with the eighteenth-century "rehabilitation of human nature" through its focus on practical theology as a means of renovating both church and society. By the 1980s, scholars such as Karl Otmar von Aretin and Peter Hersche spiritedly debated whether the failure of Catholic Enlightenment was inevitable because of the fundamental irreconcilability of religious piety and the age of reason (Lehner 2010, 6–7nn21–25).

In view of such trepidation about the unassailable chasm separating secular and Catholic Enlightenment, many if not most historians have come to prefer the term "Reform Catholicism" in lieu of "Catholic Enlightenment." Moreover, much of the Catholic Enlightenment—from its emphasis on continued moral reform of the church, an educated clergy and parish, and social reform—is often viewed as the epiphenomenon associated with the eighteenth-century working out of Catholic Reformation. Such a perspective is often evident in the writings of Derek Beales, Marc Forster, R. Po-Chia Hsia, and Louis Châtellier (Beales 2000; Forster 2007, 184–97; Hsia 2005; Châtellier 1989, 253–56). Even scholars such as Harm Klueting and Bernhard Schneider, who have continued to self-consciously evoke the term "Catholic Enlightenment," have generally stressed its continuity with the spirit of the Council of Trent, which took more than a century to reach its culmination—a climax that, as Derek Beales has astutely argued, makes the eighteenth century as much an age of religion as it is an age of reason (Lehner 2010, 6–7nn21–25; Forster 2007, 199–201; Beales 2000; Châtellier 1989, 25–26). By the turn of the twenty-first century, in many quarters of the academy, the notion of

Catholic Enlightenment had been assailed from all sides as scholars both secular and religious chipped away at the orthodoxy, the confessional uniqueness, and the very appropriateness of using the substantive "Enlightenment" if modified by "Catholic."

The notion of a Catholic Enlightenment, however, did receive a robust reinjection of scholarly attention during the 1970s, emanating at first from French academe. The most notable harbinger of this French school of Catholic Enlightenment study remains Bernard Plongeron, who maintained that eighteenth-century apologists and Catholic prelates selectively adopted concepts of social utility, *bienfaisance,* and *bon morale* from wider Enlightenment discourse in order to renew and promote the salutary role of the Catholic Church in the advancement of sociopolitical reform. In essence, Plongeron spoke of Catholic Enlightenment as having promulgated a new "religious anthropology" and "political theology" that tempered obedience with rationality; affirmed the possibility of substantial human progress in the arts, sciences, and morality despite the fall of humanity; and often favored more conciliarist, collegial styles of governance (for example, German Febronianism, French Gallicanism, or international Jansenism) (Plongeron 1969, 555–605; Van Kley forthcoming, 1).

Many religious historians of eighteenth-century Catholicism, including Plongeron himself, found their revival of Catholic Enlightenment scholarship buttressed by the convocation of the Second Vatican Council (1962–1965). In the prologue to his landmark *Théologie et politique au siècle des Lumières* (*Theology and Politics in the Century of Enlightenment*), Plongeron surveyed affinities between the Catholic Enlightenment and the era of Vatican II, thereby drawing attention to a common dilemma he believed had united the eighteenth century with the late twentieth century, namely, the question of just how much "the Church could abandon an all-encompassing ideology (*idéologie enveloppante*)"—its historic "political theology"—in order to achieve a "theological autonomy from the political" (Plongeron 1973, 11). The constitution of Vatican II, *Gaudium et Spes,* spoke of the "autonomy of terrestrial realities" in the sense that "created things and societies themselves have their laws and their own values" even if "the autonomy of the temporal" cannot mean that "created things do not depend upon God" (Plongeron 1973, 11). The Catholic Enlightenment, Plongeron subtly implies, is thereby a historical movement fundamentally in accord with the essential problems and promise of Catholic reform through the ages (Plongeron 1973, 12).

In addition, Plongeron's treatment of Catholic Enlightenment often emphasized the Gallican or Jansenist roots of the movement. Jansenism and Gallican independence often stressed the decentralized legal autonomy of Catholic parishes, ideally more free from papal juridical control. For such Catholic Enlightenment reformers, social reform was rooted in the moral regeneration of individuals through a reformed Catholic piety purged of purportedly irrational forms of popular devotion characteristic of "Baroque Catholicism" (Forster 2007, 187–89). Since the 1970s, and increasingly since the 1990s, the Catholic reform advocated by Jansenists has received significant attention from scholars of eighteenth-century Europe and from historians of France in particular. Admittedly this debate has focused less specifically on Catholic Enlightenment as such, and often has been more specifically concerned with explaining the distinctive trajectory taken by prerevolutionary France—a realm whose monarchs were ostensibly committed to Gallican principles of regal and episcopal independence from the Vatican, and yet ham-fistedly supportive of the papal bull *Unigenitus,* which conflated Gallicanism and Jansenism in an attempt to censure the latter. The Bourbon monarchy, however, condemned Jansenist reformers for largely unrelated reasons of foreign and domestic policy. The literature on Jansenism and the eighteenth century has become increasingly vast (Plongeron 1976, 1637–55; Groethuysen 1968, 7–24, 38–44; Garrioch 1996, 1–102). Among the pioneers in this regard are Dale Van Kley, David Bell, Monique Cottret, Catherine-Laurence Maire, Robert Kreiser, Peter Campbell, and recently Brian Strayer, whose painstaking research has mapped out manifold ways in which Jansenist influence undermined the Bourbon monarchy and proved a major cause célèbre of Enlightenment radicalization and revolutionary politics (Van Kley 1996, 1–14, 369–76; Bell 2001; Cottret 1998; Maire 1998; Kreiser 1978; Strayer 2008, 156–295). The focus on Jansenist and Gallican Catholic Enlightenment has also facilitated deeper understanding for the trajectories of Enlightenment in Eastern, Central, and Southern Europe. Many Enlightened absolutists like Maria Theresa, Joseph II, and Carlos III, who variously favored moral education, promotion of public instruction, and increased legal oversight over both secular and regular clergy, often found supporters and counsel from Jansenist or Gallican Catholic reformers. The concerns of such reformers, often advocates of a more collegial style of church administration under the oversight of secular rulers for the purpose of promoting social utility and individual moral reformation, often overlapped with the designs of their rulers (Paquette 2008; Noël 2001, 119–53; Smidt 2010, 403–52; Fantappiè 1986, 399–403; Miller 1978, 1–17; Souza 2010, 359–402; Van Kley 2008a).

Notwithstanding the many productive developments in the history of eighteenth-century Catholicism, especially since the 1970s, scholarly discussions of Catholic Enlightenment have only just begun (in the last twenty years) to move beyond the framework of the movements within Catholic tradition from which they emerged, namely, the prevalence of Catholic Counter-Enlightenment impulses in the late nineteenth century, the impact of the *Kulturkampf* on early German scholars like Merkle, and modern-day reformist impulses expressed at Vatican II. This halting and sometimes insular historiography of Catholic Enlightenment has (to some extent justifiably) shaken scholarly confidence in the whole notion of Catholic Enlightenment, as many historians such as Helena Rosenblatt and David Sorkin have most recently preferred to speak of a transconfessional "Christian Enlightenment" or "Religious Enlightenment" (Rosenblatt 2006; Sorkin 2008, 1–21). This approach is far from lacking merit, for in moving beyond the fold of the strictly Catholic Enlightenment, scholars have fruitfully noted transnational similarities between Protestant and Catholic Europe in the eighteenth century—developments which have inspired other scholars to engage in fascinating work on the ways in which Orthodox Europe and Rabbinical Judaism also integrated Enlightenment thought (Feiner 2004; Tsapina 2001; Ghitta 2001). But it seems a single taxonomy for a monolithic "Catholic Enlightenment" movement is, at least on the surface of things, more elusive than ever.

Enlightenment Catholicism in the Process and Style of Enlightenment

This volume then begs the important question of just why it should be necessary to retain and expand upon any notion of Catholic Enlightenment when the study of "Enlightenment Christianity," "Reform Catholicism," and "Religious Enlightenment" have all in fact proven so fruitful. The authors of the present volume will not attempt to supersede or deny the importance of existing research in these areas, and yet we remain convinced of the utility of a concept of "Catholic Enlightenment" for three significant reasons. *First,* the study of eighteenth-century Catholicism still too often inadvertently reinforces the perception within mainstream Enlightenment histories that Enlightenment Catholicism is reactive, philosophically unstable and defensive, and ipso facto destined for collapse into Counter-Enlightenment trends (Israel 2006, 10–14; Israel 2011, 1–35).

Second, the focus, especially in the past three decades, upon the Jansenist or Gallican contributions to Reform Catholicism throughout Europe, while important, has obscured the fact that various institutions and individuals, including some Sorbonne theologians, some Jesuits (especially in France), Oratorians, Lazarists, and Benedictines, all participated in their own networks and regional variations of Catholic Enlightenment (Burson 2010b, 1–135; Lehner 2011, 1–6; Burson 2010a). R. R. Palmer's *Catholics and Unbelievers in Eighteenth-Century France* (1939) remains a classic harbinger of new approaches that have emphasized the multiplicity of participants (including the Jesuits) in the crafting of Catholic Reform apologetics that creatively answered the charges of superstition, political corruption, and irrationalism that so many *philosophes* had posed (Palmer 1939, 117–25). We now understand the extent to which, far from simply a dress rehearsal for Counter-Enlightenment and counterrevolution ideologies of the period after 1789, an "Enlightened Theology," as Thomas O'Connor has called it, reignited the Catholic Reformation in the eighteenth century with a renewed focus on historical criticism, universal history, Newtonian science, Lockean epistemology, and the quest for a socially utilitarian positive theology (O'Connor 1995, 176; Everdell 1987, 79–183, 281–82; Masseau 2000, 19–26, 419–21; Chopelin-Blanc 2009, 107–276). In short, to confine the impetus for Catholic Reform almost entirely to one brand of Catholic Enlightenment thought risks succumbing to an excessively Whiggish and overly monolithic Catholic Enlightenment that is, by definition, only partially descriptive of the panorama of eighteenth-century Catholic discourses.

Third, however vital it is to examine transnational, transconfessional patterns at work within Enlightenment religion, to speak merely of "Religious Enlightenment" without a more carefully nuanced picture of the diversity existing within the Protestant, Catholic, or Jewish Enlightenment throughout Europe over time is to risk portraying those similarities in excessively static and reductionist ways. In other words, the nature of "Religious Enlightenment" (or for that matter, of the Enlightenment process as a whole) depends upon scholars being attentive not just to the special diversity of national and confessional Enlightenment contexts, but to the temporal diversity of Catholic Enlightenment tendencies in transnational context. David Sorkin has wisely cautioned scholars to "resist the impulse to hypostatize the religious Enlightenment as a separate entity" as opposed to seeing it as a position along a spectrum of Enlightenment. Yet the very concept of "Religious Enlightenment" presupposes an elaborate transconfessional taxonomy that compares hypostatic Protestant, Catholic, and Jewish affinities during the century of lights. While this comparative approach has merit, favoring only "Religious Enlightenment" insufficiently accounts for the diachronic evolution of Catholicism throughout the eighteenth century (Sorkin 2008, 19).

In diverse ways, therefore, the chapters of the present volume speak precisely to this trifold impetus, taking care to distinguish between the largely untenable notion of the Catholic Enlightenment as monolithic movement and the recognition of variegated Catholic Enlightenment tendencies present in unequal and evolving measure throughout Europe and its peripheries. Not all Catholics were enlightened, but the persistent quest for a univocal Catholic Enlightenment movement has left us with the largely impossible task of distinguishing too sharply and arbitrarily between the Catholic Enlightenment and the Enlightenment more generally. Thus, in what follows, we define Catholic Enlightenment both as a style and discursive field on the one hand and as part of a broader Enlightenment process on the other. What unites the whole of the Catholic Enlightenment as such (despite its own extreme internal diversity) is the very same quality that remains definitive of the unitary Enlightenment itself. Enlightenment is a unity of style and tone that Mark Goldie has referred to as the taste for "sensibility," and a quest for moral improvement and happiness as John Robertson and Darrin McMahon have demonstrated (Goldie 1993, 210; Robertson 2005, 1–61; McMahon 2006, 197–252). What remains of the Enlightenment project is, first, a new form of sociability—the Western world's first "information revolution"—and secondly, a style of scholarship, literature, and even religious thought that valorized the practical improvement of humanity, education, and social reform. Such values and projects were anchored in the bedrock of a more historicized, philosophical, and spiritual quest for the fundamental nature of humankind insofar as knowable in global perspective. As so defined, Catholic Enlightenment becomes a vital participant in the Enlightenment process. Far from seeing in this definition a narrowing of intellectual horizons from Peter Gay's notion of a familiar project of Enlightenment, or Cassirer's philosophy of Enlightenment in the singular, scholars have become increasingly willing to recognize unity of discursive field and process amidst a plurality of philosophical approaches, movements, and contexts—the fruits of scholarly investigations undertaken very much in the spirit of Kant's admonition "*sapere aude*." As scholars have come to know much more about the contours of the eighteenth century, is it so surprising that we should now be faced with a prospect similar to that which has long confronted our colleagues in the field of sixteenth-century studies? Much evidence now suggests for the eighteenth century what Paul Oskar Kristeller once wrote of Renaissance humanism: that it may be best conceived and united as much by style and process as by a unity of philosophical project (Kristeller 1964, 147–65).

But the Catholic Enlightenment must be more than one aspect of a nebulous Enlightenment discursive field. The second way in which the authors of this volume understand Catholic Enlightenment is as a vital participant in the process of Enlightenment as such (Burson 2010b, 1–29; Burson 2012; Lehner 2010, 5; Reinalter 2006; Möller 1986, 16–18). Just as it is difficult to speak of a unitary Enlightenment throughout the continent without anachronistically privileging a region (Scotland and Naples in John Robertson's recent *The Case for the Enlightenment* [2005], for example) or a discourse (Spinozism as in Israel's *Radical Enlightenment* [2001]), so also is it difficult to continually bisect the Enlightenment into national or confessional variations without disregarding the transnational cosmopolitanism so self-consciously dear as much to the *philosophes* as to many Catholic and Protestant participants in the Enlightenment public sphere (Robertson 2005; Israel 2011, 1–38). Thus, the Enlightenment is perhaps best framed as a transnational process characterized by secular and religious motives and implications, and by which a constantly evolving series of movements dynamically intersect and dialectically constitute one another. At the intersection of these movements—significant nodes of controversy and causes célèbres—important connections among national or religious enlightenments, the Radical Enlightenment, and the Counter-Enlightenment are thrown into stark relief, and new discourses of Enlightenment can be observed as they crescendo and decrescendo across time and geography. In like manner also do new phases of Catholic Enlightenment emerge from this larger process of Enlightenment (Burson 2010b, 1–29; Burson 2012).

Accordingly, the contributions to this volume collectively dramatize the manner in which Catholic Enlightenment is a shifting constellation of discourses emergent from the whole of Europe—the voice of men and women, laymen and clergy, periphery and metropole—a significant manifestation of the wider transnational process of Enlightenment underway within the eighteenth century. The editors of and contributors to this volume have therefore elected to utilize the term "Enlightenment Catholicism" interchangeably with "Catholic Enlightenment," inasmuch as the former better captures the plurality and evolving panorama of Catholic tendencies from the Council of Trent until the early nineteenth century, with significant turning points clustering about the international expulsion of the Jesuits (1759–1773) and the French revolutionary era of 1789–1815. Second, we have chosen to eschew *l'esprit de système* alongside so many of the eighteenth-century authors themselves, whose voices we seek to resurrect, and instead to collectively embrace the diversity of approaches which have sprung forth from further investigation of eighteenth-century Catholicism. Consequently, we remain satisfied with a relatively minimalist definition of Catholic Enlightenment, understanding it to encompass the work of any author (lay or cleric), statesman, monk, secular clergy, philosopher, or apologist from within Catholic Europe who participated in burgeoning networks of publication and eighteenth-century sociability with a view toward integrating eighteenth-century science, philosophy, philology, or political thought into their understanding of Catholic teaching, and the reform of church and society. We additionally understand Catholic Enlightenment as appertaining to any eighteenth-century writer whose work considered the moral vitality of a reformed Catholic Church to be fundamental to the Enlightenment pursuit of happiness and social justice.

Admittedly, such an expansive approach to the definition of Catholic Enlightenment involves risks, and in what follows, this introduction sketches the outline of a more systematic portrait of the institutional and geographic nodes, periodization, and common concerns associated with Enlightenment Catholicism. But the state of the scholarship requires the important caveat that all such schema must be understood as provisional. At times, history demands acquiescence to the conflictive plurality and irreducible complexity of human experience. While historians such as John Robertson have been right to caution against the risks of excessively balkanizing and broadening Enlightenment scholarship, thereby diluting the term itself, the greater danger remains the *dix-huitièmiste* urge to cling to a priori formulations of Enlightenment, which thereby risks privileging one style of Enlightenment—one political, or one philosophical, program—over other inconvenient, discordant tendencies (Robertson 2005, 1–14, 43–44; Pocock 1999, 9; Porter 2000, xvii–xviii; Kors 1987, 1–10). Indeed, the very nature of the eighteenth-century "information revolution"—a revolution by which European clergy, bourgeoisie, and nobles exchanged manuscripts, traded in suspect books, devoured celebratory accounts of new scientific achievements reported in the periodical press, or hobnobbed in salons and clubs—makes it difficult to confine any study of Enlightenment Catholicism to an excessively narrow confessional, philosophical, or national paradigm. Some of our subject authors, like the cosmopolitan Jesuit natural philosopher Ruggiero Boscovich, studied by Jonathan Wright, identified at various points of their career with philosophers and *gens des lettres* as much as they did with other Catholic prelates. In the case of Boscovich, the extent of his travels and patronage makes him impossible to link strictly to the Italian Enlightenment. Nearly all of our subjects shared a zeal for the modification or abandonment of Thomistic scholasticism by the selective appropriation of Descartes, or of Protestant Enlightenment writers such as Christian Wolff, John Locke, or Isaac Newton. Therefore, excessively monolithic constructions of Enlightenment Catholicism as nothing more than a species of "moderate mainstream" Enlightenment, separate from the true Enlightenment of more radical writers and publicists, tend to wither the complexity of the social networks and intellectual formation of many eighteenth-century Catholic authors themselves (Israel 2011, 1–35).

That there are great risks in considering the Catholic Enlightenment as largely circumscribed by the milieus of the dynastic states or nations from which its authors emerged becomes especially evident in light of the burgeoning scholarship on the participants in the Irish, English, or Scottish Catholic Enlightenment, areas that have been woefully underdeveloped until recently, until the work of Mark Goldie, Thomas O'Connor, and Gabriel Glickman, some of which is featured in this volume. With respect to these Catholics enmeshed within Atlantic empires and composite monarchies dominated by Protestants, transnational and diasporic dimensions have proven as decisive and significant as national context. As cultural minorities in England or Scotland, or legally disenfranchised majorities in Ireland, British Catholics looked as much to the continent as to the British Isles for their influences, and accordingly, Scottish and Irish Catholics may have been all the more significant in transnational debates on toleration. The cosmopolitan influences of Andrew Ramsey, an example of the Scottish Catholic Enlightenment, enabled him to become the author of a truly universalist conception of Catholic Christianity. Ramsey emerges as a Catholic defender of Masonry and a supporter of Matthew Tindal's argument that Christianity was synonymous with the oldest natural religion of man (a view he in fact shared with many Catholic authors of eighteenth-century France, including Pierre-Daniel Huet, Jean-Martin de Prades, and Nicolas-Sylvestre Bergier, to name but a few) (Shelford 2008, 114–43; Burson 2010b, 64–70, 218–19).

Enlightenment Catholicism: Affinities, Geographical and Institutional Loci, and Periodization

Notwithstanding the expansive definition of Catholic Enlightenment employed in what follows, there are some common characteristics of Enlightenment Catholicism across the length and breadth of the long eighteenth century, from approximately 1670 to 1815. First, Catholic Enlightenment is characterized by a relatively more expansive confidence in the possibility of the moral and intellectual improvement of humankind. Second, many Catholic reformers, especially the Jesuits and those influenced by them, stressed the freedom of the will to know and choose the good. Third, and especially evident among the Benedictines, Maurist Benedictines, Jansenists, and Jesuits, is the near fixation upon social and moral utility as a leading measure of church reform, alongside historical-critical scholarship as a tool in unveiling the primitive church, the anthropology of human religious experience, and the need for revealed religion. Fourth, nearly all Catholic Enlighteners hoped to significantly reform Thomistic scholasticism, often by synthesizing it with insights from Descartes, Wolff, Leibniz, Locke, or Newton. Fifth, all Catholic Enlightenment reformers shared a belief in the need to simplify and purify Baroque Catholicism in favor of a more literate, introspective, internal, or sedate piety. Sixth, it was often believed that the ultimate pursuit of happiness and social reform depended on a reformed church, governed (in terms of ecclesiology) by bishops, national synods, or kings, even if still spiritually led by the papacy. These last two characteristics are properly associated with Gallicanism, Jansenism, and Febronianism in parts of Italy, the Low Countries, France, and Austria, and they gain greater currency in the latter half of the eighteenth century.

Seventh, and also characteristic of many Catholic Enlightenment writers within the Gallican or Jansenist traditions, is the long heritage of late medieval and Renaissance conciliarism from which they drew (Parsons 2004). Such influences dovetailed with and in turn reenergized eighteenth-century understandings of Renaissance republican thought. In this essential continuity between Renaissance civic humanism and the Enlightenment, Catholic Enlighteners among the Gallican jurists and curés in late eighteenth-century France, Italy, and Utrecht have much in common with the republicanism that inspired the writings of Bolingbroke, Montesquieu, Boulainvilliers, and the Marquis d'Argenson (Van Kley 2008a; Linton 2001, 1–22, 42–45, 201–14; Hammersley 2010, 1–12, 198–204; Israel 2006, 225–64). Finally, many Catholic Enlighteners wrote for a wider public of readers and were often actively engaged in interconfessional dialogue (Lehner 2010, 18–46). Inasmuch as one might define the Catholic Enlightenment by what it is *not,* it seems reasonable to assert that it was uniformly hostile to Spinoza, at least rhetorically.

Certainly not all of the above eight characteristics are uniformly present across the period from the seventeenth-century crisis to approximately 1815. Wide variation in characteristic emphases emerges from region to region, among Jansenists, Benedictines, lay Catholic apologists, Jesuits, or other groups. Finally, inasmuch as the Enlightenment itself evolves substantially over the course of the eighteenth century, so also does the Catholic Enlightenment, as though in a kind of dialogic, diachronic dance with other discourses of Enlightenment, from one node of controversy to another. Scholars continue to revise the score, but tentatively, we can say this dance occurs in two movements. The first, an early Catholic Enlightenment, begins variously with the aftermath of the Catholic Reformation and the seventeenth-century crises (c. 1648–1700) and extends until the transitional decades of the middle eighteenth century, when Enlightenment reform (secular and religious) becomes more mainstream, reaching a bombastic crescendo in the decades surrounding the international expulsion of the Jesuits (1759–1773). The second movement overlaps the period corresponding to the rise and fragmentation of "patriot reform" and Enlightenment absolutism (1760s–1780s) and can be considered a time of creative adaptation to a more expansive public, with secular and religious reformers drawing upon one another's ideas—especially ideas associated with Jansenism and Gallicanism. It is also, however, a time of dissonant harmonies in that a more defensive rhetoric of anti-*philosophie* stood toe-to-toe with the radicalization of Enlightenment thought; first in France, and then, with the spread of the French Revolution, throughout the rest of Europe (Darnton 1982, 1–21, 39–40; Israel 2006, 699–871; Burson 2010b, 275–309; Van Kley 2008b, 252–95). Even at that, the more strident rhetorical polarization of the 1780s and following decades was accompanied by a more subtle counterpoint—the ongoing integration of secular and Catholic Enlightenment discourse. In some cases, the scholarly picture of the end point of Enlightenment Catholicism cannot yet be determined very clearly. However, this introduction will suggest a coda to this great dance by flashing forward into the nineteenth century.

Within the Holy Roman Empire and the Habsburg hereditary lands, early eighteenth-century clerics pursued the spirit of the Council of Trent by seeking to simplify Baroque Catholicism, thereby minimizing the proliferation of pilgrimages, shrines, confraternities, and medieval superstition that had become such a large part of early modern Catholic devotion. These developments were in large measure common to much of Western and Central Catholic Europe as a direct continuation of the social disciplining of popular piety and the withdrawal of courtly and urban elites from popular devotion characteristic of late Renaissance Christian humanism and the seventeenth-century Catholic Reformation (Schilling 1995; Burke 2009; Rabb 1975, 1–28, 74–82; O'Malley 2002). But by the eighteenth century, post-Tridentine Catholic reformism had begun to inspire other projects of clerical and reformist laymen who identified as enlightened. Among such related reformists were followers of the Jansenists in Austria and the Austrian Netherlands, in addition to partisans of the various strains of "Febronianism." Following Nikolaus von Hontheim, who wrote under the pseudonym Justus Febronius, Febronian episcopalists believed that forged decretals of the ninth century had illegitimately vaunted the political supremacy of the pope in contradistinction to the original, primitive church organized around the orthopraxis worked out through all bishops of the church (Forster 2007, 184–89). The outlook of this post-Tridentine spirit of reform gave rise to an emphasis on practical Christian teaching, vernacular services, and a more activist parish life detailed in the writings of Italian historian and Catholic reformer Lodovico Muratori (especially *On Well-Ordered Catholic Devotion*). Muratori's ideas were rapidly dispersed throughout southern German states and Austria thanks to his following among the Benedictines of Salzburg. Indeed, to a great extent, it is through Benedictine influence that many Catholic Enlightenment tendencies knit together Italian, German, and (to an extent) French influences, as Ulrich Lehner has recently argued. Alongside those influenced by Benedictine developments were Muratori, other Italian intellectuals such as Genovesi, and a broad network of correspondence and association linking Bavarian with Austrian and other South German Benedictine monks. Benedictine monks often taught outside of their decentralized monastic structure, and were pioneers in the integration of works by Nicolas Malebranche, German Pietists, Christian Wolff, and new methods of empirical science and critical scholarship they imported from early eighteenth-century French Maurists (reformed Benedictines) (Forster 2007, 184–86; Lehner 2011; Lehner 2010, 1–25; Blanning 1981, 118–26).

The Catholic Enlightenment in the Iberian peninsula has recently been the subject of great attention by a new generation of scholars including Andrea Smidt, Gabriel Paquette, and Charles Noël. Much like the early German Catholic Enlightenment, Benedictines seem to have played a prominent role, even if Enlightened Jesuits, Dominicans, Augustinians, and Jansenists were all at various points major players in the Spanish Catholic Enlightenment. By the dawn of the eighteenth century, many Spaniards were animated by revulsion toward the deeply evocative, often seemingly decadent Baroque piety that had become quite insular, inbred, and defensive in the waning years of Habsburg rule. From illiterate peasant to highly educated statesman, Baroque piety reigned supreme in Spain and Portugal alike. In Spain, the twin forces of scholasticism and the Inquisition remained bulwarks against new natural philosophy emanating from the works of Galileo and Descartes. However, papal support of the Austrian Habsburg claimant during the war of the Spanish Succession induced the first Bourbon king, Philip V (1683–1746), to break off communication with the curia. In addition to unresolved marriage dispensations and unfilled episcopal vacancies, this regalist turn within the Spanish church inadvertently fostered a softening of the arterial sclerosis that had beset Spanish Catholicism by the early 1700s. The standoff between the new Spanish royal family and the papacy helped illuminate Catholic thought throughout the 1720s–1740s, as intellectuals such as the noted Benedictine harbinger of Spanish Catholic Enlightenment, Benito Jerónimo Feijoo, wrote *Universal Theater of Criticism* (*Teatro critico universal*; 1726–1740), and *Curious and Erudite Letters* (*Cartas eruditas y curiosas*; 1742–1760), in which he popularized writers such as Descartes, Bacon, and Newton, thereby questioning the hegemony of scholastic learning (or any one received philosophical authority in fact). Feijoo favored a more eclectic, sober, and rational balance between skepticism and devotion, but he was far from a voice crying in the wilderness. Other voices, including those of many Jesuits, promoted empirical methods in medical science and scriptural study in the vernacular. Many nobles and Spanish statesmen promoted the dissemination of such Catholic Enlightenment notions in salons and discussion clubs known as *tertulias,* where there could be found, alongside new respect for new scientific pursuits, a burgeoning interest in critical ecclesiastical history inspired by the furtherance of Erasmian humanism during the Catholic Enlightenment (Smidt 2010, 414–23; Noël 2009, 145–65).

The early French Catholic Enlightenment also emerged from the crises of the seventeenth century, but its trajectory was far more complicated by an unusually early and contentious politicization of dueling Catholic Enlightenment tendencies: one "pro-Augustinian" and the other "pro-Molinist." To say as much is not to suggest that all French Benedictines, Lazarists, Oratorians, or secular clergy invariably fell into one "camp" over against another, nor is it to suggest that all those accused of harboring Jansenist or Molinist proclivities were actually beholden to either. Rather, I am suggesting that from early in the eighteenth century the distinctive way in which the papal condemnations of Jansenism broke across institutions of the Bourbon monarchy led to a rapid politicization of many Gallican Catholics in ways that fundamentally placed the monarchy in an ambivalent position toward the Jesuits.

Royal policy, in turn, was frequently at loggerheads with Jansenists, who, elsewhere in Europe, often emerged as the vanguard of regalist Catholic Enlighteners in league with reformist monarchs. In ways reminiscent of the ideological divisions between Laudians and more Puritanical "godly" in the British kingdoms, or the Remonstrant and Counter-Remonstrant divisions in the Dutch Republic, "Augustinian" and "Molinist" became ideological labels that poisoned theological and Enlightenment discourse, often forcing Enlightenment writers toward extreme positions and marginalizing moderate or more nuanced positions. The two sides of the French Catholic Enlightenment differed concerning moral philosophy, and over time they began to differ significantly concerning political thought and engagement with different aspects of Enlightenment science before the early 1760s (Van Kley 2006b, 653). Jansenism and the more Augustinian types among French Enlightened Catholics considered the essential sinfulness of humankind to be foundational to their Enlightenment reformism. From this pessimistic appraisal of human nature derived an emphasis on a rigorous culture of frequent confession, rigorous penance and catechetical instruction, and bookish piety alongside the drive to render the popular devotion more pristine and sober. Between around 1650 and 1709, with the destruction of the pro-Jansenist convent of Port-Royal, the Jansenist movement drew its adherents from among the professional bourgeoisie, nobles of the robe, bishops, and a number of reformers within the Sorbonne (Van Kley 2006b, 660–65; Michel 2000, 196–98, 442; Gres-Gayer 1991, 203–10).

Between 1670 and the 1750s, however, clergy of all stripes could be found in the many clubs and salons of the Regency period (1715–1726) engaging in debates over the nature of the ancient constitution of France, the aggressive foreign policy of the last years of Louis XIV, and economic reform. Between the 1720s and the 1760s, Oratorians,

Jesuits, and Benedictines alike were all (at different points) enthusiastic about Newtonian physics and the sensationalism of Locke's *Essay concerning Human Understanding*. In particular, the Jesuits and some Benedictine, Dominican, and secular clergy among the professorate throughout France considered Locke fraught with potential for reinvigorating the scholastic synthesis that had been damaged by the French vogue for Descartes, whose logic, method, and substantial dualism continued to appeal to many Jansenists (Burson 2010b, 55–136; Tuilier 1994, 390–91; Brockliss 1987, 185–90, 220–27; Cotoni 1984, 124–25). As in central Europe, the Jesuits of France often took a keen interest in natural philosophy and epistemology. In France, these efforts led to creative attempts to synthesize Malebranche and Locke in order to fortify theology against Spinoza, while promoting concerted engagement with experimental physics. Whereas Jansenists' concern for moral philosophy and promoting the improvement of humanity derived from their tragic understanding of the essential sinfulness of human nature and their attendant need to base reform on "enlightened self-interest," non-Jansenist Catholic Enlightenment in France, especially that of many Jesuits, emerged from a relative confidence that the essence of human nature, though demented by original sin, was unchanged. Therefore, to a limited extent, individuals—even those outside the church—possessed the ability to know and choose the good (Van Kley 1987; Ehrard 1981, 434–43; Burson 2010a, 66–91; Northeast 1991, 217–18; Burson 2010b, 33–135).

The French situation became more complex, however, because of Louis XIV's support for the bull of Clement XI condemning Jansenism and, at least obliquely by implication, the cherished Gallican liberties themselves of the French Church. *Unigenitus* (1713) initiated a firestorm of criticism in France, where the juridical edifice uniting the French Catholic Church to the monarchy since the rise of the Bourbons had been built on a foundation of Gallicanism. After numerous luminaries of the Sorbonne and the episcopacy attempted to appeal the bull to a national council, the new royal favorite for Louis XV, Cardinal de Fleury, and subsequent pro-bull archbishops (most famously Christophe de Beaumont, Archbishop of Paris) attempted to excise Jansenist influence root and branch from the University of

Paris, monasteries, and the parishes such as Saint-Etienne du Mont, where such influence had grown entrenched thanks to multigenerational family networks uniting lower bourgeoisie, local parish priests, pro-Jansenist bishops, and churchwardens. The emotion of this institutional purge stirred up enthusiasm for the Jansenist hero, Abbé de Paris, at the parish of Saint Médard, which became known for the waves of parishioners who fell into convulsions and other ecstatic states, claiming that the saintly spirit of the abbé had confirmed their faith and been the mediator for many other signs and wonders. Predictably, men of letters—Jesuit, Benedictine, and *philosophe* alike—unleashed intricate arguments questioning the validity of these miracles' claims. However laced with arguments from Bayle, Malebranche, and Locke, as well as eighteenth-century understanding of church fathers from Tertullian to Origen, the polemics over miracles did little more than fuel the denial of miracles from the radicalizing Enlightenment in France (Israel 2001, 684–720; Kreiser 1978, 342–49, 399)—an Enlightenment radicalized, in part, by this very campaign. Between 1749 and the late 1750s, the campaign against the Jansenists escalated under Archbishop Beaumont and his Jesuit and Benedictine allies (like Bishop Mirepoix) to include the refusal of the sacrament of extreme unction to those who could not verify having confessed to a priest who assented to the condemnation of Jansenism (Burson 2010b, 136–61).

Paradoxically, however, the suppression of Jansenism briefly resulted in the proliferation of the pro-Molinist side of Catholic Enlightenment, as Newton, Locke, and sensationalism more generally became more easily ensconced within Parisian seminaries (especially those of Saint-Sulpice) and within the Sorbonne itself, where several of its bachelors (such as the Abbé Yvon, Abbé Pestre, and Abbé de Prades) found ready employment even as writers of metaphysical and theological pieces for Diderot's *Encyclopédie*. Yet between 1752 and 1759, the Jesuits became ensnared by their increasingly strident assault on Diderot as editor of the *Encyclopédie*. This latter campaign, when combined with the Jesuits' own attempts to maintain ascendancy at court and maintain leverage over the University of Paris following the attack on Prades's Sorbonne thesis by Jansenists, helped rally unlikely defenders among the *philosophes* (Voltaire, Diderot, and the Marquis d'Argens, for instance). The Prades Affair also consequently opened a period of retrenchment during which the Augustinian and Molinist camps grappled over censorship of an increasingly assertive "third force" of anticlerical and militant secular Enlightenment writers who had migrated further into outright hostility because of the viciousness of the undeclared religious warfare between partisans of *Unigenitus*. In short, well before any similar trends are visible in the rest of the Continent, the Enlightenment of more radical *philosophes* became comfortably entrenched in the Académie française, the ministries, and the organs of the Bourbon regime in France. This more innovative, more radical, but also more self-consciously anticlerical French Enlightenment advanced its proposals for the improvement of humanity from the ashen no-man's-land between trenches dug by warring politicized ideologies that splintered the once more unified Catholic Enlightenment in France (Darnton 1982, 1–21, 39–40; Van Kley 1996, 135–248; Israel 2006, 814–62; Burson 2010b, 136–77, 239–309; Shovlin 2009, 47–61).

In no other European country did the monarchy find itself set against the conciliarist, regalist, or Jansenist strain of Enlightenment Catholicism, and much scholarship now exists suggesting that this situation within France explains the uniquely militant "family of *philosophes*" described by Peter Gay's magisterial synthesis of Enlightenment, or the uniquely prescient penchant for a more radical species of Enlightenment in France as described by Jonathan I. Israel. The work of Dale Van Kley and other scholars additionally points in the direction of seeing the suppression of the Jesuits by Portugal (1759), France (1764), Spain (1767), and by Clement XIV's bull *In emminenti* (1773) as the most significant multinational turning point in the transnational Catholic Enlightenment (Van Kley 2006a). With the Jesuits gone, many Gallican, Febronian, and Jansenist reformers became ascendant, and between the 1760s and 1780s, the more Augustinian Catholic Enlightenment ideals of these reformers evolved and inspired reforms in places as far afield as the Spain of Carlos III, the Habsburg hereditary lands of Joseph II, and parts of Italy such as Tuscany under Duke Leopold. Joseph II hoped to channel revenues from confraternities and monasteries into educational, bureaucratic, and pastoral reform. Monasteries were closed, and feast days and processions were reduced, because—so Josephine reformers argued—they detracted from discipline and piety, and also reduced the economic productivity of the realm (Van Kley 2006a)

The suppression of the Jesuits in Austria was shortly followed by an attack on the mendicant orders and a move to bring education under the purview of the state. Reforms such as these garnered support from Febronian and regalist thinkers, and, it is now known, these reformers frequently found inspiration in a wider network of pro-Jansenist Catholic reformers in France, Utrecht, Northern Italy, and Austria (Van Kley 2006a). Moreover, the vogue for historical and scientific research long underway in southern Germany and Bavaria under the aegis of the Benedictines reinforced the concerns of the German professional bourgeoisie, who grew increasingly enthusiastic in their support for individualized and internalized worship in preference to Baroque excesses. Overall, despite the proliferation of German reading clubs and a reservedly more critical and occasionally anticlerical public sphere by the 1790s, the state was generally seen as the locus of reformism. The German *Aufklärung* (Protestant or Catholic) generated precious little of the anti-Christian overtones seen in France until the era after the Napoleonic wars. In effect, even the reaction against Joseph II's reforms did not stifle middle-class desires for further reform, since many middle-class citizens ultimately rallied to the secularization of church lands and to the reform of education and monasticism characteristic of the Napoleonic occupation (Forster 2007, 189–95; Gagliardo 1991, 375–95; Outram 2005, 26–46).

As in France, Central Europe, and the Italian states, Catholic Enlightenment in Spain also changed significantly between 1747 and 1767, culminating in the high-water mark of a Jansenist and Gallican influence supportive of a regalist Catholic Church under Carlos III, whose policies became militantly anti-Jesuit and who was zealously diligent about creating a Spanish Atlantic Empire at once more efficient, modern, and effectively governed. At first, however, the regalist orientation of Philip V and Fernando VI (1746–1759) benefited the Jesuits, who, as in France in those same years, often combined optimism about human nature with support for a powerful papacy and a strongly bureaucratic absolutism of the monarch. The Concordat of

1753 effectively granted to the Bourbon monarchy control over all but fifty-two of the vacant Spanish benefices; such dominance, in turn, solidified the position of the Spanish king's Jesuit confessors and ministers, such as Francisco Rávago (1685–1763) and José Carvajal y Lancáster (1698–1754). As a result of the 1753 Concordat, Jansenists and Augustinians were effectively blocked from leadership positions in the Spanish Church (Smidt 2010, 423–32).

As in France in the early years of Louis XV (c. 1726–1764), however, the Jesuits allied themselves to a shifty monarch dominated by factious ministers and favorites. Fernando VI effectively abdicated responsibility for economic reform and gave ministerial appointments to his queen, María Bárbara da Braganza, whose untimely death in 1758 sank the king into a deep depression from which he never recovered. By 1759, the king of the Two Sicilies succeeded as Carlos III of Spain, and proceeded to lean upon Jansenists, Dominicans, and Augustinians, whose interest in regal control over a national Catholic Church favoring a more activist episcopacy (at the expense of the papacy and the regular clergy) made them natural allies in Carlos III's Enlightened absolutism. By 1767, the Society of Jesus was suppressed in Spain, and Carlos III's Enlightened absolutism entered a phase wherein Augustinian and Jansenist Catholic Enlightenment tendencies intertwined with state policies ever more closely. During the era of 1767–1793, Spanish Augustinians linked up with Jansenists and Gallicans in France—not to mention the schismatic Gallicans associated with the Dutch Council of Utrecht (1763)—and defended traditional liberties of the church against papal interference. In Spain, as distinct from the France of Louis XV and Louis XVI, such arguments buttressed the Enlightened absolutism of Carlos III (Smidt 2010, 423–32). This export of Gallican-Jansenist discourse even intensified the polarization of Enlightenment Catholicism in the Italian states, where, by the middle 1770s, many Augustinians and those identifying lately as Jansenists contributed to reform in secular Italian states like Tuscany or Naples-Sicily, while "Zelanti" or propapal Catholics opposed state-sponsored Catholic reform, even while sharing the same sensationist empiricism and optimistic appraisal of the human penchant for moral and religious progress that had characterized their pro-Jesuit counterparts in France (Van Kley 2006a; Van Kley forthcoming).

To conclude our discussion of the institutional, geographical, and temporal loci of Catholic Enlightenment, it seems necessary to pose an important question begged by many of the essays in the present volume: Where does it all end? To be too dogmatic about periodization—especially endpoints—is risky business given the present state of research on Enlightenment Catholicism, but clearly the 1790s in general, and the French Revolution in particular, constitute a significant rupture. As Richard Butterwick has recently reminded us, Catholic Enlightenment notions of church reform remained vital to the ecclesiastical reforms that emerged from the stillborn "revolution" in Poland-Lithuania (1788–1791), and considerable research on the apologetics of the Constitutional Church in France has often noted the vitality and creativity of French Catholic Enlightenment thought, which animated the attempt to bring the church under the authority of the revolutionary nation. The events throughout Europe from 1792 to 1794 seem most significant, however. Not only was the Polish Revolution squelched by the Third Partition, but farther south, the death of Joseph II in 1790 in the midst of the acerbic reactions against many of his Enlightenment reforms in the Austrian Netherlands, Bohemia, and Hungary gradually splintered Catholic Enlightenment reformers. Consequently, Jansenist-inspired patriotic rhetoric can be found among partisans of regal centralization, as well as among partisans of the gentry nationalism animating Bohemian and Belgian rebels (Butterwick 2012, 6–14, 316–31; Van Kley 2008b). Nevertheless, the radicalization of the French Revolution after 1792 ultimately superseded events in Habsburg Europe and Poland. The bloodbath of the September Massacres (1792), the regicide of Louis XVI (January 1793), and the Jacobin-inspired Terror (1793–1794), when coupled to the trauma of general war, ultimately dealt a fatal blow to many strands of Catholic Enlightenment. The situation in Spain furnishes a clear example of the effects of the revolutionary rupture on Enlightenment Catholicism. Therein, the excessively close collaboration between the policies of Carlos III and the support of Jansenists and Augustinians alienated Dominicans in the late 1780s, as well as more radical reformers. This state of affairs left the pro-Gallican element vulnerable to an onslaught of ultramontane criticism emanating from ex-Jesuits who had congregated in the Italian states and received support from Pius VI in condemning the French Civil Constitution of the Clergy and other Jansenist-like reforms throughout Italy, Spain, and the Austrian Empire (Smidt 2010, 432–49). Jansenism as such became synonymous with ultramontane attacks on Catholic reformers, who were more often accused of having naïvely paved the road to the violence of the Revolution in France after 1792. The execution of Louis XVI and the war between Spain and France spelled the downfall of the Spanish official support for Catholic Enlightenment, even as constitutional apologetics in France were overwhelmed by the purge of the Girondin and by an upsurge in counterrevolutionary violence that equated Enlightenment with Revolution (Chopelin-Blanc 2009, 552–797).

Nonetheless, while it is possible to speak of a sudden volte-face in official support for Enlightened Catholicism in the face of the French revolutionary and Napoleonic years, much evidence exists that Enlightened Catholicism had a rather lengthy denouement throughout the period from 1815 to 1848. Carlo Fantappiè, Mario Rosa, and Dale Van Kley have each in their own way reframed the rootedness of the *Risorgimento* in various strands of Enlightened Catholicism (Rosa 1999, 149–84; Fantappiè 1986, 399–403; Robertson 2009, 23–32). Van Kley has provocatively suggested that the *Risorgimento* drew "energy" from "Gallican Jansenist" aspects of Enlightened Catholicism "that by the 1790s had come to stand for 'national' Catholic churches in the name of the early church," as well as from pro-Jesuit tendencies that had come to "associate the papacy with the possibility of something like religious 'progress'" (Van Kley forthcoming). Concerning the Holy Roman Empire, Michael Printy has drawn continuities between the nineteenth-century German Catholic revival and the Catholic Enlightenment in central Europe that sought to forge a national German Catholicism (Printy 2009, 1–22). The remnant of this latter-day Catholic Enlightenment was strongest among educated, urban Rhenish "Old Catholics" even as late as the *Kulturkampf,* and many of their number continued to advocate stoic and individualistic popular Catholicism, as well as a close alliance between secular authority and the German Church (Sperber 1984, 233–40).

In connection with the period from the 1780s through the revolutionary and Napoleonic period, we must also stress that Catholic Enlightenment does not lead inevitably to Counter-Enlightenment. Indeed, much scholarship points to the creativity of conservative thought in the period from 1780 through the Restoration. Carolina Armenteros's work on Joseph de Maistre shows the extent to which de Maistre's theory of history inspired certain Saint-Simonians, August Comte, and even socialists of the Proudhonian persuasion (Armenteros 2011, 283–305), and scholars such as Darrin McMahon, James Schmidt, and I have suggested elsewhere that the stark dichotomy between Counter-Enlightenment and Enlightenment is far from clear, nor in every way useful to viewing the origins and long-term trajectories of the Enlightenment in general (McMahon 2001, 189–204; Burson 2008, 955–65, 1001–2; Schmidt 2006, 5–28). Dale Van Kley and Mircea Platon have gone so far as to the discuss the controversial existence of a kind of "Enlightened Conservatism" straddling the period from the Jesuit suppression and expulsion (1773) to the Restoration era (1815–1848) (Van Kley forthcoming; Platon 2012, 182–85). Many authors assumed to have been anti-*philosophe* or Counter-Enlightenment—such as Spedalieri, de Maistre, and Bergier—emerge upon closer reading as creative synthesizers of the early Catholic Enlightenment discourses deriving from both Jesuits and Jansenists; in addition, as Mircea Platon has argued, many of these authors borrowed in rather sophisticated ways from secular Enlightenment political economy and universal history. Though clearly no friend of radical *philosophes* like Baron d'Holbach, Nicolas-Sylvestre Bergier, for example, moved in the direction of supporting universal salvation by criticizing some of Augustine's oeuvre. Bergier also criticized the shortsightedness of the French nobility in their incapacity to relinquish some of their privileges for the sake of the national interest after the calling of the Estates General. As this volume demonstrates, therefore, it can be especially problematic in the context of Catholic Enlightenment scholarship to speak too casually of the univocal conservatism of Counter-Enlightenment or counterrevolutionary discourse, without some recognition of the evident creative integration and diversification of Catholic Enlightenment apologetics in the 1760s to 1815 that led to it, even beneath the veneer of harsh criticism for the latent atheism and materialism of Radical Enlightenment (Chopelin-Blanc 2009, 7–20; Burson 2010a, 106–15; Lefebvre 2000, 95–107; Albertan-Coppola 2010, 199–242). Even in France, arguably the most distinctive of Catholic Enlightenment polities, the expulsion of the Jesuits had the unintended effect of blunting the ideological edge of the earlier ideological polarization of the 1750s even as it paradoxically ensured the diversification and evolution of Catholic Enlightenment writings (Van Kley 1975, 235; Van Kley 2006a; Burson 2010a, 106–17). As Dale Van Kley, Jeffrey D. Burson, William Everdell, Didier Masseau, and Caroline Chopelin-Blanc have argued, many styles of Catholic Enlightenment apologetics drew from both Augustinian and Molinist moral philosophy; others argued for the veracity of the Catholic revelation based on its moral utilitarianism. Still others seasoned their attacks on materialism and atheism with a nearly Rousseauian reliance upon the heart-centered natural human connection to Catholic religion, in a way foreshadowing what Alan Spitzer has called "Romantic Catholicism." Such patterns remain evident at least through the period of the Constitutional Church until the radicalization of the first republic (1792) (Everdell 1987, 79–183, 281–82; Plongeron 1976; Masseau 2000, 237–70; Masseau 2002, 121–30; Nakagawa 2002, 67–76).

Two brief caveats are warranted by way of conclusion. *First,* as the historiography of Catholic Enlightenment continues to advance, one significant gap is the field's relative and egregious inattentiveness to gender. Much work remains to be undertaken concerning gendered theological rhetoric in the Enlightenment, or women's participation in Catholic Enlightenment piety and intellectual life. This volume issues a call to redress this scholarly lacuna, and we hope that the essay by Mazotti on the historical significance of Maria Agnesi will be a small step toward more systematic and thorough investigation of gender and women within Enlightenment Catholicism. *Second,* what we view as a relative strength—the reliance on short biographies as a means of revealing connections within transnational Enlightenment

Catholicism—may be viewed by some as a potential Achilles' heel. While the genre of historical biography is by no means the only way of approaching this topic, it has certain advantages. While some of these chapters concern well-known elites, others concern figures previously marginalized in the history of the Enlightenment. Insofar as biography reveals the intersection of individual subjective experience with wider sociocultural trends, it is ideal for dramatizing how Catholic writers experienced the sweeping changes of the eighteenth century, actively choosing from among so many discursive options characteristic of the *siècle des Lumières*. Insofar as all individuals, regardless of class, gender, confession, or ethnicity, construct their subjectivities within the context of complex social networks, it becomes all the more illuminating to undertake this preliminary trek through Enlightenment Catholicism with a guidebook authored by individual lives. The individuals surveyed in this volume lived embedded within transnational networks of commerce, consumption, correspondence, and friendship that constitute the very tissues of eighteenth-century culture. The lifeblood energizing that culture is the process of Enlightenment itself (Caine 2010, 1–7, 122).

Note

For the convenience of readers, many foreign titles have been translated into English. This does not necessarily imply that all works with foreign titles have been translated into English. Readers are encouraged to consult the bibliography of each essay for the availability of English translations. Moreover, throughout this book, all quotations from foreign language sources have been rendered into English as well. In every instance, unless otherwise noted, translations of foreign language quotations into English are those of the contributors themselves.

Bibliography

Albertan-Coppola, Sylviane. 2010. *L'Abbé Nicolas-Sylvestre Bergier (1718–1790): Des Monts-Jura à Versailles, le parcours d'un apologiste du XVIIIe siècle*. Paris: Honoré Champion.

Armenteros, Carolina. 2011. *The French Idea of History: Joseph de Maistre and His Heirs, 1794–1854*. Ithaca: Cornell University Press.

Baillon, Jean-François. 1994. "La Reformation permanente: Les Newtoniens et le dogme trinitaire." In *Le Christ entre orthodoxie et lumières: Actes du colloque tenu à Genève en août 1993*, edited by Maria-Cristina Pitassi, 123–37. Genève: Droz.

Beales, Derek. 2000. "Religion and Culture." In *The Enlightenment Century: Europe, 1688–1815*, edited by T. C. W. Blanning, 131–77. Oxford: Oxford University Press.

Bell, David A. 2001. *The Cult of the Nation: Inventing French Nationalism, 1680–1800*. Cambridge, MA: Harvard University Press.

Blanning, T. C. W. 1981. "The Enlightenment in Catholic Germany." In *The Enlightenment in National Context*, edited by Roy Porter and Mikuláš Teich, 118–26. Cambridge: Cambridge University Press.

Brockliss, L. W. B. 1987. *French Higher Education in the Seventeenth and Eighteenth Centuries: A Cultural History*. Oxford: Clarendon Press.

Burke, Peter. 2009. *Popular Culture in Early Modern Europe*. 3rd rev. ed. London: Ashgate.

Burson, Jeffrey D. 2008. "The Crystallization of Counter-Enlightenment and Philosophe Identities: Theological Controversy and Catholic Enlightenment in Pre-Revolutionary France." *Church History* 77:955–1002.

———. 2010a. "The Catholic Enlightenment in France from the *Fin de Siècle* Crisis of Consciousness to the Revolution, 1650–1789." In *A Companion to the Catholic Enlightenment in Europe*, edited by Ulrich L. Lehner and Michael Printy, 63–125. Leiden: Brill.

———. 2010b. *The Rise and Fall of Theological Enlightenment: Jean-Martin de Prades and Ideological Polarization in Eighteenth-Century France*. Foreword by Dale Van Kley. Notre Dame: University of Notre Dame Press.

———. 2012. "Reflections on Enlightenment Pluralization and the Notion of Theological Enlightenment as Process." *French History* 26 (4): 524–37.

Butterwick, Richard. 2012. *The Polish Revolution and the Catholic Church, 1788–1792*. Oxford: Oxford University Press.

Caine, Barbara. 2010. *Biography and History*. Basingstoke, UK: Palgrave Macmillan.

Châtellier, Louis. 1989. *The Europe of the Devout: The Catholic Reformation and the Formation of a New Society*. Cambridge: Cambridge University Press / Paris: Editions de la Maison des Sciences de L'homme.

Chopelin-Blanc, Caroline. 2009. *De l'apologétique à l'Église constitutionelle: Adrien Lamourette (1742–1794)*. Paris: Honoré Champion.

Cotoni, Marie-Hélène. 1984. *L'Exégèse du Nouveau Testament dans la philosophie française du dix-huitième siècle*. Oxford: Voltaire Foundation.

Cottret, Monique. 1998. *Jansénisme et lumières: Pour une autre XVIIIe siècle*. Paris: Gallimard.

Darnton, Robert. 1979. *The Business of Enlightenment: A Publishing History of the Encyclopédie, 1775–1800*. Cambridge, MA: The Belknap Press of Harvard University Press.
———. 1982. *The Literary Underground of the Old Regime*. Cambridge, MA: Harvard University Press.
Ehrard, Jean. 1981. *L'Idée de Nature en France dans la première moitié du XVIII siècle*. Geneva: Slatkine. First published 1969.
Everdell, William R. 1987. *Christian Apologetics in France, 1730–1790: The Roots of Romantic Religion*. Lewiston and Queenston, ON: Edwin Mellen.
Fantappiè, Carlo. 1986. *Riforme ecclesiastiche e resistenze sociali: La sperimentazione institutionale nella diocese di Prato alla fine dell'antico regime*. Bologna: Società editrice il Mulino.
Feiner, Shmuel. 2004. *The Jewish Enlightenment*. Translated by Chaya Naor. Philadelphia: University of Pennsylvania Press.
Forster, Marc R. 2007. *Catholic Germany from the Reformation to the Enlightenment*. Basingstoke, UK: Palgrave Macmillan.
Gagliardo, John. 1991. *Germany under the Old Regime, 1600–1791*. New York: Longman Publishing Group.
Garrioch, David. 1996. *The Formation of the Parisian Bourgeoisie 1680–1830*. Cambridge: Cambridge University Press.
Gay, Peter. 1966. *The Enlightenment: An Interpretation*. Vol. 1, *The Rise of Modern Paganism*. New York: Knopf.
Ghitta, Ovidiu. 2011. "Modalités de communication en Transylvanie au XVIIIe siècle." *Transylvanian Review* 20:24–34.
Goldie, Mark. 1993. "Priestcraft and the Birth of Whiggism." In *Political Discourse in Early Modern Britain*, edited by Nicholas Phillipson and Quentin Skinner, 209–31. Cambridge: Cambridge University Press.
Gres-Gayer, Jacques M. 1991. *Théologie et pouvoir en Sorbonne: La faculté de théologie de Paris et la bulle "Unigenitus," 1714–1721*. Paris: Klincksieck.
Groethuysen, Bernard. 1968. *The Bourgeois: Catholicism vs. Capitalism in Eighteenth-Century France*. Translated by Mary Ilford. London: Barrie and Rockliff the Cresset Press.
Hammersley, Rachel. 2010. *The English Republican Tradition and Eighteenth-Century France: Between the Ancients and the Moderns*. Manchester: University of Manchester Press.
Hsia, R. Po-Chia. 2005. *The World of Catholic Renewal, 1540–1770*. Cambridge: Cambridge University Press.
Israel, Jonathan I. 2001. *Radical Enlightenment: Philosophy and the Making of Modernity, 1650–1750*. Oxford: Oxford University Press.
———. 2006. *Enlightenment Contested: Philosophy, Modernity, and the Emancipation of Man, 1670–1752*. Oxford: Oxford University Press.

———. 2011. *Democratic Enlightenment: Philosophy, Revolution, and Human Rights, 1750–1790.* Oxford: Oxford University Press.

Jacob, Margaret. 1991. *Freemasonry and Politics in Eighteenth-Century Europe.* New York: Oxford University Press.

———. 2007. *Strangers Nowhere in the World: The Rise of Cosmopolitanism in Early Modern Europe.* Philadelphia: University of Pennsylvania Press.

Kitchen, Martin. 2006. *A History of Modern Germany 1800–2000.* Oxford: Blackwell Publishing.

Kors, Alan C. 1987. Introduction to *Anticipations of Enlightenment in England, France, and Germany,* edited by Alan Charles Kors and Paul J. Korshin, 1–10. Philadelphia: University of Pennsylvania Press.

Kreiser, Robert. 1978. *Miracles, Convulsions, and Ecclesiastical Politics in Early Eighteenth-Century Paris.* Princeton: Princeton University Press.

Kristeller, Paul Oskar. 1964. *Eight Philosophers of the Italian Renaissance.* Stanford: Stanford University Press.

Lefebvre, Philippe. 2000. "Le regard sur l'incrédule dans les sermons de la deuxième moitié du dix-huitième siècle: Evolution." In *Religions en transition dans la seconde moitié du dix-huitième siècle,* edited by Louis Châtellier, 95–107. Oxford: Voltaire Foundation.

Lehner, Ulrich L. 2010. "The Many Faces of Catholic Enlightenment." In *A Companion to the Catholic Enlightenment in Europe,* edited by Ulrich L. Lehner and Michael Printy, 1–61. Leiden: Brill.

———. 2011. *Enlightened Monks: The German Benedictines, 1740–1803.* Oxford: Oxford University Press.

Linton, Marisa. 2001. *The Politics of Virtue in Enlightenment France.* Basingstoke, UK: Palgrave Macmillan.

Maire, Catherine-Laurence. 1998. *De la cause de Dieu à la cause de la Nation: Le Jansénisme au XVIIIe siècle.* Paris: Gallimard.

Masseau, Didier. 2000. *Les ennemis des philosophes: L'antiphilosophie au temps des Lumières.* Paris: Editions Albin Michel.

———. 2002. "La position des apologistes conciliateurs." *Dix-huitième siècle* 34:121–31.

McMahon, Darrin. 2001. *Enemies of Enlightenment: The French Counter-Enlightenment and the Making of Modernity.* Oxford: Oxford University Press.

———. 2006. *Happiness: A History.* New York: Grove Press.

Merkle, Sebastian. 1909. *Die katholische Beurteilung des Aufklärungszeitalters.* Berlin: K. Curtius.

Merriman, John. 2010. *A History of Modern Europe from the Renaissance to the Present.* New York and London: W. W. Norton.

Michel, Marie-José. 2000. *Jansénisme et Paris, 1640–1730.* Paris: Klincksieck.

Miller, Samuel J. 1978. *Portugal and Rome, c. 1748–1830: An Aspect of Catholic Enlightenment.* Rome: Università Gregoriana Editrice.
Möller, Horst. 1986. *Vernunft und Kritik: Deutsche Aufklärung im 17 und 18 Jahrhundert.* Frankfurt: Suhrkamp.
Nakagawa, Hisayasu. 2002. "J.-J. Rousseau et J.-G. Pompignan: La 'Profession de foi du vicaire Savoyard' et 'De la religion civile' critiques par l'*Instruction pastorale.*" *Dix-huitième siècle* 34:67–76.
Noël, Charles C. 2001. "Clerics and Crown in Bourbon Spain, 1700–1808: Jesuits, Jansenists, and Enlightened Reformers." In *Religion and Politics in Enlightenment Europe,* edited by James E. Bradley and Dale K. Van Kley, 119–53. Notre Dame: University of Notre Dame Press.
———. 2009. "In the House of Reform: The Bourbon Court of Eighteenth-Century Spain." In *Enlightened Reform in Southern Europe and Its Atlantic Colonies, c. 1750–1830,* edited by Gabriel Paquette, 145–65. Burlington, VT: Ashgate.
Northeast, Catherine M. 1991. *The Parisian Jesuits and the Enlightenment, 1700–1762.* Oxford: Voltaire Foundation.
O'Connor, Thomas. 1995. *An Irish Theologian in Enlightenment France: Luke Joseph Hooke, 1714–96.* Dublin: Four Courts Press.
O'Malley, James W. 2002. *Trent and All That: Renaming Catholicism in Early Modern Europe.* Cambridge, MA: Harvard University Press.
Outram, Dorinda. 2005. *The Enlightenment.* 2nd ed. Cambridge: Cambridge University Press.
Palmer, R. R. 1939. *Catholics and Unbelievers in Eighteenth-Century France.* Princeton: Princeton University Press.
———. 1976. *The Age of the Democratic Revolution: A Political History of Europe and America, 1760–1800.* Vol. 1, *The Challenge.* Princeton: Princeton University Press.
Paquette, Gabriel. 2008. *Enlightenment, Governance, and Reform in Spain and Its Empire, 1759–1808.* Basingstoke, UK: Palgrave Macmillan.
Parsons, Jotham. 2004. *The Church in the Republic: Gallicanism and Political Ideology in Renaissance France.* Washington, DC: Catholic University Press.
Platon, Mircea. 2012. "Physiocracy, Patriotism and Reform Catholicism in Jean-Baptiste-Louis Gresset's Anti-*Philosophe* Enlightenment." *French History* 26 (2): 182–202.
Plongeron, Bernard. 1969. "Recherches sur l'Aufklärung catholique en Europe occidental, 1770–1830." *Revue d'histoire moderne et contemporaine* 16:555–605.
———. 1973. *Théologie et politique au siècle des Lumières.* Genève: Droz.
———. 1976. "Bonheur et 'civilisation chrétienne': Une nouvelle apologetique après 1760." In *Transactions of the Fourth International Congress*

of the Enlightenment VI, edited by Theodore Besterman, 1637–55. Oxford: Voltaire Foundation.
Pocock, J. G. A. 1999. *The Enlightenments of Edward Gibbon, 1737–1764.* Vol. 1, *Barbarism and Religion.* Cambridge: Cambridge University Press.
Porter, Roy. 2000. *The Creation of the Modern World: The Untold Story of the British Enlightenment.* New York: W. W. Norton.
Printy, Michael. 2009. *Enlightenment and the Creation of German Catholicism.* Cambridge: Cambridge University Press.
Rabb, Theodore K. 1975. *The Struggle for Stability in Early Modern Europe.* Oxford: Oxford University Press.
Reinalter, Helmut. 2006. "Einleitung: Der Ausgangspunkt; Die Ambivalenzen der Afklärung." In *Aufklärungsprozesse seit dem 18. Jahrhundert,* 11–27. Würzburg: Verlag Königshausen & Neumann.
Robertson, John. 2005. *The Case for the Enlightenment: Scotland and Naples, 1680–1760.* Cambridge: Cambridge University Press.
———. 2009. "Enlightenment, Reform, and Monarchy in Italy." In *Enlightened Reform in Southern Europe and Its Atlantic Colonies, c. 1750–1830,* edited by Gabriel Paquette, 23–32. Burlington, VT: Ashgate.
Roche, Daniel. 1978. *Le siècle des lumières en province, academies et académiciens provinciaux, 1680–1789.* 2 vols. Paris: École des Hautes Études en Sciences Sociales.
Rosa, Mario. 1999. "'L'Aufklärung' cattolica." In *Settecento religioso: Politica della ragione e religione del cuore.* Venice: Marsilio.
Rosenblatt, Helena. 2006. "The Christian Enlightenment." In *Enlightenment, Reawakening and Revolution, 1660–1815,* edited by Stewart J. Brown and Timothy Tackett, 283–301. Cambridge History of Christianity 7. Cambridge: Cambridge University Press.
Schilling, Heinz. 1995. "Confessional Europe." In *Handbook of Early Modern Europe, 1400–1600: Late Middle Ages, Renaissance and Reformation,* edited by Thomas A. Brady, Heiko A. Oberman, and James D. Tracy, 2 vols., 2:641–81. Leiden: Brill.
Schmidt, James. 2006. *What Is Enlightenment? Eighteenth-Century Answers to Twentieth-Century Questions.* Berkeley: University of California Press.
Shelford, April G. 2008. *Transforming the Republic of Letters: Pierre-Daniel Huet and European Intellectual Life, 1650–1720.* Rochester: University of Rochester Press.
Shovlin, John. 2009. "Rethinking Enlightened Reform in a French Context." In *Enlightened Reform in Southern Europe and Its Atlantic Colonies, c. 1750–1830,* edited by Gabriel Paquette, 47–61. Burlington, VT: Ashgate.
Smidt, Andrea J. 2010. "*Luces por la Fe:* The Cause of Catholic Enlightenment in 18th-Century Spain." In *A Companion to the Catholic Enlighten-*

ment in Europe, edited by Ulrich L. Lehner and Michael Printy, 403–52. Leiden: Brill.

Sorkin, David. 2008. *The Religious Enlightenment: Protestants, Jews, and Catholics from London to Vienna.* Princeton: Princeton University Press.

Souza, Evergton Sales. 2010. "The Catholic Enlightenment in Portugal." In *A Companion to the Catholic Enlightenment in Europe,* edited by Ulrich L. Lehner and Michael Printy, 359–402. Leiden: Brill.

Sperber, Jonathan. 1984. *Popular Catholicism in Nineteenth-Century Germany.* Princeton: Princeton University Press.

Strayer, Brian. 2008. *Suffering Saints: Jansenists and Convulsionnaires in France, 1640–1799.* Brighton, UK: Sussex University Press.

Tsapina, Olga A. 2001. "Secularization and Opposition in the Time of Catherine the Great." In *Religion and Politics in Enlightenment Europe,* edited by James E. Bradley and Dale K. Van Kley, 334–90. Notre Dame: University of Notre Dame Press.

Tuilier, André. 1994. *De Louis XIV à la crise de 1968.* Vol. 2, *Histoire de l'Université de Paris et de la Sorbonne.* Paris: Nouvelle Librairie de France.

Van Kley, Dale K. 1975. *The Jansenists and the Expulsion of the Jesuits from France, 1757–1765.* New Haven: Yale University Press.

———. 1987. "Pierre Nicole, Jansenism, and the Morality of Enlightened Self-Interest." In *Anticipations of the Enlightenment in England, France, and Germany,* edited by Alan Charles Kors and Paul J. Korshin, 69–85. Philadelphia: University of Pennsylvania Press.

———. 1996. *The Religious Origins of the French Revolution from Calvin to the Civil Constitution, 1561–1791.* New Haven: Yale University Press.

———. 2006a. "Jansenism and the International Suppression of the Jesuits." In *Enlightenment, Reawakening and Revolution, 1660–1815,* edited by Stewart J. Brown and Timothy Tackett, 302–28. Cambridge History of Christianity 7. Cambridge: Cambridge University Press.

———. 2006b. "The Rejuvenation and Rejection of Jansenism in History and Historiography: Recent Literature on Eighteenth-Century Jansenism in France." *French Historical Studies* 29 (4): 649–84.

———. 2008a. "Civic Humanism in Clerical Garb: Gallican Memories of the Early Church and the Project of Primitivist Reform, 1719–1791." *Past and Present* 2008 (1): 77–120.

———. 2008b. "Religion and the Age of Patriot Reform." *Journal of Modern History* 80:252–95.

———. Forthcoming. "From the Catholic Enlightenment to the Risorgimento: The Debate between Nicola Spedalieri and Pietro Tamburini, 1791–1797." *Past and Present.*

PART 1
Catholic Enlightenment and the Papacy

1

Pope Benedict XIV (1740–1758)

The Ambivalent Enlightener

MARIO ROSA

The biographical profile of Benedict XIV allows us to understand many aspects of the Catholic Enlightenment and its history, in the light of numerous studies of a general nature from recent decades. It is significant that these aspects initially find their place in the framework of the Tridentine tradition but, under pressure from an Enlightened Catholicism (especially a Catholicism enlightened by the "regulated devotion" of Ludovico Antonio Muratori), find expression in some encyclicals from the first decade of Benedict's papacy, which treated the pastoral commitments of the bishops and the training of the clergy, and in several interventions regarding the critical updating of hagiography and ecclesiastic historical studies. This dynamic conception of culture would soon open up greater initiatives by Benedict XIV, such as reform of "La Sapienza" University in Rome, restoration of classical and Christian monuments like the Colosseum and Santa

Maria Maggiore, and relationships with Italian and foreign learned men—from Muratori to Maffei, Boscovich to Fontenelle, and the much-discussed one with Voltaire. The reform of the Congregation of the Index, made by Benedict XIV in 1753, was meant to signify on Rome's part a new way of looking at modern scientific culture and a more liberal development of debates within Catholic culture itself.

At the same time the work of Benedict XIV allows us to track the ways in which the Roman Church, aware of the new political realities that had come into being in Europe following the wars in the first half of the century, made an important reply through a series of concordats with some Italian states and with Portugal and Spain. It would be this awareness of contemporary developments by Benedict XIV that opened new perspectives to the then-emerging power in Europe, the Protestant Prussia of Frederick II, by redefining relationships between Catholics and Protestants, thus easing the century-old rifts deriving from the Reformation. In the same constructive spirit, the pope intervened within the Papal States, bringing about a series of economic and social reforms in order to root out entrenched financial and administrative difficulties. Such reforms were in agreement with what was happening in the Europe of the Enlightenment with regard to reforming its culture. As a result, Benedict XIV become renowned not only as a "philosophic" pope, as the Enlightenment press already called him, but as an enlightened sovereign of a state that, according to European public opinion, seemed characterized by a particular backwardness.

On this intertwining of different eighteenth-century elements Benedict XIV also based other interventions, relating to the economic and commercial reality of the world: for example, the problem of the lawfulness of a loan at interest, about which the pope, in his encyclical *Vix pervenit* of 1745, took a mediatory stance between the contrasting motivations found in the Catholic world. We again find a mediatory stance in his other decisions; for example, those regarding the missionary practice followed in China and India between 1742 and 1744, or issues concerning French Jansenism, upon which he took a conciliatory position in another encyclical of 1756. Benedict XIV often used encyclicals in dialogue with the Catholic world, and his pontificate was thereby instrumental in giving that world the modern form we know today.

However, the work of Benedict, especially as he shifted during the second decade of his papacy (from 1750 onward), followed a precarious course between the weight of the past and the requirements of a present at the threshold of modernity. This shift derived not so much from the swing away from the initial surge of reform characteristic of his pontificate, nor from the reaction of more conservative organs of the Curia with regard to the development of the Enlighteners—instead, Benedict XIV himself grew increasingly aware of the need to address aspects of the new culture of Enlighteners that could subvert Catholic values, and to do so in a way that would give the church greater internal cohesion and a more solid defense against the outside world. A sign of this change would be the stance toward the Jewish world taken by the Papal States, a stance that changed from relative tolerance to more repressive intolerance, even at the risk of a wider repositioning of traditional anti-Semitic stereotypes, as in the papal bull *Beatus Andreas* of 1755. Almost at the same time would follow clearer distancing from Enlightenment culture, with the condemnations of Montesquieu (1752) and Voltaire (1753–1757). Such condemnations would negatively condition, and for a longer period of time, the stance of the Catholic world toward the "modernity" to which Benedict XIV had opened the doors.

This is why this chapter discusses an "ambivalence" by the pope, one that swings between acceptance of the "new" and deep concern for the future of the church on the one hand and a Catholic faith increasingly in conflict with the autonomous development of Enlightenment culture and the process of secularization of society on the other. Certainly, limits and even contradictions existed in the work of Benedict XIV, but with regard to his personality the myth of an open, tolerant pope, one disposed to fruitful dialogue with his own time, has prevailed. This myth surrounding his pontificate forms an integral part of his history and allows us to present Benedict XIV among the most important interpreters of a Catholic Enlightenment, as one who showed, from the very brink of modernity, a way to live religious values in a manner that would most nearly correspond with man's nature and the aspirations of humanity.

Family and Educational Background

Born in Bologna on 31 March 1675 to a noble family, Prospero Lambertini attended school at the Order of Somaschi's Collegio Clementino in Rome. He graduated in 1694 with degrees in both theology and law. His curial career led to his appointment as Promoter of the Faith in the Sacred Congregation of Rites in 1708, and in 1720 he became Secretary to the Congregation of the Council. In both these positions he demonstrated exceptional common sense and moderation. He was not, however, devoid of a certain rigorism; for example, in the Congregation of Rites he presented an objection to the new Jesuit devotion to the Sacred Heart of Jesus.

Appointed titular bishop of Theodosia in 1724, Lambertini then became archbishop of Ancona in 1727, and was created cardinal in 1728. He moved to the extremely important archepiscopal see of Bologna in 1731. Tridentine tradition and the examples of Charles Borromeo (1538–1584) and Gabriele Paleotti (1522–1597) (his predecessor as archbishop of Bologna) inspired Lambertini's pastoral actions. He was greatly committed to the control of ecclesiastical institutions, the training and customs of the clergy, and the spiritual growth of the laity. To increase and foster devotion, he developed the practice of town and diocesan missions.

The Scholar and Reformer in Bologna

Fundamental for understanding Lambertini's work at Bologna is the *Collection of Some Notifications, Edicts and Instructions, Published for the Good of Governing His Diocese* (*Raccolta di alcune notificazioni, editti ed istruzioni pubblicate per buon governo della sua diocesi*), published in five volumes (Bologna, 1733–1740), which went through several printings. He wrote it in preparation for a future diocesan synod, which never took place. The result of the aforementioned undertaking, his work *On the Diocesan Synod* (*De Synodo diocesana*), foresaw greater autonomy in local religious life than there had been under the

Roman centralism that had emerged at the height of the Counter-Reformation. Like the presynodal work, this book went through numerous editions and remains a crucial source for understanding Lambertini's pastoral administration, both as bishop and, later, as pope. However, because of the Curia's opposition to its publication, *De Synodo diocesana* came out only in 1748, after Lambertini had become pope.

In the meantime, another important work had appeared in print—*Beatification of the Servants of God and the Canonization of the Beatified* (*De Servorum Dei beatificatione et Beatorum canonizatione* [Bologna, 1734–1738])—into which Lambertini distilled twenty years of experience gained in the Congregation of Rites. This is another valuable source for understanding Lambertini's historical-critical attitude in regard to the cult of saints and his receptivity toward modern scientific knowledge—an attitude that often led him to express distinct reservations in regard to miraculous events and mystical visionary phenomena exhibited in the lives of some candidates for sainthood. This opus immediately met with great interest and approval even beyond the Catholic world, triggering, among other things, a detailed positive review in the prestigious Protestant periodical *Acta eruditorum* of Leipzig. It remained the basis of procedural practice for canonization by the Catholic Church until the recent reforms of Paul VI (1967) and John Paul II (1983).

The Pope of Careful Reform

Lambertini was elected pope following the death of Pope Clement XII. The conclave of 1740 had lasted six months because of the crisis the Catholic Church was undergoing, given the waning Counter-Reformation and the spreading Enlightenment. Immediately following his election, having taken the name of Benedict XIV, Lambertini forcefully expressed his desire to reclaim positions that had been lost to the church and to remodel relationships with political powers and European society in response to changing conditions. The new pope's statement set the stage for his much-celebrated policy aimed at a concordat. In this and in other cases, the pope had recourse to advisers and trusted experts, among whom were Secretary of State Silvio Valenti Gonzaga (1691–1756) and Cardinal Pompeo Aldrovandi (1686–1752), who headed the Apostolic Dataria. Their support helped him to overcome the powerful and persistent resistance of more traditional sections of the Curia against the pope's new course of ecclesiastical policy and his religious reformism.

In 1741, following a new formulation of the concordat with the kingdom of Sardinia (Lambertini also had collaborated on Sardinia's 1727 concordat), the far more important concordat with the kingdom of Naples was signed. The political and social needs of that southern state, which recently had come under the Bourbon monarchy, were favorably treated in the delicate areas of ecclesiastical property and its exemptions, of the right to asylum reserved for churches and sacred places, and of the personal immunity given to clergymen guilty of common crimes. In 1745, the concordat with Portugal followed, and in 1753, the concordat with Spain. Although the concordat with Spain transferred to the sovereign the pontifical right of appointing almost all the ecclesiastical benefices in the kingdom (in return for substantial financial compensation), it did allow Benedict to make drastic reforms to the Roman Datary, eliminating the endless abuses that had developed around the traffic in Spanish benefices of papal appointment. Both of the concordats with the Iberian countries reinforced the traditional rights of secular sovereigns, and consequently, those sovereigns relaxed their anticurial policies—but only temporarily. Under Benedict's successors, these policies would resurface with renewed vigor pertaining to the Jesuit problem.

The preceding concordats or agreements, as well as the final Austrian Lombardy concordat in 1757, which dealt with the taxation of church endowments, contributed much to forming the image of an enlightened and tolerant pope, keen to reconcile the church with the modern world. Benedict would consciously foster this image through other initiatives, and by continuing to build good relationships with other European powers, including the Austria of Maria Theresa (reigned 1740–1780) and the Prussia of Frederick II (reigned 1740–1786), both during and after the War of Austrian Succession (1740–1748) and the Seven Years' War (1756–1763).

Thanks to his flexible realism, Benedict succeeded in securing constructive dialogue with the Habsburgs and Frederick II to safeguard the rights of Catholics in Silesia as they passed from Austria to Prussia. His flexibility also extended to issues between Catholics and Protestants in general. Nevertheless, he retained toward Protestants the long-standing Roman attitude of condemnation. Indeed, he was decidedly critical of some of Cardinal Angelo Maria Querini's (1660–1755) irenic efforts toward unity. Likewise, the pope was quite hostile to the religious tolerance supported by Cardinal Philipp Ludwig von Sinzendorf (1699–1747), archbishop of Breslau. Benedict confirmed his dim view of those relapsed to Calvinism, especially in France, by his approval of the repressive policy of Louis XV (reigned 1715–1774) toward them. Thus, the pope's response to the problem of tolerance in Germany and relations with Sinzendorf demonstrates the papal stance toward Calvinists in general. It stood in strange contrast to the troubled, irenic, and ecumenical call that the Bishop of Soissons, François Fitz-James (1709–1764), would direct to Benedict in a letter of March 1755 (Appolis 1960).

However, in the course of complex negotiations with Prussia to resolve intricate political-religious and institutional problems at the end of the War of Austrian Succession, an absolutely new element emerged in the history of relations between the papacy and Protestant countries. For the first time since the Reformation, the representative of a Protestant prince was nominated in 1747. This Prussian agent, appointed privately, would negotiate with the Holy See on behalf of the Palatinate. This resulted in a modus vivendi that, in 1747, surmounted previous opposition (which dated at least as far back as the Peace of Westphalia of 1648) and led to general agreement on problems of matrimonial legislation and the subject of benefices. Moreover, concerning matrimonial legislation, Benedict was able to refer to his own provision of only a few years earlier. In 1741, with great wisdom, he had issued a special encyclical, *Satis Vobis,* relating to the sacraments in the Low Countries. This document followed the canonist tradition, while departing from Tridentine legislation. It addressed some important aspects related to the validity of the bond of matrimony among Protestants, if a couple had converted to Catholicism; as well as the validity of mixed marriages, if the non-Catholic spouse had converted to Catholicism (Greco 2011).

Concurrently with these somewhat political or diplomatic concerns, Benedict instituted numerous religious reforms, issued as encyclicals between 1740 and 1750. Reflecting an Enlightened Catholicism, these encyclicals would consolidate Benedict's fame. Various documents reminded bishops of their episcopal duties, emphasizing pastoral visitations, training of clergy, and bishops' duty of residence (*Ubi primum* in 1740 and *Ad universae Christianae republicae* in 1746). These also regulated the open competition for access to ecclesiastic appointments (1742). During these years, Pope Benedict also pursued, albeit less successfully, the reform of the Roman breviary. Driven by the erudite historical criticism of the Benedictines of Saint-Maur, as well as Muratori (1672–1750) and the biblical patristic preferences of the rigorist culture, further studies by Benedict stimulated the development of hagiography and ecclesiastic history. Nevertheless, the pope was unable to implement a reform of the Breviary, although his other liturgical initiatives moved forward, inspired by the "regulated devotion" of Muratori. In this context, the ceremonies of worship were simplified. The days of obligation were reduced (1742–1754), resulting in an increase in the number of working days, and thus the possibility for workers to earn more. The more elaborate forms of popular devotion were restored, as much as possible, to a simpler style more related to Christ than to Counter-Reformation and Baroque pomp (1746). The liturgical reforms that simultaneously accompanied the devotional changes likewise showed positive results. The revision of the Roman Martyrology was concluded in 1748. In 1754, the revision of the ancient Glagolitic missal for the Slavonic countries was completed. The edition of the Greek prayer book, which had been planned under Urban VIII, finally was made available to the Greek Uniate Church in 1756, confirming Benedict's interest in the liturgy and rites of the eastern communities. His interest in unionist tradition also facilitated the institution of the patriarchate of the Armenians of Cilicia in union with Rome.

Another major document was issued during the 1740s, important because of its social, economic, and moral implications: the encyclical *Vix pervenit* (1745), addressed to the Italian bishops. With this document, Benedict intervened in a lively debate ongoing at that time, especially in Holland and Italy, regarding usury and the lawfulness of collecting interest on loaned capital. The work *On Licit and Illicit Usury (De usuris licitis et illicitis,* 1743), by the Utrecht Jansenist Nicolas Broedersen, responding to the demands of Dutch commerce, and above all the work *The Use of Money (Dell'impiego del denaro,* 1744), by the learned Scipione Maffei (1675–1755) from Verona, gave impetus to this encyclical. In response to both these works of "latitudinarian" inspiration, which had already sparked responses by the more rigid French Jansenism and the rigorist front, Benedict's encyclical simultaneously reasserted the prevailing thesis of traditional canon law forbidding even moderate collection of interest and accepted the rigorist thesis. Nevertheless it accepted the age-old practice of permitting "extrinsic" interest, that is, interest that was not intrinsic to the contract of a loan. This could mean, for example, extra compensation for damage and loss. In all other instances, "whatever is received over and above what is fair is a real injustice," the pope wrote.

Benedict's broadening of Catholic doctrine to address the needs of contemporary society did not prevent opposing sides from subjecting the papal document to conflicting and restrictive readings. Indeed, the question would continue to be debated among theologians and Catholic moralists even into the subsequent century (Vismara 2004). Benedict's intervention on this front took on a paradigmatic value for his contemporaries, because it seemed to best express the mediatory, well-balanced positions of this pope. It was similar to his approaches to other problems that divided the Catholic world at that time. Benedict always tried to alleviate the often deep rifts and to encourage a common Catholic evangelization effort against the ideas of the Enlightenment. His concern in this regard increased markedly in the second decade of his papacy.

The Chinese and Malabar Rites Controversies and the Relationship to Jansenism

Benedict's previous well-balanced interventions, some years earlier and outside of Europe, demonstrate the particular attention this pope gave to mission territories. In 1741, in a papal brief instructing the Portuguese bishops of South America, Benedict had taken sides in favor of the human rights of the South American Indians. He also took decisive measures concerning missions in China and India, where disputes recurred regarding the "accommodating" missionary methods of the Jesuits. In the first Chinese case, Benedict confirmed the Roman ban of the "Chinese rites," those customs rooted in Chinese society, such as ancestor worship, which the Jesuits had been permitting. With the papal bull *Ex quo* (1742), he put an end to the age-old disputes between the Jesuits, on one hand, and the Franciscans and Dominicans on the other. These disputes had been tackled in various ways by previous popes, most recently by his predecessor Clement XII (1730–1740). However, interpretative uncertainties had remained in regard to the various previous instructions. In a second case connected with Indian missions, in the papal bull *Omnium sollicitudinum* (1744), Benedict showed himself, contrary to the recent bans by Clement XII (1734 and 1739), to be willing to recognize the legality of the "Malabar rites"—certain local traditional civil observances—allowing a further ten-year adjournment for the benevolent Jesuit missionary approach.

A decade later, Benedict would continue along these mediatory lines regarding a grave political-religious crisis in France that was dividing the monarchy, parliament, and public opinion. In his encyclical *Ex omnibus Christiani orbis* (1756), Benedict published an emblematic decision about the difficult matter of *billet de confession*. Archbishop Christophe de Beaumont of Paris was requiring Jansenists, while in health, to obtain a written statement from a priest of proven anti-Jansenist faith to document their repentance and confession as a prerequisite to receiving viaticum when on their deathbed. The bitter dispute in France had reached very high levels. Addressing the encyclical *Ex omnibus* to the French bishops, Benedict first affirmed his respect for the papal bull *Unigenitus,* which had in 1713 renewed the condemnation of Jansenism. He then proceeded to resolve the issue by defining, with particular moderation, the procedure for the concession of absolution to the dying. Prior to this encyclical, absolution had been refused by anti-Jansenist clergy as well as by bishops, even on the basis of mere suspicion that the penitent still adhered to banned doctrines. Following this sign of the pope's generosity and particular attention to the movement, the response in Jansenist circles to the encyclical's call for "peace in the church" would lead to a more liberal explanation of *Unigenitus* and a more general definition of the Catholic doctrine on themes connected with the past bans. Successive debates, from France to Utrecht, dealt with reuniting European Jansenist dissenters with Rome. This topic was discussed in the Curia and even in Pope Benedict's entourage. A notable proponent was Cardinal Fortunato Tamburini (1683–1761), who not only was the pope's friend but had been among his most-heeded collaborators in drafting the encyclical. Moreover, influential French parliamentarians, as well as members of the court and highly placed state administrators, also followed the issue with interest. Their requests led to an unofficial mission to Rome by the Jansenist canon of Auxerre, Augustin-Charles-Jean Clément. Despite careful preparation, his mission did not achieve the desired success. A series of mishaps prevented Clément from reaching Rome until August 1758, a few months after Benedict's death (Rosa 1999).

Reforms in the Papal States

Compared to the above-mentioned problems, to which Benedict responded by renewing his commitment to governing the universal church, the reforms he initiated in his role as sovereign of the Papal States between 1754 and 1756 were more intermittent. These were the years of peace following the end of the War of Austrian Succession and preceding the start of the Seven Years' War. As early as the decade 1740–1750, he clearly intended to resolve the very grave financial situation of the State, an unavoidable precondition for any other kind of reform at an economic and administrative level. Also, to this end, Benedict had recourse to advisers and trusted experts, from the banker Girolamo Belloni, the general customs administrator, to the already mentioned Aldrovandi and Valenti Gonzaga, to Clemente Argenvilliers, who inspired various papal attempts aimed to draw on the network of tolls, monopolies, and local privileges and to facilitate trade through the ports of Ancona and Civitavecchia. The constitution *Apostolicae Sedis aerarium* (1746) was a comprehensive intervention that defined a common method of administration, prescribing the recording of revenues and expenses of the Camera Apostolica, the use of annual balance sheets, and periodic audits. Other papal documents between 1748 and 1753 tended to liberalize internal trade, not only trade in grain but also the developing business of agricultural and manufactured products. Although the structure of the state and uncertainties in implementation did limit the reforms, nevertheless—accompanied and stimulated by contemporary publicity—the interventions and related economic debates achieved some results and gave the public a sense that the papal government was in tune with what was then taking place in European society.

Benedict's cultural policy of this time can be viewed within the framework of his reform efforts. He focused especially on the city of Rome, but also on his hometown Bologna and its Institute of Science, to which Benedict left his own personal library. There was the founding of academies in the center of Catholicism (Donato 2000), the reform of the University of Rome, *La Sapienza* (thanks to Argenvilliers), the enlargement of the Vatican Library, and the organization of new museums, including the Christian Museum, the *Museo Cristiano*. These measures also often demonstrated clear apologetic and even triumphalist intentions, whether related to restoration of ancient sacred monuments like the basilicas of Santa Maria Maggiore and Santa Maria degli Angeli or to the restoration of ancient classical monuments like the Pantheon and the Colosseum (the latter famous as the location of the persecutions of the first Christian martyrs). Alongside such accomplishments, the personal friendship and protection Benedict extended to men of culture—from Maffei to Muratori, from Boscovich (see Jonathan Wright's article in this volume) to Bernard de Fontenelle (1657–1757), from Francesco Algarotti (1712–1764) to Pierre-Louis Maupertuis (1698–1759), who facilitated contact between Benedict and Frederick II in the middle of the century—would set the definitive seal on European admiration for Benedict. Indeed, even in the Anglican world, which remained still so strongly antipapal, Horace Walpole (1717–1797) would praise this pope in a commemorative epigraph on the papacy of Lambertini.

The Conservative Turn after 1750

The holy year of 1750 seems to mark the height of Benedict's reign, and can also be considered as a turning point between the first and second decades of his long pontificate. Certainly, other innovative stimuli of the pope were not lacking; for example, the reform of the Congregation of the Index through the constitution *Sollicita ac provida* in 1753, which influenced the new 1757 edition of the *Index of Prohibited Books* (Delpiano 2007). These were interventions stemming from Benedict's legal sense and remarkable cultural sensibility, and through them, the traditional strictness of book censorship was significantly eased. For example, it became permissible for a Catholic author to defend a work subjected to examination by the Congregation. It should be noted that this disposition was soon ignored in the restrictive climate of the papacy after Benedict's death. Moreover, the ban on writings in defense of the Copernican system was canceled, and, consequently, there was an implicit suspension of the banning of Galileo's writings. Likewise, the translation of the Scriptures into vernacular languages was more broadly allowed, albeit only with the approval of the Holy See; and the age-old post-Tridentine restrictions on direct reading of the biblical text in the "vulgar" language by the faithful were lifted. This liberalization particularly affected the field of culture and Italian religious life.

Despite these advances, however, Benedict's general administration of the universal church after 1750 seems to have become more rigorous. In any case, the burden of new problems began to restrain his earlier momentum and to set the pope on a decided course of controlling and defending the institution internally, while externally, the ecclesiastic structure would respond more rigidly on a disciplinary and doctrinal level. Some restrictive directions were already obvious by the end of the preceding decade, especially in regard to the Jewish communities located within the Papal States. Indeed, regrettably, not only did he confirm and increase the traditional bans and the segregationist policy, but two of his letters in 1747 and 1751, one addressed to the deputy religious administrator of Rome and the other to the councilor of the Holy Office, further encouraged the Catholic attitude toward conversion of the Jewish community by extending and legalizing the sphere of "offering" to the Catholic faith Jewish babies, a practice until then limited to the Jewish parent who had converted. Now, he extended the practice to paternal and maternal grandparents who had converted to Catholicism (Rosa 1997; Caffiero 2012), despite the opposition of the parents who remained Jews. He took up a similar attitude in the encyclical *A quo primum* (1751), addressed to bishops in Poland. While condemning violent forms of persecution of the Jews, *A quo primum* also acknowledged the age-old anti-Jewish repressive practices still existing in that country. Nevertheless, it was on his command that Lorenzo Ganganelli, the future Pope Clement XIV (1769–1774), investigated and, after the pontiff's death, refuted the claims of Jewish "ritual murders" in Poland (Roth 1934). Benedict, however, seems to have endorsed in one of his last documents, the papal bull *Beatus Andreas* of 1755, the recurrent accusation against the Jews of the "ritual murder" of Catholic children. Benedict's pronouncement in the case of the fifteenth-century incident of Andreas from Rinn, whom the pope recognized as being beatified *per viam cultus* and not by a formal canonical trial, presupposes a well-tested anti-Jewish propaganda paradigm, destined to last within the Catholic Church up into the twentieth century (Cusumano 2002; Caffiero 2012).

Likewise, Benedict's limits of tolerance with respect to the Enlightenment became increasingly evident. After some individual prohibitions of minor works in the new culture, the papal bull *Providas Romanorum Pontificum* (1751) renewed the condemnation on Freemasonry already formulated by Clement XII in 1738. The ban of Montesquieu's *Spirit of the Laws* would follow in 1752, not without political difficulties put forward by France, given the author's fame, so that the work was not affected by a special decree, but was inserted in the annual list of the *Index of Prohibited Books*. Such a proscription was more difficult to enforce upon works already published by Voltaire. In his case, this was not only because of the writer's reputation but also because of the dedication of the tragedy *Mahomet the Prophet or Fanaticism* (*Le phanatisme ou Mahomet le prophète*), which Voltaire had, without prior consent, inscribed to the pope and which Benedict had accepted with words of praise for the author. Faced with the Catholic public's negative reaction to this compromising step, Benedict tried to clarify his motivations in a confidential letter addressed to Cardinal de Tencin, his intermediary with the French court (Morelli 1955). Yet that clarification did not prevent various Roman pronouncements between 1753 and 1757 banning Voltaire's works. As early as 1752, however, the formal censure of the thesis presented at the Sorbonne by Abbé de Prades, one of the collaborators of the *Encyclopédie,* had initiated the definitive crisis, ending hope of a possible dialogue between the heads of the church and the Enlightenment (Burson 2010). This led to the break between Catholicism and modern culture that would remain unbridgeable for a very long time.

One of Benedict's last acts, shortly before he died, was to appoint on 1 April 1758—at the request of the Portuguese government—an Apostolic Investigator and reformer of the Portuguese Jesuits in the person of the new Cardinal and Patriarch of Lisbon, Francisco Saldanha (1723–1773). Already by September, after an assassination attempt on King Joseph I, the Jesuits were accused of conspiring against the government and expelled from the Lusitanian Empire. This paved the way for the suppression of the Society of Jesus under Pope Benedict's successor, Clement XIV, in 1773. In this climate, at the beginning of the crisis around the Jesuit problem, Benedict died on 3 May 1758.

The Ambivalent Heritage of Pope Benedict XIV

While the importance of Benedict as a person and of his works in the history of the Catholic Church during the eighteenth century is undeniable, it nevertheless remains no easy task to evaluate, through close historical analyses, the characteristic features and directions of his papacy. Pope Benedict definitely left some uncertainties to his successors, but he also consciously delineated potential ways for the Roman Catholic Church to develop and renew itself. Despite the difficulties of continuing various relationships with European Catholic dynasties, in accordance with the European concordats and in the light of newly developing requirements, the Papal States continued a cautious openness to reforms in the spirit of Enlightenment. Such reforms were even more restricted under the papacy of Pius VI (1775–1799), and they primarily focused on practical and "economic" areas.

Other positive marks he left on the church include his ongoing dialogue with Jansenism, in which he employed the strategy of isolating its extreme proponents while persuading its less intransigent members to remain in conversation with the Church of Rome. Another lasting influence was the promotion of more interconfessional dialogue with the Protestant world, which had already achieved good results on the level of ecclesiastic policy, and thus brought about a more peaceful coexistence in terms of practice and juridical elaboration. Despite Benedict's reaffirmation of closure toward the Jewish world in some of his pronouncements, he permitted the continuation of some important liberties, such as the possibility for Jews to move around within the state while practicing certain activities, which Clement XIV would allow to proliferate in his brief papacy (1769–1774). Such practices were soon abandoned during the reign of Pius VI. Benedict's program was wide ranging and entailed contradictions, a fact of which he was completely aware, but this reality was common in the "moderate" climate of the first half of the century. These contradictions, especially those relating to the Jewish world and Enlightenment culture, however, gradually revealed the deep deficiencies and real crisis in eighteenth-century Catholicism, despite the positive forces of reform of the church in its institutions and religious life. Faced with the Jesuit problem, the ever more aggressive ecclesiastical oversight and secularizing policy of the enlightened monarchs toward Catholicism, and the changes that were taking place in the evolution of European society in the second half of the eighteenth century, Benedict's successors responded differently to the stimulus provided by him, abandoning his choices, and soon almost totally closing the rich prospects opened up by his papacy.

Despite the very real contradictions and difficulties I have mentioned, the image of a tolerant, benevolent pope remained untarnished after Benedict's death and was even strengthened by contrast to the papacies of his successors, Clement XIII (1758–1769) and Pius VI (1775–1799). The origins of the posthumous historiographical myth of the pope are to be found in *The Praise of Pope Benedict XIV* (*Delle lodi di papa Benedetto XIV,* 1758), by the Neapolitan Enlightenment thinker Ferdinando Galiani (1728–1787), and *The Life of Pope Benedict XIV* (*La vie du pape Benoît XIV,* 1766 and 1783), by the Jansenist Louis-Antoine Caraccioli (1719–1803). The first praised the optimism and reason that Benedict had introduced into the dialogue of his own time; the second viewed the figure and actions of the pope in the light of the ecumenical and tolerant spirit of some factions of late European Jansenism. Soon, however, criticisms based on a rigidly moralist and "ecclesiastic" criterion began to surface, in regard to Benedict's yielding to European powers and the antireligious forces of the Enlightenment. Initially such criticism circled only within the Curia, but soon it was heard from traditional, and, later, from antirevolutionary and reactionary, sectors of Catholicism. However, it is not by chance that the positive interpretation of the personality of the pope was cultivated during the nineteenth and twentieth centuries, particularly by Protestant historians, like the German Leopold von Ranke (1795–1886) and the Englishman Thomas Macaulay (1800–1859), as well as such liberal moderates as the Swiss Jean-Charles Sismondi (1773–1842) and the Italian Cesare Balbo (1789–1853), along with modernist writers like Alfred Loisy (1857–1940). In contrast, the negative interpretation was defined by the conservative historian Ludwig von Pastor (1854–1928) in the last part of his monumental *History of the Popes*. Such opposing stances have posed a real obstacle to any deep historical analysis of the figure and work of Benedict XIV: on the one hand Benedict's historiographical image, which nevertheless has historical origins and an important history, and on the other hand, the dispute that has continued to feed the more general evaluation of the eighteenth-century political, ecclesiastical, and religious events from the papacy of Lambertini to the French Revolution, and more widely, the events of the relationship between the Catholic Church and the modern world. Only since my article in the *Biographical Dictionary of Italy* (Rosa 1966), based upon more recent research, is the personality and work of Benedict XIV beginning to be viewed with a perspective of "ambivalence" (Garms-Cornides 1997)—between a "rigorism differentiated in various ways" and a "conservative reformism" (Greco

2011)—thus opening the way to a careful historical reconstruction, based on a sound analysis of the sources, of the personality of Pope Benedict, who remains a central figure in the history of the Catholic Church and Catholicism in the modern age.

Bibliography

Appolis, Émile. 1960. Le "Tiers parti" catholique au XVIIIe siècle. Paris: Picard.
Benedict XIV. 1747–1748. Opera. 12 vols. Rome.
———. 1787. Opera omnia. 15 vols. Venice.
———. 1839–1856. Opera omnia. 17 vols. Prato.
———. 1904. Opera inedita. Edited by Franz Hainer. Freiburg i. Br.
Burson, Jeffrey. 2010. The Rise and Fall of Theological Enlightenment: Jean-Martin de Prades and Ideological Polarization in Eighteenth-Century France. Notre Dame: University of Notre Dame Press.
Caffiero, Marina. 2003. "Benedetto XIV e gli ebrei: Un parere del consultore Lambertini al Sant'Uffizio." In Religione, cultura e politica nell'Europa moderna: Studi offerti a Mario Rosa dagli amici, edited by Carlo Ossola, Marcello Verga, and Maria Antonietta Visceglia, 379–90. Florence: Olschki.
———. 2012. Forced Baptisms: Histories of Jews, Christians, and Converts in Papal Rome. Translated by Lydia G. Cochrane. Berkeley: University of California Press. Originally published as Battesimi forzati: Storie di ebrei, cristiani e convertiti nella Roma dei papi (Rome: Viella, 2004).
Cecchelli, Marco, ed. 1981–1983. Benedetto XIV (Prospero Lambertini): Convegno internazionale di studi storici; Cento 6–9 dicembre 1979. 3 vols. Cento (Ferrara): Centro studi "Girolamo Baruffaldi."
Cusumano, Nicola. 2002. "I papi e le accuse di omicidio rituale: Benedetto XIV e la bolla Beatus Andreas." Dimensioni e problemi della ricerca storica 1:7–35.
De Angelis, Maria Antonietta. 2008. Prospero Lambertini (Benedetto XIV): Un profilo attraverso le lettere. Vatican City: Archivio Segreto Vaticano.
Delpiano, Patrizia. 2007. Il governo della lettura: Chiesa e libri nel settecento. Bologna: Il Mulino.
Di Carlo, Carla. 2000. Il libro in Benedetto XIV: Dalla "domestica libraria" alla biblioteca universale. Bologna: Pàtron.
Donato, Maria Pia. 1997. "Gli 'strumenti' della politica di Benedetto XIV: Il 'Giornale de' letterati,' 1742–1759." In Dall'erudizione alla politica: Giornali, giornalisti ed editori a Roma tra XVII e XX secolo, edited by Monsa-

grati Giuseppe and Caffiero Marina, 39–61. Numero monografico di *Dimensioni e problemi della ricerca storica* 51.

———. 2000. *Accademie romane: Una storia sociale (1671–1824).* Naples and Rome: Edizioni Scientifiche Italiane.

Fattori, Maria Teresa. 2004. "L'episcopato bolognese di Prospero Lambertini (1731–1740): Rassegna bibliografica." *Cristianesimo nella storia* 25:929–46.

———. 2007a. "'Acciò i vescovi latini siano ben informati di tutto': La seconda edizione del *De Synodo diocesana* di Benedetto XIV." *Cristianesimo nella storia* 28:543–608.

———. 2007b. "Lambertini a Bologna, 1731–1740." *Rivista di storia della Chiesa in Italia* 61:417–61.

———. 2008. "Documentos, Archivos y Memoria: Lambertini y el reino de España." *Studia Historica, Historia moderna* 30:33–62.

———. 2010. "Chiesa sacramentale e fede nei sacramenti nelle decisioni di Benedetto XIV sui cattolici orientali." In *Tutto è grazia: In omaggio a Giuseppe Ruggieri,* edited by Melloni Alberto, 417–40. Milan: Jaca Book.

———. 2011. *Le fatiche di Benedetto XIV: Origine ed evoluzione dei trattati di Prospero Lambertini.* Rome: Edizioni di Storia e Letteratura.

Garms-Cornides, Elisabeth. 1997. "Benedikt XIV—Ein Papst zwischen Reaktion und Aufklärung." In *Ambivalenzen der Aufklärung: Festschrift für Ernst Wangermann,* edited by Gerhard Ammerer and Hanns Haas, 169–86. Vienna: Verlag für Geschichte und Politik / Munich: R. Oldenburg.

———. 1999. "Storia, politica e apologia in Benedetto XIV: Alle radici della reazione cattolica." In *Papes et papauté au XVIIIe siècle: VI colloque franco-italien, Chambéry, 21–22 septembre 1995,* edited by Koeppel Philippe, 145–61. Paris: Champion.

Greco, Gaetano. 2011. *Benedetto XIV: Un canone per la Chiesa.* Rome: Salerno Editrice.

Morelli, Emilia, ed. 1955. *Le lettere di Benedetto XIV al card. de Tencin: Dai testi originali.* Vol. 1 (1740–1747). Rome: Edizioni di Storia e Letteratura.

Nanni, Stefania. 1997. "'Anno di rinnovazione e di penitenza': Anno di riconciliazione e di grazia; Il giubileo del 1750." In *La città del perdono: Pellegrinaggi e anni santi a Roma in Età moderna, 1550–1750,* edited by Stefania Nanni and Maria Antonietta Visceglia, 553–87. Numero monografico *Roma moderna e contemporanea* 5. Rome: Archivio G. Izzi.

Rosa, Mario. 1966. "Benedetto XIV, papa." In *Dizionario biografico degli Italiani,* 8:393–408. Rome: Istituto della Enciclopedia Italiana.

———. 1997. "La Santa Sede e gli ebrei nel settecento." In Storia d'Italia, annali 11, vol. 2, *Gli ebrei in Italia,* edited by Vivanti Corrado, 1067–87. Torino: Einaudi.

———. 1998. "Il Tribunale della santità." In *Diventare santo: Itinerari e riconoscimenti della santità tra libri, documenti e immagini,* edited by Giovanni Morello et al., 65–72. Vatican City: Biblioteca Apostolica Vaticana / Cagliari: Events.

———. 1999. *Settecento religioso: Politica della ragione e religione del cuore.* Venice: Marsilio.

———. 2000. "Benedetto XIV, papa." In *Enciclopedia dei papi,* 3:446–61 (with updated bibliography). Rome: Istituto della Enciclopedia Italiana.

———. 2003. "Benedict XIV (Prospero Lambertini, 1675–1758), Pope (1740–1758)." In *Encyclopedia of the Enlightenment,* edited by Adam Kors, 1:134–36. Oxford: Oxford University Press.

———. 2008. "Le contraddizioni della modernità: Apologetica cattolica e Lumi nel settecento." *Rivista di storia e letteratura religiosa* 44:73–114.

———. 2010. "The Catholic Aufklärung in Italy." In *A Companion to the Catholic Enlightenment in Europe,* edited by Ulrich L. Lehner and Michael Printy, 215–50. Leiden: Brill.

Roth, Cecil. 1934. *The Ritual Murder Libel and the Jew: The Report by Cardinal Lorenzo Ganganelli.* London: Woburn Press.

Schmidt, Bernward, and Hubert Wolf, eds. 2010. *Benedikt XIV und die Reform des Buchzensurverfahrens: Zu Geschichte und Rezeption von "Sollicita ac provida."* Paderborn: Schöning.

Tabacchi, Stefano. 2007. *Il buon governo: Le finanze locali nello Stato della Chiesa (secoli XVI–XVIII).* Rome: Viella.

Vismara, Paola. 2004. *Oltre l'usura: La Chiesa moderna e il prestito a interesse.* Soveria Mannelli: Rubbettino.

PART 2
Catholicism and the Siècle des Lumières in France and Savoy

2

Nicolas-Sylvestre Bergier (1718–1790)

An Enlightened Anti-Philosophe

JEFFREY D. BURSON

Born into relative obscurity in the diminutive town of Darney near the headwaters of the Sâone River on 31 December 1718, Nicolas-Sylvestre Bergier would ultimately climb to the summit of the Gallican Church as one of the most prolific and celebrated apologists of eighteenth-century France before his death just one year after the storming of the Bastille. At age ten, Bergier began his studies at the Jesuit college of Colmar; thence at age fourteen (1732) he was relocated to Besançon, where he continued his studies at that city's Jesuit college before completing his education at the University of Besançon and its Great Seminary. While in Besançon, he studied with a Father Bullet and became further acquainted with many of Bullet's students, most notably Joseph Trouillet, with whom Bergier would carry on a lifelong friendship (Jobert 1987, 15–16).

Nicolas-Sylvestre Bergier was at last ordained as priest in March 1743, just before receiving his doctorate in theology at the University of Besançon (5 October 1744). Bergier's talents secured for him a brief tenure as chair of philosophy at Besançon, but just as much did they quickly suggest to his mentor, Bullet, that his former student should more profitably pursue further study in Paris (indeed, Bullet himself had been a pupil of Jean Hardouin, S.J., in Paris). Although Bergier took his advice and resided in Paris from 1745 to 1749, no indication remains as to his exact whereabouts in these years. However, by July 1749 Bergier soon reemerges as the Curé de Flangebouche, a benefice near the Swiss border that he would retain for some fifteen years. While he seems to have longed for an end to his provincial sojourn, Bergier made the very best of his years in Flangebouche. He immersed himself in his parish, wrote extensive refutations of the works of both Bishop Chillingworth and Pierre Bayle, and was several times laureate of the Academy of Besançon, to which both he and Joseph Trouillet belonged. On two occasions, Bergier won prizes from the Academy of Besançon. Shortly thereafter, the Academy bestowed upon Bergier the honor of pronouncing the Panegyric of Saint Louis in 1754. By the end of his Flangebouche years, Bergier had published his first work, a dissertation entitled *How Many Morals Make Talent Resplendent* (*Combien les moeurs donnent d'éclat au talent*) that concluded with a brief, albeit veiled, portrait of Voltaire (Saint-Croix 1844, v; Jobert 1987, 16–17).

Bergier's Early Works I: Natural History and Philology

Bergier delved enthusiastically, and with considerable acumen, into the study of natural history and the development of language and mythology. In fact, it was during Bergier's Flangebouche years that he completed much of the research material for his first major works of philology, published between 1763 and 1769. The very first fruit of this research was his celebrated *Primitive Elements of Language* (*Les éléments primitifs des langues,* 1764). In *Elements,* Bergier defined language much as John Locke had done: it "is in general the image of the objects of our thoughts.... All other words ... are, so to speak, ... so many metaphors that become naturalized in the end through a long course of habit and usage" (Bergier 1837, 10). Accordingly, to understand the history of language was for Bergier, as much as for Claude G. Buffier, Abbé Condillac, and so many Enlightenment writers, the surest artifact of natural history, and the most certain route to tracing the history of human morals, customs, and the progress of human understanding (Buffier 1732, v–xvi, 893–1257; Wilkins 1969, 31–39). Bergier maintained that people begin in childhood to mimic the sounds they hear around them, and as primitive peoples progress to adulthood, "the things of first necessity from nourishment, to clothing, to agriculture, to their herds, to the sensible and ordinary phenomena of nature are the first to be named" (Bergier 1837, 11–12). Language bubbles up from the common man, in other words, and not from erudite writers, philosophers, and priests.

Bergier further asserted that the history of humanity's religious and secular understanding can be charted by means of philology. In the history of language Bergier also found evidence for the corruption of the original revelation of God among all peoples—an idea he developed most fully in his last published work, *Dictionary of Theology* (*Dictionnaire de théologie;* Bergier 1781–1790, 1:x–xiv). For in the same way as "insensible objects, functions, affections of the soul [passions]" are named according to "divers symptoms of the body they characterize," so also are such concepts as soul, mind, spirit, and life referred to as breath, and later confused with matter (Bergier 1837, 6–7). Thus, those authors who see in primitive humankind evidence of an original materialism, only later abstracted to include erroneous notions of incorporeal deities and intelligences, have put the cart before the horse: "I should hope that those who have seriously made such an objection should tell us how else one might possibly give a characteristic name to a spiritual object?" (Bergier 1837, 6–7n1). Finally, Bergier's *Primitive Elements* contends that the original language of all humanity must still survive in all human languages, and the primary thrust of his discourse is a preliminary attempt to reconstruct that language by determining the etymological laws that have resulted in its diversification (Bergier 1837, 14–20). In so doing, Bergier sought "to return to . . . our common origin, to renewed signs of fraternity among all peoples" (Bergier 1837, 15).

Bergier's *Primitive Elements of Language* helped earn him further critical renown, and it inspired similar works by such writers as the noted Protestant philosopher Court de Gébelin, who built upon the edifice of Bergier's system in his own work, *Young Earth* (*Monde Primitif*). Bergier's erudition was thereafter sufficient to bring him to the attention of the Besançon notables and Archbishop Choiseaul Beaupré, who, having just then been granted oversight of the College of Besançon after the suppression of the Jesuits in France, appointed Bergier headmaster of his one-time alma mater (Saint-Croix 1844, v; Jobert 1987, 17–18).

Bergier's second major work of philology and natural history, *Origin of the Gods of Paganism* (*Origine des dieux du paganisme*), published in 1767, further developed his method in *Éléments primitifs*. In this work, which he dedicated to the Count of Clermont, Prince of the Blood, Bergier took up the question of the origin of Greek polytheism. This seemingly arcane analysis is fraught with interest, however, for it adapts the philology of *Primitive Elements* to the study of religion only to conclude that the fables of Greek myth, and in particular Hesiod's *Metamorphosis,* do not derive from history but from the process of linguistic development. Bergier's *Origin of the Gods of Paganism* displaces the history of paganism as something to be emulated (as so many radical Enlightenment *philosophes* had begun to do in their studies of primitive religion and philosophy) and resituates it as something that derived from the inevitable corruptibility of human perceptions in ages of ignorance and barbarism (Israel 2006, 436–96; Leddy and Lifschitz 2005, 1–11).

In dialogue with both Rousseau's *Émile* and Voltaire's *Philosophical Dictionary* (*Dictionnaire philosophique*), and with the consensus opinion of many within the Royal Academy of Inscriptions (Académie des Inscriptions)—that the Greek gods and heroes actually derived from deified early Greek monarchs—Bergier alternatively insisted that the Greeks, like all peoples on earth, had worshiped one true God, which Hesiod had named Ouranos, or in Latin, Coelus (Bergier 1767a, 1:5–12, 15, 23–24, 29–33). Hesiod's references to the reigns of Ouranos/Coelus, of Chronos/Saturn, and of Zeus/Jupiter all referred to different stages of Greek religion. During the reign of Ouranos, the Greeks had retained their belief in the one true God as passed to them by the tradition of their own patriarchs from the descendants of Noah; with greater sophistication in their understanding of the natural world, Ouranos (heaven) became Chronos ("He who turns the heavens"). In the age of Chronos/Saturn, the Greeks, like all peoples, referred to the vital principle that animated nature, collectively, by names found in Hesiod such as "Titans," yet in the third stage of Greek religion, these nymphs, genies, and Titans were understood to be divinities and worshiped as such by the Greeks, who had by then already begun to refer to their high god as Zeus/Jupiter, the Heavenly Father. However, Greek religion, Bergier asserted, actually degenerated further than most forms of polytheism, to the extent that certain illustrious men from history attained the status of heroes and were venerated as divine progeny of the gods. Lack of understanding of the natural world in the age of Chronos and Zeus, coupled with the forgotten origins of metaphorical references to natural forces later personified and deified in the age of Zeus, had jointly conspired in the degeneration of original Greek monotheism into polytheism (Bergier 1767a, 1:38–44). In miniature, this process is the very thing that Bergier, in consort with many scions of Catholic Enlightenment in Europe, had assumed was the driving force behind the need for divine revelation itself—namely that every individual was a prisoner to his or her passions and sense perceptions. Lockean sensationism is, in this sense, both the key to the progress of enlightenment and the *Deus ex machina* behind the corruption of morals and natural revelation. The *Origin of the Gods of Paganism* in turn helped secure Bergier's election as an associated member of the Royal Academy of Inscriptions (22 January 1768).

Bergier's Early Works II: The Frontal Assault on Jean-Jacques Rousseau

In 1762, Jean-Jacques Rousseau published *Émile,* a work that rapidly drew the critical ire of mid-century men of letters and Catholic apologists alike (Masseau 2000, 25, 109–270). Even Christophe de Beaumont, Archbishop of Paris, responded to Rousseau with a famous archepiscopal *mandement* that, in turn, sparked further controversy when Rousseau himself replied in the scathing *Letters to Monsignor Beaumont* (*Lettres à Monseigneur de Beaumont*) and followed these same rebuttals with yet a third piece in 1765 entitled *Letters from the Mountain* (*Lettres de la Montagne*). It was at this time that Bergier published one of his first, most famous apologetical works, *Deism Refuted by Itself, or Epistolary Examination of the Principles of Unbelief Disseminated throughout the Works of Jean-Jacques Rousseau* (*Le Déisme réfuté par lui-même, ou Examen, en forme de lettres, des principes d'incrédulité répandus dans les ouvrages divers de M. Rousseau*), a three-part, comprehensive, critical refutation of Rousseau's *Émile*, his *Letters to Monsignor Beaumont,* and his *Letters from the Mountain.* After having written the first two parts, Bergier presented his manuscript to Archbishop Beaumont, who then enthusiastically embraced its publication in 1768 (Jobert 1987, 18).

Deism Refuted by Itself reveals the internal inconsistencies of Rousseau's doctrines across two volumes of intricate and spirited prose. Chiefly, Bergier tests the sincerity of Rousseau's claim that, in the words of the Savoyard Vicar from *Émile,* the gospel was divinely inspired, and that Jesus was the worthiest of all moral philosophers. "Is it truly incontestable, according to you, that the pure and sublime moral teachings of the Gospel come from God insofar as it is also certain, according to you, that the absurd dogmas it contains do not?" (Bergier 1768, 1:108; Masseau 2000, 239–50). "Could God," Bergier continues, "who is wisdom and truth itself, reveal to us a mixture of truth and falsehood, reason and absurdity" (Bergier 1768, 1:109)? Bergier considers Rousseau's notion of Jesus to be internally contradictory—a "sublime fool" or "virtuous fanatic." But if he is a fanatic, however virtuous, how were so many miracles and absurd doctrines also able to accomplish so much good in the world (Bergier 1768, 1:110)? For Bergier, the revelation of the Gospels (morality as well as seemingly miraculous and unnatural occurrences) is verified by the chain of witnesses—the tradition of the church—that derives ultimately from the deposition of witnesses to the events described. In this, Bergier's argument solidly comports with those of late seventeenth- and early eighteenth-century apologists who contended that, if the chain of tradition that created and interpreted the Scriptures through history was valid and historically sound, the revelation was reasonable, if not in every way rational a priori. This highly empirical and historico-critical bent of early apologetics is the very same out of which Locke's *Reasonableness of Christianity* emerged, but it is likewise the source of Richard Simon, Pierre-Daniel Huet, the Abbé d'Houtteville, the Jesuit Claude G. Buffier, and the Maurist Benedictines (Shelford 2008, 1–13, 184–191; Burson 2010b, 38–76, 208–17; Lehner 2011, 11–25). The sum total of the revelation within the New Testament is a fact that is true insofar as it has been verifiably reported as true through time in ways amenable to historical analysis. Ironically, Bergier continually quoted the Abbé de Prades's heterodox article "Certitude" from volume 1 of the *Encyclopédie* back to Rousseau, to prove his point that miraculous facts like the resurrection of Jesus Christ need nothing more to be accepted as true than a crowd of consonant eyewitness testimony, and the transmission of that witness through time in a historically sound tradition, preserved and embodied in the verifiable fact of a church magisterium (Bergier 1768, 1:133–48). By comparison, Bergier exposed Rousseau's line of reasoning as an absurdity predicated upon an article of faith in the omniscience of the individual, himself: "I understand all, and there is in fact no truth that I should not understand; now, I do not understand this doctrine," so argues Rousseau, "and therefore it must be false" (Bergier 1768, 1:149).

Bergier and the Anti-D'Holbachian Apologetics

With the plenitude of resources afforded him at the formerly Jesuit college in Besançon, and at exactly the same time in which the anti-Rousseauian works were composed, Nicolas-Sylvestre Bergier thoroughly digested an anonymous work by Baron d'Holbach entitled *Examination of the Apologists* (*Examen des apologistes*). Emanating from the famous publishing house of Marc-Michel Rey at The Hague in 1766, and attributed to an author with the mercurial name of "Fréret," the *Examination* is now known to have been adapted from a much longer manuscript of Lévêque de Burigny. In response, and with astonishing rapidity, Bergier published his landmark *Certitude of the*

Proofs of Christianity (*Certitude des preuves du Christianisme*) in 1767, a chapter-by-chapter, point-by-point refutation of the *Examination* (Bergier 1767b, 1:6). The piece was favorably received by Grimm's *Correspondance littéraire* in April 1767 and ascended to such critical acclaim that three editions were published in 1767 alone before the work was rapidly translated into Italian and Spanish (Jobert 1987, 18n12; Saint-Croix 1844, vi).

Bergier chiefly "sustained that Christianity was established by persuasion, empirical evidence, and the intrepid courage of the first apostles" (Bergier 1767b, 1:9). Subverting one of d'Holbach's major points—that Christianity had been adapted in late antiquity only by those who were uneducated and superstitious—Bergier instead argued that this fact, insofar as it was even accurate, was actually a point attesting to the natural universality of the faith. "Among the Jews as among the Pagans," he wrote, "the people tend to be generally more attached to their religion, and are more naturally the enemies of Christianity than the well educated," and this is known experientially from universal histories, even by Enlightenment men of letters themselves (Bergier 1767b, 1:203–31, esp. 204). Moreover, he unmasks d'Holbach's assertion as little more than fanatical invective since from the earliest times, Pharisees, Roman centurions, and some of the preeminent philosophers of the late Roman period such as Origen and Tertullian adapted Christianity. More recently still, Bergier continued, "many of the literati and members of the imperial family [of China] had embraced Christanity," and the founder of the Qing Empire itself, Emperor Kangxi, deeply admired the Jesuit missionaries and Christian teachings (Bergier 1767b, 1:216).

Bergier additionally emerges as something of a populist in these most famous works of apologetics, arguing in essence that one need not be a philosopher to become Christian. In fact, Bergier contends that philosophy, however important, points only to confusion, intellectual as well as sociopolitical. "The Platonists maintained the existence of a spiritual God, the Stoics believed this spiritual God to be corporeal . . . the Epicureans eschewed all such dogmas . . . [whereas] the Skeptics and Pyrrhonists overthrew all system in general" (Bergier 1767b, 2:71–72). Such confusion, Bergier concludes, could yield no agreement respecting the existence of rewards and punishments in this life or the next. In their lack of any clear sanction for divine justice in the afterlife beyond confused hypotheses, Bergier maintains, ancient philosophers had no consistent rule of public morality. "What sanction could they give to their lessons or their laws?" "What motive could they furnish to humankind to render them faithful?" (Bergier 1767b, 2:81–82). To revive ancient philosophy as that which comports most to natural reason and human nature, a project dear to many radical Enlightenment philosophers, would be, Bergier warns, nothing more than to revive the sociocultural dead end into which the Christian revelation had interposed itself (Israel 2006, 436–71). Moreover, and in contrast to d'Holbach's apotheosis of philosophy, Bergier reminds his readers that "the philosophers banished from their schools the simple people; whereas, Jesus Christ desired that they be preferred because the people has the most need of instruction" (Bergier 1767b, 2:85). "The miracles of Jesus Christ were sufficiently attested to by all the world through the monuments which were passed down by the Church," and "the infallibility of the Church is a necessary consequence of its divine establishment by Jesus Christ and his Apostles, [an] establishment demonstrated by facts" (Bergier 1767b, 2:183, 193). Most surprisingly of all, however, Bergier defends the presumed intellectual egalitarianism of the Gospels by invoking a passage from *Émile*: "'See,' says the celebrated Rousseau speaking of the Gospel, 'see how the books of the Philosophers with all of their pomp and circumstance pale by comparison to the Gospel!' How could it be that a book at once so sublime and so simple be the work of men?" This fact is all the more surprising since it coincides with the very same year in which Bergier's anti-Rousseauian apologetics appeared (Rousseau, quoted in Bergier 1767b, 2:86–87).

The success of *Certitude* led the forty-nine-year-old Principal of Collège Besançon to attempt to surmount the royal pension of 600 livres that the Archbishop of Choiseaul, now Cardinal, had secured for him in 1764. Bergier thus again determined to attract the good graces of the Archbishop of Paris's extensive patronage, so he returned to Paris and briefly took up residence with his brother, François Bergier (then a marginally successful *litérateur*), and there he submitted to his publisher the *Defense of the Christian Religion* (*Apologie de la religion chrétienne*), published in December 1768. The *Defense*, like the *Examen,* was a systematic rebuttal to the more recent, more acerbic, as yet still anonymously published work of Baron d'Holbach, this time to his *Christianity Unveiled* (*Christianisme dévoilé*) (Jobert 1987, 18–19). In many ways, the *Defense* is the quintessence of utilitarian apologetics spoken of by William Everdell and Bernard Plongeron—apologetics designed to demonstrate the natural affinity between natural religion and the universality of the Christian faith, as well as its social necessity in "purifying morals and supporting the government" (Bergier 1769, 1:12; Everdell 1987, 128–32; Plongeron 1976). Whereas d'Holbach's *Christianity Unveiled* attempted to prove that Christianity ineluctably led to barbarism by undermining natural virtue, morality, and sound politics, Bergier took great pains to prove that all peoples, as though by nature, had established a religion that would inspire devotion to one God as the foundation of law, duty, and right. "How, then," Bergier asks by way of conclusion, could institutionalized atheism be anything but a violation of "this universal consent of nations, this general cry of nature" (Bergier 1769, 2:244–45)? Repeating a leitmotif of political as well as moral philosophy that remained constant throughout his works, Bergier again argued that Christianity, uniquely true because its historicity is verifiable through the continuity provided by the Catholic Church, teaches "that virtue alone can secure our Happiness (*Bonheur*) in this world and the next," and so "to place irreligion on the throne is to place, as sovereign of the people, the most terrible kind of despotism" (Bergier 1769, 2:249, 251).

In a way that was becoming increasingly characteristic of Counter-Enlightenment ideology—and indeed, its successor, counterrevolutionary thought in France at least—Bergier and many late eighteenth-century apologists argued that reason and philosophy could not compel virtuous behavior because philosophy had no clear notion of divinity, no clear notion of spirit, no historically verifiable truth claims linking it to divine origins, and no clear concept of an afterlife during which virtues unrequited in this world might be rewarded in the next. For all his engagement with Enlightenment natural history, philology, epistemology, and intellectual sociability, Bergier's later and most famous writings are quite clear—that atheism and radical Enlightenment are political and not simply intellectual crimes.

The *Defense* earned Bergier the acclamation of Pope Clement XIII on 31 January 1769. More to the point, perhaps, Bergier's desired end—the ability to pursue a life of scholarship based in Paris—was at last achieved. Bergier's *Defense* secured for him the everlasting gratitude of Archbishop Beaumont, who was seeking to appoint to his archepiscopal council canons with a distinguished record of apologetic experience to oppose the increasingly ardent anticlericalism of radical Enlightenment writers. As a candidate with such a record, Bergier became a canon of Notre Dame in Paris on 29 December 1769 and would remain such until his death in 1790 (Jobert 1987, 19; Saint-Croix 1844, vi).

Bergier Invictus: The Counteroffensive of the General Assembly of the Clergy and the *Examination of Materialism*

At the same time in which Bergier was finalizing the *Defense of the Christian Religion*, he established liaison (through his brother, François) with members of the D'Holbach Circle (Kors 1976, 114–17). Through some combination of curiosity and perhaps literary espionage (such was Grimm's suspicion in any case), Bergier frequented the salons of the rue Saint-Roch, including the salon of Baron d'Holbach himself. This, at exactly the same time in which he composed his most systematic apologetic endeavor to date—a work that, as it happened, was to became a lavishly patronized semiofficial rebuttal to d'Holbach's own 1770 monumental tract of radical Enlightenment materialism, *System of Nature* (*Système de la Nature;* Jobert 1987, 15–20). Despite Grimm's more conspiratorial interpretation of Bergier's dalliance with the D'Holbach Coterie, there is in fact considerable evidence in surviving letters sent by the dévot Prince Louis Eugene of Würtemburg to the Abbé Bergier indicating that Bergier was chiefly interested in gaining a more intimate understanding of what motivated France's radical Enlightenment apostles of *incrédulité*. Bergier seems to have been convinced that they would be persuaded by his own dialectical, persuasive, and apologetical approach to Catholic apologetics—an approach that owes much to his own lively interest in language, natural history, and the eighteenth-century republic of letters. The Prince of Würtemburg wrote in reply to a letter of Bergier (that tragically no longer exists), "I think as you do, Sir, that your connections to the Baron d'Holbach can be very useful.... You should have little trouble confounding [these men of letters] by reasoning.... The portrait that you have painted for me of M. the Baron d'Holbach merely inspires me with more compassion for him" (Migne 1855, 8:1566–86).

That Bergier seems to have had a somewhat conflicted relationship to the so-called *incrédules* he so often refuted is further supported by an obscure passage written by Diderot to his brother, Abbé Pierre Diderot. "You are apparently acquainted with the Abbé Bergier, the great refuter of modern Celsius," the *Encyclopédiste* wrote his clerical brother. "Unless he is engaged by the doctors of the Sorbonne, he delights himself in never speaking of religion except with a tone of beneficence agreeable to honorable men who simply disagree" (Jobert 1987, 20n18). Perhaps it was in this spirit—the quintessence of the apologetical sensibilities of a Catholic Enlightenment that valued synthesis, debate, and engagement with the burgeoning public sphere—that Bergier sent the first part of his apologetic in manuscript to Diderot and to d'Holbach as well. Neither Diderot nor d'Holbach dignified it with much beyond the dismissive retort that Bergier had not understood the *System of Nature* because, in effect, "not fifty people in all of Paris were capable of understanding the language" (Bergier to Trouillet, 6 June 1770, in Jobert 1987, 54–58). However, the tenor of the reply to Bergier suggests that all of them—Bergier, d'Holbach, and Diderot—understood exactly who was the author of *Christianity Unveiled* and *System of Nature,* even though d'Holbach published both anonymously. Only after his death in 1789 did d'Holbach's authorship become formally public (Jobert 1987, 20).

Even though the channels by which Catholic Enlightenment writers and apologists appropriated aspects of Enlightenment science, moral philosophy, and epistemology were still relatively porous in the late 1760s, these channels would become increasingly circumscribed by rhetorical polarization as radical Enlightenment apologists circled the wagons in the aftermath of official censorship of both the *Encyclopédie* and Claude Adrien d'Helvétius's *On the Spirit* (*De l'Esprit*) between 1758 and 1759 (Burson 2008). The General Assembly of the Gallican Clergy held an extraordinary meeting in 1758 and adopted on 25 October of that year a resolution to organize a more concerted campaign against the effect of new philosophy among the youth. Louis XV's response on 13 November supported the assembly's initiative and additionally pledged to appoint stricter royal censors while cracking down on the clandestine book trade (Chopelin-Blanc 2009, 121).

In the years following 1758, the burgeoning rhetorical polarization between a more radical and yet increasingly mainstream Enlightenment anticlericalism in France on the one hand and a more assertive and self-conscious Counter-Enlightenment effort on the other was only enhanced by the furor unleashed in response to the publication of Rousseau's *Émile* in 1762 and Voltaire's *Philosophical Dictionary* (*Dictionnaire philosophique*) in 1764 (Masseau 2000, 23–26; Israel 2006, 814–72; Burson 2010b, 64–125). Subsequent General Assemblies in 1760, 1762, and 1765 only multiplied resolutions, and by 1765, a list of the most egregious books had been compiled for censure, including Bayle's *Analysis,* Helvétius's *On the Spirit,* Rousseau's *Émile,* and several works by Voltaire, including *The Philosophical Dictionary, Philosophy of History,* and *Oriental Despotism* (Chopelin-Blanc 2009, 121). Finally, the near simultaneous suppression of the Jesuit order in 1764 rocked the French republic of letters just as much, and without the supposedly Molinist, politically corrupt, ultramontane, and intellectually profligate Jesuits to kick around anymore, Gallican apologists of a Jansenist persuasion were able to close ranks, at least rhetorically, with Gallican bishops and former Jesuit writers in conjoint assaults on the intellectual and moral despotism they all increasingly associated with "unbelief," much as even more moderate Enlightenment writers like Voltaire and d'Alembert found it easier to ridicule the church and command the attention of French public opinion (Van Kley 1975, 231; Van Kley 2006, 302–28; Burson 2010b, 287–309). As scholars have begun to argue recently, the "free thinker" (*esprit-fort*) and the sect of "unbelief" (*incrédulité*) emerged in both apologetics and even in sermon literature of the late eighteenth century as a rather one-dimensional stock character, a straw man, a hermeneutical other by which clergy and apologists might juxtapose their conception of piety, morals, and the proper reformation of society in light of Catholic Enlightenment principles (Lefebvre 2000, 95–107).

Accordingly, the General Assembly of the Gallican Clergy convened in 1770 and resolved to orchestrate a coordinated, officially sanctioned apologetical counterthrust against the most disconcerting works of "materialism" and "atheism." As Caroline Chopelin-Blanc has recently written, the assembly "virulently believed, as illustrated by the recent publication of Holbach's *System of Nature*, that his was 'one of the last productions [where] pure atheism [was] taught with an audacity even Hobbes, Vanini, and Spinoza would never have dared indulge'" (Chopelin-Blanc 2009, 122). Because of the importance of *System of Nature,* then, Loménie de Brienne, then Archbishop of Toulouse, called upon all bishops to round up those theologians and apologists most proficient in practical and historical theology and prepare for literary battle with the radical Enlightenment. In short, Brienne helped ensure that the General Assembly would prioritize apologetical writing, thus inaugurating a lavish and competitive system of compensation designed to acquit apologists of their benefices while allowing them to devote their full attention to apologetics that would respond to "unbelief" in light of a concrete program drawn up by Brienne and approved by the Assembly itself: (1) the divine inspiration and veracity of the revealed tradition of the church and the Scriptures was to be defended, along with (2) the necessity of revelation, and (3) the "sublime liaison" of Christianity with the social order. Despite, or perhaps because of, Nicolas Bergier's acquaintance with Denis Diderot, Baron d'Holbach, and the salons they frequented, the Canon of Notre Dame was awarded the task of matching wits with the Baron d'Holbach's *System of Nature* (Chopelin-Blanc 2009, 122–23; Jobert 1987, 102, 105).

The *Examination of Materialism* repeats and augments many of the points addressed in Bergier's earlier anti-Holbachian apologetics (*The Certitude of Proofs* as well as *The Defense of the Christian Religion*), but it focuses, as the title suggests, more specifically on the metaphysical principles underlying d'Holbach's *System of Nature*. D'Holbach had asserted that religion arose from ignorance of natural causes and that the gradual personification of natural forces into multiple deities ultimately abstracted, with the advancement of arts and sciences, into the idea of a single God. Secondly, d'Holbach had argued that all humankind from China, to the South Pacific, to the ancient Greeks, Romans, and Germans had originally worshiped nature itself because nature was self-actualizing, self-motivating, and vital (Reill 2005, 1–16). Bergier considers all of this to be contradicted by historical facts and the evidence of ancient beliefs derived from seventeenth- and eighteenth-century study of the natural history of religion in light of the eighteenth-century quest for universal history. The ancients did personify nature, Bergier agrees, but they also, at some distant point in their ancient histories, believed in a single force, agent, or intelligence which they worshiped as the one true God—a belief passed down by family tradition from the descendants of Noah after the flood (Bergier 1771, 2:8–19). By means of linguistic confusion, as he earlier described in *Primitive Elements of Language* and *Origins of the Gods of Paganism*, combined with scientific ignorance, all humankind had succumbed to polytheism. In other words the primitive natural religion of man was monotheistic. Moreover, Bergier insisted, it was not materialistic, for—contra d'Holbach—polytheists, ancient and modern, did not and do not worship matter as such, but the genies and spirits of nature they believe are the primary source of natural and supernatural causes (Bergier 1771, 2:51–59, 197–203). Thus to assert dogmatically that human societies and religious history in particular derive from a natural materialism worthy of revival in an age of Enlightenment is, for Bergier, to generalize prescriptively from a belief that was far from universally held, and is, moreover, the enemy of the common sense of humankind. For Bergier argues repeatedly in parts of the *Examination of Materialism* that internal sense tells us all that our soul and other active forces, both natural and divine, are substantially other than matter. In this respect, Bergier's apologetics remains rooted in the traditions of the early Catholic Enlightenment in France—a synthetic epistemology found in writers as diverse as the Abbé Condillac and the Jesuit Claude Buffier—traditions according to which empiricism and common sense can validate, a posteriori, the substantial duality of spirit and matter, Creator and creation, and this, even though no one could observe and apprehend the essence of things directly as Thomism had once suggested (Burson 2010a, 63–106).

The publication of the *Examination* is significant for still another reason: it marks the end of a period of more open engagement and amicable relations between Abbé Bergier and some of the more radical writers his work refuted. As might perhaps be expected, Bergier's dealings with d'Holbach, Diderot, d'Alembert, and Voltaire noticeably cooled after 1771, and at least the public oeuvre of Bergier emerges as considerably more characteristic of the Counter-Enlightenment styles of apologetics Darrin McMahon has noted after 1770 (McMahon 2001, 5–31; Jobert 1987, 22). In this respect, Nicolas-Sylvestre Bergier's career comes to epitomize the fate of the process of theological Enlightenment in France more generally. This French theological Enlightenment was characterized by the sometimes amicable, sometimes hostile interaction of eighteenth-century writers with diverse varieties of Catholic Enlightenment authors across the institutions of the public sphere until the middle third of the eighteenth century, when rhetorical polarization between a recognizably coherent party of philosophy and a recognizably coherent Counter-Enlightenment ideology is increasingly evident. Bergier is instructive concerning this late theological Enlightenment process as well, for the institutional and rhetorical polarization in which his purportedly anti-*philosophe* apologetics participates belies much deeper complexity at the heart of late-century Catholic Enlightenment writings in France. As discussed in what follows by way of conclusion, Bergier's productive engagement with the Enlightenment *philosophes* for the purpose of updating and modernizing the tenor of Catholic Enlightenment apologetics was far from over.

Bergier's Last Decades and His Attack on Augustine

Bergier's *Examination of Materialism* left him a profoundly wealthy and prominent man: the General Assembly of the Clergy granted to

Bergier the sum of 2,000 livres, and the king granted him an additional benefice (the Abbey of Sauve in the Diocese of Alès) worth 2,400 livres. Christophe de Beaumont, however, refused to accept Bergier's resignation from the Canonry of Notre Dame, so he remained in possession of that already lucrative benefice as well. As though these benefices were insufficient, Beaumont soon appointed Bergier to be Confessor to the Countess of Provence on 23 March 1771 (he became confessor to the Countess of Artois in 1775), and finally, less than two months later, Bergier was granted the office of Confessor to the Queen. In February 1776, at the death of Abbé La Roche-Aymon, Bergier was offered the very prestigious Folio of Benefices (*feuille des benefices*)—a position of royal favoritism within the Gallican Church that would have placed him in direct succession to Cardinal Fleury (1726–1743), and to the Bishop of Mirepoix (1743–1755) as the font of ecclesiastical patronage in France. Yet Bergier declined this last honor, preferring rather to spend his days writing, discharging his duties at Versailles and in Paris, and taking long walks in the evening whereby he would gather his thoughts for the next day's writing. In the spirit of a *bon cure,* moreover, Nicolas Bergier made frequent visits to Notre Dame to discharge his duties as canon even though he now resided at the court of Versailles, and he was also quite generous with his largesse. Bergier once confided to the Abbé Trouillet that he had given the total sum of 68,000 livres in charity to his former parishioners in Flangebouche, many of whom lived in poverty. Abbé Bergier became, in addition, the main source of support for his brother, François, who, for all of his connections to the D'Holbach Circle, and despite his having contributed to Abbé Raynal's *History of the Two Indies* (*Histoire des deux Indes*), had fallen on hard times (Joubert 1987, 22–23).

From Versailles, Bergier would compose two of his last, most compendious, and to date less well-studied, works: the twelve-volume *Historical and Dogmatic Treatise concerning True Religion* (*Traité historique et dogmatique de la vraie religion*) in 1780 and the three-volume *Dictionary of Theology* (*Dictionnaire de théologie,* 1781–1790). The *Treatise* sold nearly 2,500 copies in fewer than three years, was reissued in a revised edition of 1786, and continued to be published occasionally until 1890. The *Dictionary,* on the other hand, emerged from an offer from Panckouke, editor of a methodologically arranged late edition of the *Encyclopedia* (*Encyclopédie méthodique*), requesting that Bergier revise the theological articles from Diderot's original *Encyclopédie*. With the permission of the Archbishop of Paris, Bergier went to work, and ultimately created his own *Dictionary of Theology,* a work that would ultimately appear in thirty-one French editions, seven Italian editions, and four Spanish editions by 1882, when it was published for the last time during the French Third Republic (Jobert 1987, 24–28). The scope of the *Treatise,* however, is incredibly vast. Spanning twelve volumes, it contains systematic refutations of ancient moral philosophy, d'Holbach, Helvétius, Epicurean atomistic materialism, Humean skepticism, and Spinozist materialism, yet it is also among the first places in which one glimpses Bergier's increasingly strident assault on Saint Augustine's theology of grace, characteristic of some of his posthumous works (Bergier 1827, 3:53–79, 283–91; 2:342–62). In the *Treatise,* Bergier implies that the bountiful grace of God must extend to all humankind, since even so-called infidels possess the natural light of reason and the inner voice of conscience (Bergier 1827, 2:96–105). Thus, Bergier concedes that "Savages" of the Americas and Oceania who have had no understanding of Catholic revelation and are scarcely capable, he thinks, of holding a clear idea of God are still just like the mentally ill or children—incapable of being guilty of sin because they have no knowledge of revelation. While this is certainly far from the Enlightenment myth of the noble savage, and still farther from anything we would consider Enlightened sensibility today, it still, in historical context, represents a significant revision of early church tradition to reflect the possibility that salvation is accessible to those beyond the Roman Catholic Church based on natural revelation and morality alone (Bergier 1827, 3:157; Jobert 1987, 32–33). This teaching was, in effect, not entirely new to Bergier, for he had already written in *Deism Refuted by Itself* that, for infidels who had not been instructed anew in the true religion, those "who follow exactly and in all things the law of God written at the foundation of their Heart" would be elevated to an understanding of God (Bergier 1768, 1:228; Jobert 1987, 32–33). Bergier further identifies this position with the earlier writings of Augustine of Hippo and with the Epistle to the Romans, wherein Paul writes that "those who have not received the law will not be judged by the law" (Romans 2:12).

Bergier shed his mortal coil with his potentially most scandalous composition unpublished, and his last days were troubled by the collapse of the Old Regime in the final months of his life. Generally speaking, Bergier seems to have taken a very dim view of the elevation of privilege and particular interests over the well-being and happiness of France as a whole. He is known to have expressed sympathy for the Maupeou Coup, which temporarily abolished the French *parlements* because of their obstruction to ministerial efforts to reform and manage the public debt and thereby avert further royal bankruptcies. For similar reasons, Bergier expressed support for the abolition of all privileges as early as the 1786 Assembly of Notables when Minister Calonne proposed only a land tax and a stamp tax to be levied on the privileged nobles and third estate, alike. In fact, Bergier considered the National Assembly and the failure of the 1789 Estates General to have been the inevitable comeuppance for a privileged nobility so blinded by hauteur that it could not attend to the urgency of the moment and the poverty of so many Frenchmen. Notwithstanding these quite progressive political positions as of 1786–1789, Bergier grew unnerved at the discourse of the social contract he detected in the rhetoric of the early revolutionary governments, and one of his last works, the uncharacteristically short brochure *What Is the Source of All Authority? (Quelle est la source de toute authorité?*, 1789), denounces the social contractarian thought made vulgar and accepted by Rousseau. For Bergier, all authority was divine, so to suggest that it could derive from a social contract based in a (Bergier argued fictive) state of nature is, he argued, a position that would only lead to dictatorship. If neither natural rights nor duties can be clearly adduced and compelled based in natural law, and if natural law is not, itself, understood to be the emanation of the sovereign will of God, then force becomes the only law. God alone "is thus evidently as much the author and institutor of authority as the society that, itself, is created by social contract" (Bergier 1789, 6). It may seem excessively uncharitable to assert, along the lines of Bernard Plongeron, that Bergier's little brochure helped calcify the reactionary position that democracy, revolution, and atheism are all inextricably linked—a view which prevailed in many European states from 1815–1848. Nevertheless, Bergier does at least seem to have foreseen one of the major (if now more nuanced and problematic) criticisms Francois Furet and R. R. Palmer directed at the rhetoric of Revolution—that by abstracting and transferring the unitary sovereignty of the monarchy to the revolutionary general will of the nation, legitimate dissent becomes treason against the will of the people expressed only through the "fatal purity" of the Terror (Plongeron 1973, 119; Palmer 1989, 75–76; Scurr 2006, 5–13; Furet 1981, 132–63).

Bergier's last days were clearly spent in relative turmoil. He accompanied the royal family and the National Assembly back to Paris after the October Days in 1789, and very soon thereafter, his health declined until, finally on 9 April 1790, he exhaled for the last time, leaving behind one of his most provocative works of Catholic Enlightenment ever. Before his death, then, Bergier entrusted to his friend, Demandre, two manuscripts. The first, presented while the *Treatise concerning True Religion* was in the pipeline, was refused approbation by the censor in 1779. This piece was ultimately published in 1821 as *Portrait of Divine Mercy Drawn from Holy Scripture* (*Tableau de la miséricorde divine tiré de l'Écriture sainte*), and as Ambroise Jobert has summarized, Bergier argued in the *Portrait* that God gives his graces to all, and whoever, then, makes use of them will achieve salvation. Those who do not utilize this divine grace available to all will not be justified by their own fault (Jobert 1987, 35; Bergier 1821, 112–90, 264–84).

In many ways, Bergier's position in the *Portrait* restates exactly the Tridentine position on the relationship of grace and good works. The second piece he entrusted to Demandre never achieved publication, though Bergier confided to his friend, Abbé Trouillet, that he considered it his greatest work. Its contents appear significantly more provocative, reflecting perhaps a more intimate understanding of just what had generated the surge of unbelief and atheism characteristic of a handful of his late eighteenth-century *esprit-fort* counterpoints in the first place. Tragically enough, this enigmatic *Treatise of Redemp-*

tion (*Traité de Rédemption*) was lost in the mêlée of revolutionary fervor, and it has never fully resurfaced. However, its basic structure, some of its passages, the whole of its argument, and Bergier's own purpose in writing it can all be reconstructed from the often heated correspondence with his friend Abbé Trouillet between 1770 and 1790, published in 1987 by Ambroise Jobert and prefaced by Jean Delumeau (Jobert 1987, 34–37; Delumeau 1987, 9–12).

Abbé Trouillet earnestly felt that Bergier's work verged on heresy, and he admonished his friend not to publish it, and to pray for repentance. Trouillet's position was simply that faith in Jesus Christ and baptism are indispensible for salvation, and tragically, the inevitable result of this doctrine will result in the majority of humanity being lost eternally. Nicolas-Sylvestre Bergier, who began work on the *Treatise of Redemption* around 1781 and finished it in the final months before his death in 1790 (perhaps in part, after the October Days), simply could no longer conciliate this with the infinite compassion of a supremely good deity he found established in the Gospels and in many works of the church fathers themselves. His conclusion? Simply that Saint Augustine's post-Pelagian works had been exaggerated during the European dark ages, especially within the Western, Latin church. The eighteenth-century Catholic Enlightenment, in defending itself against the likes of Rousseau, Voltaire, and d'Holbach, had gradually understood that the eighteenth-century church needed to return to the doctrines that represented the consensus tradition of the primitive apostolic church (Jobert 1987, 37–40). In his letters to Trouillet, Bergier refers to Saint Augustine with nearly the same rhetorical venom that he unleashed on Baron d'Holbach and Voltaire, calling Augustine's later writings a "cruel dogma" and "mystery of iniquity" largely responsible for presenting God in such detestably harsh terms that men and women fled in terror into the arms of Protestants, Jansenists, and now, a sect of atheist philosophers for two centuries. Instead, Bergier grounds his more inclusive sense of primitive church tradition in the first three centuries of Greek fathers, who, as Ambroise Jobert notes, Bergier thought had "founded themselves on Scripture [and] celebrat[ed] highly the bounty of God" (Jobert 1987, 37–38; Bergier to Trouillet, 9 October 1781 and 18 October 1781, in Jobert 1987, 251–60).

Apart from the published correspondence between Trouillet and Bergier, the oft published *Dictionary of Theology* is, itself, a source of Abbé Bergier's mature thoughts on redemption, grace, and the tradition of the primitive church: "Because Christian doctrine is revealed by God, Theology is not a science of invention but of tradition. Consequently, positive Theology is the only true Theology. . . . The first of the Church Fathers, Saint Irenaeus, had been instructed by the immediate pupils of the apostles. . . . The fathers of the following centuries made the best case of his erudition and doctrine" (Bergier 1781–1790, quoted in Jobert 1987, 39).

Bergier continues, in his article on Augustine, to argue that he was "'one of the greatest geniuses of all time,' but that his work is not exempt from contradictions." "The best means of reducing the enemies of Saint Augustine and of the Church in general to silence," Bergier maintains, "is not to attribute to this Father a species of infallibility that he was, himself, far from affecting" (Bergier 1781–1790, 1:172). "In fact," he continues, "Augustine let himself import into his writings against the Pelagians outrageous affirmations" later augmented by Pope Leo the Great in spite of himself, if only because Leo's pontificate corresponded with a harsh and barbaric age when arts, letters, and clear communication were compromised (Bergier 1781–1790, 1:172–77; Jobert 1987, 39). To Bergier, "an excessive zeal for Saint Augustine can appear suspect," and it is simply not possible to reconcile Augustine's belief in the final damnation of the majority of humankind due to original sin with the teachings of Jesus himself, and with those of the church fathers, including, in places, Augustine's own statements. Bergier seems clearly to have written before his death in 1790 that the true and primitive Catholic tradition teaches that the ultimate will of God is to redeem the world (Bergier 1781–1790, 1:173, 177). In his letters to Trouillet, Bergier is even more direct: "It is absurd to preach a general, complete, superabundant redemption, and to suppose that the evil still subsists as if it had not been repaired; or at least that the repair is only capable of being accomplished through a means that has only been made available to perhaps a quarter of humanity at all" (Bergier to Trouillet, 11 December 1781, quoted in Jobert 1987, 281–83).

In many ways, Nicolas-Sylvestre Bergier has been well studied, having been the subject of a recent book by Sylviane Albertan-Coppola (Albertan-Coppola 2010, 237–39). Bergier has additionally featured in a handful of studies, including those of John McManners, Paulette Charbonnel, Alphonse Lods, and Alfred J. Bingham, all dating before the middle 1980s and most well before then (Jobert 1987, 394–95). Bergier has most recently been addressed in Didier Masseau's *Les ennemis des philosophes* (Masseau 2000, 237–73), Jonathan Israel's *Enlightenment Contested* (Israel 2006, 661–62), and more extensively in his *Democratic Enlightenment* (Israel 2011, 1033). Bergier's place in the transformation of French theological Enlightenment has been covered in my *Rise and Fall of Theological Enlightenment* (Burson 2010b, 302–4) and Alan C. Kors's now classic work on the coterie of d'Holbach (Kors 1976, 114–17), as well as classic works on late eighteenth-century apologetics and Counter-Enlightenment, including those of Bernard Plongeron (Plongeron 1973, 119) and William Everdell (Everdell 1987, 128–32). Bergier's indebtedness to eighteenth-century travel literature, and the work of Jesuit missionaries has been insightfully addressed by Clorinda Donato (Donato 2003). Short biographical summaries of Abbé Bergier appear in Ambroise Jobert's editorial introduction, and in Jean Delumeau's preface, to the published correspondence between Bergier and Abbé Trouillet from 1770 to 1790 (Jobert 1987, 13–44; Delumeau 1987, 1–12). Nevertheless, the sheer bulk of Bergier's total publications (well over twenty volumes, discounting the *Dictionary of Theology*), and the extent of his political prominence and patronage after 1771, will certainly give scholars much to chew on and digest in the future.

Bibliography

Albertan-Coppola, Sylviane. 1998. "Cet autre versant des Lumières: L'Abbé N.-S. Bergier et ses confrères apologistes." *Revue de l'histoire de l'Église de France* 84 (212): 237–39.

———. 2010. *L'Abbé Nicolas-Sylvestre Bergier (1718–1790): Des Monts-Jura à Versailles, le parcours d'un apologiste du XVIIIe siècle.* Paris: Honoré Champion.

Bergier, Nicolas-Sylvestre. 1767a. *Origine des dieux du paganisme et le sens des fables découvert par une explication suivie poesies d'Hésiode*. 2 vols. Paris: Humblot.

———. 1767b. *La certitude des preuves du Christianisme, ou Réfutation de l'Examen critique des Apologistes de la Religion chrétienne*. 2 vols. Paris: Humblot.

———. 1768. *Le Déisme réfuté par lui-même, ou Examen, en forme de lettres, des principes d'incrédulité répandus dans les divers ouvrages de M. Rousseau*. 2 vols. Paris: Humblot.

———. 1769. *Apologie de la religion chrétienne contre l'auteur du Christianisme dévoilé, et contre quelques autres critiques*. 2 vols. Paris: Humblot.

———. 1771. *Examen du materialism, ou Réfutation du Système de la Nature*. 2 vols. Paris: Humblot.

———. 1781–1790. *Dictionnaire de théologie*. Nouvelle ed. 4 vols. Lille: Lefort, 1838.

———. 1789. *Quelle est la source de toute autorité?* Paris: no pub.

———. 1821. *Tableau de la miséricorde tiré de l'Écriture sainte, ou motifs de confiance en Dieu pour la consolation des âmes timides*. Besançon: J. Pétit.

———. 1827. *Traité historique et dogmatique de la vraie religion*. 12 vols. Tournay: Ch. Casterman-Dieu. First published 1780.

———. 1837. *Les éléments primitifs des langues, découverts par la comparaison des racines de l'Hébreu avec celles du Grèc, du Latin, du François*. Nouvelle ed. Besançon: Lambert. First published 1764.

[Buffier, Claude G.]. 1732. *Cours de sciences sur des principes nouveaux et simples pour former le langage, l'esprit, et le coeur dans l'usage ordinaire de la vie*. Paris: E. Guillaume Cavelier et Pierre-François Giffart.

Burson, Jeffrey D. 2008. "The Crystallization of Counter-Enlightenment and Philosophe Identities: Theological Controversy and Catholic Enlightenment in Pre-Revolutionary France." *Church History* 77:955–1002.

———. 2010a. "The Catholic Enlightenment in France from *Fin de Siècle* Crisis of Consciousness to the Revolution, 1650–1789." In *A Companion to the Catholic Enlightenment in Europe*, edited by Ulrich L. Lehner and Michael Printy, 63–125. Leiden: Brill.

———. 2010b. *The Rise and Fall of Theological Enlightenment: Jean-Martin de Prades and Ideological Polarization in Eighteenth-Century France*. Foreword by Dale Van Kley. Notre Dame: University of Notre Dame Press.

Chopelin-Blanc, Caroline. 2009. *De l'apologétique à l'Église constitutionnelle: Adrien Lamourette (1742–1794)*. Paris: Honoré Champion.

Curran, Mark. 2009. "Mettons toujours Londres: Enlightened Christianity and the Public in Pre-Revolutionary Francophone Europe." *French History* 24:40–59.

Delumeau, Jean. 1987. Introduction to *Un théologien au siècle des Lumières: Bergier correspondence avec l'abbé Trouillet, 1770–1790*, edited by Ambroise Jobert, 1–12. Lyon: Centre André Latreille.

Donato, Clorinda. 2003. "Le Nouveau Monde et l'apologie du catholicisme dans le *Dictionnaire de théologie* (1789–1790) de l'abbé Bergier." *Tangence* 72:57–73.

Everdell, William R. 1987. *Christian Apologetics in France, 1730–1790: The Roots of Romantic Religion*. Lewiston and Queenston, ON: Edwin Mellen.

Furet, François. 1981. *Interpreting the French Revolution*. Translated by Elborg Forster. Cambridge and London: Cambridge University Press.

Israel, Jonathan I. 2001. *Radical Enlightenment: Philosophy and the Making of Modernity, 1650–1750*. Oxford: Oxford University Press.

———. 2006. *Enlightenment Contested: Philosophy, Modernity, and the Emancipation of Man, 1670–1752*. Oxford: Oxford University Press.

———. 2011. *Democratic Enlightenment: Philosophy, Revolution, and Human Rights, 1750–1790*. Oxford: Oxford University Press.

Jobert, Ambroise. 1987. "Avant-Propos." In *Un théologien au siècle des Lumières: Bergier correspondence avec l'abbé Trouillet, 1770–1790*, edited by Ambroise Jobert, 15–44. Lyon: Centre André Latreille.

Kors, Alan C. 1976. *D'Holbach's Coterie: An Enlightenment in Paris*. Princeton: Princeton University Press.

Leddy, Neven, and Avi S. Lifschitz. 2005. "Epicurus in the Enlightenment: An Introduction." In *Epicurus and the Enlightenment*, edited by Neven Leddy and Avi S. Lifschitz, 1–11. Oxford: Voltaire Foundation.

Lefebvre, Philippe. 2000. "Le regard sur l'incrédule dans les sermons de la deuxième moitié du dix-huitième siècle." In *Religions en transition dans la seconde moitié du dix-huitième siècle*, edited by Louis Châtellier, 95–109. Oxford: Voltaire Foundation.

Lehner, Ulrich L. 2011. *Enlightened Monks: The German Benedictines, 1740–1803*. Oxford: Oxford University Press.

Masseau, Didier. 2000. *Les ennemis des philosophes: L'antiphilosophie au temps des Lumières*. Paris: Editions Albin Michel.

McMahon, Darrin. 2001. *Enemies of the Enlightenment: The French Counter-Enlightenment and the Making of Modernity*. Oxford: Oxford University Press.

Migne, M. l'abbé, ed. 1855. *Oeuvres complètes*. 8 vols., 8:1555–86. Migne: Petit-Montrouge.

Palmer, R. R. 1989. *Twelve Who Ruled: The Year of the Terror in the French Revolution*. Bicentennial ed. Princeton: Princeton University Press.

Plongeron, Bernard. 1973. *Théologie et politique au siècle des Lumières*. Genève: Droz.

---. 1976. "Bonheur et 'civilisation chrétienne': Une nouvelle apologetique après 1760." In *Transactions of the Fourth International Congress of the Enlightenment VI,* edited by Theodore Besterman, 1637–55. Oxford: Voltaire Foundation.

Reill, Peter Hanns. 2005. *Vitalizing Nature in the Enlightenment.* Berkeley and Los Angeles: University of California Press.

Saint-Croix, Baron de. 1844. "Elogé historique de l'abbé Bergier." In *Dictionnaire de théologie,* 3:v–ix. Lille: Lefort.

Scurr, Ruth. 2006. *Fatal Purity: Robespierre and the French Revolution.* New York: Henry Holt and Co.

Shelford, April G. 2007. *Transforming the Republic of Letters: Pierre-Daniel Huet and European Intellectual Life, 1650–1720.* Rochester: University of Rochester Press.

Van Kley, Dale. 1975. *The Jansenists and the Expulsion of the Jesuits from France, 1757–1765.* New Haven: Yale University Press.

---. 2006. "Jansenism and the International Suppression of the Jesuits." In *Enlightenment, Reawakening and Revolution, 1660–1815,* edited by Stewart J. Brown and Timothy Tackett, 302–28. Cambridge History of Christianity 7. Cambridge: Cambridge University Press.

Wilkins, Kathleen. 1969. *A Study of the Works of Claude Buffier.* Oxford: Voltaire Foundation.

3

Giacinto Sigismondo Cardinal Gerdil (1718–1802)

Enlightenment as Cultural and Religious Achievement

DRIES VANYSACKER

Born in Samoëns-en-Faucigny in the Haute-Savoie on 23 June 1718, the son of notary Pierre and Françoise Perrier, Gerdil received his early education at Bonneville and at Thonon, and was entrusted by his uncle, Jean Gerdil, a mathematician, to the Barnabites (Regular Clerics of Saint Paul) of Annecy in order to follow studies in rhetoric and philosophy at the local royal college. In 1734, he entered the noviatiate of the Barnabites at Bonneville, and he took his solemn vows on 25 September 1735. Sent by his order to Bologna, he studied philosophy, Italian, and experimental sciences over the course of three years, but the systematic study of the works of Saint Augustine and Saint Thomas would influence his own later work in apologetics. The intellect of the young Barnabite was noted by Prospero Lambertini (1675–1758), Archbishop of Bologna and future Pope Benedict

XIV (1740–1758); ultimately the future Cardinal Gerdil's knowledge of French became useful when he was publishing Lambertini's juridical and liturgical works. On 27 May 1737, Gerdil received his "minor orders," and from that moment on, he was a professor of philosophy at the college of the Barnabites of Macerata (1737–1738) and at the Royal College of Casale Montferrat (1738–1748). On 11 June 1741, he was ordained a priest at Casale.

On 15 September 1749, Gerdil was appointed professor of practical philosophy at the University of Turin, and in 1754, he took possession of the vacant chair of moral theology. The renown of his publications brought him membership in the Institute of Science (*Istituto delle scienze*) of Bologna on 13 March 1749, the Royal Society of London, the Academy of Arcadia, and various other literary and scientific institutions. In 1757, Gerdil became one of the earliest members of the Privy Society of Turin (*Società privata torinese*), later known as the Royal Society (*Società reale*), in 1769. Ultimately, Gerdil became a member of the Royal Academy of Science in Turin (*Accademia reale delle scienze di Torino*) in 1783, founded by Marquis Giuseppe Angelo Saluzzo (1734–1810), together with Giovanfrancesco Cigna (1734–1790) and Giuseppe Luigi Lagrange (1736–1813). His participation in the Società contributed to the publication of the academy's findings in European scientific circles and a widespread network of correspondences.

Gerdil also managed to attract the attention of the grand chaplain of the king of Sardinia, Carlo Vittorio Amedeo Cardinal Delle Lanze (1712–1784), and Crown Prince Vittorio Amedeo (1726–1796) by offering insights on the upbringing of the latter's sons. Consequently, on 21 September 1758, Gerdil was appointed tutor of the crown prince's firstborn son, later Duke Carlo Emanuele IV (1751–1819). Subsequently, on 31 July 1768, he became responsible for teaching the future king, Vittorio Emanuele I (1759–1824), and Maurizio, Duke of Montferrat (1762–1799). Like other university professors in his day, Gerdil participated in the Turin diocesan synod of 1755 as a synodal examiner. However, he soon became increasingly burdened by practical responsibilities, so he left the university in 1759. In 1764, he was elected the provincial superior of the Piedmont-Savoy Barnabites, and was reelected to this position for another three-year term in 1767.

When the Barnabite superior general died the following year, the General Chapter considered Gerdil as a possible successor, but he was not elected.

During the consistory of 26 April 1773, Clement XIV (1769–1774) named Gerdil a cardinal *in pectore*, and Angelo Maria Durini (1725–1796), who was sent as a papal legate to Avignon, informed Gerdil of this while passing through Turin. Within the framework of Savoy politics, the presence of Gerdil in Rome supported the continuation of the concordat strategy established by Vittorio Amedeo III (1773–1796), which included negotiations over the liquidation of wealthy monasteries in order to obtain and utilize their goods. Gerdil was explicitly called to Rome by Pius VI (1775–1799) in March 1776. Having arrived the following April, he took up permanent residence at the *Casa generalizia* of the Barnabites in San Carlo ai Catinari, and he was immediately employed as a consultor to the Holy Office (Wolf 2010).

Papal Censor and Adviser

On 17 February 1777, Gerdil was promoted to titular bishop of Dibona (Dibbon) and was consecrated a bishop in San Carlo ai Catinari by Cardinal Vicar Marcantonio Colonna (1724–1793). On 23 June of the same year, he was named cardinal, given the titular church of San Giovanni a Porta Latina (later changed to the titular church of Santa Cecilia in December 1777), and appointed cardinal prefect of the Congregation of the Index. Also in the same year, the king of Sardinia appointed him abbot of the Abbey of San Michele della Chiusa; in 1781, he would also become abbot of the Abbey of Muleggio, whereupon Gerdil would find himself tending to the pastoral care of both of these two distant abbeys via pastoral letters, and utilizing a large portion of their income to aid the poor (Favaro 2001).

In keeping with the initiatives of Benedict XIV displayed in his reforms of 1753, the Congregation of the Index under the prefecture of Gerdil acquired greater status within the Roman Curia, while gaining greater autonomy than the Holy Office. Given the theological and canonical sensitivity of the secretaries and the consultors, works that defended a materialistic vision of reality were discussed and condemned, in addition to books containing the marks of late Italian Jansenism, Febronianism, and Josephism. Together with Giovanni Francesco Albani (1720–1803), Leonardo Antonelli (1730–1811), Filippo Campanelli (1739–1795), and Francesco Saverio de Zelada (1717–1801), Gerdil was a member of the cardinal's committee that studied and refined the finalized text by Giuseppe Garampi (1725–1792), Francesco Antonio Zaccaria (1714–1795), and others against the Punctuation of Ems (Vanysacker 1995, 238–39). It was published in Rome in 1790 as *Response of His Holiness, Pope Pius VI to the Archbishops of Mainz, Trier, Cologne, and Salzburg on the Issue of Apostolic Nuncios* (*Sanctissimi domini nostri Pii papae sexti responsio ad metropolitanos Moguntinum, Trevirensem, Coloniensem et Salisburgensem super nunciaturis apostolicis*). The appreciation for Gerdil's work did not go unnoticed. In anticurial circles, he was regarded as "the only one with common sense and was moderate-minded" (Scipione de' Ricci [1741–1810] in a letter to Grand Duke Pietro Leopoldo, 29 March 1787; Stella 1999, 395).

Between 1790 and 1794, Gerdil was a member of the cardinal's committee at large (Zelada, Albani, Garampi, and others) as well as the core committee (together with Albani and Antonelli), which prepared the final text of the papal bull *Auctorem fidei* (28 August 1794), which condemned the proposals of the Synod of Pistoia. The use of the conditional formula ("sic intellecta" and "quatenus innuit") in this bull can be viewed as unique in the history of papal condemnations in the modern era (Stella 2001, 24). Also in the same year, Gerdil sat on the Congregation Overseeing Ecclesiastical Regulations of the French Kingdom (Congregatio super negotiis ecclesiasticis Regni Galliarum, officially established on 28 May 1793), which prepared papal documents to deal with the problems associated with the Civil Constitution of the Clergy, civil oaths imposed on clergy, and other inventions of the French revolutionaries. In addition to these responsibilities, he was also a member of the Congregation of the Rites, the Congregation of the Council, the Congregation for the Erection of Churches and Consistorial Provisions, and the Commission for the Correction of Books of the Oriental Church.

At a special meeting of the cardinals on 24 September 1790, where some requests made by the king of France were discussed, Gerdil acknowledged the exceptional circumstances in which France found itself and proposed to the Ecclesiastical Committee of the Constitutional Assembly an acceptable territorial division of dioceses. However, he did not think it was appropriate or necessary to ask the permission of the French bishops; Gerdil's position was consistent with the vision of a pope-friendly ecclesiology that was supported over and against Febronianism; this position was also the basis of future negotiations that would eventually lead to the Concordat of 1801.

On 27 February 1795, Gerdil was appointed prefect of the Congregation of the Propaganda Fide, while Stefano Borgia (1731–1804) succeeded him as the prefect of the Index. He came to this congregation in order to guide it through circumstances where normal relations with missions *in partibus infidelium* were no longer possible; many of these missions, especially in the Middle and Far East, were at risk of collapse. Given the financial difficulties caused by the war with France, Gerdil was cut off from his financial sources in Rome and had to sell books from his own library and other objects of his personal property. In spite of the great financial problems in Piedmont, Vittorio Amedeo III intervened and provided him with the revenues of the Abbey of S. Stefano d'Ivrea in December 1795.

On 10 February 1798, French troops occupied Rome, and on February 20 Pius VI was exiled to Siena; Gerdil traveled to Piedmont on March 21. In Siena, he received extraordinary powers from the pope in cases of emergency relating to ecclesiastical discipline. In Turin, he was received by and resided with former student and newly crowned prince Carlo Emanuele IV (r. 1796–1802) then residing with the Oratorians and later with the Barnabites (San Dalmazzo). Unlike other prelates, he used his extraordinary powers sparingly, but he did allow the use of church property for the financial gains of the state. When Carlo Emanuele IV, under the pressure of the circumstances of the times, renounced his throne and retreated, Gerdil retreated from the territory of the Abbey of San Michele della Chiusa. Completely isolated, he asked Cardinal Stefano Borgia (who fled to Padua) as well as his secretary, Cesare Brancadoro (1755–1837), to replace him as prefect of the Propaganda Fide (Favaro 2001).

After the death of Pius VI in Valence, France, Gerdil went to Venice for the papal conclave, arriving on 21 October 1799. During the initial rounds of voting, the Spanish party threw their support behind him. However, when Cardinal Franziskus von Paula Herzan von Harras (1735–1804) arrived on December 6, Gerdil lost his candidacy because of the right of exclusion exercised by Herzan von Harras on behalf of the Austrian emperor. Following the election of Pius VII (1800–1823) on 14 March 1800, Gerdil departed from Venice and arrived in Rome on September 12. He resumed his position as prefect of the Propaganda Fide, with the support of Borgia and Brancadoro. At the same time, he and cardinals Antonelli and Filippo Carandini (1729–1810) were delegated by the pope to the preparatory negotiations leading up to the Concordat of 1801. For more than eighty years, he lived in good health with a lucid mind. After a brief illness, Gerdil died at San Carlo ai Catinari in Rome on 12 August 1802 (Chevailler 1984; Stella 1999).

Gerdil and the *Philosophes*: The Piedmont Period (1747–1774)

During his years as a professor at the colleges of Macerata and Casale Monferrato, Gerdil was acquainted with the philosophy of Plato, Aristotle, Galileo Galilei (1564–1642), the Peripatetics, René Descartes (1596–1650), Isaac Newton (1642–1727), Gottfried Wilhelm Leibniz (1646–1716), John Locke (1632–1704), and the French Oratorian Nicolas Malebranche (1638–1715). In Italy, indeed, philosophical and theological thinking was moving from the learned theological research of the Maurists and the anti-Protestant controversies toward a confrontation with modern philosophy. Gerdil could read Locke through the French translations by Pierre Coste (1668–1747).

In 1747, Gerdil reached out with *Immateriality* (*L'immatérialité*) (Gerdil 1747)—dedicated to the young Crown Prince Vittorio Amedeo di Savoia—a model of apologetics that is not based on the fruitless contrast with modern thought, but rather accepts the theoretical principles arising from fair and honest discussion about the new philosophy of the eighteenth century. His attempt at a moderate revisionism was evident in a subsequent publication dedicated to Cardinal Delle Lanze (Gerdil 1748), in which he defends Malebranche's vision against Locke.

Through this visionary openness to further engagement with modern eighteenth-century thought characteristic of the *philosophes,* and his avoidance of alignment with the Jansenism of Antoine Arnauld (1612–1694) and Laurent-François Boursier (1679–1749)—both explicitly criticized in *Défense* (Gerdil 1748)—Gerdil made a good impression on those most responsible for Piedmontese political culture. He debuted as a professor of practical philosophy at the University of Turin in the midst of the turmoil concerning apologists who faced condemnation of Montesquieu's *De l'esprit des loix* (*The Spirit of the Laws*; 1751) by the *Index of Prohibited Books*. His inaugural lecture, *Concerning Political Virtue* (*Virtutem politicam*) (Gerdil 1750), was a polemical reflection based on the concepts of "patriotism" and "governing talents." Shortly thereafter, Gerdil distinguished himself in scientific treatises, displaying his versatility and intelligence, which resonated beyond the Alps (Gerdil 1752; Gerdil 1754b).

His inaugural lecture as professor of moral theology at Turin concerned a moral theological theme that was closely tied to a flood of books in which the followers of Daniello Concina (1687–1756) and their opponents—probabilists and benignists—were pitted against one another (Gerdil 1754a). It was especially the contributions by Piedmontese Jesuits that tested the nerves of the Savoy government, since the court did not take kindly to these frontal assaults on Daniello Concina and the Augustinian-Thomistic doctrine.

Gerdil continued his teaching assignment, combining literary and scientific output. In 1755, he published an introduction to the study of religion, a very scholarly work, long in the making and dedicated to Benedict XIV. Among others, he cited Jean le Rond d'Alembert (1717–1783), deeming him to be "one of the most important persons of this age" (Gerdil 1755b, 40)—a passage which he left untouched in later editions, despite the condemnation of the *Encyclopédie* in the *Index of Prohibited Books* (1758; 1759). He also labeled Galileo as "immortal" (Gerdil 1755b, 45, 84) during the period in which the Dominican Tommaso Maria Mamachi (1713–1792) and Jesuit Benedetto

Plazza (1677–1761) expressed doubts about the Copernican heliocentric theory while supporting the Ptolemaic system as being more in harmony with the Bible. Free thought, according to Gerdil, is incoherent if it is not ordered to (subordinate to) the knowledge of truth; so-called natural religion cannot even imagine being opposed to the supernatural insofar as the former is ordered (subordinate) to the latter (Gerdil 1755b, 122). His basic thesis was that the reality of God was shown as an archetype of an ideal order to be pursued, and of which one should be aware. In the eyes of those within the church, such as the pontiff, Benedict XIV, then preoccupied with so many conflicts between groups of theologians, *Introduzione* was a good apologetic model (Lapponi 2001).

South of the Alps, the tracts of his *Introduzione*, which were devoted to the ideas of order, the existence of God, and aesthetic beauty (Gerdil 1755a), were in fact very fruitful: they inspired the architectural projects and analyses of the Barnabite Ermenegildo Pini (1739–1825), as well as the work of Count Gianfrancesco Galeani Napione (1748–1830). In Europe, his philosophical and theological publications in Paris were well received (Gerdil 1760, 1761). During this period of the 1750s–1760s, his participation in the meetings of the Società reale was rather minimal, but at the heart of the group, he continued to be regarded as an expert for his familiarity with the Enlightenment movement in Turin. This was a time in which a significant shift from philosophical and political debate toward applied mathematics and physics was under way. In effect, Gerdil's lectures in 1774, several months after Vittorio Amedeo III's ascent to the throne, were important in this respect. Gerdil intervened with a proposal to the scientific research editors of philosophical vocabulary in order to coordinate with other literary activities that focused on a sort of "reintroduction of several encyclopedic ideals concocted by philosophers in the middle of the century" (Gerdil 1774a).

Gerdil's literary production from these years must be viewed against the backdrop of his relation to the royal offspring, the sharing of the political and religious concerns of the area surrounding the royal court, and his responsibility as provincial of the Barnabites—by then a religious order dedicated to education and study of many forms of knowledge. Gerdil wrote about the politics of social control in the State of Savoy (Gerdil 1759), but he was also willing to defy the political model outlined in the *Social Contract* (*Contrat social*), which the Barnabites considered tantamount to the "universal overthrow of social order," and the individualistic "spontaneity" of the pedagogical ideas of Jean-Jacques Rousseau (1712–1778) (Gerdil 1763). Gerdil's views confirm the natural sociability of mankind and the need for education to be extended to the lower classes. The result was the *Réflexions* (Gerdil 1763), later reissued under the title *Anti-Émile*, containing a very broad range of pedagogical ideas that would dominate south of the Alps during the Risorgimento (Italian movement for unification, c. 1750–1870). In addition to that, Gerdil also published a brief tract that began as a text designed to meet catechetical needs but turned out to be an organic explanation inspired by the *Historical Catechism Containing an Abridgment of Sacred History and Christian Doctrine* (*Catéchisme historique, contenant en abrégé l'histoire sainte et la doctrine chrétienne*; 1679), attributed to Claude Fleury (1640–1723) (Gerdil 1768a). Within the Italian catechetical environment, the well-known *Breve esposizione* had a long publication history well into the twentieth century. In 1768, Gerdil took a stand against exorbitant wealth and once again proposed themes that added a new dimension to the proposals concerning free trade proposed by Adam Smith (c. 1723–1790) and others (Gerdil 1768b). Finally, Gerdil also reiterated the common concept of the social nature of man, which he already addressed in his response to *Émile* (Gerdil 1769; Gerdil 1774b).

By 1774, Gerdil's intellectual interests quickly turned to theology, law, society, and the authorities. In his *On the Elements* (*Elementorum*) (Gerdil 1774c), he clearly demonstrates that his ideas continued to be shaped by Malebranche. In terms of theology, he mostly quotes the Dominican Alexander Natalis (1639–1724); his direct use of the works of the Oratorian Louis Thomassin (1619–1695) and of the *Summa Theologiae* of Thomas Aquinas (1225–1274) is evident throughout his theological writings. Many of Gerdil's works of political theology are dominated by references to Jacques-Bénigne Bossuet (1627–1704), while the use of the Oratorian Jacques-Joseph Duguet (1649–1733) is less explicit. In short, we can conclude that during the period of

1747–1774 Gerdil's most important philosophical and pedagogical ideas were left to posterity (Fasciolo Bachelet 2001).

Gerdil and the Theological Challenges of Jansenism and Episcopalism (1776–1803)

During the years 1776–1798, Gerdil's writings were all linked to the state of emergency created by the initiatives of reform-minded princes, especially those influenced by Jansenism and the French Revolution.

Gerdil published a treatise on persuasive theological instruction, a welcome reference tool for the supervision of the Irish and Fucciolio colleges, both centers of Jansenism under headmasters Pietro Tamburini (1737–1827) and Giuseppe Zola (1739–1806), both of Brescia (Gerdil 1776). He also delivered a lecture concerning the nature and consequences of exorbitant wealth in Arcadia; these lectures gained a special significance in confrontation with the local customs of the nobility and the high clergy (Gerdil 1777).

His signatures show that he was involved with important papal documents, such as *Mediator Dei et hominum* (21 November 1784) and *Super soliditate* (28 November 1786), concerning the condemnation of the works of Joseph Valentin Eybel (1741–1805). He continued to defend the priority of the pope and the Holy See against the writings of Tamburini (Gerdil 1789b), as well as the Synod of Pistoia (Gerdil 1789a), both of which had favored greater episcopal governance. Gerdil also defended the cult of the Sacred Heart of Jesus, which had been questioned by the Synod of Pistoia (Gerdil 1794).

The inspiration of Thomism and Malebranche, which is in the spirit of the unifying element of human reality, is passed on through Gerdil's papal-friendly apologetic discourse: physical realities lead to diversification, but they are also divisive; it is the spirit that desires and strives for unity. He respectfully quoted Bossuet's posthumous work, but he presented the arguments in such a way that they could not open the door to a nationalistic organization of the universal church. Gerdil eschewed the excessively militant and provocative style characteristic of some apologetic writings. Thus, Gerdil's writings were totally opposed to those of Zaccaria and Giovanni Marchetti (1753–1829) because the writings by these two men were disturbing in tone and rather aggressive, and leaned dangerously toward a contrahistorical theocratic papal policy. During his retreat on the grounds of the Abbey of San Michele della Chiusa, Gerdil worked on a tract he had begun in the 1770s concerning the rights of the sovereign in the exercise of administrative authority (Gerdil 1799). When he returned to Rome, he wrote more than eighty articles on various comments concerning the papal bull *Auctorem fidei* (Gerdil 1800; Gerdil 1802) and marriage within the church (Gerdil 1803).

The Eclectic "Modernity" of Cardinal Gerdil

In summation, we can say that Gerdil was an eminent and complex personality. His vision of respect toward Enlightenment culture should be viewed in the context of his broad view of theological, philosophical, and scientific culture. While many of his Catholic contemporaries saw in the Enlightenment only an antireligious process that contradicted the doctrinal positions defined by the church, Gerdil appreciated the Enlightenment as a process of disseminating culture. However, from the principle of divine origin of authority, Gerdil resolutely rejects the contractual theories of society and of sovereignty, both defended by the philosophers. From this perspective, one must find the inspired motivation behind the critique of Rousseau's *Émile*; for Gerdil, this is nothing but a preparation at the pedagogical level for a universal overthrow of the bourgeois order. Also, Gerdil's appreciation of economic phenomena has a direct link with religion. Witness, for example, his rejection of interest on loans based on the proscriptions in the Holy Scriptures and conciliar canons; witness also his condemnation of exorbitant wealth, a condemnation emergent from the wellspring of moral philosophy and social utilitarianism applied to theology. Then finally there is Gerdil's refutation of Raynal's *Philosophical and Political History of Commerce* (*Histoire philosophique et politique du commerce*), which, according to Gerdil, contained dangerous attacks on Christian doctrine. Gerdil kept a close eye on the utilitarian inclination of modern studies, and viewed with alarm the escalating trend of universities and institutions of higher learning preferring birth and wealth to talent, thus giving rise to a swelling group of frustrated and unemployed intellectuals rather than craftsmen "working for the good of the country." Therefore, Gerdil argued that access to a university education should depend on merit and not on social status.

Gerdil was not a man who only paid attention to the past. In scientific terms, he was attentive to the modern theories of Newton and saw useful tools at the academies toward the development of science. He was also interested in the socioeconomic situation of the state of Savoy, and he gave concrete proposals for the cultural enhancement of farmers and, in general, the lower classes of society. Gerdil certainly cared about social issues, and his concern could have opened up innovative perspectives on present reality, but unfortunately he was unable to pursue these perspectives sufficiently before he died.

However, one should keep in mind that Gerdil avoided the "progressive" de-Christianization by the Enlightenment. This anti-Christian trend had made him mistrust some aspects of the contemporary culture of his day. His polemic not only addresses a few "free thinkers" and their philosophical systems, but insists that contemporary culture has gone awry. This key to anti-Enlightenment reading has obviously left its mark south of the Alps. Gerdil believed that only hard-core action aimed at preserving the doctrines and the institutions of the past could safeguard people against the onslaught of new theories, which were hazardous to religion and state. From this perspective, Gerdil supported censorship by the authorities against the contemporary *"libertas philosophandi."* He was convinced that only the powerful mark of Christian culture could form the basis of a moderate reform that, far from any excesses and led by the authorities, would lead to a progressive improvement in terms of the economy and education (Valabrega 2001, 2004).

Gerdil is impossible to summarize in simple studies on the history of philosophical and pedagogical thought. Recent studies have shown that one cannot ignore the importance of his activities under the pontificate of Pius VI (Pelletier 2001). They also have integrated the information concerning Gerdil's earlier Piedmont days. A biography of Gerdil would most surely need to identify and measure the role he played during an important historical period marked by the absolutist reforms of Vittorio Amedeo III and the authoritarian centralism of Napoleon, a period marked by the religious and political ascent of Jansenism, Enlightenment reforms, and the French Revolution.

In looking at the "modernity" of the Barnabite Cardinal, it can be said that he accepted without question the role of mathematical and empirical knowledge. Moreover, Gerdil fully accepted rational arguments for the existence of God and accepted the existence of the immaterial and spiritual order necessitated by such arguments, an order in which human beings were participants. Gerdil's lectures concerning the atheists and materialists of his time, mostly within the context of French philosophers, stated his position in a modern methodological way that adapted much from the *philosophes*, even in the process of arguing against them. All of this Gerdil accomplished with the respect of the people, respect that he earned by never resorting to violent rhetoric and assumptions concerning the morality of the commoners. Confident in his mastery of experimental sciences, Gerdil fraternized with other scientifically minded intellectuals who had institutional roles within the church and the state, such as Celestino Galiani (1681–1753), Guido Grandi (1671–1742), Paolo Frisi (1728–1784), Roger Joseph Boscovich (1711–1787), and Lazzaro Spallanzani (1729–1799). All of the aforementioned attempted to maintain the bond between the church and the sciences at a time when philosophers seemed to be severing this intimate early modern liaison. Finally, one cannot ignore the fact that Cardinal Gerdil cultivated a very deep and intimate personal religiosity despite his engagement with the Enlightenment (Stella 2001).

Gerdil's vision of Enlightenment culture has to be seen in the context of his general view of theological, philosophical, pedagogical, and scientific culture. Contrary to many of his Catholic counterparts, who viewed the Enlightenment as a purely antireligious experience that endangered the doctrines defined by the church, Gerdil understood the Enlightenment as a process of disseminating culture. Nevertheless, based on the principle of divine origin of authority, Gerdil rejects outright the contractual theories of society and of sovereignty, both defended by the philosophers. As a real adept of the Enlightenment, Gerdil kept a close eye on the utilitarian inclination of modern studies, and argued that access to a university education should depend on merit and not on social status. In scientific terms, as previously noted, the modern theories of Newton informed Gerdil's work, and he saw the academies as useful for the development of science. It can also be said that he accepted without question the role of mathematical and empirical knowledge, as well as rational arguments for the existence of God that Gerdil believed necessarily implied the existence of the immaterial and spiritual order necessitated by such arguments.

Gerdil's attempt to eschew the de-Christianization by the Enlightenment often led to his own suspicions about some aspects of the culture of his day—suspicions that made an impression throughout Italy. Gerdil was a firm believer that the only way people could be protected against the tidal wave of new theories that were hazardous to religion and the state was to engage in a fierce preservation of the age-old doctrines and institutions. Concerning Gerdil's lectures, which focused on contemporary atheists and materialists mostly from the ranks of French philosophers, he made his point of view clear in a modern and methodological way, by his willingness to adapt many things from the very same philosophers he was criticizing. He strove to maintain the connection between the church and the sciences at a time when most philosophers appeared to be severing this intimate early modern liaison.

In his ecclesiological and theological thinking, Gerdil zealously advocated the rights of the Roman Church, while he opposed the superiority of the state over canon law, Gallicanism, Febronianism, and antireligious movements within the Enlightenment. As an enlightened ultramontane and a man of learned diplomacy, Gerdil preferred those treatises that were neither too aggressive nor too offensive, but that always stressed Rome's dominance in its temporal and spiritual powers, culminating in a complete independence from the rest of the world. Notwithstanding his openness toward the Enlightenment, Gerdil possessed a true religious personality with deep convictions.

Bibliography

Boffito, Giuseppe. 1933. *Scrittori Barnabiti*, 2:169–214. Florence: Olschki.
Cagni, Giuseppe M. 2001. "L'epistolario gerdiliano conservato nell'Archivio Storico dei Barnabiti a Roma." *Barnabiti Studi: Revista di ricerche storiche dei Chierici Regolari di S. Paolo (Barnabiti)* 18:321–57.
Celli, G. 1844–1851. *Opere edite ed inedite del Card. G. S. Gerdil.* 8 vols. Florence: G. Celli.
Chevailler, Louis. 1984. "Gerdil (Jean-François) en religion Hyacinthe-Sigismond, cardinal (1718–1802)." In *Dictionnaire d'histoire et de géographie ecclésiastiques*, 20, fascicules 117–18:852–57.
Fasciolo Bachelet, Silvia. 2001. "Il pensiero filosofico di Giacinto Sigismondo Gerdil." *Barnabiti Studi: Revista di ricerche storiche dei Chierici Regolari di S. Paolo (Barnabiti)* 18:29–96.
Favaro, Oreste. 2001. "Gerdil abate di San Michele della Chiusa." *Barnabiti Studi: Revista di ricerche storiche dei Chierici Regolari di S. Paolo (Barnabiti)* 18:265–320.
Gerdil, Giacinto Sigismondo. 1747. *L'immatérialité de l'âme démontrée contre m. Locke par les mêmes principes par lesquels ce philosophe démontre l'existence et l'immatérialité de Dieu, avec des nouvelles preuves de l'immatérialité de Dieu et de l'âme tirées de l'Écriture, des Pères et de la raison.* Torino.
———. 1748. *Défense du sentiment du Père Malebranche sur la nature et l'origine des idées contre l'Examen de m. Locke.* Torino.
———. 1750. *Virtutem politicam ad optimum statum non minus regno quam republicae necessariam esse oratio.* Torino.
———. 1752. *Mémoire sur la cause physique de la cohésion des hémisphères de Magdeburg aux auteurs du Journal des savants.* Paris.
———. 1754a. *De causis accademicarum disputationum in theologiam moralem inductarum.* Torino.
———. 1754b. *Dissertations sur l'incompatibilité de l'attraction et des ses différentes loix, avec les phénomènes et sur les tuyaux capillaires.* Paris.
———. 1755a. *Dissertazioni spora l'origine del senso morale e sopra l'esistenza di Dio ecc. In dichiarazione di alquanti punti del primo volume dalla Introduzione allo studio della religione.* Torino.
———. 1755b. *Introduzione allo studio della religione.* Torino.
———. 1759. *Traité des combats singuliers.* Torino.
———. 1760. *Recueil de dissertations de philosophie et de religion.* Paris.
———. 1761. *De l'infini absolu considéré dans la grandeur.* Paris.
———. 1763. *Réflexions sur la théorie et la pratique de l'éducation contre les principes de m. Rousseau.* Torino. Translated with introductory essay by William A. Frank as *The Anti-Emile: Reflections on the Theory and*

Practice of Education against the Principles of Rousseau. (South Bend, IN: St. Augustine's Press, 2011).

———. 1768a. *Breve esposizione dei caratteri della vera religione.* Torino.

———. 1768b. *Discours de la nature et des effets du luxe.* Torino.

———. 1769. *Discours philosophiques sur l'homme considéré relativement à l'état de la nature.* Torino.

———. 1774a. *Considerazione sopra i lavori accademici.* Torino.

———. 1774b. *De l'homme sous l'empire de la loix, pour servir de suite aux discours philosophiques sur l'homme . . .* Torino.

———. 1774c. *Elementorum moralis prudentiae iuris specimen.* Torino.

———. 1776. *Saggio d'instruzione teologica per uso di convitto ecclesiastico.* Rome.

———. 1777. *Discorso della natura e degli effetti del lusso.* Rome.

———. 1789a. *Abbatiae S. Michaelis de Clusa Nullius Dioecesis uni S. Sedi Apostolicae subjectae Synodi constitutiones, manadato Hyacinthi S. R. E. Cardinalis Gerdil a Francisco Ferrerio Abate S. Jacobi de Bessia, Vicario Generali, habitae in aede S. Laurentii, VII. VI. V. Cal. Oct. MDCCLXXXIX.* Torino.

———. 1789b. *Confutazione di due libelli diretti contro il breve "Super soliditate."* Rome.

———. 1792. *In commentarium a Iustino Febronio in suam retractationem editum animadversiones.* Rome.

———. 1794. *Animadversiones in notas quas nonnullis Pistoriensis synodi propositionibus damnatis in dogmatica constitutione . . . Auctorem fidei Cl. Feller . . . adiiciendas censuit.* Rome.

———. 1799. *Précis d'un cours d'instruction sur l'origine, les droits et les devoirs de l'autorité souveraine dans l'exercice des principales branches de l'administration.* Torino.

———. 1800. *Esame de'motivi della opposizione fatta da m. vescovo di Noli alla pubblicazione della bolla Auctorem fidei.* Venice.

———. 1802. *Appendice all'Esame de' motivi ecc.* Venice.

———. 1803. *Trattato del matrimonio o sia Confutazione de' sistemi contrari all'autorità della Chiesa circa il matrimonio.* Rome.

(For a complete overview of Gerdil's writings, see Boffito 1933 and the four editions of Gerdil's complete works: Tosselli 1784–1791; Scati and Grandi 1806–1821; Celli 1844–1851; Milone and Vercellone 1853–1856.)

Lapponi, Massimo. 2001. "Religione naturale e religione rivelata nel pensiero del Card. Gerdil." *Barnabiti Studi: Revista di ricerche storiche dei Chierici Regolari di S. Paolo (Barnabiti)* 18:97–125.

Milone, Gaetano, and Carlo Vercellone. 1853–1856. *Opere edite ed inedite del Card. G. S. Gerdil.* Nuova collezione. 7 vols. Naples: Diogene.

Pelletier, Gérard. 2001. "Un Cardinale savoiardo nella crisi rivoluzionaria." *Barnabiti Studi: Revista di ricerche storiche dei Chierici Regolari di S. Paolo (Barnabiti)* 18:203–64.

Pititto, Rocco. 2009. "Teorie pedagogiche e pratica educativa: La ratio studiorum dei Barnabiti." *Barnabiti Studi: Revista di ricerche storiche dei Chierici Regolari di S. Paolo (Barnabiti)* 26:85–109.

Scati, Leopoldo, and Antonio M. Grandi. 1806–1821. *Opere edite ed inedite del Card. Giacinto Sigismondo Gerdil*. 20 vols. Rome: V. Poggioli.

Stella, Pietro. 1999. "Gerdil, Giacinto Sigismondo." In *Dizionario Biografico degli Italiani*, 53:391–97 (with extensive bibliography).

———. 2001. "Appunti per una biografia di Giacinto Sigismondo Gerdil." *Barnabiti Studi: Revista di ricerche storiche dei Chierici Regolari di S. Paolo (Barnabiti)* 18:7–28.

Toselli, Filippo M. 1784–1791. *Delle opere dell'Eminentissimo sig. Card. Giacinto Sigismondo Gerdil: Nuova edizione illustrata di note e accresciuta di opere inedite*. 6 vols. Bologna: Istituto delle Scienze.

Valabrega, Roberto. 2001. "Gerdil e la critica alla cultura dei Lumi." *Barnabiti Studi: Revista di ricerche storiche dei Chierici Regolari di S. Paolo (Barnabiti)* 18:127–202.

———. 2004. *Un anti-illuminista: Dalla cattedra alla porpora; Giacinto Sigismondo Gerdil; Professore, precettore a corte e cardinale*. Torino: Palazzo Carignano.

Vanysacker, Dries. 1995. *Cardinal Giuseppe Garampi (1725–1792): An Enlightened Ultramontane*. Brussels and Rome: Belgisch Historisch Instituut te Rome.

Wolf, Hubert. 2010. "Hyacinthe-Sigismond Gerdil B." In *Prosopographie von Römischer Inquisition und Indexkongregation, 1701–1813, A–L* volume, edited by Hubert Wolf, 578–83. Paderborn: Ferdinand Schöningh.

Adrien Lamourette (1742–1794)

The Unconventional Revolutionary and Reformer

CAROLINE CHOPELIN-BLANC

Today, the name of Adrien Lamourette arouses little reaction. An almost forgotten figure of the past, Lamourette is, at best, known for his revolutionary commitment. This misappreciation partly explains the peremptory judgments issued against him. In his biography of Bishop Marbeuf, archbishop of Lyons before the revolution, Father Charles Monternot describes Lamourette's political line as "wavering, tortuous, and flexible." Pierre de la Gorce, in his famous religious history of the French Revolution written in the 1920s, calls him "the most lachrymose" and "the most cruel" of men.

Yet he deserves better. Lamourette was a brilliant intellectual of his time, and the negative memory of him that has remained is due to the failure of the Constitutional Church and to the violent political context surrounding the time in which he served as a member of the Legislative Assembly. Since the 1960s, the revival of eighteenth-century religious history and the history of the French Revolution has made it possible to rediscover some ecclesiastical figures whose commitment to the Constitutional Church was hitherto considered to have tarnished their image: this is true, of course, of Abbé Gregoire. But Lamourette also deserves a new critical biography in the light of available sources. The main advantage of such biographical approaches is to clarify the initially surprising link between the apologetic activity to which he dedicated himself in the 1780s and his revolutionary commitment as citizen bishop. How did Lamourette become a revolutionary, or more precisely, how did he do so when he began as an apologist, that is, a defender of Christian religion against the attacks of the philosophers of the *Lumières* (Enlightenment)? In short, how did he come to support the revolution actively, whose partisans drew their inspiration from the very ideas of the *Lumières*? Such questions demand that we ask just what Lamourette's conception of the revolution was, and how this conception shaped his participation in it.

1742–1789: The Origin of the Revolutionary Commitment, a Deep Spiritual Malaise

Lamourette did not become revolutionary on sudden impulse. Skimming through the first stage of his religious journey helps one understand the way in which the genesis of a deep spiritual malaise led him to an Enlightened Catholicism capable of coping with revolutionary ideas.

Adrien Lamourette was born on 31 May 1742 in Frévent, a small town in Artois, located in the present *département* (county) of Pas-de-Calais. He came from the rural middle class; his father was a *peigne-rant* (a maker of combs for the wool industry). In 1759, like many young people in the area, he entered the Congregation of the Mission (also known as Vincentians or Lazarists), and he made his vows two years later in May 1761. Lamourette pursued his training at the congregation's house located within the Saint-Lazare Quarter in Paris until 1765, when he became a deacon. From there, he was sent to Lorraine, first to the seminary of Metz, where he taught mathematics and physics until his ordination to the priesthood in 1769. From his ordination until 1772 or 1773, he served as a lecturer in theology before being transferred to another prestigious Lorraine seminary, the seminary of Toul, where he continued to teach theology. In early 1776, at the age of only thirty-four, Lamourette was appointed superior of the seminary. Yet he resigned a mere two years later, presumably because of strong disagreements with his older colleagues about the education of the younger generations. Against the advice of more experienced teachers, Lamourette would have liked to modernize the courses at the seminary, with respect both to teaching methods and to the subjects taught, in order to train priests to be more prepared for the changes they would face in the society of the *Lumières*.

Lamourette was allowed to leave by the superior-general of the Congregation, and, under the protection of the Bishop of Toul, he was appointed priest of Outremécourt, a rural parish in the diocese of Toul. Arriving in early 1778, Lamourette then gave up his parish in the summer of 1783. However, it was in the calm of this rural community that he would begin to write his first apologetic works. Because of a gap in historical records, the years 1783–1786 remain unclear, although one letter states that he finally left the Congregation of the Mission in 1784, to the great regret of the superior-general. In 1785 he is known to have published his first book, *Reflections on the Spirit and Duties of Religious Life* (*Considérations sur l'esprit et les devoirs de la vie religieuse*), which is dedicated to Madame Louise, the daughter of Louis XV who entered a Carmelite convent in 1770. This work was generally intended for nuns, to help them lead an exemplary life according to their religious rule. The same year he published *Thoughts on the Philosophy of Unbelief* (*Pensées sur la philosophie de l'incrédulité*), dedicated to *Monsieur,* the future Louis XVIII, a patron of writers. In this book for the general public, he defended the Catholic religion against the attacks of philosophers. In the second half of 1786, most likely because of the favorable response by the archbishop of Paris's social circle to the publication of his two books, he was appointed chaplain of the royal abbey of the Perrines de Chaillot, where he devoted himself more fully to his apologetic writings. By the late 1780s, Lamourette had achieved a certain literary fame, as evinced by his entry into the Academy of Literature of Arras, one of the most prestigious academies of the late eighteenth century, which included Lazare Carnot among its members. In 1788, at his own expense, Lamourette also published a devotional book entitled *The Delights of Religion* (*Les délices de la religion*), subtitled *The Power of the Gospel to Make Us Happy* (*Le pouvoir de l'Évangile pour nous rendre heureux*). This book was extremely successful, being reprinted the very same year, and again in the following year by the Catholic publisher Merigot. Lamourette's apologetic writing was finally interrupted by revolutionary events. His fourth and latest apologetic work, however, was entitled *Thoughts on the Philosophy of Faith* (*Pensées sur la philosophie de la foi*), and received the *privilège* in May 1789; this work, far more difficult to digest, was probably intended for ecclesiastical readers already well versed in theology.

After this first stage of his religious path, it is helpful to bear in mind three things. The first element is the considerable amount of time—some twenty-five years—that he spent with the Congregation of the Mission, founded by Vincent de Paul in 1625. It is likely that the Catholicism of Tridentine inspiration in which Lamourette was trained did not satisfy his spiritual concern. Accordingly, Lamourette actually severed ties with the Congregation in the early 1780s. It seems that his stay in Lorraine was certainly a cultural shock, and it eroded his trust in the Lazarist masters, leading Lamourette toward an amended Christianity. This key moment in Lamourette's life opened his mind to new ideas—like those of the Gallicano-Jansenist movement, the Febronian movements (stressing the enhancement of episcopal power at the expense of the papacy), and the Richerist movement (advocating the egalitarianism of priests and bishops because of their common vocation and authority). In addition, it was ultimately in Lorraine, at the seminary of Toul, where Lamourette made contact with the Enlightenment movement through Brocquevielle, the director of the seminary, who was also the author of the censures (*mandements*) of the archbishop of Paris, Monseigneur de Beaumont, against the philosophers. Lamourette thus nursed a growing malaise within the Congregation, a malaise both material (as he struggled to comply with the rule of community life) and spiritual, for to him, the

Catholicism professed by the Congregation, paralyzed by the legacy of the Counter-Reformation, did not seem suited to the contemporary world. Instead, Lamourette wished to employ the intellectual structures of the Enlightenment in thinking of Christianity, in order to respond more easily to the questions of his time. This amended Catholicism, therefore, emerges from within his apologetics and would only sharpen during the Revolution.

There is a second element, although less important, to remember from the first stage of Lamourette's religious path: his pastoral experience. Like Abbé Gregoire, parish priest of Embermesnil, another rural community of Lorraine, Lamourette held a certain retrospective nostalgia, probably embellished with age, concerning his four and a half years spent at Outremécourt. This parish became for him the symbol of Christian harmony or even the new primitive church, both in his apologetic and his revolutionary works. For example, in his *Decree on Church Properties* (*Décret sur les biens du clergé*), written in 1790, he provided the portrait of the ideal pastor and stated in an explanatory note, "I have taken the model from what I saw with my own eyes in a Lorraine village."

Finally, the third fundamental element of this period 1742–1789 is the nature of Lamourette's apologetics, a nature that enables us to understand his idea of Catholicism and with what conceptual tools he approached the revolution. To give a simple definition, Catholic apologetics in the eighteenth century refers to any speech aiming to defend against attacks from deistic and materialistic philosophers the dogmas and mysteries of religion, mainly the idea of one God embodied in three persons, whose word is the gospel. Lamourette stood apart from his contemporaries by favoring moderation and appeasement rather than frontal attack. He placed himself on his opponents' ground by favoring their preferred themes, such as happiness, reason, and nature. Above all, his apologetics appears original compared with the discourse of other contemporary apologists, because it was based on a renewed theology and anthropology: Lamourette tried indeed to bridge the gap between natural and revealed religion, and somehow to naturalize the revealed religion. He acknowledged the right to reason and to revalue the earthly world. This apologetic, apparently conciliatory approach was indeed very ambiguous. Lamourette retained the ultimate goal of apologetics—namely to safeguard the superiority of Christianity and win over the philosophers to his ideas. However, the really innovative content of his apologetics partly explains the passage of Lamourette from apologist to a committed revolutionary.

Thus, our brief overview of the years 1742–1789 shows us that a *"catholicisme des Lumières"* (Catholicism of Enlightenment) gradually emerged from Lamourette's pen in an innovative apologetic discourse. Before June 1789, because of the minority position of Lamourette among apologists, his will to create a space for dialogue seems doomed to failure. However, with the proclamation of the National Constituent Assembly by the Estates-General and the progression of the revolution, this volition became a desire to unite Christianity and the revolution. The revolution seemed to him the opportunity to renew Christianity, both in its theological approach and in its cultural practices.

1789–1791: Lamourette behind the Scenes of the Revolution

Between 1789 and late February 1791, when he was elected bishop of Rhone-et-Loire in accordance with the new Civil Constitution of the Clergy, Lamourette became a defender of the revolution. His commitment remained at first relatively discreet, for he was not yet in the forefront of the revolutionary drama, but instead preferred to remain behind the scenes. Before leaving for Lyons in April 1791, he attended several types of social gatherings in Paris. In the late 1780s, he associated with rather traditional social institutions that favored the revolution. He was found in the salons of Madame de Lameth and Madame de La Reynière, and most especially in the famous salon of the widow of Helvétius, known as the *Société d'Auteuil* (Auteuil Society). Thanks to these salons, he was able to participate in a very fruitful exchange of ideas and to build relationships with important people, particularly Mirabeau, whom he would have met at the salon of Madame Helvétius and who is known to have chosen him as his theological guide in 1790. From autumn 1790, he favored a structure of sociability that was revolutionary in the fullest sense of the term: the *Cercle Social* (Social Circle). Founded by the priest Claude Fauchet, future constitutional bishop of Calvados; Freemason Nicolas de Bonneville; and the philosopher Condorcet, the Social Circle defined itself as a place of open debate compared to clubs and political societies that defended particular ideas and favored a more exclusive clientele. The Social Circle advocated peace, tolerance, reconciliation between freedom and the gospel, and a diversity of views provided they did not contradict freedom. Such ideas, in addition to the personal relationship he maintained with Fauchet, help explain Lamourette's participation in the Social Circle until his departure for Lyons.

From 1789 to April 1791, Lamourette also grew closer to another future constitutional bishop, Abbé Gregoire. As evinced by a few letters, the links between these two figures include not only intellectual affinities but also emotional relationships. They actually met early in 1772, when Gregoire, a seminarian at Metz, attended the philosophy class of Lamourette, then still a young professor. After a long interruption between 1772 and 1789, the two became reacquainted, and from 1789 onward, the emotional relationship of master and pupil gave way to a friendly relationship based on intellectual equality. They worked together closely on two issues: first, on the question of civil equality of Jews—Lamourette in his *Observations on the Civil Status of Jews* (*Observations sur l'état civil des Juifs*) defended Grégoire's *Essay on the Physical, Moral and Political Regeneration of Jews* (*Essai sur la régénération physique, morale et politique des Juifs*)—then, on the nationalization of the church property, passed by the Assembly in November 1789 and proclaimed publicly by the Civil Constitution of the Clergy of July 1790. In spring 1791, their itineraries again diverged as Lamourette left for Lyons while Gregoire, elected constitutional bishop of the Loir-et-Cher, settled in Blois. The destruction of their correspondence by Gregoire makes it impossible to specify the nature of their relationship from 1791.

Not only did Lamourette form relationships with the patriotic Parisian milieu, but also in the year 1790 he put his talents to use as a writer in the service of the Constituent Assembly. He wrote the *Civic*

Sermons (*Prônes civiques*) in an effort to show "how the spirit of the constitution relates closely to that of religion." A total of six sermons were published: the first five in the second half of 1790, the sixth in March or April 1791. These *Prônes civiques* were one of the crowning achievements of the constitutional literature of that period, insofar as they address a very crucial and central dilemma of the day, namely the compatibility of the new revolutionary order of 1789–1791 with Christianity. Far from being antonyms, Christianity and the revolution were, as Lamourette demonstrated, essentially compatible and mutually supportive. It is thanks to the revolution, he contended, that the practice of evangelical morality and virtue will be revived on earth. With these works, the conciliatory apologetics set up before the revolution is seen to have matured and demonstrated its efficiency, and in 1790 when he compose the *Prônes,* Lamourette considered the reconciliation of Christianity and revolution to be effective. The publication of the *Civic Sermons* (*Prônes civiques*) was also praised by several newspapers, including Brissot's *French Patriot* (*Patriote français*) and the *Mercure de France*. These reviews helped to popularize Lamourette and hoist him to the status of theologian of the Civil Constitution of the Clergy. Therefore, it is no coincidence that in 1790 Mirabeau chose him for his theological guide.

The collaboration between the two men, especially evident during the fall and winter of 1790–1791 until Mirabeau's death on April 2, focused on the question of the Civil Constitution of the Clergy. Mirabeau gave two speeches strongly inspired by Lamourette, the first on 26 November 1790, and the second on 14 January 1791. These interventions reflect a shared resolve by Mirabeau and Lamourette to reform ecclesiastical and political structures as part of a sweeping project that would unite freedom and Christianity. This ambition failed, however, and the two speeches did not gain the support of the assembly. Beyond this, the motivations of the two authors did not coincide. In close correspondence with the court, Mirabeau worked for the institution of a monarchy with a strong executive but established within a liberal and constitutional frame. He considered religion only an instrument of his political design; that is, he wished to use the religiosity of the people in order to win their support and strengthen the executive. In contrast to Mirabeau, and without aspiring to erect a theocratic organization, Lamourette wanted religion to be returned to the purity of its evangelical precepts, permeating all aspects of social and political life.

Despite these differences of views, a strong friendship did eventually link the two men, as demonstrated by the support provided by Mirabeau for Lamourette's election to the bishopric of Rhone-et-Loire. It was at his request that the Société Populaire (Popular Society) of the Friends of the Constitution of Lyons defended Lamourette's candidacy before the voters of the *département* convened to elect the new bishop of Rhone-et-Loire after the removal of Bishop Marbeuf for refusing to take the oath of allegiance. This support explains the electoral success of Lamourette in Lyons on 1 March 1791 over the favored and far more locally prominent candidate, Charrier de la Roche.

However, the cooperation with Mirabeau would ultimately prove to be a double-edged sword for Lamourette. In retrospect, it can actually be said to have fed the "black legend" of Lamourette, since it would be easy for the refractory priests (*réfractaires*), especially after his episcopal appointment, to criticize him not only for his commitment to the Civil Constitution of the Clergy but also for his dedication to a philosopher of questionable repute. During his trial in January 1794, Lamourette saw the reversal of Mirabeau's image. Since November 1792 and the discovery of the "iron chest" (*l'armoire de fer*), which vividly confirmed his collusion with the court, Mirabeau was considered a traitor to his country. The friendship Lamourette had maintained with Mirabeau was a major foundation of the charges against him at his trial. However, in March 1791, it was thanks to Mirabeau that Lamourette was pushed to the front of the revolutionary stage as constitutional bishop of Rhone-et-Loire. Six months later, he became a member of the Legislative Assembly, but his aims remained unchanged: Lamourette remained committed to promoting the newly enacted constitution and the gospel. For him, it was no longer the time for the revolution's continuation, but rather for its stabilization.

1791–1792: Lamourette in the Forefront of the Stage as Bishop and Member of the Legislative Assembly

Lamourette arrived in Lyons on the evening of April 11 and left for Paris on September 27 to sit at the Legislative Assembly. During this first short visit, he worked on the organization of the Constitutional Church. According to the law, he was surrounded by a board of sixteen vicars he had personally chosen. The main concern Lamourette showed in the organization of the Constitutional Church was physically to occupy both the public and the religious space. He concerned himself with ordinary functions (such as celebration of the mass at St. John's Cathedral and regular preaching as parish priest of the cathedral) and more public tasks such as presiding over the major religious ceremonies in the city (Easter, Corpus Christi, patronal feasts) and attending civic celebrations (such as the 14 July Feast of the Federation on Brotteaux plain, or the blessing of the Lyons volunteers' flags in September). Lamourette thus assumed a very public profile, aiming to assert himself by showing his zeal and thwarting the *réfractaires,* who slowly moved their opposition underground.

Lamourette also participated in literary debates. He wrote not less than six ecclesiastical acts between April and September (May 12, May 20, June 29, July 16, September 16, and September 25). He additionally defended the ecclesiastical work of the assembly, thereby justifying his election. Lamourette tried to reassure the congregations and encourage them to attend constitutional churches; he responded to attacks from opponents, whom he tried to rally to the Constitutional Church, and more generally, he concerned himself with restoring peace and harmony in his diocese. In particular, Lamourette rejected the pastorals of the last ancien régime archbishop of Lyons, Bishop Marbeuf, then in exile in Brabant. These acts were published by Amable le Roy, official printer of the constitutional clergy in Lyons, and then sent to the priests of the *département,* who theoretically should have displayed them on church doors and read them from the pulpit.

The second important issue in the day-to-day establishment of the new church relates to the formation of a constitutional clergy.

Many parishes had no priests because of the outright refusal of most priests to take the oath, and because of their recantations, most numerous between April and June 1791. Thus, a new training center for constitutional priests was established to help curb these problems. Nevertheless, faced with the pressing needs of the *départements* for constitutional priests combined with the relative paucity of candidates eligible for priesthood in the new constitutional seminary of Lyons, Lamourette was forced to ordain young and poorly trained priests. He would thus preside over four ordination ceremonies between April and late September 1791.

Among the last tasks of the evolving Constitutional Church was the reorganization of worship and liturgy, with the aim of moving the existing church closer to the simplicity of early centuries. Lamourette began to diminish the splendor of traditional ceremonies in favor of their greater sobriety. He also sought a reduction of the hierarchical distance separating clergy and laity, by moving the celebrant closer to the congregation. The sacral space was reorganized, the rood screen of St. John's Cathedral was demolished (this rood screen had nothing to do with the original construction, and was part of a movement in church architecture associated with the mid-eighteenth century). The former altar at the back of the chancel was replaced by a new altar installed at the transept crossing and elevated by five stone steps. Thanks to these modifications, the congregation could see and hear the celebrant better. They could also more easily understand the meaning of his words, thanks to a major liturgical innovation, the translation into French of certain passages of the Mass, for which Lamourette solicited help from Abbé Rozier, the parish priest of Saint Polycarp's.

Finally, as other constitutional bishops had done in their cathedrals, Lamourette centralized all the relics in St. John's Cathedral in order to bring together the faithful in a clearly defined urban sacred space, and prevent pilgrimages to convent chapels owned by *réfractaires* (priests who refused to take the oath). He then placed under the new altar of St. John's the head of Saint Irenaeus, and debris from the chair of Innocent IV, dating to the time of the Council of Lyons in 1245. At the same time, he fully confirmed his much-contested place within the long line of apostolic succession by renewing his communion with the papacy. However, the bishop's room was quite narrow and difficult to maneuver in, as a result of the the permanent control maintained by the various administrative bodies (the municipality of Lyons, the district of the city of Lyons, and the *département*), pressure from the popular societies, and repeated attacks from the *réfractaires*. Actually, because of his episcopal dignity, which made him both head of the Constitutional Church of Lyons and usurper of Bishop Marbeuf's see, Lamourette became the target of the *réfractaires* in the print war they waged against the supporters of the Civil Constitution of the Clergy. Aggressiveness remained relatively subdued, controlled when it was expressed in print or in the theft of liturgical objects from the opposing side. But it could also occasionally result in outbursts of physical violence, as was the case in the brawl at St. Nizier's Church on 16 March 1791. This brawl pitted members of the popular society of the Friends of the Constitution, supporters of Lamourette, against faithful followers of Archbishop Marbeuf.

After this first six-month period, it is difficult to assess the success of Lamourette's undertaking, for lack of evidence. However, his election to the Legislative Assembly on 31 August 1791, as second member out of fifteen, suggests that he undoubtedly acquired popularity, at least among active citizens. He seldom spoke within the assembly. However, one of his rare speeches aroused great enthusiasm: it is known as the famous "Kiss of Lamourette" of 7 July 1792, and it occurred within a very tense period between the invasion of the Tuileries by an armed mob on June 20, the proclamation of national emergency on July 11, and the fall of the monarchy on August 10. On July 7, Lamourette delivered a heartfelt speech in which he called upon his colleagues to unite around the constitution and to be wary of both bicameralism and the republic. His speech inspired scenes of kissing between parliamentarians of all opinions. However, the excitement quickly faded, and on that evening tensions revived. Interpreting this episode is problematic: it is perceived, both by contemporaries and historians, either as the kiss of peace or as the kiss of Judas, and Lamourette has often been suspected of serving the interests of the court. The interpretation varies depending on one's point of view. In the light of the political past of its author, the "kiss" appears indeed as a kiss of peace, that is to say, as the final attempt, inspired by sincerity, to create a national unity and save a constitutional monarchy guaranteeing religious and political regeneration faithful to the gospel. Nevertheless, after July 7, Lamourette was labeled as a supporter of the constitutional monarchy, or even an instrument of the royalist party. Therefore, after the fall of the monarchy on August 10, he took care to change that image. He then himself distorted the meaning of the "kiss." A kiss of peace became a kiss of Judas. In the letter of 29 August 1792 addressed to one of his episcopal vicars and published on September 7, he explained that the speech was purely tactical: he aimed to break opposition, to lay the blame on the king and ultimately bring about the republican regime. Lamourette was reduced to reconstructing a recent past that had become embarrassing to him, and to modifying the interpretation of his own July 7 speech. Fear, but also perhaps the conviction of the need for a complete change of regime, can explain such a process. With his conversion to the republic, Lamourette hoped to save the achievements of the revolution. His term ended on 20 September 1792, when the convention succeeded the Legislative Assembly. However, Lamourette would not return immediately to Lyons, but instead waited until later in the fall of 1792.

1793–1794: Lamourette alongside the "Federalists"— Henceforth "Counterrevolutionary"?

The situation of the Constitutional Church of Rhone-et-Loire declined significantly during the absence of its bishop. At the end of winter 1793, Lyons entered a terrible cycle of violence. From 29 May 1793, the date of the overthrow of the Jacobin municipality by the moderate sections, Lyons is generally thought of as a home for the federalists. Faced with the rebels' persistent opposition, the convention ordered the city besieged (August 7 to September 29). The conflict explains the scarcity of Lamourette's public appearances and the retreat of the Constitutional Church, which was also faced with competition from illegal structures set up by the *réfractaires*. Nevertheless, Lamourette did publish five episcopal acts after his return, between

8 December 1792 and 14 July 1793; in one especially, published after May 29, he praised the victims of the moderate camp (December 8, February 10, April 29, June 12, July 14). These acts revealed the author's increasing revolutionary disenchantment. He deplored the alteration of two key principles of the 1789 revolution: the union of the social body and its necessary attachment to Christianity, which was, according to him, the only religion capable of giving proper order and meaning to society. His support of federalist convictions during the spring and summer revolt of 1793 should be read as the ultimate attempt to influence the course of the revolution, in a direction favorable to his own wishes for an alliance between the revolution and the gospel that would be able to firmly establish the unity of society.

Along with this ideological support, or even intellectual and religious guarantee, that he gave the rebels, Lamourette also became physically involved by participating in some missions assigned by the section *Porte-Froc* under the purview of which the bishop's palace fell. For example, on June 14 he was charged with five other *commissaires* to write a justificatory report on the events of May 29; on August 25, also with five fellow citizens, he was forced to acknowledge the message sent to Lyons by the representatives of the people then besieging the city, Dubois-Crancé and Kellermann. Overall, Lamourette's missions appear limited, even infrequent. He was appealed to mainly because of his episcopal dignity, which established him as a character of great importance in the *chef-lieu* and in the Rhone-et-Loire, but also for his personal qualities of conciliation and dialogue.

Lamourette's commitment to the side of the Lyons *fédéralistes* reflects personal convictions and not a united policy of the constitutional clergy, who did not unanimously support the insurgents—some preferring to stay behind the scenes, others siding with the Jacobins. As the troops of the convention entered Lyons on September 29, they arrested Lamourette that same day. He was then transferred to the Conciergerie prison in Paris on October 8 to be tried by the revolutionary court. In Paris, he had become the best-known character of the Lyons revolt and the ideal culprit around whom to build the myth of a counterrevolutionary conspiracy plotted and prepared long ago by Mirabeau and then by the Girondins, to whom Lamourette was close. After he had been imprisoned three months in the Conciergerie, the verdict was given on 11 January 1794 (or, according to the new calendar, on *nivôse* 20 Year II). Lamourette was accordingly sentenced to death on two major grounds: his close ties with Mirabeau and his role in the revolutionary "plot" of Ville-Affranchie. The execution took place the same day. In his last moments, he bravely uttered these few words: "What is the blade of the guillotine? A flip on the neck."

A mystery remains as to the reality of his reported retraction a few days before his death. Copies of a letter of retraction dated 7 January 1794 and signed by Lamourette have been found. However, their authenticity remains unresolved because of the disappearance of the original, if any such document ever existed. The question of Lamourette's retraction has been addressed by each of the two parties, *réfractaire* and constitutional, and integrated into their strategy to strengthen their legitimacy. Some, convinced of the reality of the letter, belong to the *réfractaire* camp; others, on the contrary, believe that this retraction is pure fantasy, and they have tended to side with the *constitutionnels*. For the latter, the issue of this retraction was fundamental, because at issue was the very continuity of the apostolic chain of succession, and thus the survival of their church was at stake. In the final analysis, Lamourette's image remains the same: he is presented as an ecclesiastic of steadfast vocation, strong faith, and exemplary lucidity. Thus, the summer of 1792 emerges as a turning point in the years 1789–1794: Lamourette's revolutionary hopes vanished, and he became tragically aware of the duplicity of the revolution. His death on the scaffold meant the final divorce between Christianity and revolution.

Are there ultimately two Lamourettes, one an apologist, the other a revolutionary? It does not seem so at the end of our biographical study. The year 1789–1790 did not establish a sharp break in Lamourette's religious path. He did not become a revolutionary suddenly or impulsively. Actually, some of his ideas before 1789 predisposed him to advancing a Christianity in love with freedom and equality, willing to accept the new political system based on national sovereignty. His *christianisme des Lumières* (Christianity of the Enlightenment) makes him prone to dialogue and friendly cooperation, even if he eventually stood his ground in defending and promoting Christianity. His theology, which valued the greatness of man and the goodness of God, emphasized the idea of freedom, an idea at once ontological and applicable to the temporal sphere. Similarly, his theological ideas allowed him to move quickly from the idea of anthropological equality to the idea of political equality. Yet in order to be productive and result in a real political commitment to the revolution, this theological ground required a high dose of opportunism on Lamourette's part. The revolution appeared to him as an opportunity to carry out his vocation. He felt invested in a mission—that of establishing an evangelical Christianity on earth through "Christian democracy." Lamourette was arguably the inventor of this expression, which would have a long posterity. He also used the less common expression "evangelical democracy" (*démocratie évangélique*). At the time, Christianity seemed to him the best education for democracy. In the longer term, it was through this "evangelical democracy" that the spirit of Christ would be revived on earth and that God's transcendence and terrestrial humanity would be reunited. Perhaps to this call for "evangelical democracy," considered to be of divine ordination, may be added a desire to extricate himself from the shadows, a thirst for recognition, as evinced by his increasing fame, and the supreme honor of being elected as both the head of one of the largest dioceses in the kingdom and as a delegate to the Legislative Assembly. Thus, sincere convictions, sincerely and rationally defended, coupled with extraordinary circumstances and personal motivations, prepared Lamourette to become a revolutionary.

However, Lamourette is not the conventional example of a great man. His physical fragility contrasts with the health of Grégoire. Several times in his writings, Lamourette complained about the weakness of his constitution and his health problems. His fragility, however, was mainly psychological. Lamourette consistently strove to fit his deep convictions with reality, to be in line with current events and to try to reconcile all parties, as illustrated by the famous "kiss." However, from mid-1792, this position was increasingly difficult to maintain. He then became hostage to events. He is still used as a negative figure by counterrevolutionary historiography. Nevertheless, his apologetic work survives him, through his devotional book *The Delights of Religion* (*Les délices de la religion*), reprinted in the nineteenth century. There is a Lyons edition of 1829, but it is anonymous, for reasons one can easily guess. Under his own name, though, several new editions were published in Spain in the first half of the nineteenth century. His name was recently given to a street in a housing district of Frévent, his hometown: the ultimate and inadequate tribute to a man who was a talented theologian and sincere reformer!

Bibliography

Chopelin-Blanc, Caroline. 2009. *De l'apologétique à l'Église constitutionnelle: Adrien Lamourette (1742–1794)*. Paris: Honoré Champion.

Lamourette, Adrien. 1785a. *Considérations sur l'esprit et les devoirs de la vie religieuse dédiées à la R. M. Thérèse de Saint-Augustin*. Paris.

———. 1785b. *Pensées sur la philosophie de l'incrédulité*. Paris.

———. 1788. *Les délices de la religion, ou le pouvoir de l'évangile pour nous rendre heureux*. Paris.

———. 1789. *Pensées sur la philosophie de la foi*. Paris.

———. [1791]. *Prônes civiques, ou Le pasteur patriote*. Paris.

———. 1792. *Projet de réunion entre les membres de l'Assemblée Nationale, par M. Lamourette, député du dép. de Rhône-et-Loire*. Paris.

Menozzi, Daniele. 1976. *Philosophes e chrétiens éclairés: Politica e religion nella collaborazione di G. H. Mirabeau e A. A. Lamourette (1774–1794)*. Brescia: Paideia.

Ravitch, Norman. 1978. "Catholicism in Crisis: The Impact of the French Revolution on the Thought of the Abbé Adrien Lamourette." *Cahiers internationaux d'histoire économique et sociale* 9:354–85.

Sorkin, David. 2008. *The Religious Enlightenment: Protestants, Jews, and Catholics from London to Vienna*. Princeton: Princeton University Press.

5

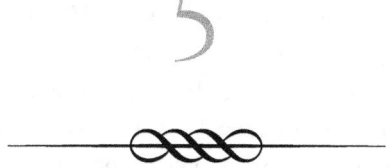

Joseph de Maistre (1753–1821)

Heir of the Enlightenment, Enemy of Revolutions, and Spiritual Progressivist

CAROLINA ARMENTEROS

Were it not for the French Revolution, Joseph de Maistre (1753–1821) might never have become a figure in intellectual history. Scion of a recently ennobled Savoyard family, he spent the prerevolutionary years of his life pursuing a legal career as a magistrate and senator; socializing in Freemasonic lodges, such as Chambéry's Three Jurist Caps (Les Trois Mortiers) and Jean-Baptiste Willermoz's Rectified Scottish Rite (Rite écossais rectifié); collecting the books and journals that would one day compose Savoy's best library; and starting a family. Although before the revolution he published two essays and some occasional pieces that circulated in manuscript form, he gave few signs of aspiring to become a published author.

Prerevolutionary Work and Masonry

Yet from an early age, Maistre displayed an exceptional inclination to read, muse, and write on moral issues. His adolescent notebooks show him deeply preoccupied with such subjects as the relationship between morality and pleasure, the suffering of the virtuous, and the edification that derives from venerating—and mummifying!—the bodies of the virtuous dead (Lebrun 1988, 10, 17–20). The *Dialogue between M. Dennis and the President on the Force of Law* (*Dialogue entre M. Dennis et le président sur la force de la loi*), a lengthy notebook entry probably composed during his twenties, is the unfinished draft of a work whose central theme—the executions of the innocent—haunted Maistre throughout his career in the justice system. Nor was this the only essay that Maistre composed on the moral implications of his legal work. At the age of thirty, he was commissioned to write the *Discourse concerning the Outward Character of the Magistrate* (*Discours sur le caractère extérieur du magistrat*; 1784), a piece reflecting on the influence that a magistrate's public image has on his ability to administer justice. Public morality is likewise at the heart of the *Elegy of King Victor-Amadeus III* (*Éloge de Victor-Amédée III*; 1775), a youthful elegiac poem about Sardinia's king with a memorable beginning: "Praise is a crime when it is prostituted to vice; it is only ridicule when accorded to mediocrity: but it is, without doubt, the sweetest of duties, when it is the prize of virtue" (Maistre 1775, 5).

Overall, these texts, which exude a sober elegance and dwell principally on issues of personal and public ethics, nowhere announce the awe-inspiring, provocative, and combative political writer that Maistre would become during the French Revolution. Before 1792, this figure can be glimpsed only in the *Memoir to the Duke of Brunswick concerning Freemasonry* (*Mémoire au duc de Brunswick sur la franc-maçonnerie* of 1782, which advises the leader of the True Scottish Rite (Rite écossais rectifié) to save the institution over which he presides by using Freemasonic themes to reconcile bickering Catholic and Protestant factions.

Denouncing Dechristianization:
Maistre's Antirevolutionary Polemics

When the revolution exploded, Maistre welcomed it at first as the harbinger of long-needed reform. However, as it unfolded and he observed the destruction of institutions, class warfare, the "vitiation of public opinion," and a dechristianization campaign (Maistre 1979, 9:11–14), he became convinced that it was all an immense scourge, the bane of a divine wrath that could not be appeased, but only endured until evil exhausted itself. The fact that God was allowing the world, as he knew it, to end filled him with anxiety and incomprehension, impelling him to find an explanation. It was in this way that accounting for the revolution became a matter of moral and spiritual survival for Maistre, that combating it became his foremost duty, and that he began, for the first time in his life, to write in earnest for publication.

Executing his new task required facing the Enlightenment and adopting revolutionary polemics. Accordingly, Maistre turned to satire and began to emulate the Grub Street philosophers that Robert Darnton has identified as the revolution's real intellectual makers (Darnton 1996). In *Benefits of the French Revolution* (*Bienfaits de la Révolution française*) and *Address of the Mayor of Montagnole to His Fellow Citizens* (*Adresse du maire de Montagnole à ses concitoyens*), written in exile in 1795, Maistre abandoned the ethic of austere dignity that he had once praised in magistrates, hurling at the revolution the kind of mockery and irreverence that had prepared its rise. Yet, quite possibly uncomfortable with the impiety that sarcasm implies, Maistre never published these texts. During his lifetime, *Adresse* and *Bienfaits* circulated only in private. Their composition served him in the development of a new style, and they marked a turn in his writing. Henceforth, elegant, hilarious, and sometimes violent scorn, conveyed by a brief, graceful, and lively prose, would punctuate his *oeuvre*. The polemical advantages of the new style would become apparent in another of his posthumous works of exile, such as *Six Paradoxes* (*Six paradoxes*), composed in 1795, a work of wit and irony that satirized the revolution's employment of Enlightenment ideals.

Revolutionary polemics also characterized Maistre's *Letters of a Savoyard Royalist to His Compatriots* (*Lettres d'un royaliste savoisien à ses compatriotes*), composed in 1793, in which he adopted the pamphlet genre for the first time in order to rally his compatriots to the counter-revolutionary cause. Although it did not achieve its immediate aims, *Lettres* prepared the pamphleteering triumph of *Considerations on France* (*Considérations sur la France*) in 1797, the stylistic masterpiece in which Maistre thundered biblically that the French Revolution was "Satanic," that it was Providence's punishment for France's sins, and that it would not last. *Considérations* was well received. It earned its author Napoleon's admiration and contributed to the Directory's inauguration of moral statistics in 1798 (Armenteros 2011b, 218–20). It would shine once more at the restoration in 1814, when it gained fame as political prophecy for predicting the king's return.

The Refutation of Rousseau and the Articulation of the Maistrian "Counter-Enlightenment"

Beyond their rhetorical brilliance and qualities of foretelling, *Considérations* was Maistre's first public attempt at articulating the main features of his mature thought. The product of a negotiation with the Enlightenment, it was intellectually founded on the refutation of Rousseau that Maistre developed in 1794–1796 in two unfinished essays: *On the State of Nature* (*De l'état de nature*), a critique of Rousseau's *Discourse on Inequality among Men* (*Discours sur l'inégalité parmi les hommes*; 1753), and *On the Sovereignty of the People* (*De la souveraineté du peuple*), a repudiation of Rousseau's *Social Contract* (*Du contrat social*; 1762). These works summed up Maistre's opinions by alternately following and chastising Jean-Jacques. Thus, they established Maistrian social theory by agreeing with Rousseau that society is a moral being capable of guilt and innocence, but insisting, against Rousseau, that no society is timeless and absolute. Society, rather, is historicized, pluralized, and concretely expressed in institutions like the church, the family, and the state. The essays also developed Maistre's political theory vis-à-vis Rousseau. They affirmed that monarchy is a form of government particularly friendly to liberty, as well as the one most suited to humanity at large, since it has been the polity most widespread since the beginning of time. Lastly, the essays on Rousseau described his historical thought. Dismissing the Rousseauian notion of a time before politics and history, they maintained that all nations have a history characterized by a game between humanity and Providence, in which God deals out the circumstances with which peoples interact in accordance with their moral character, rising to greatness and then declining as their moral force expands and is successively exhausted. The resulting trajectory of national development can be charted by a parabola. In a daring application of the lessons of the Enlightenment, then, Maistre asserted that the divine could be seized, measured, empirically detailed, and rationally understood.

The essays on Rousseau place their bets with the Counter-Enlightenment. They propose, in a way that is polemically effective but theologically dangerous, that whenever a society, culture, or political system is divinely ordained by God, it lasts through time and achieves worldly success. This was the fundamental proposition that continually informed Maistre's variety of Enlightenment, which harmonized with the Christian response to *philosophie* that emerged in France during the latter half of the eighteenth century. This response (1) objected that freethinkers reasoned only according to what they imagined, as opposed to what was real, and (2) vindicated the fact as the locus of truth. Maistre was claiming that Christianity's truth was inseparable from its status as a factual and historical, rather than a fancied, religion (Palmer 1939, 84). In *On the State of Nature* (*De l'état de nature*), Maistre extended this objection to Rousseau's second *Discours,* arguing that its fabulous account of human origins was an example of the destructive fictions that could be conjured by a hypothesizing imagination.

After *Considérations,* Maistre did not publish again for nearly two decades. Nevertheless, he continued to write assiduously, imbibing the intellectual atmosphere of St. Petersburg, where he served as extraordinary envoy of the king of Sardinia from 1802 to 1817. The subjects he treated during these years varied extremely: they included constitutionalism, epistemology, mysticism, ecclesiology, and the sociology of violence. In reflecting on them, Maistre sought consistently to detail the ways in which the divine principle manifests itself in the world, fashioning government, integrating society, and guiding history and the universe toward the good. The moral preoccupations that had been at the heart of his writings of youth thus resurfaced, but newly attired to annul the Enlightenment by defending religious tradition—especially Catholic tradition—as the most reliable, humane, and functional organizer of minds, souls, nations, polities, and societies.

Maistre's Neoplatonic, Religious Enlightenment

In 1809, a year of exceptional intellectual ferment for Maistre, he embarked on several projects. He developed the ecclesiology that would culminate in *On the Pope* (*Du pape*). He began reflecting on epistemology and composing his lengthiest work, *Examination of the Philosophy of Bacon* (*Examen de la philosophie de Bacon*), which he would complete in 1816. Additionally, he started writing his mystical works, which would be published in 1821: *The Saint Petersburg Dialogues* (*Les soirées de Saint-Pétersbourg*) and *Clarification concerning Sacrifices* (*Éclaircissement sur les sacrifices*); and he commenced the *Essay on the Generative Principles of Political Constitutions* (*Essai sur les principes générateurs des constitutions politiques*; 1814).

A defense of the idea that unwritten constitutions are superior to written ones, the *Essai* tried to save Russia from undergoing its own version of the French Revolution. It warned that nations are revitalized not by producing a plethora of written laws, as the revolutionaries believed, but by adhering to those fundamental laws that constitute the national character and are written only in hearts. In 1814, Louis de Bonald (1754–1840) published the *Essai* without Maistre's permission in Paris, where it served to swell the clamor of the ultramontanes' complaints against Louis XVIII's charter. Maistre had not intended the work for this purpose, and the publication earned him the enmity of the French king. What is most interesting from the perspective of the history of ideas, however, is the illuminist Platonism that the *Essai* upheld. Its argument that the spoken word is superior to the written one emphasizes the primacy of verbal communication. The Logos, bearer of God's infallible pronouncements—a word more active, more operative, more generative of the social and political good than a human word deadened by writing and buried in materiality. In fact, the *Essai* can be read as a lengthy, Platonic meditation on the citation of Paul that inspired the title of Montesquieu's masterpiece: "for the letter killeth, but the spirit giveth life" (2 Corinthians 3:6 King James Version).

The Saint Petersburg Dialogues (*Les soirées de Saint-Pétersbourg*) and the *Clarification concerning Sacrifices* (*Éclaircissement sur les sacrifices*) rely on Origen so consistently that scholars have argued that Maistre used the Alexandrian father to develop a Neoplatonic religious Enlightenment of his own (see Barbeau 2011; Hedley 2011; Verçosa-Filho 2011; Armenteros 2011a). Indeed, given his status as Augustine's main intellectual antagonist, Origen offered Maistre a unique opportunity. The bishop of Hippo had inspired the theology and philosophy of Latin Christendom all the way to the Enlightenment and even beyond it, since Protestantism and Jansenism, his intellectual descendants, had done much to engender the French Revolution (Maistre 1979, vol. 3)—a thesis that Dale Van Kley has demonstrated in detail nearly two centuries after Maistre first formulated it (Van Kley 1996). For this reason, Origen could serve to negate the effects of Western philosophy, down to the kind that had prepared the French Revolution. It is this logic that explains what otherwise seems incomprehensible: that in his quest to sap the intellectual foundations of the French Revolution, Maistre should seek assistance in ancient Alexandria.

Origen had the further advantage that he could help Maistre to resolve the moral problems that had absorbed him since his adolescence. *Les soirées* can be read as an attempt to answer a question that was already prominent in his adolescent notebooks: why Providence sometimes spares the guilty and allows the innocent to suffer. Plutarch had explored this subject in *On the Delays of Divine Justice,* the treatise that Maistre fell in love with as a young man and translated into French to serve as an appendix to *Les soirées*. Beyond Maistre's own interests, though, the suffering of innocence was an apt subject to be broaching after the French Revolution and the wars that followed it. Theology taught that the next life guarantees justice sufficiently and punishment is not always of this world, and personally, Maistre believed this. But he was seeking reasons to encourage virtue among those less pious, especially the young generation raised to venerate the champions of the Enlightenment—like *Les soirées'* young knight (Glaudes 2007, 436).

Consistent with Maistre's Origenism, *Les soirées* explores worldly justice by portraying nature as reenchanted and remoralized. Contrary to the transcendent God of the Augustinians—the Creator who decreed nature's laws before departing from the world—the God of *Les soirées* is an immanent God who suffuses the universe with harmonious being. Generous, he peoples creation with all manner of souls—from the animals to the angels, and even including the planets, which, as in many illuminist theodicies (and as in Origen's theology), are alive, composed of spirits and bodies. The laws of this God are not mechanical, but flexible: they respond to prayer and enable miracles. His creatures also abound with agency, especially when gathered together in groups. They pray and they prophesy, helping to overcome evil and moving the universe toward the good. Their will, in fact, is so powerful that on occasion it can contradict God's, helping to direct history and improve humanity, until history itself ends and an angel cries out in the midst of vanishing space: "THERE IS NO MORE TIME!" (Maistre 2007, 764).

Importantly, this is an extremely Pelagian, optimistic, and progressive view of moral development across time. It makes two claims: that justice will prevail and that it will do so not only through God's grace but also—indeed primarily—through human initiative. In the end, then, if not *all* the guilty are punished, at least most will be so, *on the whole*.

The *Éclaircissement* then establishes the precise process whereby this happens, again with Origen's assistance, and by relying on his theory of the soul. Origen believed that human blood had "soulfulness," and that it was the connecting point between the physical and the spiritual because it was the soul's bodily seat. It was a unique and fascinating doctrine, of which Origen himself was suspicious, and which contributed to the posthumous condemnation of his thought (Origen 1960). However, Maistre found it arresting. He saw in it the key to understanding why ancient practices of sacrifice focused so commonly on the spilling of blood. In connecting soul and body, the spiritual and the physical, blood acted as the expiatory agent that reunited societies divided by evil. When it was pure—that is, when it belonged to an innocent victim—its capacity to atone for faults was enhanced. That was why the innocent suffered—because their willing sacrifice could save the social whole from the sins of the culpable. In fact, the sacrifice of the innocent could save even those guilty individuals who wished to be saved. Rousseau's idea that society was a moral being capable of virtue and crime reappeared, but this time in the guise—of all things—of Origenist mysticism.

In addition to reintegrating society, Maistrian sacrifice mirrored and moved human history. How it did this was revealed by Maistre's history of sacrifice itself, which encapsulated human history and which he divided into two main phases: pre-Christian and post-Christian times. Before Christ, ancient peoples had practiced bloody, and sometimes even human, sacrifice. But Christ's coming had transformed immolations by introducing a new kind of victim: one that not only did not resist its own offering, but actually *willed* it for the higher good. This sweet or *"doux"* victim—epitomized by Christ himself—had revolutionized sacrifice by internalizing it, moralizing it, and rendering the gift of blood—that sentient blood that had anciently linked the physical and the spiritual—unnecessary. Henceforth, sacrifice in its highest form was any voluntary action of altruistic self-sacrifice performed for the common good. It was represented, and consummated, in the ritual of the Mass, which, insofar as it enacted the supreme sacrifice, possessed an unrivaled capacity for effecting social integration and moral progress. The Eucharist, in fact, was an eschatological machine. The divine-human blood it celebrated was the cement that repaired not only human societies, but the bodies and souls of all beings in the universe—even the planets—regenerating the cosmos and pushing history unto extinction.

The Papacy as Guarantor of Freedom and Peace

On the Pope told a complementary tale of salvation by history and, in doing so, marked a watershed in Maistre's political thought. The essays on Rousseau had adhered to the monarchical absolutism of Jean

Bodin (1530–1596) and set no concrete bounds on the king's power, assuming that he is constrained only by opinion and by a moral and religious law that he is the master of ignoring. *Du pape,* by contrast, reflected the experience and even the political point of view of the French Revolution. Drawing on an impressive amount of historical erudition, Maistre's *magnum opus* claimed that the popes had invented political freedom by creating a political system in which the spiritual and temporal powers struggled ceaselessly with one another. European Christian monarchy had emerged from the scuffle as one of the most limited and freedom-bestowing governments in the world. Importantly from the perspective of the history of ideas, this reading of church-state relations across time presupposed a radical break with Bodinian absolutism, since, *contra* Bodin, history showed that the power of European kings had been strongly constrained by the political implications of excommunication.

Maistre's philosophy of history, however, saved him from the temptation of believing that this medieval state of affairs could continue in modern times. Persuaded that humanity progresses morally across the centuries and that Providence guides history toward the good, he knew that the relationship between church and state would have to evolve in new directions. He also believed, though, that church-state relations in the future would have to be strong enough to encourage the self-restoration of postrevolutionary Europe. In particular, the popes of the future might be able to prevent both wars and the social and political violence associated with revolutions by arbitrating in cases in which a people, exhausted by duress, was on the brink of revolution. The example of Gustav IV (1778–1837), the mad king of Sweden who was dethroned by his own people after getting his country involved in a series of devastating wars, suggested the desirability of this approach. Had the Swedish people called upon the pope to intervene and oversee the change of government, Maistre argued, Gustav might have been deposed more smoothly and in a manner less precarious to sovereign legitimacy (Maistre 1966, 195–97).

Maistre's demand that the papacy acquire temporal powers in the interests of preventing political violence was revolutionary on two levels. First, it betrayed the counterrevolutionary ethic insofar as it attempted to determine the course of political events, instead of waiting piously for Providence to speak. Maistre was no longer claiming, as he had in *Considérations,* that the Revolution would exhaust itself along with its evils, that the king would return, and that political society would heal under God's guidance. He was arguing, instead, that human initiative would change the nature of European politics itself—precisely what he had once blamed the revolutionaries for doing. Furthermore, the change would be momentous. At least since the publication of Robert Bellarmine's *Treatise concerning the Supreme Power of the Popes in Temporal Matters* (*Tractatus de potestate summi pontificis in rebus temporalibus*; 1610), papal political power outside pontifical territories had been considered to be solely indirect, a secondary consequence of excommunication. Maistre proposed that it become direct, that the popes transmute into official arbiters of temporal sovereignty, international legal officers with the ability to fill and vacate thrones. Of course the idea of the popes as arbiters of peace on the European level was not novel: Leibniz, for one (whom Maistre esteemed greatly), had put it forward in the *Monadology* (*Monadologie;* 1714). What made Maistre's vision of pontifically directed international politics unprecedented was the special way in which it incorporated revolutionary politics. For *On the Pope* not only made the popes arbiters of sovereign deposition; it also rendered them the servants of popular sovereignty: Maistre made clear that the popes could intervene only at the request of nations. In this sense, they more closely resembled revolutionary leaders who deferred to the will of the people than medieval spiritual princes who forgave and excommunicated according to their judgment.

At first sight, Rousseau may seem far removed from this attempt to reinvent papal temporal power. Yet here, too, he was the starting point of Maistre's innovation. Rousseau had stood alone against the French Enlightenment in insisting that no society can survive if it lacks a religion to direct and absorb citizens' passions. *On the Pope* builds on this insight and proves it historically, demonstrating that European civilization, especially in its libertarian monarchical variants, is the masterpiece of the popes and of Christianity. However, Maistre departed from Rousseau on a crucial point. As a Catholic, he could not accept Rousseau's opinion that Christian dogma contains "superstitious" elements, much less that these should be discarded to devise a new, rational religion. On the contrary, Maistre argued, so-called superstition is nothing but the religious mysteries that stimulate the imagination and enlarge the soul, generating enthusiasm for virtue and inspiring us to behold the sublime.

Maistre's Epistemology and Philosophy of Education

Maistre explored the psychological process of learning by faith in his epistemological treatise, *Examination of the Philosophy of Bacon* (*Examen de la philosophie de Bacon*). A refutation of Francis Bacon's *Novum organum* (1620), *Examen* argued that Bacon had been wrong to try to construct a method of knowledge gathering, since the only epistemological instrument conceivable was the human mind itself. God had engraved within it all the ideas proper to humanity, so that the process of learning was in reality a process of self-revelation. Concretely, as humans experienced the world, whether individually or collectively, they came to discover the ideas that they already possessed, but of which they had so far remained unaware—Maistre's version of the unconscious. Not only that, but as Malebranche had maintained, much to Maistre's enthusiasm, faith facilitated, rather than hindered, the revelation of the innate ideas that the Divinity has engraved in us. Again echoing Rousseau, whose *Julie* (1761) argued that religious people experience nature more profoundly than atheists, Maistre suggested that faith is no obstacle to the acquisition of knowledge, as Enlightenment philosophers held. In fact, faith can further scientific discovery, as was proven by the cases of Linnaeus and Buffon. The latter despised the former and set reason against Scripture, but his work was "shelved among the poets," whereas Linnaeus, the pious Christian who discerned God's hand working in nature, became the founder of modern taxonomy (Maistre 1979, 6:407).

Maistre saw his epistemology as the foundation of his pedagogy, and pedagogy was no idle subject in Russia in the 1810s. As Alexander I (1777–1825) sought to establish a national university system and took on Mikhail Speransky (1772–1839)—a man whom Maistre described as a Kantian—as his main adviser, public education became the subject of fiery contention. Aspiring to Westernize Russia and introduce it to the Enlightenment, Speransky sought to create a homogeneous national curriculum with a scientific core. This project was anathema to Maistre, who believed that the sciences had borne the spirit of pride that animated the Enlightenment and prepared the revolution. To combat it, he proposed that the educational system privilege the humanities—especially the literary classics—postponing and subordinating the study of the sciences.

The idea was not his alone: contemporary Russian conservatives shared it too. But Maistre bolstered it more zealously than anyone by putting forward two main arguments. The first, exposed in *Examen,* was that the modern science that Bacon founded, and that the *Encyclopédie* lauded, bred a moral disorder that dissolved societies. This was why it was so friendly to revolution. The second argument appeared in one of Maistre's minor works on education, *Observations concerning the Prospectus on the Disciplines* (*Observations sur le Prospectus disciplinarum*) (1810). This was a critique of *Prospectus on the Disciplines,* which Ignatius Fessler (1756–1839), a renegade Hungarian monk and protégé of Speransky, had written as a new curricular proposal for the Nevsky seminary. *Prospectus* advocated that the seminarians should become familiar with a plethora of scientific, technical, and philosophical fields. Against it, *Observations* maintained that reading good literature along with history and the classics was the key to fashioning minds that admired virtue and were disposed to prudence, that were expert above all at learning how to learn, and that could begin, once their humanistic education was completed, to explore the sciences without peril. Only in this way, Maistre argued—only if the humanities were given priority over the sciences—could constructive members of society be formed and revolutionary personalities cease to be produced.

The idea bore fruit. Razumovsky, the Russian educational minister, adopted Maistre's recommendations when designing the curriculum of the imperial lycée at Tsarskoye Selo, which became the model for all lycées in the country. With time, Speransky's plans for a national curriculum based on the sciences were abandoned; and decades later, when Sergei Uvarov (1786–1855)—with whom Maistre had exchanged letters on knowledge from 1811 to 1814—became minister of national enlightenment under Nicholas I (1796–1855), he would become renowned as the man who gave Russia a classical university curriculum (Armenteros 2011b). Again, these policies did not reject the Enlightenment's message of self-improvement by reason, but they did snub *philosophie*'s glorification of *scientific* reason. And once more, Rousseau distantly directed them. After all, it was he who had defamed science most memorably in the eighteenth century—as Maistre himself reminded his readers when defending the classical curriculum in *Five Letters on Public Education in Russia* (*Cinq lettres sur l'éducation publique en Russie*) (composed 1810; Maistre 1979, 8:164). Moreover, it was he too who recommended, in *Julie* and *Émile, or Concerning Education* (*Émile, ou De l'éducation*; 1762), that education be founded on the sparse reading of good history and literature.

Maistre's opinions on education, however, were also shaped by his observation of religion's role in Russian politics and society. In fact, much of the writing he did in St. Petersburg can be understood as a product of the consciousness he developed as a Catholic in an Orthodox country. One of his first impressions on arriving in the land of the czars was that the national church was enslaved to the government. This is the dominant theme of the anecdotes on Russian life that he collected in the early 1800s (Grivel and Maistre 1879). Though bad in itself, enslavement to temporal authorities bred other ills. Maistre observed that, lacking independence as a spiritual power, the Orthodox Church was powerless to prevent sectarianism: he recorded with horror the stories that circulated in his aristocratic entourage about the supposedly Satanic practices of the Raskolniks (dissenters from the Orthodox Church). However, the Protestants also concerned him, especially in the early 1800s, when the Russian Bible Society became established as one of the most powerful institutions in the empire, and the influence of Pietism reached its apex at the court (Martin 1997).

Maistre's disapproval of this situation, coupled with his fear that the French Enlightenment might take over Russia, goes a long way toward explaining *On the Pope*. Although he agreed with Russian Westernizers that the empire needed to be modernized and opened up to European ideas, Maistre fought with all his strength against the possibility that the Enlightenment or its intellectual precursor, Protestantism, should mediate modernization. He watched anxiously the affinity between Orthodox and Protestants—which he ascribed to their common submission to temporal power—and determined to show Russia how attractive a Catholic road to modernity could be. *On the Pope* was his instrument in this endeavor. In recounting European history as the history of the struggle—and the equilibrium—between spiritual and temporal powers, and in identifying European kingship as the popes' creation, the book indirectly critiqued the subservience of Russia's spiritual power and argued implicitly that true liberty would blossom only if the empire returned to Rome's flock. It was not the only text Maistre wrote in support of these principles. At Alexander's request, he set them down also in *Four Chapters on Russia* (*Quatre chapitres sur la Russie*; 1811), a small work that its commissioner read with favor (Maistre 1979, vol. 8).

Maistre's recommendations for Russia's Westernization were informed by his Jesuitism, which was as compulsive to him as a verb conjugation: "My grandfather liked the Jesuits," he wrote in 1816, "my father liked them, my sublime mother liked them, I like them, my son likes them, his son will like them" (Maistre 1979, 14:426). At least as early as 1810, Maistre translated this family sympathy into practical politics and began to knit ties with the Society of Jesus, which at the time survived only in the Russian empire. He wrote *Memoir on the Liberty of Public Instruction* (*Mémoire sur la liberté de l'enseignement public*) (composed 1810), the last of his educational opuscules, with the resolve of saving the Jesuits from Speransky's reforms, and most specifically from a government monopoly on higher education. Observing that "*all exclusive privilege in the State, is nothing but the permission to do evil*" (Maistre 1979, 8:267; original emphasis), Maistre argued that allowing private education, and especially the Jesuit colleges, to exist would accelerate Russia's modernization without inviting a revolution. The Jesuits were anti-Jansenists and anti-Protestants, he reasoned, so the education they provided would help Russia to progress while protecting it from the Augustinian traditions that had paved the way to the French Revolution.

Over time, Maistre's support of the Jesuits and defense of Catholicism spelled the end of his Russian mission. The government resented his personal success at converting Russian noblewomen to Catholicism, and it was alarmed by the increasing number of Russian children who adopted Catholicism in the Jesuit schools. The conversion of the young nephew of the czar's minister, Prince Galitzin, was the straw that broke the camel's back. Alexander expelled the Society of Jesus from his lands and asked the king of Piedmont-Sardinia to recall Maistre, who departed from the Russian capital in 1817.

Settling in Turin with his family until his death in 1821, Maistre spent the last years of his life finishing *Les soirées,* preparing *Du pape* for publication, and fulfilling honorary duties for the Piedmontese government. Although his family life was happy, he felt politically despondent. In his letters, he wrote repeatedly that he was "dying with Europe" (Maistre 1979, 14:183) and he worried that his masterpiece, *Du pape,* would "only do evil" (Lovie 1978, 164). These sad thoughts intimate what was possibly the most tragic realization of his life: that if the French Revolution had ended, its ideas had subsisted, *with God's permission,* that the "spirit of negation" that characterized modernity had triumphed, and legitimated itself—just like the kings of old—*by enduring.* In his last years, a dismayed Maistre became increasingly aware that the Enlightenment and its dreadful progeny had permeated even his own works and slipped into the finest cracks of his own philosophy. After half a lifetime of combating the revolution, it was a discovery hardly suited to encourage him. He died on 26 February 1821.

An Enlightened Counter-Enlightener?

In retrospect, Maistre's counterrevolutionary career may be summarized as a continuous attempt to use Enlightenment means—the valorization of reason, the recourse to empirical evidence—to combat Enlightenment goals: the withdrawal of religion from politics and the distancing of God from human affairs. Rousseau, his master, had acted similarly, devising a compromise between Christianity and materialism and brandishing reason to put religion and the soul back at the forefront of philosophy. In this respect, both thinkers deserve well their reputation as paradigms of the Counter-Enlightenment.

Maistre's Counter-Enlightenment was uniquely Catholic, drawing on Catholic precedents to devise a Catholic synthesis. It followed in the footsteps of French Catholic apologists of the latter half of the eighteenth century by championing the fact against the imagination. However, it went further than they did, turning history into the measure of politics and identifying it as the primary means of knowledge of the human. In fact, Maistre's contribution in this area was so great that he may be deemed to have devised a specifically French way of thinking about history, whose nineteenth-century *fortuna* extended not only to traditionalists and Catholics but also—in fact principally—to socialists and positivists (Armenteros 2011b).

Maistre's Catholic Enlightenment was also the uniquely Origenist product of a desire to do away with some of Augustine's posterity, especially the transcendentalists who had declared God absent. His aim was to invite God back into the creation and to fill the world with powerful moral agents. It was an intellectual move consonant with the Pietism and illuminism of the age. *Les soirées* conjures the mystical universe of the esotericists, a spiritual cymbal that resounds with human thought. Also, it seeks to capture systematically, rationally, universally, Protestant intuitions of the divine. In this respect, Maistre was a philosopher in spite of himself: decry philosophical systems though he might, he accumulated occasional insights until he constructed a coherent whole—as an afterthought.

On the Pope's politically revolutionary propositions are also unthinkable without Maistre's encounter with Russian Orthodoxy. It was Maistre's time in Russia that suggested to him that the relations between temporal and spiritual powers in Latin Christendom had been unique, that Christian liberty had emanated from these relations, and that it now stood poised to govern the universe. Of course, the dream of Christian unity reflected in *On the Pope* was not new with him when he wrote it: that dream had inspired his zeal at least since the *Memoir to the Duke of Brunswick* (*Mémoire au duc de Brunswick*). The difference was that this time, the key to realizing it was not Freemasonry, but Catholicism-turned-revolution.

In the end, though, whether political or mystical, theorizing epistemology or bent on explaining society, Maistre's Catholic Enlightenment was governed by one idea above all others: that humanity possessed an unbounded capacity for moral progress that could not be defined and that could overcome history and the human condition. For centuries, Maistre's passionate prose and obsession with violence have disguised him as an antirational Christian pessimist (see, for the most eloquent statement of this case, Cioran 1998). But a careful examination of his thought reveals that even—or rather, especially—when reflecting on sacrifice, he was a semi-Pelagian rationalist, a man whose moral progressivism was so radical, and whose faith in humanity's capacity for self-salvation so great, that his hopes for the future exceeded even those of the heralds of progress themselves.

Bibliography

Armenteros, Carolina. 2011a. Conclusion to *Joseph de Maistre and the Legacy of Enlightenment*, edited by Carolina Armenteros and Richard Lebrun, 265–76. Oxford: Voltaire Foundation.

———. 2011b. *The French Idea of History: Joseph de Maistre and His Heirs, 1794–1854*. Ithaca: Cornell University Press.

———. 2011c. "Preparing the Russian Revolution: Maistre and Uvarov on the History of Knowledge." In *Joseph de Maistre and His European Readers: From Friedrich von Gentz to Isaiah Berlin*, edited by Carolina Armenteros and Richard Lebrun, 79–103. Leiden and New York: Brill.

Armenteros, Carolina, and Richard Lebrun, eds. 2011. *Joseph de Maistre and the Legacy of Enlightenment*. Oxford: Voltaire Foundation.

Barbeau, Aimee. 2011. "The Savoyard Philosopher: Deist or Neoplatonist?" In *Joseph de Maistre and the Legacy of Enlightenment*, edited by Carolina Armenteros and Richard Lebrun, 161–89. Oxford: Voltaire Foundation.

Burson, Jeffrey. 2010. *The Rise and Fall of Theological Enlightenment: Jean-Martin de Prades and Ideological Polarization in Eighteenth-Century France*. Notre Dame: University of Notre Dame Press.

Cioran, Emil. 1998. *Anathemas and Admirations*. New York: Arcade Publishing.

Darnton, Robert. 1996. *The Forbidden Best-Sellers of Pre-Revolutionary France*. New York and London: W. W. Norton.

Glaudes, Pierre. 2007. Introduction to *Les soirées de Saint-Pétersbourg*. In *Joseph de Maistre: Oeuvres, suivies d'un Dictionnaire Joseph de Maistre*, 405–46. Paris: Robert Laffont.

Grivel, Fidèle de, and Joseph de Maistre. 1879. *Religion et moeurs des russes*. Edited by Ivan Gagarin. Paris: E. Leroux.

Hedley, Douglas. 2011. "Enigmatic Images of an Invisible World: Sacrifice, Suffering and Theodicy in Joseph de Maistre." In *Joseph de Maistre and the Legacy of Enlightenment,* edited by Carolina Armenteros and Richard Lebrun, 125–46. Oxford: Voltaire Foundation.

Lebrun, Richard. 1988. *Joseph de Maistre: An Intellectual Militant.* Montreal: McGill-Queen's University Press.

Lovie, Jacques. 1978. "Constance de Maistre: Éléments pour une biographie." *Revue des études maistriennes* 4:141–73.

Maistre, Joseph de. 1775. *Éloge de Victor-Amédée III, duc de Savoie, roi de Sardaigne, de Chipre et de Jérusalem, prince de Piémont, etc.* Chambéry.

———. 1784. *Discours sur le caractère extérieur du magistrat.* Vol. 7 of *Œuvres complètes de J. de Maistre.* 14 vols. Chambéry. Reprint, 1885 (Lyon: Vitte and Perrussel).

———. 1966. *Du pape.* Edited by Jacques Lovie and Joannès Chetail. Geneva: Droz.

———. 1979. *Œuvres complètes.* Geneva: Slatkine. Previously published 1884–1886 (Lyon: Vitte and Perrussel).

———. 2007. *Oeuvres, suivies d'un Dictionnaire Joseph de Maistre.* Edited by Pierre Glaudes. Paris: Robert Laffont.

Martin, Alexander. 1997. *Romantics, Reformers, Reactionaries: Russian Conservative Thought and Politics in the Reign of Alexander I.* DeKalb: Northern Illinois University Press.

Origen. 1960. *Entretien d'Origène avec Héraclide.* Edited by Jean Scherer. Paris: Cerf.

Palmer, Robert R. 1939. *Catholics and Unbelievers in Eighteenth-Century France.* Princeton: Princeton University Press.

Van Kley, Dale. 1996. *The Religious Origins of the French Revolution: From Calvin to the Civil Constitution, 1560–1791.* New Haven: Yale University Press.

Verçosa-Filho, Élcio. 2011. "The Pedagogical Nature of Maistre's Thought." In *Joseph de Maistre and the Legacy of Enlightenment,* edited by Carolina Armenteros and Richard Lebrun, 191–219. Oxford: Voltaire Foundation.

6

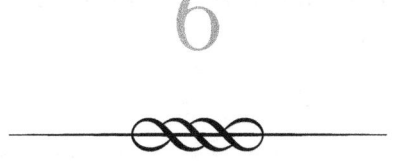

Hugues-Félicité Robert de Lamennais (1782–1854)

Lost Sheep of the Religious Enlightenment

CAROLINA ARMENTEROS

Few thinkers have had as memorable an intellectual and political trajectory as Hugues-Félicité Robert de Lamennais (1782–1854). Tirelessly prolific and unwaveringly provocative, this was the firebrand who started his writing career as an ultramontane royalist and ended it as a radical democrat and champion of socialism. The divergence of the views he held across the years, coupled with the immensity of his *oeuvre*, probably explains why no scholar has yet been found who can master his writings and sympathize with his various intellectual personas to the extent of composing the definitive intellectual biography of him. Many of the events of his intellectual life therefore remain mysterious and, in part because of the rhetorical violence and political strife that accompanied them, deeply controversial. In this brief biography, however, I will try to untangle the patterns behind the dramas of Lamennais's life, and I will argue that his intellectual trajectory was determined by two main factors. The first was his unique attempt to take the principles of the French Catholic Enlightenment to their final consequences. The second, which I expose toward the end of the essay, is the effect that his extraordinary personality had on the development of his views.

Religious Beginnings

Born at Saint-Malo in 1782, Lamennais lost his mother at the age of five and was sent, along with his older brother, Jean-Marie, to La Chênaie, the estate of his uncle Robert des Saudrais. Locked up in his new home's vast library every time he misbehaved—which was frequently—Félicité read widely according to his inclinations, becoming especially fond of the works of Rousseau and Pascal. He was attracted to philosophical rationalism, but his brother, Jean-Marie, who took holy orders and exercised a strong influence on him in his early years, instilled in him a deep sense of the value of religion. Félicité would soon follow him in his religious vocation, receiving the tonsure in 1811. During these years, Félicité and Jean-Marie also shared an intellectual life. When their father's fortune was ruined by the Continental Blockade that Napoleon formed during his wars, they both became professors at a college in Saint-Malo. It was in this period that Lamennais published his first book, a collaborative project with his brother, for which Jean-Marie provided the content and the ideas while Félicité, whose rhetorical skills became evident at an early age, did the actual writing. *Reflections on the State of the Church in France during the 18th Century and on Its Present State* (*Réflexions sur l'état de l'église en France pendant le 18ème siècle et sur sa situation actuelle*; 1809) was an ultramontanist manifesto that condemned religious indifferentism, insisted on the church's independence from the state and the need for authority in religion, and called for a clerical revival as the major means of healing the wounds of the French Revolution. The book also supported political regionalism, a theme that would recur in Lamennais's work until the end of his life, with the brothers proposing community life, provincial councils, diocesan synods, and ecclesiastical conferences as means of re-infusing the clergy with the intellectual and pastoral energies it needed to spread the Christian message and face non-Catholic opponents.

Lamennais's lifelong habit of incensing the established powers began with *Reflections*. The imperial police suppressed the book for criticizing the state's involvement in religion. Undeterred, the two brothers published, in response to Napoleon's nomination of the archbishop of Paris five years later, an even more polemical book. Announcing the rhetorical violence that would characterize Lamennais's later, more renowned works, *On the Tradition of the Church regarding the Institution of Bishops* (*De la tradition de l'église sur l'institution des évêques*; 1814) also broached classical Mennaisian themes: it thoroughly condemned Gallicanism and again denounced the interference of political authority in religious affairs, most particularly the Emperor's wish to transfer to metropolitans the right of episcopal nomination. Thankfully for Félicité and Jean-Marie, the book made it to the presses only shortly after Napoleon's fall.

Soon, Lamennais's ultramontanism would mingle with ultraroyalism. When Louis XVIII returned to the throne in 1814, Lamennais hailed him, and fled to London during the Hundred Days. While in England, he befriended Abbé Carron, a priest who ran a school for the children of *émigrés* and under whose influence he decided to be ordained as priest—which happened only after a (tellingly) long inner struggle.

The Doctrine of Common Sense

Following Napoleon's defeat, Lamennais returned to Paris and started to work on the book that would render his name immortal. The first volume of the *Essay on Indifference in Matters of Religion* (*Essai sur l'indifférence en matière de religion*), which appeared in 1817, the year of his ordination, entered the French literary scene with an explosion. Picking up again *Reflections*' condemnation of religious indifferentism, Lamennais's new opus leveled it against those who saw in religion only a practical political institution, against those who admitted the need for religion but rejected revelation, and against those—like Rousseau—who sought to reduce religion to the articles on which everyone could agree. Audacious, violent, provocative, and rhetorically brilliant, the *Essay* was an instant massive success that sold forty thousand copies in a few weeks, was translated into several languages, effected conversions to Catholicism, earned its author enthusiastic comparisons with Bossuet, Malebranche, and Pascal, and obtained for him the recognition of the ultramontanes, who invited him to write for their main journal, *The Conservative* (*Le conservateur*). Eventually, though, Lamennais grew tired of the absolute monarchism professed by one of the editors, Joseph de Villèle, and founded his own journals, *The White Flag* (*Le drapeau blanc*) and *The Catholic Memorial* (*Le mémorial catholique*), the comparatively moderate precursors of the notorious *The Future* (*L'avenir*) of 1830–1831.

In the meantime, Lamennais had started work on the second volume of the *Essai,* published in 1820, which argued that religious indifferentism was not a neutral attitude, but a form of practical atheism that caused moral disorder and social dissolution. Philosophically, Lamennais considered that atheism was the offspring of Protestantism, of the philosophy of Descartes, and most particularly of the idea of individual reason—a concept that had started off as a theological proposition, causing individual spiritual death, and ended up as a political proposition, causing the death of society. The antidote that Lamennais offered to its ravages was common sense, which he viewed as the antithesis of private judgment, as a concept incarnated in ecclesiastical authority, supported by the spiritual wisdom contained in the world's traditions, and identical with the majority opinion. According to this definition, the true religion was the one that could summon the greatest number of witnesses to the court of testimony. The prize of truth hence went instantly to Catholicism. Not only was it the world's largest religion, but its dogmas were the descendants of a primitive revelation that God had given to humankind at the beginning of time (the idea was Friedrich Schlegel's) and that had been professed, in various guises and to various degrees, by all peoples across the centuries and throughout the earth.

Lamennais's idea of common sense was at least a century old. As the Jesuits had once articulated it in their *Journal of Trévoux* (*Journal de Trévoux*), common sense was an "interior sentiment" that, when developed by experience, enables us all to intuit certain fundamental truths—like God's existence, our own freedom, the difference between body and soul, and the difference between material and spiritual (Burson 2010, 48–49, 181). In this original sense, common sense was a sentiment available to all that enabled the apprehension of the divine. Toward the middle of the eighteenth century, however, Catholic apologists faced with Helvetian utilitarianism began to lend to common sense a new meaning. The word now denoted the *actual* sentiments of the multitude, which were now assumed to be identical with the socially useful and the politically enduring. This definition was polemically effective, enabling Christian thinkers to battle the Enlightenment on its ground, and to respond to the *philosophes'* demand that Christianity not only set its eyes on heaven but also seek to improve life on earth. Common sense hence acquired new life as it slipped from Counter-Enlightenment to counterrevolution, and as heralds of reaction like Maistre and Bonald took it up in their denunciations of the new order (or, in their terms, the new disorder).

Theologically, the doctrine of common sense was problematic, and the predictable criticisms were leveled against Lamennais's version of it. Theologians objected that if collective reason afforded certitude, so must the individual reasons of which it was the sum. They also observed that, once it had been accepted that the truth of a proposition could be proven by its worldly success, it became impossible to separate the natural from the supernatural order. Lamennais was irritated but unconvinced by these arguments and published, shortly thereafter, a *Defense of the Essay on Indifference in Matters of Religion* (*Défense de l'Essai sur l'indifférence en matière de religion*; 1821), to which Rome granted an *imprimatur*. He also continued writing the *Essay* itself and devoted the last two volumes (published in 1823 and 1824) to proving his doctrine empirically.

By 1823, Lamennais had accumulated extensive materials for the purpose. In 1807, desiring to further Catholicism's fortunes, and convinced that Christianity's truths were dispersed throughout the world's cultures (another Schlegelian idea), he had undergone a personal Oriental Renaissance. He had started taking notes on the *Avesta,* the *Asiatick* [sic] *Researches,* and *The Laws of Manu* (the *Manusmriti* composed c. 200 BCE–200 CE, which Sir William Jones first translated into English in 1794), perusing them for similarities with Catholic dogma (Schwab 1984, 238). This search was no passing fad for him. Decades later, in the 1820s, he was still asking his friend Ferdinand von Eckstein, the fervent Catholic and disciple of Schlegel who brought the Oriental Renaissance to Paris, for Oriental documents suggesting belief in original sin and the Second Coming (Burtin 1931, 81).

As the restoration of the monarchy progressed, Lamennais felt despair at Louis XVIII's failure to honor what Lamennais considered to be common sense: after all, the first and second restorations were officially Gallican. The young priest expressed his grievances in the book that followed the four volumes of the *Essay, On Religion Considered in Its Relations with the Civil and Political Order* (*De la religion considérée dans ses rapports avec l'ordre civil et politique*) (1825–1826). A raging attack on the royal government, *On Religion* was Lamennais's ferocious response to a ministerial ordinance that prescribed the teaching of the Gallican Articles of 1682. Deploying an inexorable logic, the book accused the French state and all of French society of being atheist. There was no other name for those who refused to submit to Rome. For without the pope, there could be no church. Without the church, there could be no Christianity. Without Christianity, there could be no religion for all peoples who were Christian, and hence no society. In France, therefore, the state was completely outside civil and political society, and was the reason why atheism had passed from civil and political society into domestic society.

As had by now become foreseeable, Lamennais's attacks attracted the attention of the authorities. The French bishops, most of whom were moderate Gallicans, signed a complaint against the pamphlet, and Lamennais was summoned before the Tribunal of the Seine and condemned to pay a fine for insubordination to the Articles—at the time a law of the realm—as well as for insubordination to the king's government. The incident served only to deepen his hatred of the restoration.

Preparing *The Future*

The discussion so far may have suggested that Lamennais was interested solely in defending religion politically, but he devoted much of his energy to fostering Catholic devoutness as well. Since 1809, he had been publishing works of piety. He had translated Louis de Blois's *Mirror of Kings* (*Speculum monachorum*) into French, publishing it under the title *The Spiritual Guide* (*Le guide spirituel*). In 1824, he had also published a widely read edition of *The Imitation of Christ* (*Imitatio Christi*), ostensibly translated by him (but actually using the text of the 1822 translation by Eugène de Genoude) and ostensibly inserting his own commentaries (but actually using at least in part those of the Abbé Augustin-Jean Le Tourneur). Other spiritual works followed, notably the *Guide of the Early Years* (*Guide du premier âge*), the *Christian's Day* (*Journée du Chrétien*), and the *Collection of Piety* (*Recueil de piété*; 1828).

These publishing ventures were accompanied and supported by organizational initiatives. Lamennais's literary fame, coupled with his enormous personal charisma, had made him hugely popular among France's young Catholics, especially the clergy. In the mid-1820s he retreated with a group of disciples—among them Maurice de Guérin, Jean-Baptiste-Henri Lacordaire, and Charles de Montalembert—to La Chênaie. The group's goal was to combat Gallicanism and to make ultramontanism France's official religion. When the government stood once more in the way of this project, Lamennais retaliated furiously with yet another inflammatory publication. *On the Progress of the Revolution and on the War against the Church* (*Des progrès de la révolution et de la guerre contre l'église*; 1828) marked his decisive break with royalism. Defending the Jesuits, his old enemies, against the Martignac government's closing of their schools by two ordinances of June 1828, Lamennais now held that the form of temporal governments was immaterial. All that mattered was that they uphold the pope's spiritual monarchy as the true foundation of their power. The argument was colossally successful, to the point that the bishops, though attacked as usual for their Gallicanism, welcomed the book with open arms as their much-needed salvation from the government's school policy. The latter had been an unexpected blow: the church, whose public fortunes had surged during the restoration—and especially since the coronation of Charles X in 1825 (Jardin and Tudesq 1977, 63–64)—found itself suddenly used as a decoy to defuse public demands for the indictment of Martignac's predecessor, Villèle (Jardin and Tudesq 1977, 67). The bishops' consequent discontent was commensurate with their surprise: probably encouraged by Lamennais's volatile opus, they rebelled.

In 1828, Lamennais founded the Congrégation de Saint-Pierre (Congregation of Saint Peter), formed around the group that had gathered at La Chênaie, and including among its members Eugène and Léon Boré, Théodore Combalot, Olympe-Philippe Gerbet, Guérin, Jean-François de Hercé, Lacordaire, Montalembert, René François Rohrbacher, Charles de Sainte-Foy, and Antoine de Salinis. The Congrégation's main purpose was to form a scholarly clergy capable of spreading the Christian message and responding to the attacks of modern philosophy. Two years later, after the Revolution of 1830, some of its members founded *The Future* (*L'avenir*), a journal whose slogan was "God and Liberty." Its goals were various: to demand the separation of church and state; to advocate freedom of conscience, of assembly, of education, press, and religion; and to foster the provincial and municipal liberties that Lamennais and his brother, Jean-Marie, had vindicated since *Reflections*. The strategy behind these demands was to defend the church according to the zeitgeist. The Orleanist regime was far less favorable to the church than the Bourbons had been, and Lamennais, who had a gift for discerning and using the dominant ideas of every epoch, thought it best to put the church in the position of demanding the same equal rights, and the same freedoms, that the new regime promised to impart so liberally. His hopes were daring: they extended to liberating the church from the state supervision that had been its lot since the Concordat of 1801. Moreover, they included—consistently with the theses of *On the Progress of the Revolution*—weakening temporal power in order to unlock the spirit of liberty inherent in the clergy. In this way, declared the first issue of *The Future* (16 October 1830), the church could come nearer to the people and "pour on its immense miseries the inexhaustible streams of divine Charity."

The *Future*'s supporting institution was yet another Mennaisian creation, the General Agency for the Defense of Religious Liberty (Agence générale pour la défense de la liberté religieuse), an organization that monitored violations of religious freedom and battled with zeal for freedom of education, which since the revolution had been largely in the hands of the state. As expected, the Agency's activities landed the Mennaisians in court repeatedly. Yet its efforts to sway public opinion in its favor were so successful that they were crowned in 1833 by the promulgation of the Guizot law, which allowed private primary and secondary schools to exist. The Agency tried to obtain freedom of education at the university level as well, but it dissolved before it could win this fight, and to this day no private universities exist in France (on the Agency's struggles, see Grimaud 1898, 203–39).

The activities of *The Future* and the Agency brought the Mennaisians into conflict again with conservative bishops who supported Gallicanism and the monarchy, and who accused the Agency's minions of lacking orthodoxy. Lamennais, Lacordaire, and Montalembert therefore departed for Rome to obtain the pope's approval of their actions. Lamennais had already visited Rome in 1824, in the wake of the *Essai*'s publication, when Leo XII had received him very kindly. However, Gregory XVI was not disposed to welcome the nineteenth-century precursor of liberation theology. He granted an audience after much difficulty, and eventually advised the three Frenchmen to leave Rome, admitting the justice of their intentions, but refusing to bless their political program.

Exiled from the Church

As he returned home from Rome, Lamennais received *Mirari vos,* an encyclical condemning religious pluralism along with other ideas propagated by *The Future*. It was the end of both the journal and the Agency, which Lamennais and his companions dissolved immediately in deference to Gregory. It was also the beginning of Lamennais's separation from Christianity. Withdrawing to La Chênaie, he kept public silence but poured resentment into his letters, and when the Holy See asked him to submit to *Mirari vos* without qualification, he refused, renouncing his vows in 1833 and, eventually, all formal connections to the religion of his birth.

Lamennais's Catholic friends, nearly all of whom eventually abandoned him, explained his apostasy as an act of pride. I will have more to say later about how his psychological profile may have affected his religious, political, and intellectual choices throughout his life. For now I only want to observe that, from a strictly intellectual point of view, Lamennais's final renunciation of Christianity was the result of an ardent and honest attempt to take the principles of the French Counter-Enlightenment to their full conclusions. Although stylistically *The Future* was pure political provocation, intellectually its revolutionism was rooted in the innocent wish to lend common sense an empire, to realize completely what defenders of the faith had advocated since the middle of the eighteenth century, when they combated *philosophie* by brandishing the facts against the imagination. The trouble from Lamennais's point of view was that the powers of his day were not upholding the facts: they were ignoring, in other words, the truth contained in popular wisdom. At first, the offending powers were only the monarchy and the French bishops, but in the end, it was also the pope and, by extension, the Catholic Church itself. Others would have concluded from all this opposition that common sense was an imperfect doctrine. But not Lamennais: one feature of his religious fervor was that, once he had committed to an idea, he was faithful to it to the last. Therefore, after *Mirari vos,* he began looking for a new, worthy reservoir of common sense. He found it in the people—in the Catholic majority who bore the spirit of Christianity, not because it was learned, but because God had engraved within it the sublime ideas that were humanity's preserve since the beginning of time. Herein was Lamennais's final democratism; herein also his abandonment of the philosophy of history. In France in the 1820s, being a Catholic traditionalist meant adhering to historical thought, and Lamennais was no exception. At the time when he was running *L'avenir,* he collaborated with Pierre-Simon Ballanche in composing an introduction to a new historical-philosophical system that remained unpublished until the twentieth century. Entitled *Essay of a*

System of Catholic Philosophy (*Essai d'un système de philosophie catholique*; 1830–1831), it exposed a Christian speculative philosophy of history whose daring goal was to embrace "by a wholly rational method the entire order of knowledge on the basis of the most simple concept of Being" (Reardon 1975, 83). Its premises were democratic, expressing a cultural relativism that was radical for the times. Ballanche and Lamennais insisted that all religions are identical, but that Christianity is the voice of all humanity and especially of the masses; that Christianity's essence is only gradually apprehended; that it evolves progressively until all forms of social and racial exclusiveness disappear; that only through Christianity can liberty be realized for individuals and societies; and that Christianity is the universal religion of humanity (McCalla 1998, 347–48).

All of the ventures in which Lamennais engaged when he was a Catholic, even *The Future* itself, can be interpreted as *dedicatios* to a utopia at the end of time. One significant—and little-known—fact is that the notorious periodical of 1830–1831 was not the first Mennaisian publication to be called *The Future*. In the early 1820s, Lamennais had penned a little piece entitled "De l'avenir," in which he lamented that his egoistic contemporaries held on to the present for dear life, and sacrificed everything to it, because they were afraid of the future. But they needed to change their perspective, because faith's true domain was the future, the time when God's inflexible will would be expressed, and when punishments and rewards would be dealt out. In this context, the journal *The Future* emerges as an altruistic attempt at self-immersion in the future, with the goal of accelerating the time when liberty and equality will be the preserve of all and Christianity will have spread to the whole world.

Philosophical history likewise underlay the Mennaisian struggle for freedom of education. The intellectual leader of this part of the movement was Abbé Philippe Gerbet. At the request of Frédéric Ozanam and his friends, Gerbet held a series of lectures on the philosophy of history that were attended by hundreds of young people. Published in 1832 under the title *Lectures on Catholic Philosophy: Introduction to the Philosophy of History* (*Conférences de philosophie catholique: Introduction à la philosophie de l'histoire*), the lectures called upon

Catholics to sacrifice themselves for a future when there would be free universities throughout France. Gerbet referred to himself as a humble "proletarian . . . of Catholic philosophy in the nineteenth century" (Gerbet 1832, 49) and made clear that all that he could offer was an introduction, a broad, methodological sketch, of the philosophy of history that, like many of his devout compatriots, he considered to be the foundation of all Catholic philosophy. Executing the philosophy itself, however—gathering systematically all the facts that would prove its veracity—was a project so vast that only the long and collective effort of the erudite faithful could bring it to fruition. These observations were not innovations of Gerbet's. Conscious that Catholicism lacked a comprehensive, modern intellectual synthesis comparable to the one that had been achieved by *philosophie,* French traditionalists at the time sought to lend to their religion an encyclopedic, philosophical dimension. Thus the prolific writer Félicité de Genlis invited François-René de Chateaubriand and other conservatives to join her in writing a Catholic encyclopedia, while Ballanche, Augustin Bonnetty, Philippe Buchez, Eckstein, the Mennaisians, and—for as long as he was a Catholic—Lamennais himself strove to turn the philosophy of history into Catholicism's new *summa,* the depository in which all human knowledge could be stored in a manner and within a structure that would prove Christian truth of itself.

This is why, as soon as he abandoned Catholicism, Lamennais lost interest in history. The work that marked his break with the church was a collection of aphorisms, *Words of a Believer* (*Paroles d'un croyant*; 1834), which denounced the conspiracy of priests and kings against the people. *Words* replaced the thesis that truth was contained in the world's traditions, and most completely in Christianity, with the proposition that truth emerged from the voice of the people. Lamennais would henceforth maintain that it was this voice, and not theology, or the knowledge gathered up by scholars—or the historical philosophy it could constitute—that would carry the message of liberation. This epistemological change implied a political one. In deserting erudition, and hence special knowledge, as the key to regeneration, Lamennais was also rejecting a world in which a higher truth was available to those who had the privilege of studying. And in maintaining that the voice of all, regardless of their education (and perhaps thanks to their lack of it) carried divine truth, he was opening the door to a leveled and democratized society where insight into the sublime—and hence into social justice, liberty, and equality—was the prerogative of everybody.

Words prompted Gregory XVI to publish the encyclical *Singulari nos,* which condemned Lamennais as a thinker whose knowledge did "not come from God, but from the elements of the world." No greater statement could have been made of Lamennais's new, extra-Catholic status. Yet he never abandoned the Christian dream, which continued to inspire him until the end of his life. Despite its hostility toward the church, *Words* can be read as a development of the gospel's socially subversive message. This message also continued to preoccupy Lamennais, who in 1846 returned to his old habit of producing pious literature by publishing *The Gospels* (*Les Évangiles*), an edition of the Gospels that contained, like *The Imitation* of 1824, his own notes and reflections. Even more, as a deist Lamennais embarked on a philosophical project that derived from the philosophy of history. He wrote a theodicy. The difference was that, in being de-Christianized, this theodicy was also dehistoricized. He exposed it in two main writings: *Sketch of a Philosophy* (*Esquisse d'une philosophie*; 1840) and *On the First Society and Its Laws* (*De la société première et de ses lois*; 1848). In these works, the first of which he began when he was still a Catholic, Lamennais conjured a universe suffused with being and permeated by an immanent God, which unfolded irresistibly toward the good. Borrowing from Leibniz, the scholastics, and Maistre's *Saint Petersburg Dialogues* (*Les soirées de Saint-Pétersbourg*), he maintained that the universe was composed of different classes of beings that were intimately connected with each other, which presupposed each other as parts of a whole, and which together formed a vast organism, the living society of nature that extended to the planets—which Lamennais, like Maistre, Fourier, and the illuminists, believed to be alive. The development of this universe was rational and linear. Although it was punctuated by catastrophes, these made little impact and did not last. And although it contained sacrifice, it was a "mysterious banquet" of love where all beings gave themselves to all, and where all were victims and performers of sacrifice (Lamennais 1980–1981, 14:358). It was a description offering a striking contrast to traditional historiosophies, in which sacrifice was a salvific ritual that demarcated victim and executioner clearly and that possessed the power to push history along.

Lamennais's final philosophy, in short, celebrated a harmonious world where all beings communed with each other and with the universe, conspiring together to return to God. It was a universe where Providence had become so identified with nature, and with the reason of natural beings, that the three were virtually indistinguishable. Lamennais's theodicy finally achieved what his politics had always striven for: an empire of common sense in which the good dictated by each individual's reason could realize itself without being hindered by class distinction and conflicting wills, as reason conspired with reason to push the universe toward its telos in God. Original sin was absent from this universe: Lamennais followed Augustine in presenting evil as the absence of good, but denied the possibility of its inheritance. Gone with the fall were other Christian doctrines like eternal punishment and the divinity of Christ. Yet, to the end, Lamennais defended a religion of progress that he called Christian, and which he defined in *On the First Society and Its Laws* (*De la société première et de ses lois*) as true belief returned to its pure essence and freed from the vain opinions that pose obstacles to common sense. Even his doctrine of progress, his announcement of the coming of God's reign to earth, was secularized messianism. Until the end, then, Lamennais retained a Christian understanding of society as constituted by faith and influenced by Providence. The difference was that he saw the source of social cohesion no longer in a hierarchical church, but in the people as the incarnation of God in suffering.

Radical to the Last

Lamennais's new philosophy found a natural expression in his radical political commitments. Once he had identified the *vox populi* as the *vox Dei*—in a way that wholly reinvented the medieval adage—he consistently defended popular causes against the establishment. Thus he supported the Polish revolt of 1830–1831, denounced Austrian despotism, and took the side of the Italian rebels against the pope. In a sense, the decisive moment in his break with the church may be considered to be Gregory's letter to the Polish bishops of 1832, which supported the czar against the insurgents. Lamennais's *Critical Discussions* (*Les discussions critiques*; 1841), the journal of his personal spiritual crisis, shows how carefully and conscientiously he reflected during the problem of conscience that ensued, and that appeared in the version of his dealings with Gregory that he published in *Roman Affairs* (*Affaires de Rome*; 1836). His reasoning was simple: since the pope had not upheld the common sense that was inscribed in the people's voice and that was humanity's divine preserve, the Catholic Church could not be, in reality, the bearer of Christian liberty and divine knowledge. Rather, it was an enemy of both, another member of the establishment that had to be fought in order to make God's true message shine through. In the years that followed, Lamennais espoused the radical socialism and democracy that derived from these reflections in a series of works centered on the people, its current subjection, and its future liberation: *The Book of the People* (*Le livre du peuple*; 1837), *On Modern Slavery* (*De l'esclavage moderne*; 1839), *Politics for the People's Use* (*Politique à l'usage du peuple*; 1839), *On the Past and Future of the People* (*Du passé et de l'avenir du peuple*; 1841), and *Amschaspands and Darvands* (*Amschaspands et Darvands*; 1843).

This last, poetic text was a product of Lamennais's Orientalist imagination. It conjured a race of ancient, magical, and quasidivine extraterrestrials that had come down to earth, observed its inhabitants, and left behind, in the Orient, an account of their impressions. In this text, the wise authors concluded that the human race lived in a state of subjection, and lyrically recommended for its deliverance Lamennais's variety of democracy. This kind of mythical narrative owed much to that of Ballanche, whose *Essays on Social Palingenesis* (*Essais de palingénésie sociale*; 1820–1830s) sought to uncover "initiation"—Ballanche's version of the divine knowledge that was secreted in the world's cultures and confirmed by Catholicism—by poetically recounting myths, both historically existing and newly imagined. After rejecting history, then, Lamennais embraced fictional myth-poetry like that of *Amschaspands et Darvands* as a means to knowledge of the human and the divine. In doing so, he rejected the Counter-Enlightenment's guardianship of the fact. For in epistemology, Catholicism's French apologists of the last half of the eighteenth century had consistently insisted on wielding the fact, and especially the historical fact, against the imagination (Palmer 1939, 84), that *cheval de bataille* of the *philosophes*. Lamennais's final years found him as radical a politician as ever. In 1838, he changed his name from "La Mennais" to "Lamennais" to suppress the particle and the aristocratic origins it denoted. He became a republican, welcoming the fall of the July Monarchy in 1848 and the proclamation of the Second Republic. He was elected deputy for Paris and found himself, along with Victor Considérant, the only radical democrat in an assembly dominated by Orleanists and moderate republicans. He joined the committee responsible for drafting a constitution and produced a constitutional plan of his own, entitled "Constitutional Project of the French Republic by La Mennais" ("Projet de constitution de la République française par La Mennais"), which he published at the headquarters of his new, short-lived, republican journal, *The Constituting People* (*Le peuple constituant*), selling it at twenty centimes a copy. The "Project," which began "IN THE NAME OF GOD," was a deist text with Christian overtones. It eschewed the language of citizenship so common in republican constitutions in favor of an organic model of the French people, inspired by the family, which rejected all distinctions as unrepublican. Its greatest originality lay in the exceptional importance it accorded to decentralization and local autonomy (Clément 2003), those themes that Lamennais had trumpeted in *The Future* and vindicated ever since he wrote *Reflections* with Jean-Marie. Echoing Christian familialism, the "Project" described the local community as an entity almost as natural as the family, a constituted society that sustained medieval unity against revolutionary individualism.

Lamennais's regionalism did not fare well with the National Assembly's Orleanists and Jacobinist republicans, who decided to adjourn debate on the question, triggering his immediate resignation from the constitutional committee. He remained, however, a deputy in the assembly until Bonaparte's coup d'état of 1851, after which he lived estranged from politics. He returned to scholarship and undertook the translation of another Christian classic, the *Divine Comedy,* which was published posthumously. He died in 1854, having turned down various attempts to reconcile him with the church, and was buried without funerary rites at the cemetery of Père Lachaise.

Lamennais's Secret

Centuries after his death, Lamennais's story irresistibly commands the attention of all who read about him. The evocative beauty of his prose, the violence with which he defended the various positions that he adopted throughout his life, the breadth and radicalism of these, his eventual and unflinching opposition to any and all regimes, secular and ecclesiastical, and, most remarkable of all, his utter political, religious, and intellectual transformation in the early 1830s—all these features clamor for remembrance. I would like to argue here that they are consistent with what psychologists today would call histrionic personality disorder (this diagnosis has been confirmed by Agnes Muñoz de Laborde, MD). Throughout his life, Lamennais stood out in the crowd. He was enthusiastic, charismatic, dramatic, a fervent follower of parties, a man who frequently changed his style and image (in his case, the style being political and the image public); by all the accounts of his disciples and friends (and as is confirmed by his correspondence) he was a loving, devoted, kind, and enjoyable man. Whether as an ultraroyalist or as a democrat, Lamennais was always in demand. But he could get very upset over relatively small slights (as happened when the constituent assembly decided to postpone the discussion of provincial autonomy), was unshakably convinced of his righteousness (as *The Critical Discussions* abundantly illustrate), attacked inexhaustibly all who questioned this righteousness or criticized him (as happened with the Gallican bishops), was very easily influenced by others (witness his early dependence on Jean-Marie, whose philosophy he borrowed, or his friendship with Abbé Carron, or his extraordinary ability to imbibe and advocate the ideas most popular at any one time), oscillated between extremes of idealization and devaluation (as happened in regard to his attitude to the pope), and eschewed detail and specifics in preference for language that was colored, impressionistic, and exaggerated. Hence his ultimate abandonment of the traditionalist quest for an encyclopedic erudition, and his heavy reliance, in his own writing, on other people's work and ideas. The development of Lamennais's personality may have been influenced by the loss of his mother when he was five: histrionic personality disorder is associated with a death in the family at a young age (Miller and Grossman 2004, chap. 9).

I dwell on Lamennais's psychological profile because it can help to explain the mysteries that continue to baffle scholars, and that have probably delayed the composition of his intellectual biography: his sudden change of mind in the early 1830s as well as the extremely divergent political and intellectual personas that he adopted over the course of his life. Applying the categories of today's psychiatry to a nineteenth-century subject is of course a risky enterprise: to my knowledge, historians have yet to reflect systematically on how to do this. Nor can diagnoses of deceased subjects be as certain of those of live ones. I would suggest, however, that the advantages are worth the risks, insofar as science's predictive powers allow us to become "prophets of the past"—to borrow the epithet that Jules-Amédée Barbey d'Aurevilly used to describe Lamennais (Barbey d'Aurevilly 1851). That is, science's ability to foresee allows us to discern coherences that might otherwise escape us, broadening our understanding of events and—as Lamennais's case well illustrates—helping us to make sense of the otherwise incomprehensible.

My purpose, however, is not to suggest that Lamennais was only a performer, or that he committed to ideas for the sole sake of exhibiting them, as is often the case with histrionics. The reality is much more complex and paradoxical. For if Lamennais's life shows his great emotional instability, it testifies also to the profound sincerity of his convictions. Not only does this sincerity shine through his adherence to the Christian vision; it does so even through his vocation as a priest. For if, in refusing to submit to *Mirari vos,* Lamennais broke his vow of obedience, he seems to have kept until the end his vows of chastity and poverty. He slept on the floor in his final years, never married, and—with the possible exception of his adolescence—is not known to have had lovers. To the last, he tried to live in emulation of Christ and of the humble *peuple* that he believed incarnated his suffering, sacrificing everything—his religion, his status, his friends, his reputation—for the sake of an ideal of order founded on the divinization of humanity.

To this sketch of his sincerity may be added that of his intellectual consistency, which was solid to the point of extremity, and which underlay, stunningly, his radical changes of mind. Lamennais may have changed his views frequently, but he never did so without reflecting on every possible way in which they might affect the common interest. Despite the sudden twists in the road, his intellectual trajectory was marked by continuity rather than rupture, with every system he espoused developing out of the previous one and retaining the concepts and themes that he thought most worthy. Being aware of this is crucial for understanding the main idea that I have endeavored to convey in this essay: that, from an intellectual point of view, Lamennais's final, dehistoricized, socialist deism was nothing more than the strict and logical deployment of the secularizing potential of the French Catholic Enlightenment, and most particularly of the notion of common sense that it had originally developed in its combat against *philosophie*.

Bibliography

Barbey d'Aurevilly, Jules-Amédée. 1851. *Les prophètes du passé*. Paris: Louis Hervé.
Burson, Jeffrey. 2010. *The Rise and Fall of Theological Enlightenment: Jean-Martin de Prades and Ideological Polarization in Eighteenth-Century France*. Notre Dame: University of Notre Dame Press.
Burtin, Nicolas. 1931. *Un semeur d'idées au temps de la restauration: Le baron d'Eckstein*. Paris: E. de Boccard.
Clément, Jean-Paul. 2003. "La constitution de La Mennais (1848)." *Revue française de droit constitutionnel* 55:473–82.
Gerbet, Philippe. 1832. *Conférences de philosophie catholique: Introduction à la philosophie de l'histoire*. Paris: Bureaux de l'agence générale pour la défense de la liberté religieuse et chez Eugène Renduel.

Grimaud, Louis. 1898. *Histoire de la liberté d'enseignement en France depuis la chute de l'Ancien régime jusqu'à nos jours.* Grenoble: Allier Frères.

Jardin, André, and André-Jean Tudesq. 1977. *Restoration and Reaction, 1815–1848.* The Cambridge History of Modern France 1. Translated by Elborg Forster. Cambridge: Cambridge University Press.

Lamennais, Hugues-Félicité Robert de. 1980–1981. *Oeuvres complètes.* Edited by Louis Le Guillou. 21 vols. Geneva: Slatkine.

McCalla, Arthur. 1998. *A Romantic Historiosophy: The Philosophy of History of Pierre-Simon Ballanche.* Leiden: Brill.

Miller, Theodore, and Seth Grossman. 2004. *Personality Disorders in Modern Life.* Hoboken, NJ: Wiley.

Palmer, Robert R. 1939. *Catholics and Unbelievers in Eighteenth-Century France.* Princeton: Princeton University Press.

Reardon, Bernard. 1975. *Liberalism and Tradition: Aspects of Catholic Thought in Nineteenth-Century France.* Cambridge: Cambridge University Press.

Schwab, Raymond. 1984. *The Oriental Renaissance: Europe's Rediscovery of India and the East, 1680–1880.* Translated by Gene Patterson-King. New York: Columbia University Press.

PART 3
Catholic Enlightenment in the Holy Roman Empire

7

Benedict Stattler (1728–1797)

The Reinvention of Catholic Theology with the Help of Wolffian Metaphysics

ULRICH L. LEHNER

Born in Kötzting in the Bavarian Forest on 30 January 1728, Benedict Stattler first attended the school of the Benedictines in the nearby abbey of Niederaltaich before entering the Society of Jesus. From 1747 to 1751, he studied philosophy and mathematics in Ingolstadt. He became enchanted with the philosophy of the Silesian Protestant Christian Wolff (1679–1754), whose works were widely read at Catholic universities at that time. Stattler accepted Wolff's ideas as his own new way of thinking, applying them to his theological studies between 1751 and 1754. His ordination to the priesthood followed in 1759. After a few minor teaching positions, he accepted the chair of dogmatic theology in Ingolstadt in 1770, which he held even after the 1773 suppression of his order, until 1781. With stupendous erudition and breathtaking reasoning, he published many works in the fields of the sciences, philosophy, and theology (Miedaner 1983; Stattler 1769–1772). Even the Munich Academy of Sciences, which was notorious for its anti-Jesuitism, offered him one of its prestigious memberships. Always eager to lead, Stattler also served for some years as vice chancellor of his university, until 1781, when he had to resign from his chair after the Benedictines took over higher education in Bavaria. For seven years he then worked as pastor in Kemnath in the Upper Palatinate. It was probably during those years that he conceived his idea of publishing a vernacular textbook version of his main theological and ethical works. From 1788 on, he lived in Munich, where he was appointed a member of the Elector's Censorship Collegium (1790–1794). There he worked zealously to stop the dissemination of the philosophy of Immanuel Kant, who was, in Stattler's eyes, a major threat to Christian metaphysics, especially because so many Catholic theologians and philosophers began embracing his teachings (Fischer 2005). Stattler's impressive bibliography entails more than sixty voluminous books in Latin and German. Only in the last few decades has the ex-Jesuit's enormous courage in re-inventing Catholic theology and philosophy been rediscovered. Previously, he was seen as an anti-Enlightener simply because of his rejection of Immanuel Kant. His clear agenda to make use of the philosophies of his time as a tool for modern apologetics does not make him un-Enlightened any more than a materialist agenda makes Diderot Enlightened.

Theology as Scientific Discipline

Christian Wolff's metaphysics promised an answer to the fundamental questions that had challenged Christian thought in the eighteenth century. If physical necessity and freedom were compatible, was belief in a personal God and his revelation intelligible, and was true and infallible knowledge in the sciences achievable? Wolff could say an emphatic "yes" to all of these questions with the extraordinary clarity of his mathematical method (Gómez-Tutor 2004). Stattler immediately realized that Wolff's method could not only save Catholic theology from an outdated scholasticism but also defend its doctrines against the ferocious attacks of deism and atheism. Therefore, the concepts and propositions of theology and philosophy had to be tested for their intrinsic possibility, that is, for their noncontradictoriness, consistency, and coherence. This seemed theologically appropriate because it acknowledged faith as the starting point of the reflection on the logical consistency of the doctrines. The method did not prove doctrinal truths through reason, and thus it was a tool to follow the old program of *credo ut intelligam* (Eschweiler 2010, 36; Lehner 2006). Stattler saw the key to solving all theological and philosophical problems in Wolff's principle of sufficient reason (Gurr 1959, 57–67). With its application, so he was convinced, a new theology could arise, one that would be able to restore certainty among believers—a certainty that had vaporized under the attacks of naturalism, providential deism, and the like. Now theological propositions could become "almost" evident, that is, have the highest possible moral certainty, and thus could offer stronger support for the credibility of the Christian revelation (Scholz 1957, 43–56).

By following Wolff, Stattler's eclectic, empirical dogmatism navigated between Descartes (1596–1650), Leibniz (1646–1716), Locke (1632–1704), and Hume (1711–1776). It claimed that clear principles and concepts would allow for clear explanations, convincing demonstrations, and proper, chainlike connections of all doctrines (Scholz 1957, 46–51; Werner 1889, 173–77). Stattler's compelling unitary system of thought was meant to be not only a theistic counterpart to materialism or indifferentism but also a tool to reestablish theology as an exact science. With this newly discovered conceptual clarity and logical force, Catholicism, according to Stattler, could convince other Christian confessions of its truth. The Wolffian method thus became a tool for the reunification of the churches and for early ecumenism. However, the methodological and systematic strength of Stattler's work, which was imitated by neoscholastic handbooks until the twentieth century, was also its greatest weakness. Since every sentence was connected to a previous sentence, one had to reread his works over and over, or at least continually refer to previous axioms if one wanted to follow the argument. Such a structure, expressed in a graceless Latin, made Stattler's works a burden to read for many.

Stattler's plan for a reform of theology aimed to reinvent theology as a whole not only through Wolff's method but also with the help of the sciences and historical-critical exegesis. One can see this clearly in his *De locis theologicis* (Stattler 1775a), where he merged the authorities of the scholastic theologians, natural reason, philosophers, and history into a new category entitled "reasonable theology." Nevertheless, Stattler was far from being a rationalist. On the contrary, he insisted that theology was only a scientific discipline insofar as it pertained to the rational-philosophical parts of doctrine, for which sufficient reasons could be presented, but not for the revealed mysteries themselves. For the latter, only their intrinsic possibility—including coherence (*compossibilitas*)—could be demonstrated. In other words, one can prove the fact that God has revealed himself from reason, but not the content of this revelation. In his system, theology became a science of the *naturally* certain elements of revelation (Ruhstorfer 2003, 195; Scholz 1975, 15–17).

In his apologetic works, Stattler arranged his arguments according to the modalities of possibility, reality, and necessity. Therefore, his *Demonstratio Evangelica* (1770) was usually regarded as the beginning of modern Catholic apologetics because of its tripartite scheme of proving first the possibility of revelation, then its necessity, followed by the proof of its reality; after all, all textbooks in fundamental theology and apologetics used this approach until the middle of the twentieth century. Research in the last five decades, however, has established that Samuel Clarke (1675–1729) and the Irish Catholic theologian Luke Hooke (1714–1796; see Thomas O'Connor's essay in this volume) had already used this scheme. It is possible that Stattler knew of their works, although he never quoted them. Stattler's primary aim with *Demonstratio Evangelica* was to refute the criticism of deist thinkers like Edward Herbert (1583–1648), Matthew Tindal (1657–1733), Thomas Morgan (d. 1743), Jean-Jacques Rousseau (1712–1778), David Hume, and even John Locke (Stattler 1770, 25, 38). Through an abridged edition compiled by Stattler's student Johann Michael Sailer (1751–1832), the work saw four editions between 1777 and 1781 (Heinz 1984, 186–203).

Stattler rejected theological nativism, which claimed that the idea of God was innate and was usually combined with a mystical Augustinianism. Instead, he followed Wolff's philosophy because it bore significant parallels to the French Jesuit synthesis developed by Claude Buffier (1661–1739) and René-Joseph Tournemine (1661–1739). Both had attempted to merge Descartes and Malebranche (1638–1715) with Newton (1643–1727) and the empiricist philosophies of Locke, Voltaire (1694–1778), and Condillac (1715–1780) into a coherent system that they considered an epistemic overhaul of Thomism (Burson 2010). Stattler viewed even the highest ideas as deriving from sensory experience. Consequently, common sense would be likewise not innate, but rather trained by experience and reflection. If all knowledge derives from the senses, then an external, supernatural revelation could be considered something positive and not something alien to the human mind. This supernatural revelation was necessary for the first humans, who otherwise would have needed too much time to find God through reason alone and never would have reached their final goal. Stattler viewed such revelation as a necessary grace, which elevated the natures of human beings above nature alone (*natura elevata;* Stattler 1781, §206f; Eschweiler 2010, 21–33). Thus for Stattler, the primary effect of original sin was a disordered sensuality leading to wrong concepts about the world, the human person, and God.

The Divinely Instituted Office of Bishops

Charges brought by the Benedictine Wolfgang Frölich (1748–1810) of Regensburg-St. Emmeram led to the indictment of numerous works by Stattler, including *Demonstratio Catholica* (1775b). The Congregation of the Index proscribed the book on 10 July 1780, but the sentence was not carried out or published until 1796. The official decree of 1796 also included the proscription of his *Theologia Christiana theoretica* (1781), *De locis theologicis,* his published letter to Bahrdt (1780), and his public defense of the *Demonstratio Catholica,* the *Authentic Files* (*Authentische Aktenstücke*; 1796). What had been so dangerous that this most famous Catholic German theologian and philosopher was punished so harshly? The Roman Congregation of the Index tried to persuade the bishop of Eichstätt to proscribe the book *Demonstratio* quietly so that no turmoil would be caused, but it did not mention any reasons for its decision. It even stated that it was unnecessary to hear Father Stattler or to state the mistakes because they were self-evident. After all, Stattler had questioned the pope's ordinary and immediate authority over all the faithful, or so it seemed to the censors. Indeed, Stattler questioned the pope's immediate authority but in a much more sophisticated way. Stattler argued that the episcopate was of divine right, instituted by Christ, and that all bishops had their ecclesiastical authority *immediately* through Christ and *not* through the pope. They were in his view successors of the apostles and *not* vicars of the pope. The pope did have the full authority to supervise, to govern, and to judge all bishops and their subjects in all ecclesiastical affairs, but this authority was for Stattler a physical one and *not* a moral one. This meant that the pope should never have the desire to use his immediate and universal powers except in an emergency (1775b, §§160–65). Such a new ecclesiology, buttressed by up-to-date biblical scholarship, bore also a political dimension for Stattler. If Rome would follow his insight, he reasoned, the tensions with the Gallican Church could be overcome, and the schisms with other churches healed. Moreover, he was convinced that such a view of the bishop's office could have prevented the Anglican schism as well. One can see here again that, for Stattler, theology must always have the reunification of all Christian churches as its main target; even his renewed ecclesiology served the purpose of ecumenism.

This position, however, does not mean that Stattler denied the infallibility of the magisterium or the primacy of the pope. Quite the contrary, he envisioned a more *subsidiary* ecclesiology in which the office of Saint Peter would be more edifying than oppressive, and in which the genuine office of bishops would be adequately acknowledged. In fact, Stattler highly valued the magisterium and the primacy of the pope, because he feared that eventually, deism and Socinianism would overwhelm orthodox Protestantism with a widespread subjectivism in biblical interpretation, so that Catholicism would be the only true Christian church left. He therefore implored faithful Protestants to embrace the Catholic Church and its magisterium. Yet Stattler also made clear that infallibility had its limitations, and he criticized attempts to turn every papal statement into an infallible teaching: "In issues and questions that do not immediately pertain to salvation or damnation, the head of the Church can err in his judgment of human wisdom [*falli humanae prudentiae judicio potest*]. Therefore, he should not trust too much in its own cleverness and should not burden the Church with laws against the will of the subordinate bishops, especially if they regard these laws as not helpful or even harmful" (Stattler 1775b, §164/III). Although the pope would not have to consult other bishops, Stattler thought it would be opportune for him to do so, as well as to ask the bishops in a collegial way to help him govern the church. If the pope decided to subdue the bishops with illegal means, his laws would be null and void, Stattler pointed out. In cases in which the pope erred out of ignorance of facts or because of human failure (ex ignorantia certorum factorum . . . seu vitae exemplo idcirco non optimo exhibito), the bishops would not have to follow such commands, but instead should admonish the pope fraternally but persistently about his mistake (cum reverentia quidem, sed et decente cum constantia animi illum erroris admonere) (1775b, §164 VI).

Stattler never accepted the proscription of his works. Since a definitive magisterial ruling on these issues was not promulgated for the entire church, he was convinced that his punishment was illicit. Being true to himself, or stubborn, as one might call it, he did not submit to the ruling of the Congregation and never withdrew any sentences from his works, since the withdrawal of true or probable sentences would be unethical in his eyes (1796; Wolf 2011).

Philosophical and Christian Ethics

Stattler's ethics also followed Christian Wolff's opinion that certitude was indispensable in ethical questions. Stattler presented his ethics in nine volumes on six thousand pages, predominantly in his *Ethica Christiana universalis* (1772) and his six-volume *Ethica Christiana communis* (1782–1789). However, Stattler deemed that the content of

Christian ethics was only an addition to philosophical ethics and that the former was scientific only insofar as it was based on reason alone. It was unscientific when it relied on the authority of Scripture and the Fathers, but its harmony with scientific, philosophical ethics was demonstrable. For Stattler, freedom was the ability to choose between two equally strong desires without being unduly swayed by either of them. This he considered the sufficient reason of freedom. If this equilibrium was one-sided and no images or ideas of warning or encouragement were present, the person would lose his freedom and be controlled by nature.

Stattler's ethics had theological underpinnings, however. Since the world was created for those who were predestined for heaven, God must offer in the world the means for humans to achieve their ultimate goal of happiness. Because of the existence of freedom, God cannot want the happiness of all, but "must" want the maximum happiness of the highest possible number of human beings. (Scholz 1975, 22). The law was to Stattler the practical motive to do good, instituted by God so that persons could realize psychologically their potential and become aware of their own merits. Since God has bound himself to this principle of morality, he must reward merits. Thus, Stattler's statement that the beatitude achieved through natural perseverance and one's own merits is *more* valuable than a beatitude merely given gratuitously by grace (1772, §165/I: maius bonum est beatitudo proprio marte et merito morali parta, quam mere liberaliter donata) seems to contradict the Catholic doctrine of the absolute gratuity of salvation. Human beings are admonished to achieve merits through the fear of eternal damnation and the torments of hell, because only such admonitions can persuade their wills. However, Stattler went beyond this when he stated that an authority can legally oblige those commands only if it has the moral *and* physical authority to punish or reward (1772, §333). "While Wolff, together with the scholastic tradition, had found the sufficient reason in the good itself, Stattler alienates moral obligation in a shocking fashion from its source and makes it part of a radical merit and punishment morality" (Scholz 1975, 24). It was Stattler who gave Enlightenment utilitarianism a place in Catholic ethics and who first attempted to construct a utilitarian

Christian ethics (Diebolt 1926). He was also one of the most important Catholic voices on the ethical question of just wages, and between 1770 and 1886, no other Catholic theologian dealt with such precision with the issue and proposed similarly durable and fundamental norms (Healy 1966, 213–43).

Nevertheless, it would be unfair to judge Stattler's ethics from the standpoint of twenty-first-century biblically inspired moral theology. Considering the context of his time, his approach was indeed liberating because it rejected a merely "natural" and philosophical ethics that many Christian theologians already practiced. Such an approach, in Stattler's view, disrespected the intimate relationship between God and human beings brought about by Jesus Christ. A philosophical ethics alone was also insufficient for motivating persons since it lacked the unique role model of the God-man (Bruch 1997, 135–55). A principle became famous in the third volume of the *Ethica Christiana communis* (1789), which Catholic theologians had thus far either neglected or deliberately ignored. In sections 1889, 1891, and 1893 Stattler laid out that it was permissible for Christians to kill (!) an aggressor in order to prevent the spreading of evil rumors (*periculi infamiae*). How a punishment before the actual deed can be justified remains unclear. Equally questionable is section 1894, according to which infamous lies can be morally fought with other lies and rumors. These paragraphs, buried between hundreds of pages of complicated material, were found by the Bavarian priest Franz Sales Riembauer, who used them in 1807 as justification for killing his mistress (Feuerbach 1829, 43–122).

Ecumenism, Toleration, and the Christian State

The single most overlooked theme of Stattler's works, even though it permeated all of his writings, was the desire for a reunification of the churches. With everything he wrote, he wanted to serve the purpose of ecumenism. His ethics, he hoped, could show Protestant Christians the compatibility of Catholic moral thought with philosophical reason, while his conceptually purified theology should convince them of the intrinsic coherence and consistency of Catholic doctrine. It was clear for Stattler that non-Catholics were ignorant of the true authority of the Catholic Church as the one and only church of Christ, but he insisted that no sensible Catholic could reject his or her own means of salvation. He even stated that Catholic theologians should stop calling Protestants heretics, not only because German Imperial Law proscribed it but also because, in Stattler's view, Protestants were connected to the true church of Christ despite not being full members of the church of Rome (1775b, §79). If Protestants were saved, they received salvation, so he argued, through the means of the Catholic Church, which had remained in the Protestant church (e.g., baptism). Thus they were spiritually connected (*secundum animam*) with the Catholic Church, even if not institutionally. Connected with this spiritual membership comes the "right to spiritual communion in all spiritual goods of the Catholic Church, such as the ordinary power of holy public sacrifices and prayers, which they are able to use as long as they [the Protestants] pertain in their error.... They are only excluded from those spiritual goods—partly through a hypothetical natural law due to their current religion, partly through necessary and appropriate laws of protection— . . . which they would regard erroneously . . . as false goods or which they would dishonor" (1787, 392).

When Protestants visited Stattler, he was always irenic, and when they attended his lectures, he graciously addressed them in public as his "Protestant brethren" (Will 1778, 8–11). The ex-Jesuit even dedicated an entire book to his ideas about a reunion of the churches: *Plan to the Only Possible Reunion between the Protestant and the Catholic Churches* (*Plan zu der allein möglichen Vereinigung im Glauben der Protestanten mit der katholischen Kirche*; Stattler 1791). Yet he despised the universalism that the theologian and radical Enlightener Karl Friedrich Bahrdt (1741–1792) taught. Stattler found Bahrdt's indifferentism dangerous and resulting from a confused framework of metaphysics. The Ingolstadt professor even wrote a book addressed to Bahrdt in which he tried to convince him of the truth of his system. Despite his otherwise tolerant views, Stattler believed that Bahrdt was rightly persecuted and that he could not claim toleration since such right pertained only to private ideas, not to published words (1780; C. Schäfer 1992, 182).

Stattler developed his ideas about toleration and his vision of the Christian state in more detail in a book dealing with the views of the Jewish philosopher Moses Mendelssohn (1729–1786). It establishes Stattler as a person who participated in the exchange of knowledge between Protestant, Catholic, and Jewish Enlighteners and thus as a figure of a transconfessional and transcultural Enlightenment. In his famous treatise *Jerusalem* (1783), Mendelssohn had written in response to the toleration edicts of Emperor Joseph II, to which Stattler responded with his *True Jerusalem, or About Religious Power and Tolerance in All, but Especially in Catholic Christendom* (*Wahres Jerusalem, oder Über religiöse Macht und Toleranz in jedem und besonders im katholischen Christenthume*; 1787). Far from any polemic, Stattler analyzed Mendelssohn with generosity and reverence, but did not withhold his criticism. The Bavarian theologian considered the main flaw of Mendelssohn's book to be his concept of religion as an individual relationship between God and a person, which contained *no* contractual element whatsoever. Consequently, there could be no real government or authority in a church and no possibility for exterior force (e.g., excommunication). Thus, a state could never infringe the rights of religion—which is all about interior, deeply personal convictions—since it is the state's obligation *only* to enforce exterior actions, which are based on natural law and social contract theory. Therefore, it always would be illicit to enforce convictions. Stattler also disagreed with Mendelssohn about the extension of toleration to naturalists and atheists. To Stattler, these were dangerous individuals because their views undermined common morality and contributed to religious indifference. Particularly remarkable is Stattler's attempt to refute Mendelssohn in the area of biblical history, namely the history of the Old Testament. The Bavarian pointed out that Mendelssohn had misinterpreted the Old Testament narratives and had stated that the Hebrew Scriptures acknowledge a religious power to expel and punish similar to that in the Christian churches—a claim Mendelssohn had denied (Stattler 1787, x). Likewise, Stattler rejected Mendelssohn's premise that God could only give civil laws and could never order faith and conviction, because this premise would exclude God's influence on the human mind and severely limit his omnipotence (Stattler 1787, xi). The central criticism, however, was Stattler's argument that Judaism and Christianity were not religions of individual experience, but rather were communal religions that had been "learned"—*not* from reason alone, but from the teaching of an authority. Unlike Mendelssohn, Stattler was not convinced at all that reason was sufficient to find the speculative truths of natural religion; he saw the Old Testament as a proof of the opposite, namely that Judaism *was* a revelatory religion. Every "supernaturally enlightened true Jew and Christian" must admit, according to Stattler, that reason and human authority alone testify for their own impotence and instead bear witness to the supernatural revelation of the Bible (1787, xv–xvi).

In order to understand Stattler's idea of toleration properly, we must look more closely at his concept of society and state, because this concept lies at the heart of his definition of the church as a supernaturally elevated society. According to Stattler, a state is a collective of families, connected deliberately by contract to promote true happiness for all. Consequently, the more a state tries to promote such happiness, the more perfect it is. The primary reason why humans live together in families is their desire to perfect their individual pursuit of happiness through the mutual help and support of others. The secondary reason is the protection of achieved goods against evil human beings; the final reason is to secure enjoyment of property and all other achieved goods. In order for the state to be able to guarantee such demands, the individuals would have to give up certain rights, especially natural liberty (1787, 1–13). The power of the state must therefore pertain to all *three* dimensions of life, namely the augmentation of individual happiness through good order and distribution (police); the guarantee of property and rights and liberties (judicial system); and, finally, the protection of this property (military defense). An imperfect state is one that lacks one of these characteristics. The full and undivided power of the state, usually in the hand of a prince, is always a moral power insofar as he commands, proscribes, defends, or encourages. A sovereign, however, is obliged to command his subjects only to certain actions that are necessary to obtain the common good (1787, 21–29). Religion fits into this framework insofar as it is the "faculty to revere God as the Supreme Being and first cause of all happiness according to his infinite dignity. . . ." Natural religion is based on the connection of the virtues of mind (knowledge of God and wisdom) and the virtues of the will (hope for help and support, love of creation, desire for participating in the divine plan) (1787, 65). The *super*natural and revealed religion of mind and will consists also of virtues, namely of the knowledge of God's revelatory history; of the philosophical knowledge of the parts of revelation, which bring about moral certainty of the truth of revelation; and of the knowledge of the so-called articles of faith. Moreover, supernatural religion must contain a strong assent to all these articles of faith because of God's authority, a sincere hope and trust in God's promises, a growth in love for God, and, finally, the desire to participate in the eternal bliss God has promised. All virtues of natural and revealed religion are subsumed under "inner religion, because they have their home in the soul of a human being" (1787, 69). If one expresses this inner religion through signs to others, it becomes an exterior signification of the inner religion, which has two goals: to make the steady exercise of religion easier for the faithful person and to encourage others to follow the example of a believer. The more an interior religion can bring about the practice of the love of God in will and mind, which ultimately makes it possible to fulfill God's laws, the more *perfect* it is. An exterior religion is perfect if it supports the perfections of the inner religion in oneself and others (1787, 72). Such an essentially *perfect inner religion* is also necessary for an appropriate understanding of self-love and love of other human beings. Since the ordinary common good, the goal of every state, cannot be achieved without the steady execution of all virtues, which depend on a perfect inner religion, the best means to promote and maintain the main goal consists in supporting the perfect inner religion. "The inner religion . . . is the main column on which the happiness of the state rests and the best and sufficient means to achieve it. . . . For without this religion the fulfillment of the duties of orderly self-love, love of others, and justice is impossible—and thus also happiness, the final aim . . . of the state" (1787, 82). Such a religion has to be *publicly* endorsed and asserted.

After having established the rationale for a state religion, Stattler then refuted Mendelssohn's thesis that, since credibility of such a religion cannot be ordered or enforced by law, there would be no lawful force in religious matters at all (1787, 89). On the contrary, Stattler was convinced that the sovereign of a Christian state has the right and duty to support with the help of the police an essentially perfect interior religion, since it is the best means to achieve the final goal of the state. Police measures must be sufficient to produce certainty in the knowledge of God, which provides the motives and grounds for fulfilling all duties toward God and fellow human beings with the utmost diligence. There are, according to Stattler, five ways to achieve certainty in our knowledge of God: (1) through the experience of the external world, (2) through the changes of the states of our soul, (3) through rational judgments, (4) through the principles of common sense, and (5) because of the sufficient authority of a witness. Police, however, can support only the fifth way of authority. This way is, for Stattler, the ordinary path by which people become acquainted with religion because of their uninterest in theological questions. Most acquire therefore only a "respective" certainty from their teachers because they never put the learned material to the discursive test (1787, 91–100). Unlike Mendelssohn, Stattler consequently argued that teachers of religion could be requested to take an oath to teach according to the nation's religion. This does not mean that the personal belief of a teacher is enforceable, but that he can be obliged to teach a certain doctrine. Even if one cannot force a person to believe, Stattler reasons that the sovereign has the right to force his subjects to *listen* to his official religious teachers, which of course reminds one of Saint Augustine's treatment of the Donatists.

Stattler differentiated toleration into a private and a public/political sphere. His main rules for private toleration in the natural state were as follows: (1) no human being is allowed to hate a person or even to be indifferent to a person only because of some evil deed, since it is always a duty to love human beings in all circumstances; and (2) in the natural state, human beings have the right to decide for themselves according to their own insight and liking. Force is permissible only if a person's rights are violated. These rules rest on the following principles:

(1) In the natural state every human is obliged to tolerate his evil brother as long as his actions do not violate or offend him or others.

(2) It is not allowed to do evil to someone or to wish evil because someone is evil or follows the wrong religion.
(3) It is not permissible to deprive someone of the common love of benevolence or help in emergencies.
(4) Every offense of such an evil human being is forbidden by natural law.
(5) All violence done to him is sinful.
(6) However, one must try to improve the morals of the evil person and convince him of his errors.
(7) "With the intention to improve a person in the spirit of friendship, or (as one could call it) punishment, the pious friend has the right to withdraw the exterior privileges of particular love and friendship—not the common and ordinary ones—in order to demonstrate to him his disgust for the other person's errors...."
(8) "It is allowed to wish that God would interfere and save pertinacious and incorrigible persons...."

Nevertheless these principles are limited by the evil person violating one's own rights, which one is always allowed to resist. People who harm others cannot be tolerated. Even those who tempt or seduce others fall into this category. Consequently, people who cannot fulfill the natural duties of friendship or civility are dangerous. Into this latter category Stattler placed people who do not have a perfect religion of the mind and who attempt to destroy among Christian citizens the essential perfect religion. Such people should not be tolerated because they are an intrinsic risk for the state and religion (1787, 147–53). Consequently, such enemies of public peace (atheists, naturalists, indifferentists) cannot be given the same civil rights and the same protection Christians enjoy. Moreover, a Christian ruler has the duty to protect an essentially perfect religion against inimical attacks in the same way he is obliged to protect the possessions of his subjects—an idea also proposed by the Protestant Enlightener Christian Thomasius (1655–1728), whom Stattler most definitely knew. Therefore, a sovereign cannot tolerate individuals who attack religion, nor protect religions that publicly work against the state's religion. Rather, he must ban such individuals from his territory. Stattler does not accept the argument that such individuals would just follow their erring conscience by expressing their heterodox beliefs. Instead, he argues that the natural freedom of conscience has reached its limit when it attempts to refute or attack publicly the religion of a state (1787, 165).

Mendelssohn's argument that a prince does not have legal power over religion, since no individual ever gives up the right to his own religion in the societal contract, likewise was rejected by Stattler. As an individual person has the right to avoid the acquaintance of a dangerous or sick person, so can the state, as a moral entity, take measures to keep its civil society healthy. The question is therefore not whether a Christian state can force a person to embrace a creed mentally, but whether the state is allowed to take measures against *irreligion,* that is, naturalism, atheism, and deism. But if the Christian princes have the right to be intolerant against naturalists, one could make a parallel argument and say that the pagan Roman emperors were justified in their persecution of Christianity because it was inimical to the state's religion. Stattler rejected this thought, reasoning that the emperors were wrong and probably suffered from invincible ignorance, which prevented them from acknowledging Christianity as the true religion. Therefore, the Christians were allowed to resist in their minds, however not in action. The first apostles did not have the right "to resist the tyrants with violence, but had to endure . . . all suffering . . . in order to convince the heathens that . . . preaching the gospel was to their own advantage. The modern theists should do likewise, if they wish to convince us Christians of their message. . . ." (1787, 173).

Stattler adequately summarized Mendelssohn's position against any church having the right to force, but he doubted Mendelssohn's argument that a state would not have the right to forbid a religion, because Stattler rejected the private relationship between a human being and God as the basis for religion. Stattler agreed that such a relationship was indeed the basis for the construction of an inner religion but not for the public exterior religion, the church, and its duties. Moreover, the interior religion depends for its formation and its origin not only on the exterior religion of the people but also on the public authority of its teachers—the two means that are necessary for most people to gain moral certainty about the truth of religion. From these sources derive the rights and duties of exterior religion that cannot be based on the individual relationship with God. The primary duty is to show others the certainty of the true religion through one's own authority, reputation, and faith life, but also to avoid making others indifferent in their fervor for religion. "All human beings who need such actions [creedal activity] have a universal and perfect right to them. Therefore human beings should be able to oblige themselves because of their relationship with each other . . . to provide first such a universal service of love and support for the public exterior religious services . . . and secondly the negative duty . . . to abstain from any . . . attack on such a precious common good" (1787, 181–82). Stattler thus argues that religion is *not* individually based but, first and foremost, a *duty* of the community and derives from the relationship to other persons. He also criticizes Mendelssohn for viewing the church as a mere educational institution and for his inconsistency in claiming that a sovereign would not have the right to forbid religions that question the basis of such educational institutions.

Stattler, of course, now faces a problem. If the church were a society based like any other society on a contract, then it would be difficult not only to deny the state a right over the church's affairs, but also to deny the laity a voice. His solution is therefore to establish the church as a society for a common purpose, namely to achieve eternal happiness (1787, 203–4). For the ex-Jesuit, however, the church is not like a state insofar as its members do *not* contribute to the wording of the contract of the society it brought about, since the text of that contract rests *solely* on the authority of God's revelation. The same can be said, Stattler argues, about the Jewish religion but not about the Protestant churches, where he detects a contractual agreement among the members (synods). For early Christianity, however, no document suggests that the community agreed on an ecclesiastical constitution that then conceded to the apostles jurisdiction and power: "All this power the apostles and their successors did not exercise in the name of the community, but in Christ's name" (1787, 221).

For Stattler no state can bring about a perfect religion for its people, because every such religion would lack sufficient means to bring about harmony among the subjects and personal certainty about the truth of the religion. Only a divine revelation or a logical demonstration could achieve the latter. But since most people do not care for logical demonstrations, a revelation is the best way to establish a perfect religion, and, in Stattler's view, this was the way chosen by God when he revealed himself to the people of Israel and founded a church through Jesus: "All people, Jews or Heathens, whom Jesus wanted to collect in his church . . . , were supposed to constitute a church according to his intentions: all were bound to fulfill the duty to further . . . their common eternal happiness" (1787, 233). The government of this one church, however, could not have been given to a certain state, since such a step would have trivialized God's message. In addition, Scripture alone was an insufficient means to maintain that church; thus God entrusted his religion to a hierarchy and its magisterium—a Catholic standard view. The harmony of the teachings of the apostles and their successors, however, was in need of a guaranteeing principle, the guidance of the Holy Spirit. The strong trust in the continuing guidance of the Holy Spirit is the *central* column of the Catholic faith, and an attack on it is an attack on the church herself. A dissenter who denies this guidance of the Holy Spirit not only attacks Catholicism itself, but also confuses its members. Every sovereign must hinder such confusion in order to keep religious harmony and peace. Consequently, intolerance is a somewhat necessary virtue and is at least necessary in order to protect the ecclesiological trust Catholics have in the magisterium of their church (1787, 244–60).

According to Stattler, a Catholic state has the duty to protect the Catholic belief and the divine authority of the church. The attacks it needs to protect against include public preaching against Catholic doctrines or the public support of heterodox beliefs. The more harmful the error, and the lesser the person's remorse, the more severe the punishment should be. If a sovereign changes his belief, he does *not* have the right to force his subjects to do the same, even if he is a Protestant sovereign who becomes Catholic (1787, 347)! *Political toleration* of a religion that contradicts the general religion of the state is therefore possible if adherents of the other faith support the civil community of the state. Such political toleration can have different grades. It can allow the simple private creed and belief, but restrict the religious exercise to private houses; or it can allow public worship; and last but not least, it can even allow public teaching and proselytizing. According to the Peace of Westphalia (1648), Lutherans and Reformed Christians should enjoy free public toleration. However, no Catholic sovereign may tolerate a newly evolving public worship to be practiced by any non-Catholic religion unless some necessity (e.g., public unrest, economic reasons) were to demand it. If he does tolerate it, he must be sure that such a step will *not* endanger the Catholic faith. If toleration is in the interest of the state and poses no danger to the church, such a step toward free political toleration is wise, but proselytizing should be banned. Moreover, as Stattler points out, it is always better for a Catholic monarch to have a Protestant minority than to have an atheist one. After all, intolerant politics can lead to involuntary conversions but also to people who in their hearts despise Catholicism. Because they cannot practice the religion they believe in, they can easily become "victims" of atheism (1787, 399).

Stattler thought of the church in the terms of societal philosophy, not only in his *True Jerusalem* but also in his other works. This was new to Catholic thought and brought it closer to Enlightenment social contract theory, but it also created the problem that the church became an object of philosophical discussion rather than an object of faith. Certainly, Stattler distanced himself from Wolff's philosophy of society, by pointing to the supernatural end of human beings and the new law humanity had received through Christ, entrusted to the hierarchy to carry out. Yet this view was also problematic because it sees the faithful as not much more than an accessory to the hierarchy rather than as the people of God. Moreover, as the Catholic theologian Johann Adam Möhler (1796–1838) pointed out, Stattler's ecclesiology seemed to have exhibited some unhealthy "deism." As in his (problematic) understanding of deism, according to which God created the world, entrusted it with his laws, and then receded in order to watch it run like clockwork, so in Stattler's works the church seemed to be entrusted with the law of Christ and sacramental powers but be empty of God's continuous action (P. Schäfer 1974, 121–22; Geiselmann 1952, 58).

The "Destroyer" of Immanuel Kant

Most famous, but least creative, is Stattler's treatment of Immanuel Kant's philosophy in three volumes, his *Anti-Kant* (1788). The ex-Jesuit was deeply concerned that "Kant's poison" was penetrating Catholic universities, but he never engaged in a dialogue with his Catholic peers who saw in Kant's philosophy a renewal of apologetics and of a modern Christian philosophy (namely, a philosophy that made scientific determinism, materialism, and atheism impossible to uphold, especially as articulated in *Critique of Pure Reason* [1781/1787]; Hinske 2005). Moreover, it is significant that Stattler refused to read the other two volumes of Kant's critiques, because Kant had never responded to his criticism of the first volume (Sirovatka 2005). Even Stattler's student Johann Michael Sailer (1751–1832), and Sailer's friend Joseph Weber (1753–1831), as well as the ex-Jesuit Sebastian Mutschelle (1749–1800), repudiated Stattler in his harsh rejection of Kant. To this day, it remains uncertain whether Kant knew of Stattler's critique and whether he actually said that the ex-Jesuit was one of his favorite opponents because of his stringency and understanding as some sources claim (Sirovatka 2005, 273). The main point of Stattler's critique was that Kant's moral system needed neither the idea of a superior being in order to acknowledge duty, nor any other motive than the law itself to follow the law. In other words, morality did not presuppose religion. In Stattler's system, speculative knowledge of God must precede moral rules because only speculative certainty gives the moral law its universal force. Without the theoretical knowledge of God a priori, according to Stattler, one could not arrive at a practical science, because moral law was based on the certainty of God's existence as the ultimate judge, who compensates for virtues and punishes for vices (Sirovatka 2005, 275–76).

Stattler—An Enlightened Conservative?

Stattler's intellectual biography exemplifies the eclecticism of Catholic Enlightenment. The former Jesuit was fascinated with the philosophy of Christian Wolff and how it helped to modernize theology, but he rejected the philosophy of Kant as he identified it as an enemy of revelation. In his desire to mold theology with the help of a new philosophy while remaining faithful to the teachings of his church, Stattler can be associated with thinkers like Genovesi or Hooke, and other eclectic synthesizers of Enlightenment thought with ancient faith. In his support for strengthening the office of bishop, his work can be linked with the movement of episcopalism verging, at times, on an appreciation of French Gallican models. Nevertheless, Stattler's hatred of Kant, his insistence on religion as the foundation of society, and his defense of Catholic privileges align with what many scholars have hitherto referred to as Counter-Enlightenment. In what category does Stattler then belong? Was he an Enlightener or an obscurantist Anti-Enlightener? It seems that he resembles such figures as de Maistre inasmuch as Stattler also could be considered something of an "enlightened conservative," an eclectic and at times creative defender of traditional values, society, and religion by means of modern thought. Only such a categorization does justice to the complexities of Stattler's character; attempts to simplify his engagement with modern thought risk descending into mere caricature. It seems that Stattler embodies the multifaceted nature of Catholic Enlightenment—a movement characterized by a mixture of progressivism and conservatism. Yet because he attempted to reformulate old doctrines in more understandable ways, to point out their relevance for modern society while anchoring them in a sophisticated foundation of metaphysics and biblical scholarship, Stattler still found himself in serious conflict with both the Roman Curia and the Enlighteners.

Bibliography

Bruch, Richard. 1997. *Ethik und Naturrecht im deutschen Katholizismus des 18. Jahrhunderts: Von der Tugendethik zur Pflichtethik*. Tübingen: Francke.

Burson, Jeffrey. 2010. *The Rise and Fall of Theological Enlightenment: Jean-Martin de Prades and Ideological Polarization in Eighteenth-Century France*. Notre Dame: University of Notre Dame Press.

Diebolt, Joseph. 1926. *La théologie morale catholique en Allemagne au temps du philosophisme et de la restauration (1750–1850)*. Strasbourg.

Eschweiler, Karl. 2010. *Die katholischen Theologie im Zeitalter des deutschen Idealismus*. Edited by Thomas Marschler. Münster: MV Wissenschaft.

Feuerbach, Paul Anselm. 1829. *Actenmässige Darstellung merkwürdiger Verbrechen*. Vol. 2. Giessen.
Fischer, Norbert, ed. 2005. *Kant und der Katholizismus*. Freiburg: Herder.
Geiselmann, Josef Rupert. 1952. *Von lebendiger Religiosität zum Leben der Kirche: Johann Michael Sailers Verständnis der Kirche geistesgeschichtlich gedeutet*. Stuttgart: Schwabenverlag.
Gómez-Tutor, Juan Ignacio. 2004. *Die wissenschaftliche Methode bei Christian Wolff*. Hildesheim: G. Olms.
Gurr, John Edwin. 1959. *The Principle of Sufficient Reason in Some Scholastic Systems, 1750–1900*. Milwaukee: Marquette University Press.
Healy, James. 1966. *The Just Wage, 1750–1890: A Study of Moralists from Saint Alphonsus to Leo XIII*. The Hague: Martinus Nijhoff.
Heinz, Gerhard. 1984. *Divinam christianae religionis originem probare: Untersuchung zur Entstehung des fundamentaltheologischen Offenbarungstraktates der katholischen Schultheologie*. Mainz: Mathias Grünewald Verlag.
Hinske, Norbert. 2005. "Kant im Auf und Ab der katholischen Kantrezeption: Zu den Anfängen des katholischen Frühkantianismus und seinen philosophischen Impulsen." In *Kant und der Katholizismus*, edited by Norbert Fischer, 189–206. Freiburg: Herder.
Lehner, Ulrich L. 2006. "Einleitung." In *Martin Knutzen—Philosophischer Beweis von der Wahrheit der christlichen Religion (1747)*, edited by Ulrich L. Lehner, i–xlii. Nordhausen: Bautz.
Mendelssohn, Moses. 1983. *Jerusalem, or On Religious Power and Judaism (1783)*. Translated by Allan Arkush. Hanover: Brandeis University Press.
Miedaner, Michael. 1983. *Die Ontologie Benedikt Stattlers*. Frankfurt and New York: P. Lang.
Ruhstorfer, Karlheinz. 2003. "Benedikt Stattler: Theologie als System der Vernunft." In *Theologen des 18. Jahrhunderts*, edited by Peter Walter and Martin H. Jung, 181–203. Darmstadt: Wissenschaftliche Buchgesellschaft.
Schäfer, Christoph. 1992. *Staat, Kirche, Individuum: Studie zur süddeutschen Publizistik über religiöse Toleranz von 1648 bis 1819*. Frankfurt am Main: P. Lang.
Schäfer, Philipp. 1974. *Kirche und Vernunft: Die Kirche in der katholischen Theologie der Aufklärungszeit*. Munich: Max Hueber.
Scholz, Franz. 1957. *Benedikt Stattler und die Grundzüge seiner Sittlichkeitslehre unter besonderer Berücksichtigung der Doktrin von der philosophischen Sünde*. Freiburg: Herder.
———. 1975. "Benedikt Stattler (1728–1797)." In *Katholische Theologen Deutschlands im 19. Jahrhundert*, edited by Heinrich Fries and Georg Schaiger, 1:11–34. Munich: Kösel.

Sirovatka, Jakub. 2005. "Den 'Alleszermalmer' zermalmt? Der Streit um Kant: Joseph Weber, Stattler's 'Anti-Kant' und Bischof Sailer." In *Kant und der Katholizismus,* edited by Norbert Fischer, 263–82. Freiburg: Herder.
Stattler, Benedict. 1769–1772. *Philosophia methodo scientiis propria explanata.* 8 vols. Augsburg. Reprint, Hildesheim: Olms, 2011.
———. 1770. *Demonstratio Evangelica.* Augsburg.
———. 1772. *Ethica Christiana universalis.* Eichstätt.
———. 1775a. *De locis theologicis.* Weissenburg.
———. 1775b. *Demonstratio Catholica.* Augsburg.
———. 1780. *Epistola Paraenetica ad . . . Carolum Fridericum Bahrdt.* Eichstätt.
———. 1781. *Theologia Christiana theoretica.* 6 vols. Eichstätt.
———. 1782–1789. *Ethica Christiana communis.* Augsburg.
———. 1787. *Wahres Jerusalem, oder Über religiöse Macht und Toleranz in jedem und besonders im katholischen Christenthume, bey Anlaß des Mendelsohn'schen Jerusalems und einiger Gegenschriften Nebst einem Nachtrage an Hr. Nikolai in Berlin.* Augsburg.
———. 1788. *Anti-Kant.* 3 vols. Munich.
———. 1789. *Ethica Christiana communis,* pars 3, sectio 3. Augsburg.
———. 1791. *Plan zu der allein möglichen Vereinigung im Glauben der Protestanten mit der katholischen Kirche, und den Gränzen dieser Möglichkeit.* Augsburg.
———. 1792. *Allgemeine katholisch-christliche theoretische Religionslehre aus hinreichenden Gründen der göttlichen Offenbarung und der Philosophie: Hauptsächlich für die Nichttheologen unter den Studirenden in den pfalzbaierischen obersten Schulen, und für alle eine tiefere Religioskenntniß affektirende Laien.* Vol. 2. Munich.
———. 1796. *Authentische Aktenstücke wegen dem zu Rom theils beschriebenen, theils abzuwenden getrachteten Verdammungsurtheil über das Stattlerische Buch: "Demonstratio Catholica."* Frankfurt and Leipzig.
Werner, Karl. 1889. *Geschichte der katholischen Theologie seit dem Trienter Konzil bis zur Gegenwart.* Munich.
Will, Georg. 1778. *Bemerkungen über einige Gegenden des katholischen Deutschlands auf einer kleinen gelehrten Reise.* Nuremberg.
Wolf, Hubert. 2011. "'Ich hoffe, ich werde meinen Prozess bei Gott besser ausfechten, als auf Erden.' Eine Hinführung zu den Möglichkeiten der Grundlagenforschung zum 18. Jahrhundert am Beispiel des Falles Stattler." In *Inquisition und Buchzensur im Zeitalter der Aufklärung,* Römische Inquisition und Indexkongregation 16, edited by Hubert Wolf, 17–42. Paderborn: Schöningh.

8

Beda Mayr (1742–1794)

Ecumenism and Dialogue with Modern Thought

ULRICH L. LEHNER

In the German-speaking lands of the eighteenth century, it was the Benedictines who spearheaded the dissemination of Enlightenment ideas (Lehner 2011). One of the most intriguing figures among these enlightened Benedictines was Beda Mayr (1742–1794), because he was probably the first Catholic theologian to propose publicly an ecumenical theology. Contemporaries praised Mayr as a keen, enlightened, and pious thinker. Among them were such prominent figures as Johann Michael Sailer (1751–1832), the future bishop of Regensburg and groundbreaker for Romanticism in German theology; and Johann Sebastian Drey (1777–1853), the leading figure of the Catholic "Tübingen School."

Beda Mayr was born on 17 January 1742 in Taiting, near Augsburg, to an upper-middle-class family of farmers. His baptismal name was Felix Nolanus. After attending the abbey school at Scheyern and the high school in Augsburg, he studied philosophy in Munich for two years and then mathematics in Freiburg/Breisgau. In 1761, he entered the abbey of the Holy Cross in Donauwörth, where he professed his solemn vows on 29 September 1762 and received the name Beda. After three years of studying theology at the common college for Bavarian Benedictines in Benediktbeuern, he was ordained in 1766. Just a year later, he was appointed to serve as professor of philosophy and theology in Donauwörth, a duty that he fulfilled until 1785. Occasionally he also taught natural sciences and mathematics. From 1772 until 1776, Mayr worked as a pastor in the village of Mündling, where he made friendly contacts with Protestant clergy. It must have been here that he came to realize the scandal of the divided Christian confessions and the need for a reunion of the churches.

Like many others, he saw the major obstacle to such a reunion not in the beliefs about the sacraments, nor even holy orders, but in the papacy and in ecclesiastical infallibility. He was thoroughly acquainted with the writings of German, French, and even English Enlighteners. His zeal to reform Catholicism to make it more attractive to Catholics, and especially to Protestants, motivated him to argue for the vernacular in the Roman Mass as early as 1777 (1777). That same year, Mayr even found time to translate a number of volumes of Condillac's (1714–1780) monumental *Modern History*. One year later, Beda caused an enormous scandal when an essay he had sent to a friend of his, the school reformer and former Benedictine (Abbey of Tegernsee) Heinrich Braun (1732–1792), was published without his knowledge or consent under the title *First Step toward the Future Reunification of the Catholic and Protestant Churches* (*Der erste Schritt zur künftigen Vereinigung der katholischen und der evangelischen Kirche*; 1778a). It was placed on the *Index of Prohibited Books* on 31 July 1783. The uproar over this twenty-two-page pamphlet was so great that a number of theologians started to conspire against Mayr, because they considered the essay to be downright heretical. As a result, episcopal investigators were sent to the monastery of Donauwörth to interrogate Mayr and all members of the community. Only the protection of his abbot, Gallus Hammerl (1776–1793), saved Mayr from punishment. The abbot also resisted pressure from the bishop's office to remove Beda as professor in the monastery. Instead, Abbot Hammerl permitted Mayr to continue his work and granted him vast amounts of money to buy every book he regarded necessary for his work, whether written by the French *philosophes,* an English freethinker, or a saint.

Under Abbot Gallus's leadership, the monastery flourished as a center of liberal arts and a place where the dialogue between Catholicism and modern thought was sincerely attempted. However, one small concession was made to the bishop: in the future, Mayr was required to send his lecture notes and theses to the episcopal chancery for approval. In these notes, however, the censors could never find anything questionable because Mayr cited only such approved authors as Augustin Calmet, O.S.B. (1672–1757), Petrus Gazzaniga, O.P. (1722–1799), and Joseph Bertieri (1734–1804). He never taught his students his new ideas or lectured on the problems he was working on, such as how one could rebuke Gotthold Ephraim Lessing (1729–1781) or Anthony Collins (1676–1729). He reserved his creative work for the academic circles outside the monastery, and for good reasons. First, only peers could judge whether his ideas were worth discussing or not. He believed in public discourse and in the critical feedback of his peers as the ultimate censors, also in regard to his orthodoxy. Second, Beda Mayr was a monk who had seen how Enlightenment ideas had been used to undermine monastic discipline and gradually destroy communities. New ideas about freedom and human rights easily seduced young monks to adopt a libertine lifestyle and to forget about their monastic vows. The many cases in which monks had fled their monasteries out of a newly found love for the Enlightenment were for him justification enough to restrain himself in his lectures for young monks. If a monk happened to discover the value of the Enlightenment on his own, then Mayr would have regarded this as a blessing. Nevertheless, he would not have encouraged him to pursue it, because he knew very well the dynamics of living in a community and how, if old and new ways of thinking clashed, this could easily destroy a monastery. "Either all have to think—on the same level—in an Enlightened manner, which is too much to hope for, or nobody" (1790, 163). Even in his preaching, Mayr seems to have maintained his policy of not advocating his private ideas to the faithful, who might have mistaken his own fancy for the teachings of Catholicism. While he declared in his academic works that there is salvation for members of other religions (1789a, 3–6), he stated in a homily the opposite, namely that "no Jew, no Turk, no Heathen" will enter purgatory and ultimately heaven, because "they go directly after their death to hell." Purgatory was, according to this homily, only filled with Catholic Christians, because heretics were in no need of purgation; after all, he claimed, they go automatically to hell (1778b, 261). This kind of theologizing, which was not in the least directed against revelation, the sacraments, or the church, disappointed radical Enlighteners, who thought that Mayr would take their side. Mayr died on 28 April 1794 in the abbey in Donauwörth.

In Defense of Revelation

Like Benedict Stattler, S.J. (1728–1797), Beda Mayr attempted to implement Enlightenment thought in his theology in order to reform Catholicism from within and to free it from the centuries-old "burdens" of scholasticism. Mayr never questioned Christ's role as the only savior or the legitimacy and authority of the Catholic Church, since he was convinced that Christianity was the source of all *true* Enlightenment and that only the neglect and abuse of doctrines had led to the eclipse of reason. However, he was confident that in the face of the massive critique of religion in the eighteenth century, the doctrines of ecclesiastical and papal infallibility and tradition needed to be redefined with the newest means of logic and Enlightenment insights, lest they wither away altogether. Thus it is not surprising that he had no problem quoting Protestant theologians as authorities on certain problems, among them Lessing, Johann David Michaelis (1717–1791), Johann Salomo Semler (1725–1791), and Johann Gottfried Eichhorn (1752–1827), because of his conviction that Catholic theology needed updating in order to battle atheism, deism, and indifferentism successfully (cf. the subtitle of Mayr's famous trilogy, *Defense of Natural, Christian, and Catholic Religion* [*Vertheidigung der natürlichen, christlichen und katholischen Religion*], "According to the Needs of Our Time"). Among Catholics, the biggest influence on Mayr's opinions seems to have been the ingenious Nicolas-Sylvestre Bergier (1718–1790).

In defense of divine revelation—necessary because of the attacks of deism, which claimed natural religion alone was the one and true religion—Mayr developed criteria for a truly natural and truly revealed religion in the first volume of the trilogy, which followed the scheme of treating first the possibility of revelation, then the necessity of revelation, followed by the facticity of revelation.

When he defined true religion as "the true knowledge of God and the adequate affective responses of the heart" (1789b, 353), it is noteworthy that Mayr did not neglect the affective aspect of religion. Despite the oft-repeated claim that Catholic Enlighteners, like many of their contemporaries, were intellectualists, who neglected the role of feelings, the reader must bear in mind that a great number of them gave feelings a proper place in their theology. Few, however, did so as consciously as Mayr. It may be that the heart as a category was closer to Mayr's theology because of his Jansenist sympathies, and his consequent love for Blaise Pascal (1623–1662). True religion must also further the happiness of humans (very similar to Stattler's thinking), contribute to the good of the state, be intelligible, and be conformed to God's dignity (1787, 356–59). Natural and revealed religion do not differ in their origin but mainly in their mode of acknowledgment: human reason can never find the truths of revelation on its own. Here Mayr adapts a thought from Lessing's *The Education of the Human Race* (1780), in which all revealed truths are disclosed during a long education process as truths of reason, as well as Herder's (1744–1803) idea of a primeval revelation. For Mayr the truths of natural religion are recognized by humans through a primeval revelation (*Uroffenbarung*) of God, and only afterwards interpreted as truths of reason. Lessing—for whom, in reality, revelation vaporizes into reason—is thus catholicized and reconciled with traditional theology (Mayr 1787, 397; Niemann 1983, 271–76).

According to Mayr's reasoning, the most substantial criterion for a divine religion is, however, its assertion by a divine sign, namely a prophecy or a miracle. He introduced the categories of "historical accuracy," "philosophical certainty," and "power of persuasion" for his theological analysis of miracles. While his "historical accuracy" depends upon the credibility of the witness of the miracle, and tries to reject Hume's arguments, "philosophical certainty" refers to the supernatural character of a miracle. In other words, a miracle will always be impossible in the current course of nature, while the power of a miracle must correspond to and affirm the divine mission of the prophet and the truth of his sayings. Even Voltaire's sarcastic comment that a miracle should occur at the Académie francaise so that it could be properly analyzed provoked this comment from Mayr:

> As carefully as Voltaire enumerates the requirements of a trustworthy miracle, he has missed one essential point. By necessity all deists would have to be present at this miracle, otherwise somebody could again question it. Perhaps, the miracle must happen through the hands of a deist for this purpose.... These assumptions [of Voltaire] destroy all historical faith.... If somebody tells me: Caesar was assassinated in the Senate ... I will answer ... his death is not certain if he did not die in the presence of the members of the Académie francaise. (1789a, 214)

Against Hume, Mayr argued that human knowledge of nature was fragmented and that it relied on God for not interrupting its course. He also rejected Hume's notion that common experience could disprove witness accounts. If the latter was true and one based knowledge on historical experience (e.g., that in the past no such miracles occurred), then one would impede new scientific discovery and innovation. After all, Galileo found the moons of Jupiter because he trusted *his* experience and not the experience of generations of astronomers before him. Thus, experience could only prove the possibility of a thing, not its impossibility (1789a, 259, 283–85). In all likelihood, Mayr was also the first Catholic theologian who engaged with Lessing and thus with the great challenge of the unbridgeable gap between history and faith, as stated in Lessing's *On the Proof of the Spirit and of Power* (*Ueber den Beweis der Geistes und der Kraft*; 1777). This axiom denied that one could never test eternal, absolute truths of reason by means of hypothetical, historical truths (e.g., miracles). Mayr, however, lacked the theological categories to address this problem properly. Even if he could not solve the riddle, however, he deserves our respect for trying to guide Catholic theology out of the safety of a scholastic system and on to the stage of modern thought (Niemann 1983, 277–80).

Mayr was one of the few Catholic Germans, perhaps the only one, who had a thorough knowledge of non-Christian religions, including not only Islam but also Persian, Chinese, and Indian religions. This knowledge went back to the earliest days of his studies. By 1764, he had already embraced Bernard Fontenelle's critique of oracles, rejected their demonic origin, and contributed substantially to a dissertation on the topic (Mayr and Pruggberger 1764; Mayr 1789a, 337). He knew Jean Chardin's (1643–1713) travel accounts in the French original and shared admiration for him with such distinguished readers as Montesquieu, Rousseau, Voltaire, and Gibbon. Moreover, he was well acquainted with the works of Abraham Hyacinthe Anquetil-Duperron (1731–1805) and numerous others. He also knew the famous *De tribus imposteribus* well enough to quote from it in his treatment of Islam, along with the works of the English deist Thomas Morgan (d. 1743). He applied the methods of historical criticism he was aware of in his discussion of the historicity of these religions, as well as to the Old Testament and Jewish history (e.g., Mayr 1789a, 496–97). However, instead of presenting a typical demonstration of the truths of each biblical book of the Hebrew Bible in the manner of Pierre-Daniel Huet's (1630–1721) classical *Demonstratio evangelica,* he integrated these proofs into his analysis of the Jewish religion, which he treated side by side with Islam and the Chinese and Indian religions—a comparative approach unusual for theology books at that time. Mayr defended Moses' authorship of the Pentateuch by relying on the works of the Protestant exegete Johann Gottfried Eichhorn.

Mayr's relationship to historical-critical exegesis is remarkable. In his trilogy, which was written in German, and thus intended for a broad dissemination beyond the Catholic academy, whatever he presents about scriptural passages is predominantly drawn from Protestant sources. However, he carefully reviewed, assessed, and excerpted from their works, rejecting everything that would have defeated his apologetic purposes. For example, he rejected Carl Friedrich Bahrdt's (1741–1792) criticism of miracles and Hermann Samuel Reimarus's (1694–1768) charge of forgery—but never before discussing and reviewing them in detail. Despite much sensibility for historical questions, Mayr's understanding of revelation remains on an ahistorical level. For him the teachings of the church today must be identical to the beliefs and teachings of Jesus. The apostles and an eighteenth-century Christian must share the identical truths of faith, at least for the most part (Niemann 1983, 288–90; Lehner 2009).

Like Stattler's apologetic works, Mayr's served as models for the structure of neoscholastic textbooks that were in use in Catholic seminaries until the 1950s. While Stattler positively received the philosophy of Wolff, Mayr adapted all kinds of modern thinkers in his system, as well as critical biblical scholarship, which most neoscholastics rejected. Stattler's books were dry and hard to read, but Mayr's works are written in a witty yet thorough style that makes them readable even today, demonstrating that theology can seriously engage contemporary culture, challenge it, and yet remain accessible (cf. Niemann 1983, 193–297).

The Beginnings of Ecumenical Theology

It was Mayr's ecumenical theology that brought him the most fame. He was probably the first Catholic theologian who wholeheartedly committed to this cause. While a number of Protestant thinkers like Johann Friedrich Wilhelm Jerusalem (1709–1789) or Jakob Heinrich von Gerstenberg (1712–1776) were debating the possibility of a reunion of the churches, Mayr's pamphlet *The First Step toward the Future Reunification of the Catholic and Protestant Churches* (1778) was a first in Catholic theology. It said a decisive farewell to the polemical theology of the past and was a sincere theological reflection, written to a friend and never intended for publication. That Heinrich Braun published Mayr's thoughts without obtaining his permission did not destroy their friendship, but most likely put it to the test. *The First Step* encourages, first and foremost, Catholic theologians and authorities to respect the goodwill of Protestant theologians. It sets out the idea that if academies can solve riddles in science and philosophy, they can also solve the problem of a fragmented Christianity. An "Academy of Reunification," consisting of Protestant and Catholic theologians, could, in Mayr's view, slowly bring about mutual understanding and finally a reunion. For this purpose, the theologians of the academy would have to assemble all doctrines about which they disagreed and then work on possible solutions. The final drafts of the solutions should then be presented to the respective church authorities. As a formal secretary of the academy, the "professor for reunification" would have to admonish the members of the academy to be tolerant, irenic, and constructive. Like the Protestant thinkers who inspired him, Mayr considered ecclesiastical and papal infallibility as the central problem of ecumenism. Therefore, he focused on a critical examination of the concept of infallibility, concerning its legitimacy and extension. He hoped that a compromise on this subject could bring about or at least start the reunification process. He reduced other doctrines on which the churches disagreed, including sacramental confession, confirmation, and purgatory, to the level of academic school disputes (*opiniones*), which must not impede the potential reunification.

Benedikt Werkmeister (1745–1823), one of the most radical Catholic Enlighteners, considered Mayr's *First Step* a groundbreaking event of Enlightenment Catholicism because it was the first public commitment of a Catholic professor to ecumenism. The attempts at reunification by the Benedictines of Fulda (c. 1776–1783), initiated by the reformed theologian Johann Rudolf Anton Piderit (1720–1791), were influenced by Mayr's work, even if their leaders, Peter Böhm, O.S.B. (1747–1822), and Karl von Piesport, O.S.B. (1716–1800), criticized *The First Step* severely (Spehr 2005, 127–245). Böhm—like the Cathedral preacher of Augsburg, Aloys Merz (1727–1792)—considered Mayr's pamphlet to be heterodox. Some of Mayr's critics even spread the rumor of his apostasy; others remarked that even the slightest disagreement with parts of the doctrine on infallibility would lead to doubts about the indefectibility of the church and its doctrine (Lehner 2009). Germany's leading Catholic theologian, the former Jesuit Benedict Stattler, appreciated Mayr's work (Stattler 1780), even if—for his taste—it went too far. Instead, Stattler put forward his own thoughts about a possible reunification. But unlike Mayr, Stattler did not see the magisterial definitions of doctrines as a "burden" for ecumenical dialogue, and he considered the idea of common, "most fundamental" beliefs that Protestants and

Catholics could draw directly from the Bible—in the spirit of Sebastian Castellio or John Locke—to be a poor compromise. Stattler gave a detailed critique of *The First Step* and the ecumenical ideas of the *Defense* in his reunification book (1791, 159–279). However, Mayr's substantial indebtedness to the achievements of Stattler has been overlooked. He was influenced especially by Stattler's Wolffian system of Catholic theology, and an analysis of the third volume of Mayr's *Defense* proves this fact. Nevertheless, Mayr considered Stattler's early reunion proposal (Stattler 1780) to be futile because it did not make any concessions regarding that stumbling block to ecumenism: infallibility (Mayr 1789c, 384).

In the third volume of his *Defense,* Mayr gives a detailed apology for the Catholic faith but also develops basic insights from *The First Step* into a more mature ecumenical theology (1789c). A crucial hermeneutical starting point for Mayr is the difference between traditional scholastic opinions, for example, between Thomistic interpretations of church doctrines and magisterially defined doctrinal truths. Another is his ecumenical methodology: in order to achieve an interdenominational agreement, the Catholic side cannot follow the majority of its own scholastic authorities in a discussion about a doctrine *if* this majority opinion is an impediment to a reunion. Rather, it has to follow the minority opinion as long as it does not compromise on magisterially defined doctrines and is truly beneficial for ecumenism.

The most original idea of the book, however, is his concept of *limited infallibility,* whose first cautious utterances had been already contained in *The First Step*. Mayr does not sacrifice infallibility as such, but wants to show where its limitations lie, and how the Catholic Church could make compromises concerning this doctrine without giving up its *deposit of faith,* in order to enable a reunion with the Protestant churches. The discussion about the concept of infallibility has its background in early modern Catholic ecclesiology, which, as a reaction to the Reformation, was conceived almost entirely as an apologetic enterprise. It was not the doctrine of the church as God's people that was the focal point in standard ecclesiology of the time, but rather the church's hierarchical structure and its magisterium. Infallibility in this instance meant the *infallibilitas in docendo* (infallibility in teaching), which extended to the universal episcopacy alone. Only the worldwide episcopacy was considered by Mayr and the majority of the German theologians as highest and infallible judge in questions of faith and morals. He defined infallibility as follows: "I call *infallibility* the privilege which Christ gave to his church: to teach everything without the danger of falling into error and to teach what is necessary or useful for the faithful to achieve eternal blessedness. This also includes that she cannot teach anything that leads the faithful away from the order of salvation" (1789c, 369). However, if the aim of ecclesiastical infallibility is the certainty of salvation for the faithful, then it cannot extend beyond the *necessary* elements of faith and morals (1790, 210–11). Consequently, the church is not only fallible in the realm of dogmatic facts (*facta dogmatica*), but possibly also in the realm of truths about the faith. Certainly such an error could not be *material,* but only formal; for example, if the church declared an unrevealed doctrine—like purgatory—*revealed,* such a *virtual* and *formal* error would not affect the holy order of salvation, as long as the doctrine in question was useful for the advancement of saving one's soul. If somebody did not believe a doctrine that the church taught was revealed, he certainly would not lose salvation, but a good and helpful means that could have helped him to achieve his final end. Therefore, even an "erroneous" teaching—an incorrect proposition about the revelation status of a doctrine—would not be completely wrong, because the church can never err in teaching something *helpful* for achieving eternal bliss. Interestingly, Mayr saves the infallibility of the church by pointing to the primacy of ethics and praxis:

> The doctrine, which we presuppose, is good and leads us into the order of salvation. In this, the church does not err, since she recommends a certain doctrine as useful. However, whether the doctrine is of *direct divine origin,* the faithful do not need to know necessarily, because the doctrine aims at the improvement of the heart, and such a proposition does not have any necessary influence on doctrines of faith or morals. Therefore, such declarations cannot be part of ecclesiastical infallibility. Consequently, the church does not lose trustworthiness if she

errs in things that are beyond the sphere of infallibility. (1789c, 27; emphasis original)

Mayr thought such a limited version of infallibility would appeal to Protestants, and that Catholic theologians would readily agree with him that his theology did not undermine the authority of the church as an instrument of salvation. He tried to confirm the church's infallibility by introducing the differentiation of direct and indirect revelation. Even if a doctrine is not *directly* revealed through Jesus Christ and the apostles, there remains the possibility of regarding such a doctrine (if the church teaches it) as *indirectly* revealed. However, such an indirect revelation has to possess a biblical foundation, even if its main point is derived from reason. With such a distinction, Mayr distanced himself from the scholastic theologians of his time, who regarded *indirect revelation* as a necessary deduction or consequence from *directly* revealed truths. Nevertheless, doctrines of such an indirect character must not be mistaken for "scholastic opinions," he insisted. When, for example, the Council of Trent declared the seven sacraments as directly instituted by Christ, while Protestants accepted only baptism and Eucharist because of their biblical foundation as sacraments, then Catholicism could regard the latter two as directly revealed, and the other five as indirectly revealed through Christ in the church. This differentiation between direct and indirect revelation led Mayr to an ecumenical conceptualization of a hierarchy of truths, but also to the bizarre conclusion that the church had to remain absolutely silent about the revelatory status of *all* doctrines in order to avoid error (Lehner 2009).

Much more radical is Mayr's ecclesiology. In his theological system, the church cannot be regarded any longer as *mediator of salvation,* but only as a teaching force whose dogmas are helpful but *not* essential or necessary to achieve eternal joy. This reductionism is probably derived from Enlightenment theology, which had lost sight of the sacramental character of the church and regarded her only as a moral teacher. Only if the church was a pedagogue employed by God rather than a sacrament of salvation could the divided Christian brethren accept in good conscience a doctrine as an "ecclesiastical teaching" and not as a "truth of faith." Those who did not want to accept such doctrines as "ecclesiastical teachings" would not commit heresy, but an act of disobedience. In the case of speculative doctrines (for example, transubstantiation of the Eucharist), such disobedience could never be made public, Mayr insisted. After some heavy criticism, Mayr corrected his terminology, since it would allow a Protestant after a reunion to doubt the infallibility of the church: "Since the church herself does not regard speculative teachings as revealed, it must be up to the Protestant to hold them as a necessary part of the faith or not, as long as he is not doubting the truth of the teaching itself" (1790, 250–51). This means that a Protestant could—in Mayr's reunited church—believe that transubstantiation is not a necessary part of the Christian faith as long as he did not doubt the doctrine as such. We can see a twofold change in Mayr's work: a change in the understanding of what the church is and of what it means to be a member of the church. The church is no longer the mediator of Christ's salvation, but a mere pedagogical adviser. With regard to individual members, the consequence is that the church loses the authority to ask for obedience of will and intellect; her teachings are surrendered to individual judgment. Additionally, the faithful are absolved in advance from private disobedience, which harms the unity of the church, since such disobedience is an indispensable part of Mayr's ecclesiology and plan for reunification. All three volumes of Mayr's *Defense* were prohibited by a decree of the Congregation of the Index and placed on the *Index of Prohibited Books* on 17 December 1792. It is noteworthy that the censor of the work was a fellow Benedictine, namely Wolfgang Frölich (1748–1810) (Wolf 2009, 1420–23), who was also responsible for the indictment of the works of Benedict Stattler.

A close study of Mayr's works reveals an updating of Catholic theology that is bold, and yet always done in the context of the church. Even in his ecumenical theology, Mayr insisted that his work consisted of suggestions only and that the final say over his work would be in the hands of the church. He also never questioned the validity of his monastic vows or attempted to leave the cloister. Beda Mayr emerges as a faithful monk, a bold thinker, and a moderate Catholic Enlightener.

Bibliography

Bantle, Franz Xaver. 1976. *Unfehlbarkeit der Kirche in Aufklärung und Romantik*. Freiburg and Basel: Herder.

Bellinger, Dom Aidan. 1997. "Superstitious Enemies of the Flesh? The Variety of Benedictine Responses to the Enlightenment." In *Religious Change in Europe, 1650–1914*, edited by Aidan Bellinger et al., 149–60. Oxford: Oxford University Press.

Lehner, Ulrich L. 2009. "Ecumenism and Enlightenment Catholicism." In *Vertheidigung der katholischen Religion (1789)*, edited by Ulrich L. Lehner, ix–lxxxix. Leiden and Boston: Brill.

———. 2011. *Enlightened Monks: The German Benedictines, 1740–1803*. Oxford: Oxford University Press.

———. 2012. "The Ghosts of Westphalia: Fictions and Ideals of Ecclesial Unity in Enlightenment Germany." In *A Man of the Church. The Work and Witness of Ralph del Colle*, edited by Michel R. Barnes, 283–301. Eugene, OR: Wipf and Stock.

Mayr, Beda. 1777. *Prüfung der bejahenden Gründe, welche die Gottesgelehrten anführen, über die Frage, soll man sich in der abendländischen Kirche bey dem Gottesdienst der lateinischen Sprache bedienen*. Frankfurt and Leipzig.

———. 1778a. *Der erste Schritt zur künftigen Vereinigung der katholischen und der evangelischen Kirche*. N.p.

———. 1778b. *Festpredigten und Reden von dem guten Tode für das Landvolk*. Vol. 2. Augsburg.

———. 1787. *Vertheidigung der natürlichen, christlichen und katholischen Religion*. Vol. 1. Augsburg.

———. 1789a. *Vertheidigung der natürlichen, christlichen und katholischen Religion*. Vol. 2/1. Augsburg.

———. 1789b. *Vertheidigung der natürlichen, christlichen und katholischen Religion*. Vol. 2/2. Augsburg.

———. 1789c. *Vertheidigung der natürlichen, christlichen und katholischen Religion*. Vol. 3. Augsburg.

———. 1790. *Apologie seiner Vertheidigung der katholischen Religion*. Augsburg.

Mayr, Beda, and Marian Pruggberger. 1764. *Dissertatio de profanis paganorum oraculis*. Tegernsee.

Niemann, Franz Josef. 1983. *Jesus als Glaubensgrund in der Fundamentaltheologie der Neuzeit: Zur Genealogie eines Traktats*. Innsbruck: Tyrolia.

Rauwolf, Gerhard J. 1999. "P. Beda Mayr OSB (1742–1794): Versuch einer ökumenischen Annäherung." *Jahrbuch des Vereins für Augsburger Bistumsgeschichte* 33:317–53.

Schäfer, Philipp. 1999. "Beda Mayr—Ein Theologe der Aufklärungszeit." In *Aufsätze zur Aufklärung,* 69–80. Passau: Passauer Universitätsverlag.

Spehr, Christopher. 2005. *Aufklärung und Ökumene: Reunionsversuche zwischen Katholiken und Protestanten im deutschsprachigen Raum des späteren 18. Jahrhunderts.* Tübingen: Mohr Siebeck.

Stattler, Benedict. 1780. "Anacaephaleosis ad DD. Protestantes in Germania et Propositio Conditionum sub quibus solis Unio Religionis Exoptata possibilis est." In *Theologia Christiana theoretica,* vol. 6, *De sacramentis,* i–xxx. Eichstätt.

———. 1791. *Plan zu der alleinmöglichen Vereinigung im Glauben der Protestanten mit der katholischen Kirche und den Grenzen der Möglichkeiten.* Munich.

Wolf, Hubert, ed. 2009. *Systematisches Repertorium zur Buchzensur, 1701–1813: Indexkongregation.* Paderborn: Schöningh.

PART 4
Catholicism, Enlightenment, and Habsburg Europe

9

Franz Stephan Rautenstrauch (1734–1785)

Church Reform for the Sake of the State

THOMAS WALLNIG

Within the master narratives of the "Catholic Enlightenment" as well as within the relevant handbooks, Franz Stephan Rautenstrauch (1734–1785), abbot of Břevnov-Broumov, is usually referred to as the powerful Josephist reformer of the theological university curricula in the Habsburg state, and as the initiator of "general seminaries" for the religious education of all of the secular and regular clergy (Beales 1987–2009; Hersche 1977; Lehner and Printy 2010; Vocelka 2001). "German" Reform Catholicism of the late twentieth century has rediscovered Rautenstrauch as the founder of pastoral theology as an academic discipline (Klostermann and Müller 1979; Zulehner 1989–1990).

Abbot Rautenstrauch represents the exception, and alleged contradiction, of a monk propagating and enacting Josephist church policies; he is also the rare case of a monastic scholar with the necessary means at his disposal to realize his pedagogical visions. He can, without much reservation, be collocated within the context of the Catholic *"Aufklärung,"* as he himself used the term affirmatively. Yet his ideas alone would appear less original and remarkable were they to be viewed apart from their institutional context and judged according to their actual impact on state and society. Therefore, the following pages will focus on the complex relationship between these factors. Hence, what emerges is the complex portrait of a prelate becoming a state official, thereby transforming a monastic concern into a Jansenist one, a Tridentine inspiration into a Josephist effort, and, accordingly, an intellectual agenda into a bureaucratic one.

Rautenstrauch's Abbey: Břevnov-Broumov

Rautenstrauch was a monk, and later abbot, of the most powerful Benedictine monastery in Bohemia, Břevnov-Broumov. This abbey, situated near (today within the limits of) the city of Prague, was founded in 993 by St. Adalbert, in the context of the christianization of Bohemia (Hejdová, Preiss, and Urešová 1993). The Hussites had destroyed the abbey, and the religious community had fled to the northeastern Bohemian village of Broumov. In the decades following the Thirty Years' War, Břevnov was rebuilt and took an active part in the massive efforts to re-Catholicize Bohemia after the fervid Utraquist episode of the late sixteenth and early seventeenth century. Indeed, the abbot of Broumov played an important role in the prehistory of the Defenestration of Prague in 1618.

Franz Stephan Rautenstrauch entered the monastery in 1751 under Abbot Benno Löbl (abbot 1738–1752), who had inherited from his predecessor Othmar Zinke (abbot 1700–1738) two main political concerns. First, the abbey incorporated four other communities and claimed total spiritual supremacy over the other Benedictine institutes in Bohemia, Moravia, and Silesia. In the past, this had caused several conflicts, both within the larger Břevnovian community and outside it, when the archbishop of Prague saw his visitation rights diminished. These conflicts were carried out by various legal means on various institutional levels, from Vienna to Rome (Menzel 1999).

The second concern was a pedagogical one and aimed at the betterment of monastic education and discipline, for example, by the strengthening of ties with educational institutions like the Benedictine university of Salzburg. At the beginning of the 1750s, Abbot Löbl responded to Count Joseph Philipp Kinsky's (1700–1749) initiative for the creation of a Benedictine academy for young noblemen in Prague. There had already been various efforts in this direction in the southern parts of the empire (Hammermayer 1976), and Löbl could build upon the networks already established by Baron Josef Petrasch's (1714–1772) "Society of the Unknown" (Societas incognitorum) in Olomouc. Löbl invited some of the leading Benedictine scholars to Břevnov, and although the plans for an academy in Prague failed, the presence of Anselm Desing, O.S.B. (1699–1772), of Ensdorf Abbey; Oliver Legipont, O.S.B. (1698–1758), of St. Martin's Abbey, Cologne; Ulrich Weiß, O.S.B. (1713–1763), of Irsee Abbey; and Magnoald Ziegelbauer, O.S.B. (1688–1750), of Zwiefalten Abbey, contributed to an open intellectual climate in the abbey during the years of young Rautenstrauch's formation and first teaching experiences.

Desing, Legipont, and Ziegelbauer were historians, and the last was charged with writing the abbey's history. As successors to such scholars as Bernhard Pez, O.S.B. (1683–1735), of Melk Abbey, they propagated (and also practiced) two of the most "innovative" approaches to monastic scholarship: historical criticism as the critical assessment of historical facts and sources, and positive theology, which designates the superiority of alleged "primordial"/patristic spirituality over scholastic speculation. In this context, the French congregation of St. Maur should be viewed less as a model to be imitated to the letter, and rather as a generally accepted frame of reference for the justification of Benedictine scholarship (Wallnig 2010; Wallnig 2012). Weiß, finally, was among the first generation of Benedictine teachers who openly criticized Scholasticism and Thomism. Instead, he incorporated the philosophy of Christian Wolff (1679–1754) into his teachings. In 1751, Rautenstrauch's confrere Bonaventura Piter finally published a prayer book with historical notes, entitled *Benedictine Piety* (*Pietas Benedictina*), in which he adopted the Muratorian approach of a devotion based on historical criticism.

All these elements point to a heterogeneous intellectual climate in Břevnov-Broumov around the middle of the century. Additionally, it is important to mention the vivid contemporary activity in art and architecture. Rautenstrauch, though, witnessed this climate from the perspective of a monastic novice and went through a quite traditional schooling before going on to create his very own synthesis of the mentioned approaches.

Rautenstrauch's Life and Works

Franz Stephan (baptism name Johann Franz) Rautenstrauch was born in 1734 in the village of Polevsko (Blottendorf) near Česká Lípa, which was a German-speaking area of northern Bohemia. His father ran a glass-production business, which three of his brothers took over. Three other brothers became clergymen (for his biography, see Menzel 1969).

In 1751, Rautenstrauch entered the abbey and studied the traditional philosophy courses, along with mathematics, physics, and astronomy. These were followed by a Suárez-oriented theology course and canon law courses based on the late seventeenth-century manual by the Melk Benedictine Ludwig Engel (d. 1674). From 1756 to 1761, Rautenstrauch studied at the University of Prague, first at the faculty of theology (in 1758 he was ordained), then at the faculty of law. Here he had his first encounters with "established" reformers, such as the director of the legal faculty, Baron Franz Karl Kressel von Qualtenberg, and the Protestant moral philosopher Karl Heinrich Seibt (1735–1806). Through his courses with Franz Lothar von Schrodt (1727–1777), Rautenstrauch also became acquainted with Hugo Grotius's (1583–1645) and Samuel Pufendorf's (1632–1694) concepts of natural law, as well as with Paul Joseph von Riegger's (1705–1775) idea of Erastian church legislation (*Staatskirchenrecht*).

In 1773, Rautenstrauch was elected abbot of Břevnov-Broumov. His treatises on canon law (e.g., Rautenstrauch 1769a; Rautenstrauch 1769b/1772; for a comprehensive catalog of his published and unpublished works, see Menzel 1969, 11–13), published in the context of his teaching at the abbey school since the late 1760s, had provided him a good reputation at the Viennese court. This led, in 1773, to his appointment as a director of the faculty of theology at the University of Prague and, in 1774, to his appointment in Vienna.

Such "top-down" appointments of high university officials were part of the ongoing university reforms in the Habsburg lands. In this vein, the state managed to deprive the traditional lobbies—in this case the Jesuits, the bishops, and even the universities themselves—of their inherent rights. Now changed from an erudite monk into a university "functionary," Rautenstrauch had become a state official who was supposed to achieve, within the relevant structures, acceptance of Maria Theresa's and Joseph's reform agenda.

In his position as a faculty director in Prague, Rautenstrauch also became a member of the Bohemian Commission for Studies and Censorship (*Studien- und Zensurkommision*). As a faculty director in Vienna, he was also on the Court Commission for Studies (*Studienhofkommission*), responsible for the educational agenda throughout the Habsburg lands.

It was in this constellation that Rautenstrauch was charged with a thorough revision of the theological curricula (Rautenstrauch 1776a–b; Rautenstrauch 1778a–c), a reform that he put into practice from 1774 onwards. Hence, it was simply the next consequent step when Rautenstrauch was appointed "Proper Court Counselor" (*Wirklicher Hofrat*) in 1782 by Joseph II and was charged with an educational reform for the entire clergy of the Habsburg lands, both secular and regular. For this purpose Rautenstrauch designed general seminaries (*"Generalseminare"*; see Rautenstrauch 1782a/1784), twelve of which were established by the emperor in 1783 as a substitute for the recently abolished ecclesiastical schools. In these general seminaries, the main "progressive" theological authors of the time, both Catholic and Protestant, were taught, and for the sake of successful pastoral activity, the respective vernaculars became an important part of the curriculum.

Although these general seminaries were abolished in 1790 after Joseph's death, Rautenstrauch's theological curriculum remained valid until 1857, at which time it seemed more influence was granted to the state than the neoabsolutist concordat of 1855 would tolerate. The abbot himself witnessed neither the abolition of the seminaries nor the long-standing influence of his own curriculum: he died in Eger, Hungary, on a visitation journey in 1785. His agenda was left to a younger generation of "Josephist" theologians, and his "Catholic Enlightenment, Bohemian style" (Sorkin 2011), would soon start to collide with, and later be overcome by, the "Czech National Awakening" (David 2010).

"House Interests" and Jansenism: Rautenstrauch and Canon Law

Ulrich Lehner states that "it was law that fascinated Rautenstrauch most, and since it was infused with Enlightenment thought, the young monk's mind integrated enlightened natural law and canon law theory into his already existing mindset of Maurist historical-critical awareness and Muratorian piety" (Lehner 2011, 159). One might add that Rautenstrauch's interest in law—and that of his abbot consenting to his studies—was also motivated by Břevnov's above-outlined need to defend its supremacy over the rest of the Bohemian Benedictines, and especially to confront the interests of the archbishop of Prague.

A critical reevaluation of young Rautenstrauch's approach to canon law has yet to be attempted. As recently as 2011, some of his papers from the 1750s and 1760s (lecture transcripts, excerpts, and correspondence), last used by Beda Menzel in the 1930s, were confirmed to have reappeared in the archives of the now reestablished abbey of Broumov. At least one of Rautenstrauch's motivations can be identified: dissatisfaction with the existing canon law handbook written by Ludwig Engel, used in the context of the Benedictine university of Salzburg (outside the Habsburg lands and thus without respect to the Habsburgs' interest in a state education process). That work was mainly conceived for "extern" monks responsible for the monastery's "incorporated" parishes. In his own canon law courses, Rautenstrauch initially did not contradict Engel, but commented on him. The slow switch from commenting on existing authors to substituting older textbooks with original new ones was an important development for Catholic scholarship; Rautenstrauch is a good example for this paradigm shift.

Rautenstrauch, though, was enough a historian of theology to remain aware of the necessity of integrating tradition. Thus, his approach to canon law was similar to his approach to theology: it was a historical approach. By assuming the existence of a "spirit" of a certain period, he managed to explain (rather than to judge), for example, the Pseudo-Isidorian Decretals, admitting their spuriousness without doubting their validity. By admitting a factor of human development in history, he could criticize ecclesiastical policies of past centuries and explain them at the same time. Thus it is evident that "the popes, who could scarcely reject them [the Pseudo-Isidorian Decretals], would insist on their authority, and the bishops themselves would refer to them as to genuine and precious monuments of antiquity, embracing them especially at those occasions where they wanted to abscond from the jurisdiction of the metropolitans" (1769b/1772, 27; Wallnig 2012).

On other topics, Rautenstrauch was even less constrained and more explicit. The titles of his early treatises refer to both the "German practice" (*"usibus Germaniae"*; 1769b/1772) and the "hereditary lands of the august empress Maria Theresa" (*"Terras haereditarias augustissimae imperatricis Mariae Theresiae"*; 1776a). In this manner, he explicitly evoked a Jansenist frame of reference. His defense of the imperial decree imposing the elevation of age for monastery novices, first published in the year of his abbatial election (1773/1775), combined Rautenstrauch's will for monastic reform with his desire to strengthen the state's impact on monastic affairs. The same holds true for his ideas on matrimonial legislation, which reserved the contractual nature of marriage to the sphere of the state (Lehner 2011, 161).

It is no surprise that the ecclesiastical authorities resisted Rautenstrauch's canon law treatises. Above all the archbishop of Prague, Peter Count Přichovsky, in 1769–1770 tried to get Rautenstrauch's writings censored by the Court Commission for Studies. It was due to the failure of this intrigue—thanks to the intervention of Seibt—that the Viennese court first became aware of Rautenstrauch's activities and started to use him as a spearhead for educational reform. About one decade later, Rautenstrauch would be offered an occasion to return the favor to Seibt: when the same group of traditionalists in Prague tried to bar the Protestant from the university, Rautenstrauch intervened in a private audience with Maria Theresa (on the Seibt controversy, see Winter 1943; Lorman 2011).

With all due consideration for the concept of paradigmatic change in the history of ideas—be it a "change of paradigm" or a processual transformation—one should bear in mind that "ideas" always change along with their respective power constellations, and that they are used as symbolic denominations and group identities by well-defined lobbies that fight for supremacy. It is not only in the light of intellectual progress, but also from this perspective of social struggle, that Rautenstrauch's reforms should be seen.

Educational Reform and Josephism: Rautenstrauch as a Theologian

In 1773 and 1774, Rautenstrauch was appointed director of the theological faculties of the universities in Prague and Vienna, thereby becoming a member of the respective court commissions.

This situation was a unique one in centuries, since the recent abolition of the Jesuit order had created a power void in higher education that could now be filled by the institutions of the emerging dynastic state. Moreover, a large part of the contemporary development in Benedictine scholarship itself was the result of efforts to redefine monastic learning: first in the sense of positive theology, later also in the sense of modern philosophy, natural philosophy, and natural law. Finally, the university system was in a process of reform that the state itself had initiated and supported.

Therefore, it was an opportune moment to implement a thoroughly new theological curriculum with newly shaped and even newly created academic disciplines, such as pastoral theology. This subject was particularly important for Rautenstrauch, who—in agreement with Jean Opstraet (1651–1720), and with explicit reference to

Protestant models—regarded the "good shepherd" (*Pastor bonus*) as the fulfillment of enlightened priesthood, and thus as the primary goal of ecclesiastical formation (Müller 1969; Klostermann and Müller 1979). Beyond that, Rautenstrauch advocated historical-theological scholarship, positive theology, and biblical studies, and reduced the weight of speculative theology. In a draft for his reform, he wrote:

> From this main concept of dogmatic theology we see that it is a disreputable abuse to label and institute dogmatic theology "according to the mind [*ad mentem*] of Saint Augustine," "of Saint Thomas," or "of Duns Scotus." Dogmatic theology is the systematic connection of the doctrines of faith; thus, it must be taught "according to the mind of our Lord Jesus Christ"; which means that the doctrines of Jesus Christ must be presented in a systematic way. The explanations of these doctrines, that one may choose from Saint Thomas or Saint Augustine, are minor matters that should neither serve as titles, nor as core objects of theology, which, alas, has hitherto been the practice: dogmatic theses have been treated in a brief and superficial way, whereas much paper has been dedicated to scholastic questions and sentences in order to distinguish one theological sect [!] from the other, for example the Augustinian from the Thomistic sect, and that from the Scotistic one; and there has been much more interest in gaining followers for one's own sect than in forming real theologians! (Müller 1969, 153–54)

Yet Rautenstrauch did not turn theology upside down. He never abandoned the grounds of divine revelation, and accepted natural law only within the limits of the human sphere—not beyond, as did many of his fellow Benedictine scholars (see Mádl, Schlecht, and Vondráčková 2006, on an eighteenth-century Břevnov painting in which the burning of natural law textbooks is depicted). To gain a better idea of Rautenstrauch's position, it is helpful to examine his concept of moral theology as a discipline between the "static" pole of dogmatic theology and the "dynamic" pole of pastoral theology. (The following quotations are taken from a volume of Rautenstrauch's manuscript drafts entitled *Literary Notes* [*Animadversiones litterariae*], kept at the National Archives in Prague, Benedictines of Břevnov, book 92; as with all other quotations in this text, these have been translated by the author).

For Rautenstrauch, moral theology is defined by the insufficiency of moral philosophy. While the latter discusses the "pure state of human nature, the fallen and the redeemed state (or state of grace), free will, sin, and the resulting deficiency of man," the former is an "explanation of what every human being must do according to the law of God's word; it therefore is a closer and practical explanation of the general duties of a Christian." The law of the Gospels is to be understood by its spirit, by the "idea of Christian life," not by its letter. Books on moral theology should be derived "not from rivulets, most of them foul-smelling, but from the pure springs of the Bible and the Fathers." Thus, like all of the modern ethicists, Rautenstrauch bases his moral theology on the concept of a Christian duty that has to be deduced from the "facts and acts" of the biblical persons such as Saint Paul and King David.

In Rautenstrauch, one finds little consideration of the philosophical foundation of moral philosophy; he was more interested in the actual application of moral principles. Morality, the "idea of Christian life," has to involve the whole human being, and while for ethical theory Rautenstrauch recommends Protestant authors such as Johann Lorenz Mosheim, he criticizes Lutheran hymns. "They are too dry, drab, and so on—a dry morality does not serve the true betterment of the heart; it brings Christianity to the head, but not to the heart, and causes at best the morality of external actions toward other humans, not toward God."

Where Rautenstrauch does reflect on the influence of philosophy on theology, he stresses their close connection, with visibly more sympathy for the latter:

> This influence [of philosophy on theology] will always remain important, also among the Protestants, who take the Bible as the only foundation of cognition, definition, and judgment of all Christian doctrines. The Bible does deliver doctrines, but

in popular and often figurative terms, and now philosophy takes the liberty (a) of translating those terms into its language, or defining how they are to be exactly and properly understood. Furthermore, the Bible, as everyone knows, does not always present its precepts in a general way, or in connection to each other; from that, dogmatizing philosophy (b) creates general sentences, puts them in relation to each other, and for this purpose, often permits itself by means of hypotheses to fill in gaps or to resolve apparent contradictions. Then it interweaves what it has offered to theology with the relevant testimony of the Bible, which is often in comparison quite limited, in a way that leaves it very difficult to separate one from the other and to determine exactly what each of the two has contributed.

Rautenstrauch continues by stressing the "particular influence of Wolffian philosophy," which "could become a conciliator between her respective followers within the Lutheran and the Calvinist church, and tear down the fatal wall of the controversial doctrines on predestination and on the Eucharist."

In a draft entitled *Idea of Moral Theology* (*Idea theologiae moralis*), Rautenstrauch clearly defines the theological disciplines in their relation to moral theology. The latter has two main subjects, Christian ethics and Christian jurisprudence, whose limits are determined by the difference between the virtues and counsel of the Bible on the one hand and actual biblical laws on the other. "As in moral theology, and even in natural law, there are perfect and imperfect duties; only here, the arguments must be deduced less from authorities than from the Bible and the holy canons. The preconceived notions of what used to be called morals, which actually were casuistic theology, are to be abandoned entirely; nor are those doctrines to be involved that properly belong to dogmatic theology or to canon law. But above all, moral theology in the strict sense has to be separated from anything that belongs to the practice, that is the application, of moral precepts, which belongs to pastoral theology, as does the whole of casuistic theology and the doctrine of the administration and reception of the sacraments." Rautenstrauch recommends chapter ten of Augustin Zippe's

(1747–1816) *Introduction to the Ethics of Reason and Revelation* (*Anleitung in die Sittenlehre der Vernunft und Offenbarung*), dealing with the motives of virtue, to conclude a course in moral theology, although Rautenstrauch is skeptical about Zippe's concept of "moral sense" ("*moralisches Gefühl*"; cf. Lorman 2011): "Moral sense is not to be put among the principles of moral philosophy, as it seems to have too much affinity with the enthusiastic feeling of inspiration, and seems, when it is made the guideline of [human] action, to have consequences as confused as they are disadvantageous. Clear cognition has infinite preference, because it has all necessary reliability and shows at any point how far to go and where to step back."

What emerges from all these observations on Rautenstrauch's concept of theology is the image of an eclectic Benedictine scholar from Bohemia, who transformed the traditional agenda of educational reform, anti-Jesuitism, and struggle against the secular clergy into a bureaucratic action both "Jansenist" and "Josephist." In the increasingly powerful hands of Abbot Rautenstrauch (supported by the state authorities), monastic reform plans, learned ecumenism—the theological ground of pastoral theology—and the historical-critical foundation of piety became state law.

Rautenstrauch "Offstage": The Diaries

This image, though, only represents a limited part of Rautenstrauch's wide range of interests. About these we can learn from his two manuscript diaries, consisting of a "private" one and a "scholarly" one kept from 1776 onwards. Although the distinction between the two is not very clear, because both reflect Rautenstrauch's frequent reading of mainly Protestant review journals, the *Diarium privatum* provides particular insight into the abbot's close relationship with Maria Theresa and Joseph II. The frequent literal accounts of the audiences reveal both a certain atmosphere of confidence and, at the same time, Rautenstrauch's character, well aware of his impact on the heads of the empire, a fact that also Beda Menzel has noted in ambiguous terms.

Rautenstrauch's exhaustive reception of Protestant review journals stands in a tradition of contact between southern German clergymen, mostly Benedictines, and middle German scholars at the beginning of the century. While in the 1720s and 1730s the two groups found common ground in the investigation of their allegedly common "German antiquity," a generation later they engaged together in the above-mentioned academy plans that, among others, involved Johann Christoph Gottsched (1700–1766); finally, in Rautenstrauch's generation, and as a consequence of the reception of Christian Wolff's writings, Catholic scholars also started to consider the theological production of the Protestants.

Unlike similar diaries kept by other scholars, Rautenstrauch's diaries do not merely contain notes on the content of a reviewed book, but mostly his own comments, and sometimes even exclusively these. In some cases, Rautenstrauch copied such remarks, sometimes even excerpts from books he does not seem to have read, into his administrative submissions and blueprints. In this vein, again, scholarly notes were transformed into precepts of their own value.

Rautenstrauch's diaries do not show him as a theologian, and even less as a philosopher. Rather, they reveal him to be an "enlightened monarch" of his abbey, interested in any issue that could improve its state and the condition of its subjects, whether that be weather observations, matters of modern agriculture and economy, technical issues, medical innovations, or even classical authors or popular German songs. The diaries reveal the abbot of one of the monarchy's most powerful monasteries trying to keep up with the scientific state of the art in any discipline that might affect his daily business.

Rautenstrauch's agenda was clearly organizational and pedagogical. Theology must be seen as the basis for what he was really interested in: the education of the Christian individual. His philosophical enthusiasm was limited, and while natural law may have found its place within moral philosophy, it was firmly required not to contradict revelation where the biblical basis of moral theology was concerned. In spite of what Josef Hanzal has claimed (1995), Rautenstrauch had no sympathy for Voltaire (1694–1778), whose death and un-Christian burial mainly interested him in terms of canon law;

likewise, he was unsympathetic toward the Prussian king, Frederick II, who during the Seven Years' War had been in direct—unpleasant—contact with Rautenstrauch's abbey.

Scarcely a democrat, Rautenstrauch laughed at the "republic of geese where, if one starts honking, everyone honks," and at the "incorrigible nation of crabs, that angrily pinch with their claws if one tries to teach them anything." Although (or maybe because) he was interested in, and in favor of, Christian tolerance, one will find clear anti-Semitic positions when he talks about the "deeply rooted malice of the Jews, their arrogance, and the resulting proclivity to idleness and dislike of any kind of work, and their habit of always wandering about and cheating on other people."

Afterword: "Monastic Enlightenment"?

One may conclude, once again, that Rautenstrauch transformed the erudite monastic culture of his time into a theological reform program that was aimed at the betterment of society. Taken one step further, this meant that scholarship and learning had to become useful for everyone. In his diary, Rautenstrauch writes: "The academic reform at Münster is failing, in that the whole issue only aims at the formation of future scholars. It is from below that all perfection must start, and then gradually grow upwards. The Enlightenment [*Aufklärung*] must go through all classes [*Stände*], and for that purpose the country schools are the *conditio sine qua non*." At another point, Rautenstrauch notes: "The biggest advantage the sciences of our time have in comparison with the older ones may consist in their popularity, in their condescension to everyday common sense, to common life. It is according to this principle that I have established the reform of the schools of theology; [continuing in Latin] may God bring it to a good conclusion." And thus: "All monasteries without exception shall be used for education and study."

Rautenstrauch frequently quotes Jean Mabillon's (1632–1707) *Treatise on monastic studies* (*Traité des études monastiques*) as an example of monastic scholarship and erudition, while completely ignoring the deeply reflective and hortative, ascetic and spiritual intent with which it was written. Rautenstrauch and the other "enlightened monks" of his time give little or no attention to the distinguishing *monastic* aspects of monastic life—such as monastic vows (if one leaves apart the Josephist concern for raising the age of profession), the group structure of a monastery, or the spiritual aspects of monastic discipline—to name only a few examples.

This will not surprise us if we are aware of the broad support that the Josephist reforms had enjoyed, especially among the old orders. What is remarkable, though, is that historical criticism and "German Maurism," the *"Akademiebewegung,"* the combats against fictitious saints and devotional exaggerations, the propagation of Muratorian and Jansenist ideas, and all the other core topics of the monastic *culture* of the first half of the century were now interpreted as mere expressions of monastic *scholarship,* leaving aside the fundamental religious concern that previously had been the driving force behind each of these issues.

So, by the time monasticism had become truly enlightened, had it ceased to be truly monastic?

Bibliography

Beales, Derek Edward Dawson. 1987–2009. *Joseph II*. Vol. 1, *In the Shadow of Maria Theresa: 1741–1780*. Vol. 2, *Against the World: 1780–1790*. Cambridge: Cambridge University Press.

David, Zdenek V. 2010. *Realism, Tolerance, and Liberalism in the Czech National Awakening: Legacies of the Bohemian Reformation*. Washington, DC: Woodrow Wilson Center Press.

Hammermayer, Ludwig. 1976. "Die Forschungszentren der deutschen Benediktiner und ihre Vorhaben." In *Historische Forschung im 18. Jahrhundert: Organisation, Zielsetzung, Ergebnisse; 12. Deutsch-Französisches Historikerkolloquium des Deutschen Historischen Instituts Paris,* edited by Karl Hammer and Jürgen Voss, 122–91. Bonn: Röhrscheid.

Hanzal, Josef. 1995. "F. Š. Rautenstrauch ve světle svých deníků." *Český Časopis Historický* 93 (1): 86–98.

Hejdová, Dagmar, Pavel Preiss, and Libuše Urešová, eds. 1993. *Tausend Jahre Benediktiner-Kloster in Břevnov: Benediktinerabtei der Hl. Margarethe in Prag-Břevnov; Ausstellung zu den Tausend-Jahr-Feiern der Gründung des Klosters*. Prague: Benediktinský Klášter.

Hersche, Peter. 1977. *Der Spätjansenismus in Österreich.* Vienna: Verlag der Österreichischen Akademie der Wissenschaften.
Klostermann, Ferdinand, and Josef Müller, eds. 1979. *Pastoraltheologie—Ein entscheidender Teil der Josephinischen Studienreform: Ein Beitrag zur Geschichte der praktischen Theologie.* Vienna: Herder.
Lehner, Ulrich L. 2011. *Enlightened Monks: The German Benedictines, 1740–1803.* Oxford: Oxford University Press.
Lehner, Ulrich L., and Michael Printy, eds. 2010. *A Companion to the Catholic Enlightenment in Europe.* Leiden and Boston: Brill.
Lorman, Jaroslav. 2011. "The Concept of Moral Theology of Augustin Zippe, a Moral Theologian at the Turn of the Epoch." In *The Enlightenment in Bohemia: Religion, Morality and Multiculturalism,* edited by Ivo Cerman, Rita Krueger, and Susan Reynolds, 209–30. Oxford: Voltaire Foundation.
Mádl, Martin, Anke Schlecht, and Marcela Vondráčková, eds. 2006. *Detracta larva juris naturae: Studien zu einer Skizze Wenzel Lorenz Reiners und zur Dekoration der Klosterbibliothek in Břevnov.* Prague: Artefactum.
Menzel, Beda Franz. 1969. *Abt Franz Stephan Rautenstrauch von Břevnov-Braunau: Herkunft, Umwelt und Wirkungskreis.* Königstein: Königsteiner Instituts für Kirchen- und Geistesgeschichte der Sudetenländer.
———. 1999. "Die böhmische Benediktinerkongregation." In *Germania Benedictina,* vol. 1, *Die Reformverbände und Kongregationen der Benediktiner im deutschen Sprachraum,* edited by Ulrich Faust and Franz Quarthal, 591–619. St. Ottilien: Eos.
Müller, Josef. 1969. *Der pastoraltheologisch-didaktische Ansatz in Franz Stephan Rautenstrauchs "Entwurf zur Einrichtung der theologischen Schulen."* Vienna: Herder.
Muschard, Paul. 1929. "Das Kirchenrecht bei den deutschen Benediktinern und Zisterziensern des 18. Jahrhunderts." *Studien und Mitteilungen zur Geschichte des Benediktiner-Ordens und seiner Zweige* 47:225–315, 477–596.
Rautenstrauch, Franz Stephan. 1769a. *Prolegomena in ius ecclesiasticum.* Prague.
———. 1769b. *Institutiones iuris ecclesiastici cum publici tum privati usibus Germaniae accommodatae.* Prague. 2nd ed., 1772.
———. 1773. *De iure principis praefigendi maturiorem professioni monasticae solemni aetatem diatriba.* Prague. 2nd ed., 1775.
———. 1776a. *Anleitung und Grundriß zur systematischen dogmatischen Theologie.* Vienna. 2nd ed., 1776.
———. 1776b. *Synopsis iuris ecclesiastici publici et privati, quod per terras haereditarias augustissimae imperatricis Mariae Theresiae obtinet.* Vienna.
———. 1778a. *Institutum facultatis theologiae Vindobonensis.* Vienna.

———. 1778b. *Tabellarischer Grundriß der in deutscher Sprache vorzutragenden Pastoraltheologie.* Vienna. Latin ed., 1778.

———. 1778c. *Theologiae dogmaticae tractandae methodus et ordo.* Vienna.

———. 1782a. *Entwurf zur Errichtung der Generalseminare in den k.k. Erblanden.* Vienna. 2nd ed., 1784.

———. 1782b. *Entwurf zur Errichtung der theologischen Schulen in den k.k. Erblanden.* Vienna.

Sorkin, David. 2008. *The Religious Enlightenment: Protestants, Jews, and Catholics from London to Vienna.* Princeton: Princeton University Press.

———. 2011. "Afterword: The Enlightenment—Bohemian Style?" In *The Enlightenment in Bohemia: Religion, Morality and Multiculturalism,* edited by Ivo Cerman, Rita Krueger, and Susan Reynolds, 295–302. Oxford: Voltaire Foundation.

Vocelka, Karl. 2001. *Österreichische Geschichte, 1699–1815: Glanz und Untergang der höfischen Welt; Repräsentation, Reform und Reaktion im habsburgischen Vielvölkerstaat.* Vienna: Ueberreuter.

Wallnig, Thomas. 2010. "La congrégation de Saint-Maur comme modèle d'ascèse: Exercices spirituels de Jérôme Le Contat et méditations de Claude Martin dans la traduction de Franz Mezger (Salzburg)." In *Dom Jean Mabillon, figure majeure de l'Europe des lettres,* edited by Jean Leclant, André Vauchez, and Daniel-Odon Hurel, 293–307. Paris: Académie des Inscriptions et Belles-Lettres.

———. 2012. "Ordensgeschichte als Kulturgeschichte? Wissenschaftshistorische Überlegungen zur Historizität in der benediktinischen Geschichtsforschung des 18. Jahrhunderts." In *Europäische Geschichtskulturen um 1700 zwischen Gelehrtsamkeit, Politik und Konfession,* edited by Thomas Wallnig, Thomas Stockinger, Ines Peper, and Patrick Fiska, 193–212. Munich: De Gruyter.

Winter, Eduard. 1943. *Der Josefinismus und seine Geschichte: Beiträge zur Geistesgeschichte Österreichs, 1740–1848.* Brno and Munich: Rohrer.

Zulehner, Paul Michael. 1989–1990. *Pastoraltheologie.* 4 vols. Düsseldorf: Patmos.

10

Johann Pezzl (1756–1823)

Enlightenment in the Satirical Mode

RITCHIE ROBERTSON

Johann Pezzl was born in Mallersdorf, near Straubing in southern Bavaria, on 30 November 1756. The son of a baker, he was educated at the Lyzeum in Freising and in September 1775 began a novitiate in the Benedictine monastery of Oberalteich (Höschel 2006, 2007). He left it in August 1776 and then studied law at the Benedictine university of Salzburg, which was then run in a relatively enlightened spirit: an obsolete scholasticism had been replaced by the philosophy of Christian Wolff, and the study of experimental science was encouraged (Lehner 2011). At Salzburg, Pezzl became acquainted with Johann Kaspar Riesbeck (1754–1786), a congenial spirit who was writing his own *Letters on Monasticism* (*Briefe über das Mönchswesen*), published in 1779. Riesbeck encouraged him to read Enlightenment texts and introduced him to many Freemasons and Illuminati. By publishing the first volume of his *Letters from the Novitiate* (*Briefe aus dem Novizziat*) in 1780, Pezzl obtained a dangerous notoriety. The book was banned in Bavaria, and even in relatively enlightened Salzburg it became the subject of a judicial investigation, which ended when Pezzl was forced to recant his errors. In August 1780, Pezzl moved to Zurich, where in 1781 and 1782 he issued the second and third parts of the *Briefe,* and in spring 1783, his humorous novel *Faustin, or The Philosophical Century* (*Faustin, oder Das philosophische Jahrhundert*).

After 1784, however, Pezzl found a secure home in the enlightened Vienna of Joseph II. Joseph had ruled jointly with his mother, Maria Theresa, since 1765. Freed by her death in 1780 from her maternal authority, he became sole ruler of the Habsburg Empire. He was determined to introduce reforms, and did so rapidly. Among Joseph's most famous reforming measures were his Patents of Toleration, which, beginning in October 1781, granted freedom of worship to communities of Lutherans, Calvinists, and Greek Orthodox, thus removing the restrictions on their ability to buy property, join guilds, and attend university. Similar measures removed the much more extensive restrictions on Jews. In dealing with the Catholic Church, Joseph tried to bring it under state control by ordaining that the appointments of bishops would require his approval; and he dissolved the contemplative monastic orders, transferring their property to charitable use. These measures caused such alarm in Rome that in the spring of 1782 Pope Pius VI took the unprecedented step of visiting Vienna in person in order to remonstrate with the emperor, who remained steadfast (see Blanning 1994; Beales 2009).

In Vienna, Pezzl lived by his pen and also worked as a librarian to Prince Wenzel Anton of Kaunitz-Rietberg, who was Austria's state chancellor from 1753 to 1792. Pezzl socialized with Freemasons, becoming a member of the lodge "Zur Wohltätigkeit," to which Mozart also belonged (Abafi 1890–1899, 3:333). More noteworthy publications followed, including his *Journey through Bavaria* (*Reise durch den Baierschen Kreis;* 1784), his *Moroccan Letters* (*Marokkanische Briefe*; 1784), and the topographical *Sketch of Vienna* (*Skizze von Wien*), published in six parts between 1786 and 1790. On Joseph II's death in 1790, Pezzl published a biographical sketch, *The Character of Joseph II* (*Charakteristik Josephs II*), which has considerable interest as a historical source. Even combined with journalism and translation, these works seem not to have provided him with an adequate living, and—perhaps also to make up for his earlier espousal of Josephinism—at the time of the political reaction after Joseph's death he took up a post in the "Chiffre-Kanzlei," a government office concerned with intercepting and deciphering mail. He married the well-to-do Anna Maria Kurz (1764–1844) in 1793; they had no children. Pezzl published some further satirical novels and historical works, but otherwise concentrated on his career, which culminated in his becoming deputy director of the Chiffre-Kanzlei in 1820, three years before his death from what contemporary sources described as dropsy on 9 June 1823.

Concerning Pezzl's personal appearance and character we have the testimony of Caroline Pichler (1769–1843), the Viennese salon hostess, novelist, and memoirist, who as a girl met most of the leading figures of the Austrian Enlightenment in the house of her father, the distinguished civil servant Franz Sales von Greiner: "In the early days of his residence in Vienna, Pezzl was a frequent visitor to my parents' house—a small, stocky man, rather ordinary-looking if one considered only his outward appearance, but full of wit, liveliness, and knowledge" (Pezzl 1982, 118). Other witnesses confirm that though Pezzl looked like a Bavarian farmer, he was also highly intelligent, with notably bright eyes, and simple in his attire and lifestyle (Bodi 1995, 191).

The best way to present Pezzl's contribution to the Catholic Enlightenment and to the reforming ambitions of Joseph II is by surveying his main works.

Letters from the Novitiate

Pezzl presents *Letters from the Novitiate* (*Briefe aus dem Novizziat*; 1780–1782) as an authentic document sent to him by a slightly older friend during his year as a novice in a Benedictine monastery in Bavaria. This profession of authenticity is usual in eighteenth-century fiction, particularly epistolary fiction. Thus, the fictitious letters in Goethe's *The Sorrows of Young Werther* (*Die Leiden des jungen Werthers*; 1774) are presented by an editor who claims to have assembled them after collecting information about Werther from the latter's friends. This fictitious editor, then, increasingly intervenes in the text when Werther's mental disturbance requires another viewpoint to counterbalance his own. In Pezzl's *Briefe,* the narrator's introduction also explains how the letters came into his hands. The novice was able to get them smuggled out, first by a good-natured monastic servant, and later by a cousin of the novice's who resided in the same monastery. Nevertheless, since we are repeatedly told that the inmates are under constant surveillance, it is somewhat implausible that the novice could write his letters in the first place, let alone send them without having them intercepted by the authorities. However, Pezzl's profession of authenticity should not be wholly disregarded. He also tells us that the book will not be yet another scurrilous attack on monasticism. Instead, it is to be a serious and informative work based directly on experience. And although *Briefe* amounts to a very severe attack on monasticism, it is also extremely factual, presenting in circumstantial detail the training to which a novice is subjected, while also drawing conclusions about the moral and physical harm that normally results from such severity. There is no reason to doubt that these letters are a broadly faithful record of Pezzl's own experience.

The novice finds himself subjected to subordination, solitude, strict routine, and inquisitorial discipline. On requesting admission to the Benedictine order, he is obliged to kneel before the prelate. Later, the novices are often made to sit on the floor as an exercise in humility. Apart from services, meals, and an hour set aside each day for conversation, they are confined to their sparsely furnished cells. They are required normally to remain silent, to keep their eyes on the floor, to avoid eye contact with anyone, especially superiors, and to walk with their hands folded on their chests. These practices prevent the monks from developing the social virtues in which the Enlightenment reposed so much faith. A standard trope of antimonastic critiques was that solitude led to dire consequences, including madness. Accordingly, Pezzl emphasized how the monks nourished resentment against one another, played malicious tricks against one another, engaged in petty quarrels, and gathered supporters to their equally petty factions, until what should be Christ's flock had morphed into a pack of ravenous wolves. The artificial solitude imposed by monastic life is the worst possible setting in which to acquire the social virtues, conceived by Pezzl as being synonymous with Christian virtues: "Everyone must admit that people who live in solitude cannot possibly have the chance to learn social virtues: benevolence, brotherly love, and compassion" (1780–1782, 1:45).

The monks' daily routine starts at 3:30 a.m., when they are roused by the servant hammering on their cell doors, and continues, parceled up into small units, until bedtime at 8 p.m. or soon after. The time is spent in idleness, which is much less healthy than work in the fields would be. The novices are allowed no privacy: anyone can look into their cells through apertures in the door, and the area reserved for them contains a screen with holes through which they can be watched. Their inner lives are kept under equally close surveillance. They make frequent confession, though they are too tired and harassed to have any time for sinning, and each day ends with a general examination of their consciences, in which they are asked questions to which it would be very imprudent to give an honest answer—for example, which of the monastic rules they find most difficult, whether they dislike any of their fellow novices or superiors—so that they rapidly become accomplished hypocrites. They are supplied with a *cilicium,* or wire belt, full of points turned inwards, which after a few hours becomes agonizing to wear, and with whips consisting of numerous cords, with which they are required to practice ritual flagellation. They are under the direction of a novice master, who in Pezzl's hands becomes a memorable comic tyrant. We are given a dramatic scene in which a series of novices confess their faults in Latin and the novice master replies "auf gut hausknechtisch" ("like a house servant"; 1780–1782, 1:120), with abusive tirades. They are required to practice mortification by undergoing unnecessary discomfort, denying themselves food that they like, refraining from drinking when they are thirsty, and so forth. In these practices the monks have the examples of the saints to follow, and the feats of asceticism recorded in saints' lives are recounted with due ridicule: how Saint Francis talked with donkeys, rolled in the snow, and slept in a chimney; how Passidea of Siena knelt on thorns, thistles, red-hot nails, or a large grater when she prayed, and had herself hung upside down in a chimney, like a ham, to be smoked; how Saint Macarius lay buried in earth up to his throat for three years, eating nothing but the grass that was within reach: and all this for the mortification of the body. The narrator concludes: "Am I wrong, dear brother, in maintaining that the actions formerly praised as deeds of spiritual heroism, as superhuman virtues worthy of heaven, would now get one put in a madhouse" (1780–1782, 2:117).

Briefe is not just a factual report but a literary work, and as so often in the eighteenth century, it is literature—*belles lettres*—that provides a touchstone by which monastic life is condemned as unnatural and absurd. The narrator is an enthusiast for literature. Before he enters the monastery, he describes escaping from uncongenial society into the enjoyment of nature, in a manner strongly reminiscent of *Werther*: "I bow, go to a hill near the wood, read my Wieland, and in the light of the setting sun I contemplate the industrious people who must spend their days sweating in unpaid obligatory labor, in order to provide nourishment for twenty praying layabouts, while their own children at home are wailing with hunger" (1780–1782, 1:14). The original rule of Saint Benedict required the monks themselves to do manual labor, but now it is left to the laborers who are required to cultivate the monks' fields in addition to their own. This reflection on social injustice is coupled with a display of sensibility recalling Goethe, with the difference that whereas Goethe's hero reads Homer at sunset, Pezzl's narrator reads Wieland. Christoph Martin Wieland, the great humorous writer of the German Enlightenment, was a favorite of Pezzl's and is frequently cited in *Briefe* and elsewhere. When the narrator and his cousin acknowledge to each other the sexual content of their dreams, they do so by adapting some well-known lines from "Diana und Endymion," one of Wieland's *Comische Erzählungen* (Pezzl 1780–1782, 1:161):

> Sie sind auch hier von jener Art,
> Die oft, trotz Skapulier und Bart,
> Sankt Franzens fette Seraphinen
> In schwüler Sommernacht bedienen.
>   (Wieland 1964–1968, 4:113)

(Here too they [the dreams] are of the kind often employed by Saint Francis's plump seraphs, despite their scapulars and beards, on sultry summer nights.)

The theme of suppressed sexuality surfaces repeatedly in *Briefe*. The narrator notices that a hymn usually sung in the evenings contains a line which is clearly a warning against nocturnal emissions (Pezzl 1780–1782, 1:70). When relating that the novices sleep in a dormitory, the narrator notes that it is visited at night by a monk, and wonders ironically whether he is in search of homosexuals: "Surely one cannot suppose that some novices have had a fit that makes them go together at night into the stalls and do what Jupiter did to Ganymede, Socrates to Alcibiades, and what even nowadays the Jesuits have so often done to their young students" (1780–1782, 2:88). Pederasty was a standard charge against Jesuits in Enlightenment polemic (Friedel 1785, 1:52–53; Pomeau 1985, 226).

The narrator's literary tastes contrast sharply with those permitted in the monastery. He reads Wieland, Goethe, Voltaire, Sterne's *Sentimental Journey,* Friedrich Nicolai's novel *Sebaldus Nothanker,* the poems of Albrecht von Haller, and the antimonastic satire *The Ballet* (*Le Balai,* 1762), by Henri-Joseph du Laurens (1719–1793). This poem provides the whole book with an epigraph, taken from an allegorical episode set in the Temple of Monasticism:

> Tyran des coeurs, la Moinerie affreuse
> Est de ces lieux la Souveraine heureuse.
> Son diadême est la crédulité,
> Son triste sceptre est l'inhumanité.
> (du Laurens 1762, 118)

(Tyrant of hearts, frightful Monasticism is the happy ruler of this place. Her diadem is credulity, her sad scepter is inhumanity.)

In the monastery's library, however, Pezzl's narrator finds the church fathers, theologians from Aquinas to Busenbaum. There are also sermon collections, although instead of French and German sermons, which have some literary merit, there are the popular sermons by Abraham a Sancta Clara and Martin Cochem, which Enlighteners despised. Hidden away at floor level are expurgated editions of the classics. Pezzl gives broadly the same impression when describing the library at Oberalteich, where he spent his own novitiate (1784b, 36). Though excluded from the room with prohibited books, he learns that it contains Ovid, Luther's Bible, "Febronius," "Lochstein," "Neuberger," and a history of the papal bull *In coena domini* (Pezzl 1780–1782, 1:27). The joke here is that several of these works were antimonastic treatises which would probably not have been in a monastery at all. The pseudonymous work by "Febronius" argued that papal power should be restricted; those by "Lochstein" and "Neuberg[er]" argue that church property ought to be subject to taxation, while the bull *In coena domini,* issued in 1627 and read every Holy Thursday, declared that church property was inviolate (Printy 2009).

Toward the end, *Briefe* abandons the pretence of fiction and turns into a treatise on monasticism. The narrator recounts the history of monasticism from its origins in Egypt and tries to calculate its demographic ill effects. In a period when the economic doctrine of mercantilism urged that each state should maximize its population and make the entire population productive, one of the charges against monasticism was that it took large numbers of healthy adults out of economic life and forbade them to reproduce. Pezzl wrote that in 1549 there were 225,044 monasteries in the world. If each had 36 inmates, the total would be over 8,000,000. If spread across three generations, the sum total would be 24,304,752 monastic religious (1780–1782, 2:63). If each of these had married and had five children, the population would have increased in a single generation by 40,000,000. These figures may be treated with skepticism. Contemporary estimates of the numbers of monks and nuns were very unreliable. Pezzl tells us elsewhere that in 1780 there were about 63,000 monks and nuns in the Austrian territories (1803, 72), but according to Derek Beales, the leading historian of the Austrian Enlightenment, these territories contained fewer than 2,000 monastic houses with about 40,000 regular clergy of both sexes, a disproportionate number being located in the monarchy's Belgian and Italian territories (2003, 180).

Pezzl's critique of monasticism was very much in the spirit of the times. Even earlier, under Maria Theresa, her chancellor Kaunitz had argued on economic grounds for reducing the number of regular clergy. One of Joseph II's first acts was to issue a decree dissolving the monasteries of contemplative orders and imposing restrictions on the rest. Satires on monastic life were popular and were sometimes written by liberal-minded monks, such as Ulrich Petrak of Melk and Anselm Edling of St. Paul in Carinthia (Frimmel 2004; Nussbaumer 1956; Jäger 1993). Pezzl was astute in making use of his own experiences to launch himself into literature with a distinctive contribution to a familiar genre.

Faustin, or The Philosophical Century

Pezzl's novel *Faustin, or The Philosophical Century* (*Faustin, oder Das philosophische Jahrhundert*) is an updated version of Voltaire's *Candide*. The naïve hero, Faustin, comes at an early age under the influence of Father Bonifaz, an enlightened cleric. Just as Voltaire's Pangloss persists in believing, despite all evidence to the contrary, that this is the best of all possible worlds, so Bonifaz is convinced that the age he lives in is the philosophical century in which enlightenment has triumphed. Faustin goes on a whirlwind and largely involuntary tour of Europe and America, which proves overwhelmingly that ignorance, superstition, and barbarity are still rampant. In southern Germany, he finds people flocking to the alleged exorcist and miraculous healer Gassner (see Midelfort 2005). In Venice, he is expelled for mocking the ceremony in which the Doge marries the sea. In Naples, where Freemasons are persecuted, he is denounced as one, and flees to Genoa. There he gets caught up in a scheme for sending German colonists to Spain and becomes secretary to the enlightened minister Olavides, but when the latter is arrested by the Inquisition, Faustin flees to supposedly enlightened France. There he learns that the *Encyclopédie* is in the Bastille (this is literally true, as offending books, as well as people, were confined there), and that on Voltaire's death the clergy refuse to permit his burial in a cemetery. Enlightened England is no better: an imposing monument there, which Faustin thinks must be the tomb of some enlightener such as Locke or Shaftesbury, turns out to commemorate a racehorse, and on a later visit, Faustin finds London convulsed by the anti-Catholic Gordon Riots, which he considers a Protestant counterpart to the massacre of St. Bartholomew's Night. The world still drives a trade in human beings. Forcibly recruited as a soldier, Faustin arrives in America and witnesses the horrors of the slave trade, as well as seeing how European immigrants are obliged to sell themselves as indentured laborers. His disgust at European colonialism is strengthened by reading the Abbé Raynal's famous anticolonial text, *Histoire des deux Indes* (1770).

Fortunately, this benighted world has two bright spots. One is Berlin, where under Frederick the Great tolerance prevails to such an extent that a mass is said in a Catholic church for the soul of Voltaire. The other is Vienna, where Joseph II has just assumed sole rule and instituted his edicts of toleration. Faustin declares that with Joseph's accession in 1780 a new era has begun—"the era of enlightened southern Germany, the Josephian era" (1982, 378)—this is apparently the first use of an adjective derived from the emperor's name, anticipating the later *"josephinisch"* (Beales 2005, 289–90). The end of the novel sees Faustin and a like-minded friend living quietly in Vienna and greeting each of Joseph's reforms with the exclamation: "Under Joseph's government, we have the universal victory of reason and humanity, and an enlightened, tolerant, truly philosophical century!" (1982, 381).

Faustin shares the episodic structure of *Candide*. Just as Voltaire transports Candide all over the globe, from Westphalia to the Black Sea and to South America, taking in such newsworthy destinations as earthquake-ruined Lisbon and the much-discussed Jesuit reductions in Paraguay, so Pezzl sends Faustin on the slightest of pretexts to every place where superstition and oppression can be observed. Though it lacks the polish of *Candide,* Pezzl's novel is a lively narrative, which especially shows how closely he followed contemporary events: all his references, even the monument to the racehorse, can be traced to newspaper reports and travel books.

Pezzl's eye for detail is still more evident in *Journey through the Bavarian District* (*Reise durch den Baierschen Kreis*), which he published anonymously soon after arriving in Vienna and which attracted considerable interest. It is a lively travel book in a series of letters in which the author, modeling himself explicitly on Sterne's Yorick, undertakes to report on "morality, enlightenment, the people's character, and the national mentality" (Pezzl 1784b, 3) in Bavaria from Passau to near Salzburg. Towns and important buildings are characterized, the state of universities such as Ingolstadt is examined in detail, and we learn such items, valuable for the historian, as the fact that Regensburg, like all imperial cities, is full of Austrian, Prussian, and Danish recruiting officers, of which the Austrians generally get the best recruits and the Danes the worst. Monastic and religious life is the main topic. Many anecdotes are told about life in various monasteries, their financial management, their reputation for learning, the state of their libraries, and the extent to which they still promote vulgar superstition. Thus we learn that the chapel at Oberalteich, where Pezzl did his novitiate, contains "the most disgusting picture that a plebeian monk's head could ever devise" (37), in which monks spray holy water as Doctor Luther flees through the air on a pig, carrying a Bible, a full glass, and a sausage. Equally tasteless is the statue of a pregnant Madonna, in whose belly a window has been opened allowing the spectator to see the infant Jesus as a half-formed embryo. These are among many examples of superstition heightened by vulgarity.

Oriental Fictions: *Moroccan Letters* and *Abdul Erzerums Neue Persische Briefe*

Pezzl's *Moroccan Letters* (*Marokkanische Briefe*) is the most radical critique of Christianity to emerge from the Austrian Enlightenment. The work was suggested by a Moroccan embassy that visited Vienna in 1783, but, like several of his others, its literary inspiration is French. While *Faustin* is modeled on *Candide*, *Marokkanische Briefe* is inspired by Montesquieu's *Persian Letters* (*Lettres persanes*; 1721), in which two Persians visiting France comment satirically, from an outsider's perspective, on French manners and customs. In Pezzl's version, "Sidi" reports to his friend "Hamid," back home, on his impressions of Vienna. Sidi favors monarchy and approves of the freedom of the press introduced by Joseph II, but his main interest is in Christianity. He pillories not only the superstitious excesses of Baroque Catholicism, a standard target of enlightened critique, but the very foundations of Christianity in the Bible. The Old Testament is both fanciful and immoral. Sidi illustrates the former by a skeptical résumé of the early chapters of Genesis, and the latter by listing the many massacres from sacred history that, he says, have inspired assassins down the ages. The murder of Eglon, king of Moab, by Ehud with his two-edged sword (Judges 3:15–23) and Samuel's hewing Agag in pieces "before the Lord" (1 Samuel 15:33) were among the Enlightenment's favorite examples of Old Testament barbarity (e.g., Voltaire's article "Fanatisme" in his *Philosophical Dictionary* [*Dictionnaire philosophique*; 1964, 190]). Sidi knows such radical writers on the Bible as Lessing, who in *The Education of the Human Race* (*Die Erziehung des Menschengeschlechts,* 1780) argues that revelation is a gradual and still incomplete process; he mentions the Italian deist Alberto Radicati, who compared Islam with Christianity, arguing that the original purity of both religions had been corrupted by priests (see Israel 2006, 97); and he even cites the notorious *Treatise of the Three Impostors,* which represented Moses, Muhammad, and Jesus as equal charlatans.

As this suggests, the New Testament comes in for sharp criticism as well. Sidi knows the arguments presented by the Hamburg Orientalist Reimarus, published after his death by Lessing, that Jesus was a political revolutionary whose intentions were reinterpreted after his death by his followers. He questions the divinity of Christ: "The Catholics believe with dogmatic zeal that Christ was the true son of God. The Protestants are gradually beginning to say that Christ was a human being like any other, but a gifted preacher of morality, and in that sense a son of God, that is, a good person" (Pezzl 1784a, 91).

Here Pezzl steps over the boundaries of the Catholic Enlightenment, illustrating Ernst Wangermann's contention that "Reform Catholicism could be the gateway to natural religion, deism and atheism" (Wangermann 1981, 133; cf. Klueting 2010, 143). As for the institutions of the Catholic Church, Sidi is as severe as Pezzl could wish against monastic orders, Jesuits, and the practices of auricular confession and celibacy. The boredom suffered by the novice in *Letters from the Novitiate* is echoed in his critique of the church fathers:

> One is alarmed at the sight of the monstrous folio volumes of Augustine, Ambrose, Jerome, Thomas, and so on, and so forth. Apart from occasional scraps of a kind of eloquence or chattiness, everything else is unreadable. Nonsense and contradictions are in their rightful place on every page. For a thinker of our time I could imagine no more painful punishment than condemning him to read the complete works of a church father: a *bel esprit* would burst, as though he had taken rat poison.
>
> Most patristic scribblings consist of sophistical hair-splitting, word-plays, allegories taken to the point of absurdity, exaggerated morality, eccentric Bible commentaries, nonsensical monastic notions, empty platitudes, foolish declamations, and occasional deliberate absurdities and distortions. Now and again some sensible sentences are visible, but they are far from outweighing the mass of useless stuff. (Pezzl 1784a, 99–100)

No wonder that such a harsh and sweeping critique was too much even for the freedom of publication instituted by Joseph II. Deistical works were in any case treated with caution; the anti-Christian thrust of *Moroccan Letters* caused their publication in Vienna to be prohibited, and care was taken to confiscate any copies that were smuggled in from abroad (Wangermann 2004, 113–14).

It has been claimed (Gugitz 1906, 195) that Pezzl also wrote the anonymous *New Persian Letters of Abdul Erzerum* (*Abdul Erzerums neue persische Briefe*; 1787), which are based on the fiction that the grandson of Usbek, the letter writer in Montesquieu's *Lettres persanes*, likewise visits Europe and writes reports to his friends and relatives at home. However, the ascription is dubious (Bodi 1995, 315). Unlike Pezzl's other works, *New Persian Letters* is very short on specific contemporary detail. It is a tirade in which Abdul Erzerum expresses the disillusionment that, as the prefatory letter informs us, led him after his travels to drown himself. Although an acquaintance he meets while traveling gives Abdul high hopes of the Viennese Enlightenment, Abdul notes, even before reaching Vienna, the misery of the rural population, a topic to which he frequently recurs. In Vienna itself, he concludes that the humane treatment of the citizens results not from genuine philanthropy but the mercantilist ambition to maximize the number and productivity of the population. The very project of enlightenment strikes him as dubious, because it means treating everyone by the same standard and thus spreading uniformity and mediocrity, and because it deprives people of traditional beliefs while offering nothing in return. The spirit in which Abdul forms these judgments echoes that of the Sturm und Drang, and particularly *Werther*: "It is simply impossible for me to limit myself to quiet civil life, waiting for the wealth of domestic happiness to provide me with the small quantity of joy that I long impatiently to seize for myself. Why should I hide it? A heart like mine cannot easily be appeased" (Anon. 1787, 28). Passages like this suggest that Abdul's disillusionment is not the result of his Austrian experiences, however disheartening they may be, but is programmed from the outset.

Sketch of Vienna

Sketch of Vienna (*Skizze von Wien*) appeared in six installments between 1786 and 1790. In its method of describing a city, it acknowledges a debt to the *Tableau de Paris* (1781–1788), by Louis-Sébastien Mercier (1740–1814). Beginning with statistical information about Vienna's situation, climate, population, commerce, and consumption of commodities, *Skizze* continues with a miscellaneous collection of mini-essays on Viennese localities and on such aspects of urban life as theaters, newspapers, coffeehouses, prostitutes, venereal diseases, and many more. By this superficial disorder, the genre of the *tableau* differs from the older genre of the urban topography, and conveys the juxtaposition of heterogeneous realities that is characteristic of the great city (Kauffmann 1994, 210–12, 235). *Skizze* was so popular that Pezzl later wrote a sequel, *New Sketch of Vienna* (*Neue Skizze von Wien*), in three parts (1805–1812), which differs from the first series in its more negative emphases, notably on the cost of living and the growth of luxury (Kauffmann 1994, 241).

Part of Pezzl's purpose is to defend great cities as such against the strictures of moralists, who denounce them as haunts of vice, and against the primitivism of Rousseau, who is here dismissed as an idealist. Cities, Pezzl insists, are centers of arts, learning, refinement, culture, and humanity. Vienna in particular needs to be defended against the complaints of the Berlin enlightener Friedrich Nicolai (1733–1811), who in his account of his travels in southern Germany and Austria attacked the Viennese for their self-indulgent hedonism and their attachment to Catholic superstitions (Nicolai 1783–1787). Pezzl defends the ordinary Viennese against the charge of excessive eating and drinking, undue enjoyment of theater, excursions to the country, and other pleasures. After all, Vienna lies in a fertile region, and the average Viennese is well off; why should the Viennese not enjoy the abundant products of nature?

The charge of superstition is harder to rebut, for Pezzl himself, an ardent Josephinist, shares the disapproval of Catholic *"Andächtelei,"* or superstitious piety (1786–1790, 92). He welcomes the reduction in the number of regular clergy, whose establishments, he claims, used to take up one-sixth of Vienna's surface area. Surveying the state of religion in Vienna, he finds that the majority of the population are warmly attached to a religion consisting of a medley of truths, half-truths, and untruths, and that they reject any criticisms of it, while many, especially the clergy, practice religion mainly from self-interest. Among so-called freethinkers, he distinguishes those who remain Catholics but wish to purify their religion from superstitious practices; those who, loyal to Christianity, wish to modify some of its doctrines; deists, who are rare in Vienna; and French-style atheists, who have yet to appear there.

Pezzl naturally praises also the secular achievements of Josephinism. Besides freedom of speech and abolition of censorship, he includes accounts of the General Hospital (*Allgemeines Krankenhaus*), the school for the deaf, and other institutions founded by Joseph. His overall commitment to the cause of enlightenment appears in a section headed *"Aufklärung,"* where he says that many people identify enlightenment with the removal of religious abuses, but it means much more:

> For me, an enlightened man is one whose moral feeling is properly formed; who finds contentment in the profession in which chance or the laws have placed him; who acts honestly and on reflection; who has become accustomed to loving his work, reverencing the laws, readily accepting instruction, loving order in his domestic and professional affairs, and observing moderation in his diet and taking care of his health; who never longs to spend more than he can afford; who seeks constantly to perfect the talents necessary for his destined role within society; who knows and practices the virtues of the citizen, friend, husband, and father; who knows that in civil society one must inevitably bear one's individual burden and sacrifice one's private advantage for the sake of the greater whole; who never makes an immodest attack on the religion publicly sponsored by the state and, if he has acquired different beliefs, holds them in private; who, finally, enjoys his existence with pleasure, and knows how to enjoy it comfortably, quietly, and for a long time. (1786–1790, 350–51)

This is a decidedly conservative conception of enlightenment. The enlightened person, imagined only as male, is first and foremost a good citizen. He should be contented with his lot, accept his place in society, perform his domestic and public duties, and, whatever his private beliefs may be, conform to the official religion of his country. These are the ideals recommended to the middle-class readers of the moral weeklies that flourished in eighteenth-century Germany, and of which Sonnenfels's *Man without Prejudice* (*Der Mann ohne Vorurtheil*) was an Austrian counterpart (Martens 1968). The advice about religious conformity, in particular, suggests that the author of the *Marokkanische Briefe* had by now returned within the fold of the Catholic Enlightenment. Although *Skizze* makes clear that Pezzl still opposed monasticism, pilgrimages, and other customs defined as superstitious, he no longer wished to question the foundations of Christianity.

Pezzl and the Catholic Enlightenment

Where, finally, are we to place Pezzl on a map of the Catholic Enlightenment? He undoubtedly belongs on the outside left. He agreed with the Catholic reformers of late eighteenth-century Austria in attacking credulity, superstition, and intolerance. In his polemic against monasticism, he went beyond Joseph II, who closed down the monasteries of contemplative orders, and attacked the entire institution of monasticism as useless to society and damaging to its inmates. His perspective was close to that of Protestant polemics against monasticism. Similarly, in his most radical text, the *Marokkanische Briefe,* he moved beyond the limits of Catholicism by questioning the divinity of Christ, seeming closer in spirit to the liberal developments within German Lutheranism. The liberal wing of Protestant theology known as Neology did its best to dismantle the supernatural aspects of Christianity while maintaining a façade of orthodoxy; Lessing in his theological polemics sought unsuccessfully to induce the Neologists to admit that their official orthodoxy was intellectually dishonest. Pezzl referred to Lessing with sympathy. He also accepted the historical criticisms of the Old and New Testaments made by Reimarus and published after Reimarus's death by Lessing as "Fragments of an Anonymous Writer." His adoption of a non-Christian perspective in the *Briefe,* and his sympathy for such extreme views as those of Radicati, imply a deism close to that of Voltaire.

However, Pezzl remained within the Catholic Church. This sets him apart from his contemporary Ignaz-Aurelius Fessler (1756–1839), whose autobiography recounts his entry into the Capuchin order, his ordination as a priest just when he had lost his faith, his reading in radical writers such as Helvétius and Spinoza, and his conversion to Protestantism (Fessler 1824). Pezzl took a less intense interest in strictly religious questions, and was more interested in moral and political reform. Hence, writing under his own name in *Skizze von Wien,* he prudently recommended that anyone whose private beliefs differed from the religion supported by the state should keep his beliefs to himself and refrain from attacking the state religion. This indicates that Josephinism had by then reached its high-water mark, and also that many of its reforming aims, such as the reduction of superstitious practices and the dissolution of monasteries belonging to contemplative orders, had in fact been achieved. Although he approached the boundaries of the Catholic Enlightenment, Pezzl did not—publicly at least—go beyond them.

Bibliography

Abafi, Ludwig. 1890–1899. *Geschichte der Freimaurerei in Österreich-Ungarn*. 5 vols. Budapest: Ludwig Aigner.
[Anon.] 1787. *Abdul Erzerums neue persische Briefe*. Vienna and Leipzig: Stahel.
Beales, Derek. 2003. *Prosperity and Plunder: European Catholic Monasteries in the Age of Revolution, 1650–1815*. Cambridge: Cambridge University Press.
———. 2005. *Enlightenment and Reform in Eighteenth-Century Europe*. London: Tauris.
———. 2009. *Joseph II*. Vol. 2, *Against the World, 1780–1790*. Cambridge: Cambridge University Press.
Blanning, T. C. W. 1994. *Joseph II*. London: Longman.
Bodi, Leslie. 1995. *Tauwetter in Wien: Zur Prosa der österreichischen Aufklärung, 1781–1795*. 2nd ed. Vienna, Cologne, and Weimar: Böhlau.
Du Laurens, Henri-Joseph. 1762. *Le Balai: Poème héroï-comique en XVIII chants*. Constantinople [i.e., Amsterdam]: De l'Imprimerie du Mouphti.
[Fessler, Ignaz-Aurelius]. 1824. *Dr. Fessler's Rückblicke auf seine siebzigjährige Pilgerschaft: Ein Nachlass [sic] an seine Freunde und an seine Feinde*. Breslau: Korn.
Friedel, Johann. 1785. *Heinrich von Walheim, oder Weiberliebe und Schwärmerey*. 2 vols. Frankfurt and Leipzig.
Frimmel, Johannes. 2004. *Literarisches Leben in Melk: Ein Kloster im 18. Jahrhundert im kulturellen Umbruch*. Vienna, Cologne, and Weimar: Böhlau.
Gugitz, Gustav. 1906. "Johann Pezzl." *Jahrbuch der Grillparzer-Gesellschaft* 16 (1906): 164–217.
Höschel, Clarissa. 2006. "Wie Johann Pezzl vom Benediktinernovizen zum Freimaurer, Satiriker und Staatsbeamten wurde: Ein biographischer Abriss zu Pezzls 250. Geburtstag (2006)." *Literatur in Bayern* 85:38–46.
———. 2007. "*Candidatus Johann Pezzl*: Auf den Spuren eines konspirativen Salzburger Studentenlebens." *Salzburg Archiv* 32:187–208.
Israel, Jonathan. 2006. *Enlightenment Contested: Philosophy, Modernity, and the Emancipation of Man, 1670–1752*. Oxford: Oxford University Press.

Jäger, Hans-Wolf. 1993. "Mönchskritik und Klostersatire in der deutschen Spätaufklärung." In *Katholische Aufklärung—Aufklärung im katholischen Deutschland,* edited by Harm Klueting, 192–207. Hamburg: Meiner.

Kauffmann, Kai. 1994. *"Es ist nur ein Wien!" Stadtbeschreibungen von Wien, 1700 bis 1783.* Vienna, Cologne, and Weimar: Böhlau.

Klueting, Harm. 2010. "The Catholic Enlightenment in Austria or the Habsburg Lands." In *A Companion to the Catholic Enlightenment,* edited by Ulrich L. Lehner and Michael Printy, 127–64. Leiden: Brill.

Lehner, Ulrich L. 2011. *Enlightened Monks: The German Benedictines, 1740–1803.* Oxford: Oxford University Press.

Martens, Wolfgang. 1968. *Die Botschaft der Tugend: Die Aufklärung im Spiegel der deutschen moralischen Wochenschriften.* Stuttgart: Metzler.

Midelfort, H. C. Erik. 2005. *Exorcism and Enlightenment: Johann Joseph Gassner and the Demons of Eighteenth-Century Germany.* New Haven and London: Yale University Press.

Nicolai, Friedrich. 1783–1787. *Beschreibung einer Reise durch Deutschland und die Schweiz im Jahre 1781: Nebst Bemerkungen über Gelehrsamkeit, Industrie, Religion und Sitten.* 8 vols. Berlin and Stettin.

Nussbaumer, Erich. 1956. *Geistiges Kärnten: Literatur- und Geistesgeschichte des Landes.* Klagenfurt: Kleinmayr.

Pezzl, Johann. 1780–1782. *Briefe aus dem Novizziat.* N.p. [Zürich].

———. 1784a. *Marokkanische Briefe: Aus dem Arabischen.* Neue vermehrte und verbesserte Auflage. Frankfurt and Leipzig.

———. 1784b. *Reise durch den Baierschen Kreis.* Salzburg and Leipzig.

———. 1786–1790. *Skizze von Wien.* 6 vols. Vienna and Leipzig: Kraus.

———. 1803. *Charakteristik Josephs des Zweiten.* 3rd ed. Vienna: Degen.

———. 1982. *Faustin: oder das philosophische Jahrhundert.* Edited by Wolfgang Greip. Hildesheim: Gerstenberg.

Pomeau, René. 1985. *D'Arouet à Voltaire, 1694–1734.* Oxford: Voltaire Foundation.

Printy, Michael. 2009. *Enlightenment and the Creation of German Catholicism.* Cambridge: Cambridge University Press.

Voltaire. 1964. *Dictionnaire philosophique.* Edited by René Pomeau. Paris: Garnier-Flammarion.

Wangermann, Ernst. 1981. "Reform Catholicism and Political Radicalism in the Austrian Enlightenment." In *The Enlightenment in National Context,* edited by Roy Porter and Mikuláš Teich, 127–40. Cambridge: Cambridge University Press.

———. 2004. *Die Waffen der Publizität: Zum Funktionswandel der politischen Literatur unter Joseph II.* Vienna: Verlag für Geschichte und Politik.

Wieland, Christoph Martin. 1964–1968. *Werke.* Edited by Fritz Martini and Hans Werner Seiffert. 5 vols. Munich: Hanser.

PART 5
Varieties of Italian Catholic Enlightenment

11

Lodovico Antonio Muratori (1672–1750)

Enlightenment in a Tridentine Mode

PAOLA VISMARA

Lodovico Antonio Muratori was one of the most influential cultural figures in Italy in the first half of the eighteenth century. His nephew, Gianfrancesco Soli Muratori, wrote a very informative, although celebratory, biography of him. Today, after about two and a half centuries, Muratori is still waiting for another biographer. He was an extremely complex character: an active priest, the author of various scholarly works, and in correspondence with many illustrious people. He left a great intellectual heritage, and his thought has been interpreted variously. This chapter will outline in broad terms Muratori's personality in the context of his time, with a particular emphasis on the so-called Catholic *Aufklärung*, a version of the Enlightenment that spread in the Habsburg lands and in Italy. Two commonly acknowledged features of "Enlightened Catholics" are their desire for a renewal of the church with the help of secular sovereigns in order to take the church back to its roots, and the marginalization of the importance of dogma (Plongeron 1969, 1970; Rosa 1999, 149–84).

During the first decades of the eighteenth century, the cultural consequences of the Enlightenment were not completely clear, which is why, for instance, Benedict XIV accepted Voltaire's dedication of his book *Mahomet*. At that time, the opposition between the Enlightenment and Catholicism was not yet recognized. Not until the pontificates of Clement XIII and Pius VI did the fundamental tension become obvious.

In the course of Muratori's life, the first signs of the gradual political weakening of Rome appeared, but the Catholic Church continued to be very influential. Despite internal debates in the church, its religious accomplishments according to the ideals of the Council of Trent were clearly visible. At the same time, within the church some were attempting to adapt the Catholic doctrine to new sensibilities. To penetrate Muratori's thought and to evaluate his role, we must study his life and works within the broader context of the Catholic *Aufklärung*.

Intellectual Formation

Born in Vignola in 1672 to a family of artisans, Muratori studied at the Jesuit College in Modena, following the traditional *cursus studiorum*, which included classes in grammar, the humanities, and philosophy. He graduated in philosophy and, a few years later, canon and secular law. There is rich information on his early years in an autobiographical work written in 1721, a letter to Giovanni Artico, Count of Porcia, entitled *On the Method I Followed in My Studies* (*Intorno al metodo seguito nei miei studi*; Battistini 1994). The Count of Porcia, who was collecting short autobiographical descriptions of the early life of the most important living Italian men of letters, commissioned him to write it. Muratori wanted his autobiography to be published only after his death; it was eventually published in 1772 because of the premature death of the Count of Porcia.

Muratori's connections to literary salons in Modena allowed him to be in touch with the cultural environment of that town and to meet many influential people, including the marquis, Giovan Gioseffo Orsi, and the men of letters Carlo Maria Maggi and Francesco de Lemene, both members of the Arcadia (Viola 2009). Muratori soon realized that his ignorance of Greek was a problem for his intellectual formation, and he tried to overcome it. In that period, Italian culture appeared to him less developed than that of the rest of Europe.

During those years, Muratori was a pupil of Benedetto Bacchini (1651–1721) (Momigliano 1963; Golinelli 2003), who strongly influenced him. Bacchini inspired in him an interest in sacred erudition (origins of Christianity and ecclesiastical history) and the desire to create an encyclopedia of knowledge that could combine French erudition (Maurists), German culture (Leibniz), and the scientific Italian tradition (from Galilei to Malpighi) (Raimondi 1989). This is very important for understanding the evolution of Muratori's thought and the origin of his peculiar attitudes, namely, his emphasis on logic, on the vital need for research, on the sound use of reason, and on the ethical and civic responsibilities of men of letters (Cottignoli 1994).

Thanks to Bacchini, Muratori deepened his skills in philology and ecclesiastical history. During his years spent at the Biblioteca Ambrosiana in Milan (1695–1700) as a *dottore*—a scholar charged with working on the collections of the library—he devoted himself to philology (Flammini 2006). Although he did not always achieve excellent results, he developed an attitude of fidelity to philological evidence, even when such evidence was in conflict with the most celebrated traditions. The years in Milan were rich with experiences that strongly influenced Muratori's personality. He broadened his knowledge of Europe, and thanks to lively correspondences like the one with Antonio Magliabechi (1633–1714), he widened his network of connections.

Muratori and History

In 1700, Muratori moved to Modena, where he became the archivist and librarian at the court of Duke Rinaldo d'Este. His expertise in history was especially crucial in the thorny "Comacchio Affair" (Bertelli 1960). The territories of Comacchio were disputed: as property of the Holy See from 1598, they were claimed by the Este family with the support of the Holy Roman Empire. Their claims relied not only on the threat of armed intervention but also on historical documents. The writings on this topic tested Muratori's skills as a historian. He thoroughly collected and studied the sources and used all the instruments of philology and medieval historiography, as can be seen in his work entitled *Rights of the Empire and of the Este Family on the City of Comacchio* (*Piena esposizione dei diritti imperiali ed estensi sopra la città di Comacchio*; 1712), followed by *Antiquities of the House of Este* (*Antichità estensi*; 1717). Muratori understood that it was necessary, in order to study medieval Italian history, to tackle the critical knot of the historical role of the papacy (Neveu 1975, 279). He distinguished between the pope as the prince of the church and the pope as the sovereign of a state, and stated that the political choices of the pope could be openly questioned. This approach by Muratori was misinterpreted in the nineteenth century, when, for instance, the poet and man of letters Giosuè Carducci (1835–1907) wrongly considered his approach a precursor to the anticlericalism of the Risorgimento (Carducci 1900; Marchi 1998). Indeed, Muratori had ruled on a specific problem in favor of the Este family, but he was in no way hostile either to the temporal power of the pope or to the papacy itself. On the political-diplomatic front, Rome won in the dispute: the territories of Comacchio were returned to the Papal States in 1725.

Over the years, Muratori published extensive editions of sources and many historical works such as *Writers of Italian History* (*Rerum italicarum scriptores*; 1723–1751), *Italian Antiquities of the Middle Ages* (*Antiquitates italicae Medii Aevi*; 1738–1742), and *Italian Annals* (*Annali d'Italia*; 1744–1749). The Società Palatina was created to support the publication of *Writers of Italian History,* and it was an important experiment in a kind of Italian "Republic of Letters" at a time when Italy was somewhat marginalized from the rest of European scholarship. After discovering the importance of medieval history in the "Comacchio Affair," Muratori concentrated on studying the fusion of the Romans and the barbarians. In his view, this topic was extremely important for understanding both the origins of European civilization and the peculiarities of Italian history, physiognomy, and identity. Muratori emphasized that the cultural unity of Italy—a country that at the time was divided into a hundred cities—did not come from politics but from history, language, and religion. By suggesting this background of continuity, the historical works by Muratori profoundly influenced the Italians' civic consciousness (Cottignoli 1994, 97–110).

Although Muratori did not support the idyllic and mythologized vision of the Middle Ages that had great success at the beginning of the nineteenth century, he also strongly disagreed with the Enlightenment's negative interpretation. In Muratori, we can find a nonideological attention to the concreteness of history that originated in the importance he gave to sources and that, in the spirit of truth seeking, he inherited from Bacchini. According to Muratori, philology and erudition were not ends in themselves, but provided the instruments for building knowledge and prevented the historian from becoming a mere wordsmith. In Muratori's view, philological expertise, study of genealogies, knowledge of politico-diplomatic factors, and skills in juridical history were crucial for a well-rounded historiography.

Yet another field was required in order to complete historical knowledge: it is what Muratori called "philosophy," that is, the capacity to penetrate the events of the past by understanding the causes, effects, and connections among them. Only in this way, according to Muratori, was it possible to write a complete history of institutions and civilizations. In his historical research, Muratori thus overcame two widespread trends: "mere" erudition *and* the instrumental use of history. For instance, when he talked about the Catholic Church he avoided apologetic or controversialist attitudes, peculiar features of the historiography of the Counter-Reformation, and the use of history for purely polemical purposes, for example for a criticism of the church. He believed it was important to discern the true from the false in the church and its history, avoiding hypercriticism as exemplified in what Muratori considered to be the "sound criticism" of the Maurist monks. In this way, it was possible to avoid Pyrrhonian skepticism, which Muratori had condemned in his *On the Power of the Human*

Imagination (*Delle forze dell'intendimento umano*; 1745). In short, he supported a constructive rather than a "destructive" criticism.

Defending Reason

The French occupation of Modena (1702–1708) temporarily thwarted Muratori's research in the field of history and erudition, because of the impossibility of traveling and networking. During this period Muratori dedicated himself to cultural and literary projects, in particular two works with a Europe-wide horizon, *First Designs of the Literary Republic of Italy* (*Primi disegni della Repubblica letteraria d'Italia*; 1703) and *Reflections on Good Taste in Art and Science* (*Riflessioni sopra il buon gusto nelle scienze e nelle arti*; 1708–1715), whose first volume was published in 1708. In the latter, Muratori discusses the real function of research, which can never be for personal profit, literary glory, or the increase of personal knowledge. The only authentic purpose of research is the search for truth and goodness. According to Muratori, even a bitter debate with one's opponents might be useful, provided that it springs forth from the "evidence of reason" (Vismara 2002, 2011).

In Muratori's thought, the defense of logic and the exaltation of reason appear repeatedly. In his view the study of logic is crucial because it enables one to understand the rules of reasoning and because it is an indispensable instrument for all the other disciplines of letters and sciences. He thought the critical approach, a skill mandatory for reasonable men and scholars, should be limited only in matters of religion and faith. In these two subjects, reason must be subordinated to authority, yet not be trampled by it. Even religious teachings, although partially inaccessible to reason, are not unreasonable. A fortiori in all the other subjects one must always submit books and authors to the test of reason (1708–1715, 107–9, 225–26; 1767 [1734, posthumous], 350). Muratori emphasized at all times the Christian appreciation of reason, and saw in it a root of a certain stream of (religious) Enlightenment from which the majority of Enlightenment thinkers, however, eventually detached themselves. In Muratori we do not find the Enlightenment's absolute faith in reason that leads to rationalism; on the contrary, he was concerned about "the delirium of reason left to itself" (Falco 1960, 157).

In two works on this topic, *Reflections on Good Taste* and *On the Moderation of Our Cleverness in Religious Matters* (*De ingeniorum moderatione in religionis negotio*; 1714), the author developed his idea on the nature and the goals of research by appealing to good taste (*buon gusto*) and moderation (*moderazione*). The goal of erudition is to show new truths and evidence in order to respond to "wise curiosity" and, above all, to expand the private and public good. Other works develop the topic of the common good in its various facets, emphasizing the importance of civic commitments on the part of scholars. Mario Rosa highlighted the strong presence of this topic even in the final part of Muratori's life, when he composed the last part of the *Italian Annals* (1749). In this late work, Muratori—who died in Modena the following year—shows a civic and religious consciousness, one capable of measuring itself against contemporary events and finding, in the tumultuous events of the first half of the eighteenth century, motivation for renewed commitment (Rosa 1997).

Civic and Religious Commitment

The entire intellectual journey of Muratori is a crescendo of civic consciousness. In *The Defects of Jurisprudence* (*Dei difetti della giurisprudenza*; 1742) he refuses what we might call the "Pyrrhonism of jurisprudence," reaffirms the certainty of law, and describes concrete proposals for judicial reform. In the last years of his life, Muratori presented his thoughts on the responsibilities of governors in *On Public Happiness* (*Della pubblica felicità oggetto de' buoni principi*; 1749). His model for princes is the enlightened ruler, who has the duty to care for the welfare of his subjects according to the ideals of *utility* and *happiness*. These two words—crucial in the culture of the eighteenth century—occur frequently in Muratori's works. He disagrees with atheists and theists who think that happiness and the good order of the state can be reached regardless of religion, and in particular the "true religion of Christ," Catholicism. Muratori does not mythologize progress in terms of earthly happiness, but emphasizes the value of peace as "tranquility of order" (*tranquillitas ordinis*) and an ultimate longing for the everlasting kingdom (Vismara 2002, 2011).

One of the most renowned works of Muratori is *The Science of Rational Devotion* (*Della regolata divozione de' cristiani*; 1747), a pseudonymous book published during the last part of his life, in which we see the development of a decades-long intellectual path. From the beginning of his historical research, Muratori thought it was necessary to prune from religion the pagan remnants and distorted devotions that were encouraged by what he called "illiterate zeal." He assumed that the tendency to accept cults of saints uncritically had produced bad effects; for the attempt to support the popular impulses resulted in the multiplication of relics and the excess of devotions. Severity and rigor in the matter of devotions were absolutely necessary. At the same time, according to Muratori, the historical criticism of devotions also has limitations: it is important to use criticism properly and to submit the results to the judgment of the Curia. In his view, it was right to contest what did not conform to truth and to "healthy piety," but always in accordance with the church and its authorities. Muratori never abandoned this attitude of fidelity to Rome (Vismara 2011). For instance, while he was convinced the church would not proclaim a dogma of the immaculate conception, he asked the future cardinal, Fortunato Tamburini, to keep him informed in case it would be defined a dogma, so that he could speedily change his literary statements about this matter. Muratori's opinions on this topic in *On the Moderation of Our Cleverness in Religious Matters* attracted the attention of Roman censorship, but no concrete action was taken against the book (Vismara 2002).

Muratori never concealed his ideas on devotion; they were an almost ever-present leitmotif in his thought. There are many nuances in devotions. True piety and true devotion should have a christological and Trinitarian horizon: God as Father, Son, and Holy Spirit is the proper object of devotions. Muratori criticized the small devotions (what he calls *devozioncelle*) that he considered excessive and almost fanatical, but he never criticized devotions per se. On the contrary, he repeatedly affirmed that one of the duties of a good priest is to promote devotions in a proper way, and in particular christocentric ones (1747). He was not against external religious manifestations per se, provided that they did not conflict with authentic religion and civic duties. In short, he was in favor of an interior religious renewal, the practice of a "civic Catholicism," and at the same time a deeper evangelization of society (Rosa 1999, 124ff.). In this way he suggested a concrete, balanced, and practical proposal for the reform of the church, inaugurating "the age of Muratori," as it has been called by some scholars, that coincided with the papacy of Benedict XIV (1740–1758) (Rosa 1969).

Muratori, in his writings, always sees the reform of church and society as a concrete action and not as a theoretical problem. He concludes his treatise *Reflections on Good Taste in Art and Science* with the sentence, "One's knowledge is measured by one's activity" (Tantum scit homo, quantum operatur) (Falco 1960, 139). In *On Public Happiness* he proposes the inventor of the stocking handloom as the model of a "great philosopher." In Muratori's view the impetus for reform always requires a commitment to concrete daily life and the value of the human person (Falco and Forti 1964).

Praxis prevails over theory, the latter being considered useless if not realized in actual achievements. Although Muratori is in no way opposed to theoretical reasoning, in his view concrete application is not a complementary, but rather a necessary, component for establishing the validity of any theoretical system. Truth, however, is for him always superior to utility, and determines usefulness, not vice versa. He emphasizes the value of concreteness especially at the end of *Reflections on Good Taste,* in *On Perfect Italian Poetry* (*Della perfetta poesia italiana*; 1706), and in *On the Moderation of Our Cleverness in Religious Matters* (Vecchi 1968).

It is also noteworthy that Muratori was a devout and active pastor. He accompanied the Jesuit Paolo Segneri the Younger (1673–1713) on his missionary work and devoted his energies to offering the sacrament of confession. From this experience, he was able to handle the difficult work of being a parish priest in a disreputable area on the outskirts of Modena. He had no intention of living the life of an ivory-tower intellectual, but primarily concerned himself with the particular needs of his flock.

The Protestant World

Muratori came into conflict on various topics with Angelo Maria Querini, O.S.B. (1680–1755), a leading figure in the Italian literary and ecclesiastical world. Despite initial hostilities related to a discussion about the decrease in the number of holy days of obligation, the two were able to agree on what has at times been improperly called "the ecumenical question." It would better be described as peaceful, nonpolemic dialogue between denominations. Both men proved to be sensitive to rapprochement with the Protestants. Muratori was especially concerned with Marian devotion and how it was viewed by Protestants. In his opinion, excessive Marian devotions, which he considered not necessary for salvation, were mistakes that created further difficulties for a successful dialogue with Protestant Christians (Lehner 2011, 176–77). Muratori's concessions to Protestantism were indeed the most criticized aspect of his *On the Moderation of Our Cleverness in Religious Matters*. Both Querini and Muratori were trained under Benedetto Bacchini. At that time in intellectual circles there was openness to dialogue with the rest of Europe, even if Muratori's Italian contacts were the most influential and relevant for him (Rosa 1994, 96–97). The correspondence network he maintained with non-Catholic intellectuals promoted respect for Christians of other confessions and encouraged attempts at confessional reconciliation. Muratori's relationship with the pastor and scholar Jacob Brucker (1696–1770) is one such example; intellectual exchanges soon became a friendship. Originally, Muratori had even intended to dedicate *The Faults That Occur in Religion* (*De naevis in religionem incurrentibus*; 1749) to Brucker (Kraus 1975).

Muratori insisted that Protestants be treated respectfully and charitably, and not antagonistically or dismissively. He expressed these sentiments clearly in his letter to Querini on 4 February 1749, as well as in other letters of that same year that mentioned the problem of the "peace of the church." Behind the call to avoid excesses in Marian devotion there was also a warning not to scandalize the Reformers, keeping them from converting. The ultimate purpose of this moderation and charity was to invite Reformers to return to the Catholic Church. In Muratori, there was no indifferentism or leveling of the different Christian confessions—unlike in many contemporary currents of thought that found the origin of all the different churches in natural religion. He never doubted the superiority of Catholicism, but distanced himself from both superficial irenicism and the notion of tolerance.

In the course of his life, Muratori constantly affirmed the need to relieve Catholicism of the burdens that might distract the faithful from an authentic relationship with God, while at the same time not to yield in any way to the Protestant marginalization of external devotion. Since his earliest works, Muratori rejected the notion that only interior prayer was valuable and, for instance, countered the critiques of Protestant theologians through a discussion of the decoration of holy buildings, as in *On the First Christian Churches* (*De primis christianorum ecclesiis*; 1771 [1694, posthumous]). He wanted to demonstrate the legitimacy of the use of images that dated back to the origins of Christianity.

In chapter four of *On Public Happiness,* he affirmed that the true basis for peaceful coexistence in any state is Catholicism, not Protestantism. In works such as *On the Moderation of Our Cleverness in Religious Matters,* "Letter Written on Behalf of an English Catholic" ("Lettera scritta a nome di una inglese cattolica ad uno inglese protestante"; 1767 [1734, posthumous]), and *The Ancient Roman Liturgy* (*Liturgia romana vetus*; 1748), several anti-Protestant points of debate emerged in matters concerning the Eucharist. The third part of the final version of the *Liturgia romana vetus* is a small treatise dedicated to the Eucharist with an anti-Protestant goal, and it aroused some criticism in Germanic lands. G. G. Ramaggini (1715–1779), secretary to the Olmütz bishop F. J. von Troyer, while considering this work "useful" for responding to the Protestants, criticized Muratori's use of overly harsh language, which sounded offensive. Muratori certainly intended to stay open to interpersonal dialogue but was unyielding in terms of dogma. His *Letter Written on Behalf of an English Catholic* effectively shows this in how the author responded to the critiques of John Tillotson (1630–1694), the archbishop of Canterbury whose works were produced in numerous editions. Muratori's tone is gentle, but he never concedes on doctrinal points.

Echoes in Europe

Muratori's view spread far in the intellectual and cultured circles of Europe—at times independently of direct knowledge of his works—but this success did not always bring with it a widespread agreement with his ideas.

Without dwelling on the situation in France, which has received excellent scholarly treatment (Waquet 1989), it is worth noting Muratori's debt to the Maurist monks; this relationship was an opportunity for intellectual exchange, but it did not spread knowledge of all his works in France. Explicit quotations and references to Muratori's work are rather rare in great authors such as Montesquieu and Voltaire. However, both the *Mémoires de Trévoux* and the *Journal des Savants* published reviews of Muratori's oeuvre, and one major work, *On the Moderation of Our Cleverness in Religious Matters,* was published under a pseudonym in Paris (1714). According to Dupront, there were, on a deeper level, close relationships between Muratori and French culture, and he considers Muratori's thought to be a sort of "incubator" of the Enlightenment (Dupront 1976, 13).

In seventeenth-century Austria and Germany, Muratori's works were well known both in their original Italian and in several German translations. Among others, *On Christian Charity* (*La carità cristiana*; 1723), and especially *The Science of Rational Devotion,* went through numerous editions. Muratori's intellectual exchange with the German world, which began during his years in Milan and which continued later (Marri and Lieber 2010), was vibrant; his exchanges with Leibniz on historic-genealogical research provide an example. In many cases, it was Muratori himself who strongly desired these contacts, and he was helped to find them by Domenico Brichieri Colombi (1716–1787) in Vienna and by other correspondents. Some interpretations of Muratori's thought, especially as regards the regularization of devotions, at times had rigorist and Jansenist nuances (Zlabinger

1970; Garms-Cornides 1975) with intellectualistic overtones (Rosa 1999). However, it is clear that Muratori never embraced the Jansenist movement (Stella 2006, 1:34). Several Jesuits used the accusations of Jansenism as an excuse to attack him. Far from being Jansenist, Muratori increasingly embraced a positive, very moderate view of humanity, for which the Jansenist Costantino Rotigni (1696–1776) accused him of being a Molinist (Vecchi 1955; Solé 1975). Nevertheless, the legend that Muratori was a Jansenist spread into the nineteenth century and could still be found in the first studies of A. C. Jemolo in the early twentieth century (Burlini Calapaj 1997). The inspiration that contemporary rulers drew from Muratori (regarding the reduction of the number of holy days of obligation, among other points) has been well-studied (Zlabinger 1970, 112–53; Schöch 1995). Particularly under Emperor Joseph II (1780–1790), Muratori's ideas were often distorted. The same happened in Hungary, where the tendency to exaggerate the influence of certain ideas of Muratori under the impetus of Josephinism is well documented (Szauder 1975, 147). A similar phenomenon occurred elsewhere. Scipione de' Ricci (1741–1810), the famous bishop of Pistoia and Prato, required his parish priests to read *The Science of Rational Devotion,* but it is difficult to find substantive connections between Muratori and Scipione given the enormous difference in the political and religious context in which they lived. Even some of Muratori's book dedications—such as those to Johann Philip von Lamberg, Prince-Bishop of Passau; to A. J. von Dietrichstein, archbishop of Salzburg; and to Cardinal F. J. Troyer—do not so much attest to a real intellectual affinity with these personalities as to his own desire, or that of his friends, to circulate his works as widely as possible (Garms-Cornides 1975; Burlini Calapaj 1997, 168–71).

In Spain, Gregorio Mayáns (1699–1781) was one of the main promoters of Muratori's work because he shared, as reflected in their correspondences, Muratori's interests in church reform and commitment to historical research. An engaged and valued figure in the Spanish intellectual world, Mayáns played an important role in the transmission of Muratori's thought; for example, he favored the distribution of *On the Moderation of Our Cleverness in Religious Matters.* Nevertheless, some of Mayáns's works show that the two did not hold the same positions on several issues. Unlike Muratori, Mayáns was a supporter of anti-Jesuitism, regalism, and episcopalism, and he had a deep-seated aversion to the Roman Curia (Mestre Sanchis 1979, 618–50). Likewise, Nuncio Enrique Enríquez was a friend and admirer of Muratori, but the political and religious environment of the time made their mutual differences clear. Some positions expressed in Muratori's *On Moral Philosophy* (*Della filosofia morale*; 1735) were brought on charges before the Spanish Inquisition, but nothing came of them thanks to the nuncio's intervention. Muratori's hostility to the "blood vow" in favor of the immaculate conception and his skepticism that it would turn into official dogma aroused considerable negativity in Spain, where devotion to the immaculate conception was very popular (Mestre Sanchis 1975, 192; Appolis 1966, 32–33). The *Science of Rational Devotion,* which had been translated into Spanish in 1763 with some omissions, also generated a vibrant debate.

Muratori and His Times

Muratori had many faces. Some people considered him a forerunner of the Enlightenment, and others made of him a nineteenth-century "liberal Catholic." Yet as noted by Mario Rosa, it is difficult to place him in a fixed interpretive system. Since the beginning of his public life, Muratori's identity was clear but unique. Later, thanks to new relationships, reflections, and contacts, he constantly revised his theories following experience and reason, but without substantial changes. There is a line of thought that connects his various works and creates a profoundly unified picture; such basic continuity has been adequately brought to light by several scholars (e.g., Vecchi 1975; Falco 1960).

If one accepts the questionable idea that the eighteenth century is truly defined by rationalism and anti-Catholic Enlightenment thinkers, Muratori stands apart in his faithfulness to Rome and his understanding that reason is brought to perfection only through authentic faith. He placed the new culture within the realm of Catholic-Christian thought. He showed an understanding of the Catholic tradition that distinguished him from Jansenists, who were convinced of the "eclipsing of truth" in the church, as well as from many Enlightenment figures, and some eminent members of the Catholic *Aufklärung*.

Muratori has often been considered an authoritative point of reference in the Catholic *Aufklärung*. His holistic approach favoring a unification of political, cultural, and religious concerns exerted significant influence. It seems certain that the attention to the Enlightenment of some Italian Catholic thinkers matured in Muratori's wake. The difference in personalities and contexts, however, often led to an ultimate distortion of Muratori's thought and to the use of its components to construct something totally different (Rosa 1999). Muratori's thought merged with the "Christian philosophy" of the late eighteenth century, which was based on a positive regard for reality and was directed more toward socioreligious inquiry than political theology. "Christian philosophy" opened the way for further developments in the nineteenth century, especially as regards "social doctrine." Charity, a critical term in Muratorian religious thought, was interpreted with a radically Christian meaning far from nineteenth-century philanthropy; but at the same time, the importance Muratori gave to the concrete aspects of the virtue of charity is symptomatic of the age and shows a clear consciousness of social needs.

In a moment of intense reflection and great change, Muratori's thought seemed intensely willing to open the Catholic world—within the clear boundaries of post-Tridentine Catholicism—to cultural and social issues using a language that was new for the church of the eighteenth century. In many respects, Muratori also made significant social contributions that were sometimes advanced for the period. For example, his *The Defects of Jurisprudence* had a great influence on the process of codification in Italy, and in it, Muratori gave exceptional emphasis to the progress of the sciences.

Muratori's thought was the result of the rational and harmonious combination of various elements. Maintaining a link with the past was a clear priority and is particularly relevant to the inheritance of the Council of Trent. Muratori praised the council and some of its successful achievements, such as those brought about by Borromeo and the efforts within the church to correct and eliminate abuses. According to Muratori, "happy" was the man who lived in the period of the implementation of the Council of Trent; this is particularly evident in his comments in the *Annali d'Italia*. Dupront describes Muratori as "a faithful follower of Trent" (*tridentin de la meilleure observance*), for whom "the Council is a way to begin a new era" (Dupront 1976, 98). Loyalty to the institutions of the modern church and to its battle against abuses was in perfect harmony with the will to overcome excessively juridical ecclesiology. The appeal to the Scriptures and the Fathers was not presented as the exaltation of a mythical "golden age," but as the invitation to adhere to the original sources of the Christian life.

Moderation, balance, and high regard for reason have ancient roots, particularly in Italy. Muratori combined all of this with a spirit for a "new era," through a striking originality that presents three distinct components. First, knowledge of the past is essential for understanding the present, and it is no coincidence that many of Muratori's works are rooted in his own historical research. Second, one also must look toward the future because it is fitting to consider projects and perspectives for the future. Finally, all of this happens in the present, to which everything is related and where everything is realized (Bonfatti 2010, in particular 168–69; De Martino 1996). This is accomplished through a positive esteem for man, his reason, and his potential. According to Muratori, a key element of human action is Christian freedom (Solé 1975, 357). For him, reason and freedom were both crucial aspects of the human experience, a view in opposition to the Jansenist one.

Muratori's thought was deeply connected with the tradition of the early modern Catholic Church, in its "Roman" faction; his admiration for the post-Tridentine church is a clear sign of that. At the same time, Muratori was open to reality in its various facets, and he often seemed to be sympathetic to certain aspects of the Enlightenment. He underlined the value of reason, but always reinforced the importance of its connection with faith. Reason was a crucial topic for that time. In fact, during the eighteenth century, many Enlightenment intellectuals transformed the Christian understanding of reason into a radically different view of reason denying faith. Although Muratori used the eighteenth-century categories of "usefulness" and "happiness," he did not forget the importance of the afterlife.

If compared with the intellectual perspectives of other representatives of the Catholic *Aufklärung,* Muratori's was broader. His cultural understanding derived some of its ideas from the Enlightenment, which at this time still showed its Christian origins.

Muratori's view of "reasonable Christianity" is itself an expression of the Christian background of a part of the Enlightenment thought. At the same time, it is an indication that conscious Christian thinkers and some representatives of the Enlightenment could engage in dialogue.

Bibliography

Appolis, Émile. 1966. *Les jansénistes espagnols*. Bordeaux: Sobodi.

Battistini, Andrea. 1994. "'Il gran profitto' delle 'verità dissotterrate': Le ragioni di Muratori autobiografo." In *Il soggetto e la storia: Biografia e autobiografia in L. A. Muratori,* 1–23. Florence: Olschki.

Bertelli, Sergio. 1960. *Erudizione e storia in Ludovico Antonio Muratori*. Naples: Nella Sede dell'Istituto (italiano per gli studi storici).

Bonfatti, Rossella. 2010. *L'"erario" della modernità: Muratori tra etica ed estetica*. Bologna: CLUEB.

Burlini Calapaj, Anna. 1997. *Devozioni e "regolata divozione" nell'opera di Lodovico Antonio Muratori: Contributo alla storia della liturgia*. Rome: CLV.

Carducci, Giosuè. 1900. "Di Lodovico Antonio Muratori e della sua raccolta di storici italiani dal 500 al 1500." In L. A. Muratori, *Rerum Italicarum Scriptores,* edited by Giosuè Carducci, vol. 1, part 1, xvii–lxxi. Città di Castello: S. Lapi.

Cottignoli, Alfredo. 1994. *Studi sul Muratori storico*. Bologna: CLUEB.

De Martino, Giulio. 1996. *Muratori filosofo: Ragione filosofica e coscienza storica in Lodovico Antonio Muratori*. Naples: Liguori.

Dupront, Alphonse. 1976. *L. A. Muratori et la société européenne des prélumières: Essai d'inventaire et de typologie d'après l'"Epistolario."* Florence: Olschki.

Falco, Giorgio. 1960. *Pagine sparse di storia e di vita*. Milan and Naples: R. Ricciardi.

Falco, Giorgio, and Fiorenzo Forti, eds. 1964. *Opere di Lodovico Antonio Muratori*. Milan and Naples: R. Ricciardi.

Flammini, Giuseppe. 2006. *Gli "Anecdota Graeca" di Ludovico Antonio Muratori e l'indagine filologica all'alba del secolo XVIII*. Macerata: EUM.
Garms-Cornides, Elisabeth. 1975. "In margine alla relazione L. A. Muratori e l'Austria." In *La fortuna di L. A. Muratori*, 247–57. Florence: Olschki.
Golinelli, Paolo. 2003. *Benedetto Bacchini (1651–1721): L'uomo, lo storico, il maestro*. Florence: Olschki.
Kraus, Andreas. 1975. "Lodovico Antonio Muratori und Bayern." In *Bayerische Geschichtswissenschaft in drei Jahrhunderten: Gesammelte Aufsätze*, 212–32. Munich: C. H. Beck.
Lehner, Ulrich L. 2011. *Enlightened Monks: The German Benedictines, 1740–1803*. Oxford: Oxford University Press.
Marchi, Gian Paolo. 1998. "Un confronto ineludibile: Scipione Maffei e Ludovico Antonio Muratori." In *Scipione Maffei nell'Europa del Settecento*, edited by Gian Paolo Romagnani, 363–97. Verona: Cierre.
Marri, Fabio, and Maria Lieber. 2010. *La corrispondenza di Lodovico Antonio Muratori col mondo germanofono: Carteggi inediti*. Frankfurt am Main: Peter Lang.
Mestre Sanchis, Antonio. 1975. "Muratori y la cultura española." In *La fortuna di L. A. Muratori*, 173–220. Florence: Olschki.
———. 1979. "Religión y cultura en el siglo XVIII español." In *Historia de la Iglesia en España*, edited by Antonio Mestre Sanchis, 583–743. Madrid: BAC.
Momigliano, Arnaldo. 1963. "Bacchini, Benedetto." In *Dizionario Biografico degli Italiani*, 5:22–29. Rome: Istituto della Enciclopedia Italiana.
Muratori, Lodovico Antonio. 1706. *Della perfetta poesia italiana*. Modena: Bartolomeo Soliani.
———. 1708–1715. *Riflessioni sopra il buon gusto nelle scienze e nelle arti*. Part 1, Venice: Luigi Pavino, 1708. Part 2, Colonia (Naples): per Benedetto Marco Renaud, 1715.
———. 1712. *Piena esposizione dei diritti imperiali ed estensi sopra la città di Comacchio*. Modena: n.p.
———. 1714. *De ingeniorum moderatione in religionis negotio*. Paris: apud Carolum Robustel.
———. 1717. *Delle Antichità estensi*. Modena: nella Stamperia ducale.
———. 1723. *La carità cristiana in quanto essa è amore del prossimo*. Modena: Bartolomeo Soliani.
———. 1723–1751. *Rerum italicarum scriptores*. Mediolani: Ex Typographia Societatis Palatinae in Regia Curia.
———. 1735. *Della filosofia morale esposta e proposta ai giovani*. Verona: Angelo Targa.
———. 1738–1742. *Antiquitates italicae Medii Aevi*. Milan: Ex Typographia Societatis Palatinae in Regia Curia.

———. 1742. *Dei difetti della giurisprudenza*. Venice: Giambattista Pasquali.
———. 1744–1749. *Annali d'Italia*. Milan (Venice): Giambattista Pasquali.
———. 1745. *Delle forze dell'intendimento umano*. Venice: Giambattista Pasquali.
———. 1747. *Della regolata divozione de' cristiani*. Venice: Giambattista Albrizzi. Translated as *The Science of Rational Devotion* (Dublin: James Byrn, 1789).
———. 1748. *Liturgia romana vetus*. Venice: Jo. Baptistae Pasquali.
———. 1749. *De naevis in religionem incurrentibus*. Lucae: Ex Typographia Benediniana.
———. 1767 (1734, posthumous). "Lettera scritta a nome di una inglese cattolica ad uno inglese protestante." In *Opere,* 4:345–432. Arezzo: per Michele Bellotti.
———. 1771 (1694, posthumous). "De primis christianorum ecclesiis." In *Opere,* 13:32–67. Arezzo: per Michele Bellotti.
———. 1872 (1721, posthumous). "Intorno al metodo seguito nei miei studi." In *Scritti inediti,* part 1, pp. 1–31. Bologna: Nicola Zanichelli.
Neveu, Bruno. 1975. "Muratori et l'historiographie gallicane." In *L. A. Muratori storiografo,* 241–304. Florence: Olschki.
Petruzzi, Paolo. 2010. *La "regolata" religione: Studi su Ludovico Antonio Muratori e il Settecento religioso italiano*. Assisi: Cittadella.
Plongeron, Bernard. 1969. "Recherches sur l'Aufklärung catholique en Europe occidentale." *Revue d'histoire moderne et contemporaine* 16:555–605.
———. 1970. "Questions pour l'Aufklärung catholique en Italie." *Il pensiero politico* 3:30–58.
Raimondi, Ezio. 1989. *I lumi dell'erudizione: Saggi sul Settecento italiano*. Milan: Vita e Pensiero.
Ricuperati, Giuseppe. 2003. "Muratori, Lodovico Antonio." In *Encyclopedia of the Enlightenment,* edited by Alan Kors et al., 3:103–4. Oxford: Oxford University Press.
Rosa, Mario. 1969. *Riformatori e ribelli nel '700 religioso italiano*. Bari: Dedalo.
———. 1994. "Un 'médiateur' dans la République des Lettres: Le bibliothécaire; In Commercium Litterarium." In *La communication dans la République des Lettres, 1600–1750,* edited by Hans Bots and Françoise Waquet, 80–99. Amsterdam and Maarssen: Apa-Holland University Press.
———. 1997. "Rileggendo Muratori tra politica e storia." In *Politica, vita religiosa, carità: Milano nel primo Settecento,* edited by Marco Bona Castellotti, Edoardo Bressan, and Paola Vismara, 3–41. Milan: Jaca Book.
———. 1999. *Settecento religioso: Politica della Ragione e religione del cuore*. Venice: Marsilio.

———. 2009. *La contrastata ragione: Riforme e religione nell'Italia del Settecento*. Rome: Edizioni di Storia e Letteratura.
Scandellari, Simonetta. 2004. "Las relaciones españolas de la obra de Ludovico Antonio Muratori." *Analecta Malacitana* 1:117–40.
Schöch, Nikolaus. 1995. "Der Streit zwischen Angelo Maria Querini und Antonio Muratori um die Reduktion der Feiertage." *Antonianum* 70:237–97.
Solé, Jacques. 1975. "Éthique chrétienne et anthropologie: Du pessimisme de Pierre Nicole à l'optimisme de Muratori." In *L. A. Muratori e la cultura contemporanea*, 353–59. Florence: Olschki.
Soli Muratori, Gian-Francesco. 1756. *Vita del proposto Lodovico Antonio Muratori*. Venice: Giambattista Pasquali.
Stella, Pietro. 2006. *Il giansenismo in Italia*. Vol. 1, *I preludi tra Seicento e primo Settecento*. Rome: Edizioni di Storia e Letteratura.
Szauder, Jozsef. 1975. "La fortuna dei trattati della Carità cristiana e della Regolata divozione in Ungheria nel '700." In *La fortuna di L. A. Muratori*, 143–50. Florence: Olschki.
Vecchi, Alberto. 1955. *L'opera religiosa del Muratori*. Milan: Edizioni Paoline.
———. 1968. "Tradizione e teologia nel Muratori." *Studia Patavina* 15:263–89.
———. 1975. "L'itinerario spirituale del Muratori." In *L. A. Muratori e la cultura contemporanea*, 181–223. Florence: Olschki.
Venturi, Franco. 1969. *Settecento riformatore*. Vol. 1, *Da Muratori a Beccaria*. Torino: Einaudi.
Viola, Corrado. 2009. *Canoni d'Arcadia: Muratori, Maffei, Lemene, Ceva, Quadrio*. Pisa: ETS.
Vismara, Paola. 2002. "Muratori 'immoderato.'" In *Cattolicesimi: Itinerari sei-settecenteschi*, edited by Paola Vismara, 29–61. Milan: Edizioni Biblioteca Francescana.
———. 2011. "Entre romanisme et antiromanisme: L'œuvre historique de Lodovico Antonio Muratori." In *Histoires antiromaines: Antiromanisme et critique dans l'historiographie catholique (XVIe–XXe siècles)*, edited by Sylvio De Franceschi, 87–114. Lyon: Edité par l'équipe Religions, Sociétés et acculturation (RESEA) du Laboratoire de Recherche historique Rhône-Alpes.
Waquet, Françoise. 1989. *Le modèle français et l'Italie savante: Conscience de soi et perception de l'autre dans la République des lettres (1660–1750)*. Rome: École Française de Rome.
Zlabinger, Eleonore. 1970. *Lodovico Antonio Muratori und Österreich*. Innsbruck: Kommissionsverlag der Österreichischen Kommissionsbuchhandlung.

12

Antonio Genovesi (1713–1769)

Reform through Commerce and Renewed Natural Law

NICCOLÒ GUASTI

The eldest of four brothers, Antonio Genovesi was born on 1 November 1713 at Castiglione, a little village near Salerno in the Kingdom of Naples, to a landowning family of modest means (Venturi 1962, 43–44, 47–83; Zambelli 1972, 797–860; Perna 1999). Antonio's father pointed his son toward an ecclesiastical career, and after he had completed his initial studies in rhetoric and humanities, a family relative in the medical profession introduced him to the study of scholasticism and Cartesianism.

The Early Years

Antonio spent his early years reading the works of the Renaissance historians and humanists, such as Dante (1265–1321) and Petrarch

(1304–1374), along with tales of medieval chivalry (Venturi 1962, 48–49). Genovesi also developed a passion for Cartesian geometry, as well as theology and metaphysics. The authors who influenced him most during this training period, other than René Descartes (1596–1650), were Melchior Cano (1509–1560), Nicolas Malebranche (1638–1715), and François Lamy (1636–1711).

After Genovesi received minor orders, he became, at the age of twenty-four years, professor of rhetoric at the seminary of Salerno, where he taught for two years, and then in December of 1737, he was ordained a priest. Some months later, he moved to Naples with one of his brothers, and there he attended the lectures of Giambattista Vico (1668–1744) and met Paolo Doria (1662–1746). In 1739, while still in Naples, he started a private school in which he taught theology, philosophy, and ethics, and developed a teaching style that exemplified his pedagogical vision. Genovesi's lectures became so famous in the Kingdom of Naples that Major Chaplain (*Cappellano Maggiore*) Celestino Galiani (1681–1753), responsible for the direction of the university, wanted to meet him. Galiani was the protagonist of the revival of studies in southern Italy, founder of the Academy of Sciences in 1732, who had emerged as an important popularizer of Pierre Bayle (1647–1706), Locke (1632–1704), Newton (1642–1727), the Utilitarians, and the British deists. In his capacity as headmaster of the University of Naples, he reformed the curriculum and introduced the teaching of natural sciences and experimental physics (Ajello 1976; Ferrone 1982; 2007, 111–72; Stapelbroek 2008, 56–87, 127–64). Thanks to Galiani's intervention, Genovesi was appointed extraordinary professor of metaphysics at the University of Naples in 1741. Four years later, he acquired the position of professor of ethics, thereby substantially increasing the number of students that attended his lectures.

During the 1740s, Genovesi devoted himself to the research of a systematic rationalism, capable of identifying the links between theology, metaphysics, and physics; this research pushed him toward adopting an eclectic-syncretic method and a comprehensive cultural perspective. Besides his antipathy toward the scholastic tradition and his initial sympathy for the Cartesian method, he profoundly admired the Cambridge Platonists, the empiricism of Bacon (1561–1626) and Locke, and the Lockean and Newtonian orientation of much Anglo-Dutch culture. Genovesi additionally read and admired the works of Jean Le Clerc (1657–1737), Peter van Muschenbroek (1692–1761), Samuel Clark (1675–1729), Thomas Woolston (1670–1733), and Arthur Ashley Sykes (1684–1756), in addition to texts of Cocceius (1603–1669), Christian Wolff (1679–1754), G. W. Leibniz (1646–1716), Johann Franz Budde (1667–1729), Gilbert Burnet (1634–1715), and William Whiston (1667–1752).

Genovesi's acquaintance with Newton's works, particularly with the *Mathematical Principles* (*Principia mathematica philosophiae naturalis*; 1687) and the *Opticks* (1696), became important because they provided Genovesi with a key to understanding the functioning of nature and human psychology. Moreover, Newtonian methods and ideas, which Genovesi knew from reading Voltaire's (1694–1778) works, including the *Métaphysique de Newton* (1741), stimulated his interest in physics, theology, and ethics (Zambelli 1972, 1978).

Equally important for Genovesi was his encounter during the 1740s with the works of the European natural law thinkers, especially Thomas Hobbes (1588–1679), John Locke, Hugo Grotius (1583–1645), Samuel Pufendorf (1632–1694), Richard Cumberland (1631–1718), Christian Thomasius (1655–1728), Jean Barbeyrac (1674–1744), Johann Heinecke (1681–1741), Jean J. Burlamaqui (1694–1748), and Jacob Friedrich Bielfeld (1717–1770). Genovesi also became interested in debates surrounding the works of Benedict Spinoza (1632–1677) and the British deists, in particular John Toland (1670–1722), Anthony Collins (1676–1729), the third Earl of Shaftesbury (1671–1713), and Bernard Mandeville (1670–1733). Finally, Genovesi knew, from the *Encyclopédie* and other key texts, such European Enlightenment thinkers as Voltaire, Maupertuis (1698–1759), Helvétius (1715–1771), Montesquieu (1689–1755), Étienne-Gabriel Morelly (1721–?), Rousseau (1712–1778), Hume (1711–1776), and Beccaria (1738–1794) (Venturi 1962, 1969; Zambelli 1972; Pii 1984).

The wealth and heterogeneity of his own education are already easily recognizable in his first printed work, the manual entitled *Elements of Metaphysics* (*Elementa Metaphysicae*), the first volume of which appeared in 1743. In *Elements,* Genovesi condemned the backwardness of Italian academic culture due to its strong links to Aristotelianism and scholasticism, which had limited freedom of thought and thus delayed Italy's modernization. Genovesi, therefore, argued for the freedom to philosophize (*libertas philosophandi*), referring explicitly to the examples of Bayle and the British thinkers, particularly Bacon, Locke, and deists like Toland and Thomas Morgan (d. 1743). This stance provoked an immediate reaction from Neapolitan and Roman conservatives. However, Genovesi remained undeterred and did not feel threatened, only responding to the heated controversy with an *Appendix* to his *Elements,* in which he reaffirmed the necessity of discussing unorthodox authors (Genovesi 1744, 9–10).

During 1745, Genovesi cooperated with his friend and colleague Orlandi (1712–1776) in the publication of the Neapolitan edition of the *Elements of Physics* (*Elementa Physicae*), by Peter van Muschenbroek. In the introduction, Genovesi (1745a, 2001) recapitulated the history of science from ancient times to his day and gave an outline of the importance of authors like Wolff, Leibniz, Newton, and the deists (Garin 1993, 231–47; Ferrone 1982). However, his sincere acceptance of Newtonianism was linked with the Platonism of Girolamo Cardano (1501–1576) and Tommaso Campanella (1568–1639). A little while later, Genovesi published a manual of philosophy, the *Elements of Logic* (*Elementorum artis logico-criticae libri V*; 1745b), in which he combined Cartesian methods and deistic ideas on the one hand with Augustinian ethics from Antoine Arnauld's (1612–1694) and Pierre Nicole's (1625–1695) *Logic of Port Royal* (1662) on the other. At the same time, however, Genovesi remained firm in defending freedom of thought as essential to the reform of university studies. In 1745, he decided to accept a professorship of ethics, although it was a less prestigious chair than that of metaphysics, because teaching this discipline was often a stepping-stone for promotion to a theology professoriate. Nevertheless, this intended transfer did not happen because his writings were suspected of heterodoxy.

In the mid-1740s, Genovesi had become one of the most well-known intellectuals of Italy, an assessment attested to by his correspondence with the major scholars of his time. Among his most prominent correspondents were the Venetian Philosopher Conti (1667–1749) and Lodovico Muratori (1672–1750) of Modena, who had highly praised the *Elements of Logic* and the *Elements of Metaphysics* (Venturi 1969, 531, 533; Zambelli 1972, 112–63).

His notoriety guaranteed Genovesi a certain protection that allowed him to escape official condemnations or censures by the ecclesiastical authorities of the Kingdom of Naples and the Holy Offices of Rome. Apart from Galiani's support, Genovesi could also count on the Secretary of State, José Joaquín Montealegre; on numerous regalist employees of the royal court like Niccolo Fraggianni; and, finally, on the leader of Neapolitan Freemasonry, Raimondo di Sangro (1710–1771), to support him. Within the Roman ecclesiastical circles, Genovesi enjoyed the tacit protection of Pope Benedict XIV (1740–1758), to whom he dedicated the second part of *Elements of Metaphysics* in 1747. The pope shelved various indictments that the nuncio and the archbishop of Naples, Spinelli, directed to Rome about Genovesi's works (Wolf 2011, 74). Nevertheless, because of such accusations Genovesi was unable to obtain a professorship in theology, nor could he publish his *Elements of Universal Christian Theology* (*Universae christianae theologiae elementa dogmatica,* published posthumously 1771). This, and the controversy that derived from the publication of the fourth volume of his *Elements of Metaphysics* (1752) about natural law, persuaded Genovesi to abandon his speculative studies in favor of more practical endeavors.

The Florentine Bartolomeo Intieri (1678–1757) contributed to this change of interests in a very significant way. At the time, Intieri was administrator of the property and possessions of the most important Tuscan families in the Kingdom of Naples and hosted a famous salon, which attracted outstanding intellectuals to his villa at Massa Equana. As a supporter of scientific progress in agronomy and of Enlightenment thought, Intieri convinced Genovesi of the need to devote himself to the study of political economy (Venturi 1962, 15–18; 1969, 553–58; Galasso 1989, 401–29). This turning point in Genovesi's intellectual life, from metaphysics to the science of commerce, was made public in his *Discourse on the True Purpose of Literature and the Sciences* (*Discorso sopra il vero fine delle lettere e delle scienze*), inserted as an introduction to the reprinting of *Reasoning about the Best Means for Agriculture to Flourish* (*Ragionamento sopra i mezzi più necessari per far fiorire l'agricoltura*; 1754) by the Tuscan agronomist Montelatici (1692–1770). The *Discorso* was rightly considered to be related to the Intieri group of intellectuals and reformers. In it, Genovesi not only maintained that commerce was a science with its own general principles, but also asserted the urgency to the Kingdom of Naples of increasing agricultural development and factory manufacturing, in order to improve public happiness and welfare. To accomplish this objective, according to Genovesi, it was necessary to have a well-organized collaboration between the intellectuals, or "sages," of the kingdom and the sovereign, who therefore must totally reform the school curriculum with the aim of educating the youth and the privileged with a new system focusing upon the common good of the entire nation (Venturi 1962, 84–131). The profound impact of this *Discourse* is evident from the fact of its multiple reprintings.

From Metaphysics to Economy and Commerce

The reform attempts of Intieri culminated in 1754, with a proposal to the sovereign that a chair be endowed for "commercial and mechanical" (*commercio e meccanica*) studies at the University of Naples. Genovesi was Intieri's favorite candidate for the position. On 16 March 1754, after having overcome the opposition of conservative groups in his realm, Charles of Bourbon approved the professorship and, on November 4, Genovesi held his first lecture course, which was later published as *Reasoning on Commerce in General* (*Ragionamento sul commercio in universale*; Genovesi 1984, 1:119–63). The lectures, at Intieri's request, were given in Italian rather than Latin, so that they might attract a wider audience and be more easily disseminated, thus helping to establish the new discipline. Genovesi maintained this teaching appointment until his death. This academic recognition of political economy as a new scientific discipline must be considered as a key event in eighteenth-century Italian culture. In fact, the Neapolitan professorship, which soon became a role model for other institutions of higher learning, can be considered the first university position in political economy in Europe (Di Battista 1988).

During the last fifteen years of his life, Genovesi's efforts focused on the formulation and popularization of the principles of "civil economy," or the "science of commerce," by means of his lectures and publications. The authors who contributed to the formation of Genovesi's economic thought have been known for a long time (Villari 1958; Venturi 1962, 19–24; Venturi 1969, 568–71; Pii 1984, 54–68). However, unlike most other agronomists of the period, Genovesi appreciated British political arithmetic (e.g., vital statistics) and read Josiah Child (1630–1699), Gregory King (1648–1712), and William Petty (1623–1687). His reading of the late mercantile literature of Spain and Britain included John Cary (1649–1720?), Charles Davenant (1656–1714), Thomas Mun (1571–1641), Joshua Gee (1667–1730), Gerónimo Uztáriz (1670–1732), and Ulloa (d. 1740). Additional influences were early eighteenth-century French writers of economic treatises—Pierre de Boisguilbert (1646–1714), Sébastien Vauban (1633–1707), Nicolas Dutot (1684–1741), and, above all, Jean F. Melon (1675–1738); the *Political Discourses* (1753) by David Hume; and French authors from the Vincent de Gournay group, in particular Véron de Forbonnais (1722–1800), Plumard de Dangeul (1722–1777), Claude J. Herbert (1700–1758), and Gabriel F. Coyer (1707–1782). Of central importance was, however, the Paris group of civil servants, merchants, and French intellectuals headed by the *Intendant du commerce* Vincent de Gournay. Even if Genovesi was one of the few Neapolitan intellectuals of the period who learned English, French remained the basic medium for reaching British culture. Genovesi became very familiar with English and Spanish literature on political economy through the numerous translations organized by the members of the Gournay group (Murphy 1986; Meyssonnier 1989; Larrère 1992; Guasti 2000).

Since the first year of his professorship in "commerce and mechanics" and the publication of his first work on the subject of economics, Genovesi's efforts were directed toward a twofold objective. First, he worked to defend the scientific basis of the civil economy that he inserted into his new political theory of natural law, because he considered the "art of prudence" out-of-date and bound to sixteenth- and seventeeth-century thought; this thesis of his is exemplified by *Reason of State* (Genovesi 1984, 1:119, 125–27; 2005, 3–4, 261–63, 271, 509). Second, Genovesi considered civil economy a fundamental instrument in reformist policy and, therefore, an appropriate medium for the Bourbon government to transform the Kingdom of Naples from a still-feudal economy into a modern, commerce-oriented society like Britain. The strength of the "British model" is displayed in the first work on the economy that Genovesi published, the *History of Commerce in Great Britain* (*Storia del commercio della Gran Bretagna*; 1757–1758).

The core of this three-volume treatise is a translation of Cary's *Essay on the State of England* (1664) from French. It was accompanied by three essays—the already-mentioned *Ragionamento sul commercio, Reasoning about the Forces and Effects of Great Wealth* (*Ragionamento filosofico sulle forze e gli effetti delle gran ricchezze*), and *Reasoning about the Public Confidence* (*Ragionamento sulla fede pubblica*)—and by various "annotations," in which Genovesi commented in detail on some themes and concepts proposed by Cary and his French translators (Gournay and Butel-Dumont).

Finally, in the *History,* Genovesi also included a translation from the original English of *England's Treasure of Commerce* (1664), by Mun. In the annotations, he buttressed the power of the British model of society and economic policy, though he considered some suggestions for economic reform by Uztáriz and Ulloa useful, too. In fact, in addition to representing Great Britain (and to a lesser extent, the United Provinces) as an ideal point of reference for modern commercial society and as a form of economic development worthy of emulation, Genovesi considers the situation of the underdeveloped Spanish monarchy. According to Genovesi, the Spanish monarchy resembled, for many reasons, the then run-down Kingdom of Naples, a country poor in raw materials, still feudal, and at the margins of the international mercantile circuit (Venturi 1969, 564–65, 571–95; Pii 1984, 50–53; Stapelbroek 2006; Reinert 2007).

The political framework for the success of Genovesi's economic thought was strengthened by the great famine of 1764, which hit the whole of Italy and its southern regions in particular. Like many European thinkers and reformers, Genovesi was convinced—after a careful analysis of the cause of the crisis—of the necessity of a free trade policy capable of facilitating the abandonment of ancient rationing laws, while also creating a free market in land under the control of a state commission and ecclesiastical mortmain. Actually, in 1764, Genovesi edited the reprint of *The Experienced Farmer* (*L'agricoltore sperimentato*), by Cosimo Trinci, one of the most well-known agricultural works printed in Italy in the first half of the 1700s. This edition was accompanied by a preface (Venturi 1962, 164–76; Trinci 1764, i–ix; Genovesi 1984, 2:875–86), as well as an appendix entitled *Idea of a New Method of English Farming* (*Idea del nuovo metodo di agricoltura inglese*; Trinci 1764, 327–58), which in reality is a translation of the *Treatise on the Cultivation of Land* (*Traité de la culture des terres*; 1750) by Duhamel du Monceau (1700–1782). In addition to reaffirming the necessity of spreading the new agricultural techniques through the foundation of agrarian academies for rural farmers and landowners, Genovesi's appendix asked for the expansion of small-holding properties and the leasing of property. The following year, Genovesi tried to support a bill for the liberalization of the grain trade by the Neapolitan Secretary of State, Tanucci, by his editing of the *Reflections on the Overall Economy of Grains* (*Riflessioni sull'economia generale de'-grani*; 1765), a translation of Herbert's *Essai sur la police générale des grains* (1775). In the "Preliminary Discourse" to this translation and in the commentary, Genovesi asked the government to guarantee the institutional and legislative framework of the future free-trade policy (Di Gregorio 2009). Nevertheless, despite the enormous efforts of Genovesi and his supporters, the bill was rejected.

Between 1765 and 1769, that is, during the last five years of Genovesi's life, his political and cultural commitment intensified; the priest from Salerno had in fact become the point of reference for the intelligentsia and for the reformist groups in the Kingdom of Naples (Genovesi 1774; Rao 1984; Imbruglia 2000). Besides teaching, he still published numerous works and consulted on the Council of Infringement (*Giunta degli Abusi*), a new administrative organization that was supposed to accelerate reformist policy. The reports given by Genovesi were concerned with the most pressing issues of the time: other than the already-mentioned liberalization of the grain trade, his reports treated monetary policy, commercial treaties, new curricula for the former Jesuit schools, the abolition of the Naples University Chair of Papal Decretals, the limitation of mortmain, and the defense of royal privileges against the Holy See (Genovesi 2008b, 406–573). It was during this phase of his career that Genovesi's regalism, inspired by Giannone (1676–1748), matured into the conviction of a deliberate jurisdictional superiority of the state over the church (Ricuperati 1970; Ajello 1980; Galasso 1989, 369–99; Rosa 2009, 145–66).

Works on Civil Economy and Commerce

This heterogeneous political-cultural commitment culminated in the most important and famous of all Genovesi's works—*Lectures on Commerce or on Civil Economy* (*Delle lezioni di commercio o sia di economia civile*; 2005, 257–892). The success of Genovesi's treatise was immediate, and it affected the whole of Italy. The first Neapolitan edition was published in 1765–1767, followed by a second edition published in Milan in 1768 and edited by his disciple Troiano Odazi, and a third (1768–1770) printed again in Naples (Venturi 1969, 620–21; Genovesi 2005, 908–19). Parts of the lectures derived from a much earlier university course he had taught in 1757–1758, entitled *Elements of Commerce* (*Elementi di Commercio*; 2005, 3–256). The reasons for the importance of the *Lectures* within the framework of the Enlightenment culture and Italian reform in the second half of the 1700s are numerous. First, Genovesi emphasized that this work was meant as a textbook that could be adopted for courses by every professor of civil economy. Moreover, the *Lectures* can be considered a summa of Genovesi's thought. In fact, in them he went so far as to reflect on the laws of civil economy and themes of current political affairs through the analysis of human psychology and political regimes (2005, 272–376). Therefore, the treatise proposed a full explanation of political economy through a precise historical and contextual analysis of the links between moral philosophy, politics, and economics (2005,

262–63). The fact that some of his other texts—for example, *Academic Letters* (*Lettere accademiche*; 1764b/1769), *Logic* (*Logica*; 1766), *On Justice* (*Delle diceosina* [the title is a neologism created by Genovesi from the Greek words δίκαιος/δικαιοσύνη (*dikaios/dikaiosunē*): that is, it is "a philosophy of Justice and Honesty"]; 1766–1771), *Metaphysics* (*Delle scienze metafisiche*; 1767), the unedited *Moral Dialogues* (*Dialoghi morali*), and Genovesi's notes to the Neapolitan translation of *The Spirit of the Laws,* by Montesquieu (1777; Genovesi 2008a, 73–376; De Mas 1971; Pii 1984, 76–84; Imbruglia 2000, 2005)—echoed thoughts of the *Lectures* demonstrates that in reality, during these five years Genovesi was writing only one major encyclopedic text on links between epistemological principles and the various disciplines of scholarship. Thus, the *Lectures* were "a type of encyclopedia of everything that was discussed, meditated on and done in Italy on the subjects of moral theology, ethics, political theory, science and political economy" (Venturi 1969, 621).

Such an encyclopedic effort was evident above all in the first part of the *Lectures,* which were dedicated "to the practical principles of civil economy" (Genovesi 2005, 271–652), while the second part, centered on monetary questions, appeared more technical (Genovesi 2005, 657–892). Civil economy, according to Genovesi, formed the essence of a new civil philosophy that should aim at human happiness. This happiness, whether private or public—far from the paternalistic definition that Muratori gave it—followed the more recent utilitarian theories maintaining that it depended on the development of the "improving arts" (*arti miglioratrici*) and on luxury (Bellamy 1987; Ferrone 2000, 2:159–61, 188–92, 307–8; Wahnbaeck 2004; Jossa and Patalano 2007; Trampus 2008, 153–56). To show that the progress of knowledge was indissolubly linked to that of the arts and trade, Genovesi redeveloped, in an original way, the stadial theory taken from *Political Discourses,* by Hume, from *The Spirit of the Laws* by Montesquieu, and from *On the Origins of Laws* (*De l'origine de lois*) by Antoine Goguet (1716–1758). To argue with Rousseau and the supporters of a cyclic philosophy of history (the first amongst them, Vico), Genovesi maintains that the arts and sciences represent the driving force of the historical process. This theoretic outline served Genovesi as a point of reference when it came to analyzing the economic situation of Italy, and of the Kingdom of Naples in particular; it was at this moment that he adopted a political perspective. If the civil economy supports itself on precise laws and general principles, obtained empirically from "the history of commerce" of individual countries, it was necessary to bring them into line with particular contexts. It is up to the enlightened sovereigns and governments, Genovesi suggested, to apply such principles through an economic policy that takes into account the peculiarity and the specificity of the contexts in which those authorities govern (Pii 1984, 49–53). In the particular case of the Kingdom of Naples, Genovesi (2005, 610–50) recommended various measures to be taken, in particular the expansion of small-holding property, the liberation of the grain trade, the reorganization of the public administration, and the launch of an equalizing fiscal levy. His recommendations, therefore, deal with a series of reforms that, if adopted, would produce a radical change to the society of the ancien régime.

The innovative meaning of the proposal put forward by Genovesi was confirmed also by the semantic care that constantly accompanied his considerations. For example, to define the kind of reform he recommended for different ranks of the society in which he lived, at the end of the first part of the *Lectures* he used the expression "constitutional law" (Genovesi 2005, 649), a concept that would become familiar to his followers and the Neapolitan reformers during the late Enlightenment period. According to Genovesi, this reorganization of contemporary society on new foundations could be carried out only through a firm alliance between the crown and the *élites*: the nobility, the clergy and the "middle rank." They must rethink their current position and their established roles in office for the public good, abandoning their rank, order, and professional selfishness accordingly as needed. Moreover, and above all, the state should be able to create the conditions to educate the youth and working classes through a general reform of studies and a greater diffusion of practical knowledge throughout these working ranks, thanks to the foundation of the agrarian societies, scientific academies, professional schools, libraries, and new manuals and catechisms (Pii 1984, 271–85; Chiosi 1992, 79–88).

A Renewal of Natural Law Philosophy

In addition to his interests in political economy, which proved central to his teaching activity, Genovesi continued to be interested, broadly speaking, in philosophy between the end of the 1750s and 1769. In particular, Genovesi aspired to the transformation of moral philosophy into a new science coupled with economics and politics (Genovesi 2005, 3–4). He maintained a clear distinction, therefore, between the form of ethics that was determined to attain eternal happiness through religion and the more secular form of ethics, understood as honest education and respect for natural rights, human rights, and citizens' rights. Accordingly, Genovesi founded morality on natural law and Stoicism, insofar as Stoicism maintained that the twin forms of public happiness could reunite exclusively through strict respect of social duties and through a precise correspondence between natural laws and civil laws (Arata 1978; Pii 1984, 121–29; Trampus 2008, 147–50). The first step in this direction was fulfilled by *Philosophical Meditations* (*Meditazioni filosofiche*), published in 1758. But Genovesi, who had tried to demonstrate the orthodoxy of his thought in his *Elements of Metaphysics,* only to have his work denounced again by the Congregation of the Index and by his friend Pasquale Magli (1720–1776), had failed in this first attempt of defining a moral science, because it remained too traditional (Venturi 1969, 595–97).

However, such a project was realized between 1764 and 1769, during a phase of intellectual and political hyperactivity that was the last glorious moment of Genovesi's life. Also in the sphere of moral and philosophical reflection, Genovesi finished by singling out his actual privileged readers among the young generations. In fact, it was to the "youngsters" (*giovanetti*) that he dedicated his first treatise in Latin on moral philosophy, *On Rights* (*De iure et officiis in usum tironum libri II*; 1764a), which he followed with a genuine philosophy course divided into three parts: *Logic* (*La logica*; 1766); *Della diceosina* (1767–1771), that is, the part concerning moral philosophy; and *Metaphysics* (*Delle scienze metafisiche*; 1767). This trilogy, in which Genovesi reelaborated and popularized through the Italian language the concepts already developed in previous works, had a broad and prolonged success across the whole peninsula—a fact confirmed by the many republished editions that followed. In these texts, and in particular in *On Rights* and *Della diceosina,* Genovesi tried to apply mathematical laws of nature to human science (Marcialis 1994). In this, he closely followed natural law and the Newtonian method, where it sustained a perfect coincidence between the principles of physics, beginning with the conflict of forces, and the weakness of human behavior. Polemicizing against Hobbes, Genovesi redeveloped Stoic thought and Shaftesbury's ideas (along with the new interpretation that Diderot had given them in his *Pensées philosophiques*; 1746), as well as thoughts of Maupertuis and Helvétius, maintaining that egoism is not the only weakness in human behavior, but that there also exists a natural inclination to help, to be charitable, and to be humanitarian. Therefore, the rational control of one's own love, which is at the foundation of natural law, also springs from the simple calculation of convenience—to not invade other people's rights and to help one's neighbor. In essence, Genovesi was the first Italian to arrive at a conscious definition of the subjective rights of man (Ferrone 2003, 131–33; Guasti 2006; Genovesi 2008b; Trampus 2009, 152–53).

Genovesi—A Pioneer of Italian Enlightenment Culture

Even after Genovesi's death in Naples on 12 September 1769, Italian publishers continued to print his works. His works circulated equally widely abroad. In particular, *Lectures, Logic,* and *Metaphysics* all succeeded hugely in Germany, Portugal, Spain, and Latin America, where they were translated, discussed, and adopted as textbooks in the universities and other gatherings of Enlightenment society (Venturi 1969, 534–37, 632–44; Astigarraga and Usoz 2007). That Genovesi's works were not so well known in France and England did not necessarily mean that they were not in accordance with more mature Enlightenment thought (Venturi 1969, 634–44). On the contrary, that they fit the Enlightenment and reformist nature of the time explains their foreign success. The knowledge he provided of the injustices in the society of the ancien régime and the solutions that he outlined to reform it were adaptable to many European and non-European contexts of the period, so they were appreciated in those countries that aspired to the renewal of their own economy, society, and culture.

In conclusion, Genovesi combined two epochs, "the crisis of the European consciousness" and the one of the Enlightenment itself. The labels "Catholic *Aufklärung*" and "moderate Enlightenment" seem insufficient in defining exactly his cultural project. Undoubtedly, Genovesi had used an eclectic method with the aim of recovering various elements of Aristotelian and Thomist political theory (like the concept of "family," considered as the cellular base of the political body). Nevertheless, this cannot be assimilated easily into the defensive strategy and opportunist choice by some sectors of Italian Catholicism that had accepted a few Enlightenment ideas only in order to weaken their subversive significance and undermine Enlightenment in the long term (Rosa 1999, 151–64; Israel 2001, 56–58). In the case of Genovesi, the eclecticism was functional, insofar as it allowed him to develop a cultural project that, far from restraining the diffusion of modern science and European Enlightenment, instead facilitated it. Above all, he considered economic thought as a means for spreading contemporary Enlightenment culture (Robertson 1997; 2005, 347–60). Genovesi must therefore be considered, along with Beccaria, as the most remarkable figure of the first generation of the Italian Enlightenment. His importance does not reside so much in having realized an epistemological break within the sphere of the culture of southern Italy; this was in fact realized during the first thirty years of the 1700s by his protector Galiani, through the introduction of texts and thought by Newton, Locke, and the British deists. Instead, Genovesi guaranteed a political platform rather than that of a cultural revolution. Such a commitment produced, within the Kingdom of Naples, a true and genuine Genovesian "school," and it is commonly believed that it attempted, after his death, to achieve the reforms that he recommended (Galanti 1772).

Bibliography

Ajello, Raffaele. 1976. *Arcana juris: Diritto e politica nel Settecento italiano.* Naples: Jovene.

———, ed. 1980. *Pietro Giannone e il suo tempo: Atti del convegno di studi nel trecentenario della nascita.* 2 vols. Naples: Jovene.

Arata, Fidia. 1978. *A. Genovesi: Una proposta di morale illuministica.* Padua: Marsilio.

Astigarraga, Jusús, and Javier Usoz. 2007. "From the Neapolitan A. Genovesi of Carlo di Borbone to the Spanish A. Genovesi of Carlos III: V. de Villava's Spanish Translation of 'Lezioni di commercio.'" In *Genovesi economista: Nel 250° anniversario dell'istituzione della cattedra di "Commercio e Meccanica,"* edited by Bruno Jossa, Rosario Patalano, and Eugenio Zagari, 193–220. Naples: Istituto Italiano per gli Studi Filosofici.

Bellamy, Richard. 1987. "'Da metafisico a mercatante': Antonio Genovesi and the Development of a New Language of Commerce in Eighteenth-Century Naples." In *The Languages of Political Theory in Early-Modern Europe,* edited by Anthony Pagden, 277–302. Cambridge: Cambridge University Press.

Chiosi, Elvira. 1992. *Lo spirito del secolo: Politica e religione a Napoli nell'età dell'Illuminismo.* Naples: Giannini.

De Mas, Enrico. 1971. *Genovesi e le edizioni italiane dello "Spirito delle leggi."* Florence: Le Monnier.

Di Battista, Francesco. 1988. "Per la storia della prima cattedra universitaria d'economia." In *Le cattedre d'economia politica in Italia: La diffusione di una disciplina "sospetta" (1750–1900),* edited by Massimo M. Augello, Marco Bianchini, Gabriella Gioli, and Piero Roggi, 31–46. Milan: Franco Angeli.

Di Gregorio, Adriano. 2009. "Fra *Commerce* e *police des grains*: Echi del dibattito francese nel Meridione d'Italia; Il caso di Herbert." In *Modelli d'oltre confine: Prospettive economiche e sociali negli antichi Stati italiani,* edited by Antonella Alimento, 113–30. Rome: Edizioni di Storia e Letteratura.

Ferrone, Vincenzo. 1982. *Scienza Natura Religione: Mondo newtoniano e la cultura italiana nel primo Settecento.* Naples: Jovene. Translated as *The Intellectual Roots of the Italian Enlightenment: Newtonian Science, Religion, and Politics in the Early Eighteenth Century* (Atlantic Highlands, NJ: Humanities Press, 1995).

———. 2000. *Il profeti dell'Illuminismo: Le metamorfosi della ragione nel tardo Settecento italiano.* Rome and Bari: Laterza.

———. 2003. *La società giusta ed equa: Repubblicanesimo e diritti dell'uomo in Gaetano Filangieri*. Rome and Bari: Laterza. Translated by Sophus A. Reinert as *The Politics of Enlightenment: Constitutionalism, Republicanism, and the Rights of Man in Gaetano Filangieri* (London: Anthem Press, 2012).

———. 2007. *Una scienza per l'uomo: Illuminismo e Rivoluzione scientifica nell'Europa del Settecento*. Turin: Utet.

Galanti, Giuseppe Maria. 1772. *Elogio storico del Signor Abate Genovesi* . . . Naples.

Galasso, Giuseppe. 1989. *La filosofia in soccorso de' governi: La cultura napoletana del Settecento*. Naples: Guida.

Garin, Eugenio. 1993. *Dal Rinascimento all'Illuminismo: Studi e ricerche*. Florence: Le Lettere.

Genovesi, Antonio. 1743–1752. *Elementa Metaphysicae in usum privatorum adolescentium mathematicum in morem adornata ab Antonio Genuensi in regia napolitana Academia philosophiae professore,* 4 vols. Naples. 2nd ed., 5 vols., Naples, 1760–1763.

———. 1744. *Appendix ad priorem Metaphysicae partem qua quaedam paullo obscuriora clarius explicantur* . . . Naples.

———. 1745a. "Dissertatio physico-historica de rerum corporearum origine et constitutione." In *Elementa physicae conscripta in usus academicos . . .* , by Petrus van Muschenbroek. Naples.

———. 1745b. *Elementorum artis logico-criticae libri V.* Naples.

———. 1753. "Discorso sopra il vero fine delle lettere e delle scienze." In *Ragionamento sopra i mezzi più necessari per far fiorire l'agricoltura,* by Ubaldo Montelatici. Naples.

———. 1757–1758. *Storia del commercio della Gran Bretagna scritta da John Cary mercante di Bristol, tradotta in nostra volgar lingua da Pietro Genovesi.* 3 vols. Naples.

———. 1758. *Meditazioni filosofiche sulla religione e sulla morale.* Naples.

———. 1759. *Lettere filosofiche ad un amico provinciale per servire di rischiaramento agli elementi metafisici.* Naples.

———. 1764a. *De iure et officiis in usum tironum libri II.* Naples. 2nd ed., Naples, 1767.

———. 1764b. *Lettere accademiche su la questione se sieno più felici gl'ignoranti che gli scienziati* . . . Naples. 2nd ed., Naples, 1769.

———. 1765. "Idea dell'opera o discorso preliminare dell'abate Genovesi regio cattedratico di commercio." In *Riflessioni sull'economia generale de' grani tradotte dal francese . . .* , by Claude-Jacques Herbert. Naples.

———. 1765–1767. *Delle lezioni di commercio o sia d'economia civile da leggersi nella cattedra interiana dell'ab: Genovesi regio cattedratico.* 2 vols. Naples. 2nd ed., Naples, 1768–1770.

———. 1766. *La logica per gli giovanetti*. Naples.

———. 1766–1771. *Della diceosina o sia della filosofia del giusto, e dell'onesto per gli giovanetti*. 2 vols. Naples. 2nd ed., 3 vols., Naples, 1777.

———. 1767. *Delle scienze metafisiche per gli giovanetti*. Naples.

———. 1771. *Universae christianae theologiae elementa dogmatica, historica, critica*. Venice.

———. 1773. *Lettera scritta su gli Elementi teologici dell'abate D. Antonio Genovesi*. N.p.

———. 1774. *Lettere familiari dell'Abate Antonio Genovesi*. Edited by Doenico Forges Davanzati. 2 vols. Naples.

———. 1779. *Elementa physicae experimentalis usui tironum*. Naples.

———. 1973. *Della Diceosina o sia della filosofia del giusto e dell'onesto*. Edited by Francesco Arata. Milan: Marzorati.

———. 1984. *Scritti economici*. Edited by Maria Luisa Perna. 2 vols. Naples: Istituto Italiano per gli Studi Filosofici.

———. 2001. *Dissertatio physico-historica de rerum origine et constitutione*. Edited by Maurizio Torrini and Sara Bonechi. Florence: Giunti.

———. 2005. *Delle lezioni di commercio o sia di economia civile con elementi del commercio*. Edited by Maria Luisa Perna. Naples: Istituto Italiano per gli Studi Filosofici.

———. 2008a. *Della Diceosina o sia della filosofia del giusto e dell'onesto*. Edited by Niccolò Guasti. Venice: Centro di Studi sull'Illuminismo europeo G. Stiffoni.

———. 2008b. *Dialoghi e altri scritti intorno alle lezioni di commercio*, edited by Eluggero Pii. Naples: Istituto Italiano per gli Studi Filosofici.

Guasti, Niccolò. 2000. "Forbonnais e Plumard traduttori di Uztáriz e Ulloa." *Il pensiero economico italiano* 8 (2): 71–97.

———. 2006. "Antonio Genovesi's *Diceosina*: Source of the Neapolitan Enlightenment." *History of European Ideas* 32 (4): 385–405.

Imbruglia, Girolamo. 2000. "Enlightenment in Eighteenth-Century Naples." In *Naples in the Eighteenth Century: The Birth and Death of a Nation State*, edited by Girolamo Imbruglia, 70–94. Cambridge: Cambridge University Press.

———. 2005. "Due opposte letture napoletane dell'*Esprit des lois*: Genovesi e Personè." In *Montesquieu e i suoi interpreti*, edited by Domenico Felice, 1:191–210. Pisa: ETS.

Israel, Jonathan I. 2001. *Radical Enlightenment: Philosophy and the Making of Modernity, 1650–1750*. Oxford: Oxford University.

Jossa, Bruno, and Rosario Patalano. 2007. "Genovesi, la ricchezza e l'umana felicità." In *Genovesi economista: Nel 250° anniversario dell'istituzione della cattedra di "Commercio e Meccanica,"* edited by Bruno Jossa, Rosario Patalano, and Eugenio Zagari, 91–107. Naples: Istituto Italiano per gli Studi Filosofici.

Larrère, Catherine. 1992. *L'invention de l'économie au XVIIIe siècle.* Paris: Presses Universitaires de France.

Marcialis, Maria Teresa. 1994. "Legge di natura e calcolo della ragione nell'ultimo Genovesi." *Materiali per una Storia della Cultura Giuridica* 24 (2): 315–40.

Meyssonnier, Simone. 1989. *La Balance et l'Horloge: La genèse de la pensée libérale en France au XVIIIe siècle.* Paris: Les Éditions de la Passion.

Montesquieu, Charles-Louis de Secondat de. 1777. *Spirito delle leggi del signore Montesquieu con le note dell'abate Antonio Genovesi.* Naples.

Murphy, Antonin E. 1986. "Le développement des idées économiques en France (1750–1765)." *Revue d'histoire moderne et contemporaine* 33:521–41.

Perna, Maria Luisa. 1998. "L'universo comunicativo di Antonio Genovesi." In *Atti del convegno Editoria e cultura nel XVIII secolo,* edited by Anna Maria Rao, 391–404. Naples: Liguori.

———. 1999. "Genovesi, Antonio." In *Dizionario Biografico degli Italiani,* 53. Rome: Istituto dell'Enciclopedia Italiana.

Pii, Eluggero. 1984. *Antonio Genovesi: Dalla politica economica alla "politica civile."* Florence: Olschki.

Rao, Anna Maria. 1984. *Il Regno di Napoli nel Settecento.* Naples: Guida.

Reinert, Sophus A. 2007. "Emulazione e traduzione: La genealogia occulta della Storia del Commercio." In *Genovesi economista: Nel 250° anniversario dell'istituzione della cattedra di "Commercio e Meccanica,"* edited by Bruno Jossa, Rosario Patalano, and Eugenio Zagari, 155–92. Naples: Istituto Italiano per gli Studi Filosofici.

Ricuperati, Giuseppe. 1970. *L'esperienza civile e religiosa di Pietro Giannone.* Milan and Naples: R. Ricciardi.

Robertson, John. 1997. "The Enlightenment above National Context: Political Economy in Eighteenth-Century Scotland and Naples." *Historical Journal* 40 (3): 667–97.

———. 2005. *The Case for the Enlightenment: Scotland and Naples, 1680–1760.* Cambridge: Cambridge University Press.

Rosa, Mario. 1999. *Settecento religioso: Politica della Ragione e religione del cuore.* Venice: Marsilio.

———. 2009. *La contrastata ragione: Riforme e religione nell'Italia del Settecento.* Rome: Edizioni di Storia e Letteratura.

Stapelbroek, Koen. 2006. "Preserving the Neapolitan State: Antonio Genovesi and Ferdinando Galiani on Commercial Society and Planning Economic Growth." *History of European Ideas* 32 (4): 406–29.

———. 2008. *Love, Self-Deceit, and Money: Commerce and Morality in the Early Neapolitan Enlightenment.* Toronto: University of Toronto Press.

Trampus, Antonio. 2008. *Il diritto alla felicità: Storia di un'idea*. Rome and Bari: Laterza.
———. 2009. *Storia del costituzionalismo italiano nell'età dei Lumi*. Rome and Bari: Laterza.
Trinci, Cosimo. 1764. *L'agricoltore sperimentato di Cosimo Trinci con alcune giunte dell'abate Genovesi*. Naples. 2nd ed., Naples, 1769.
Venturi, Franco, ed. 1962. *Illuministi italiani*. Vol. 5, *Riformatori napoletani*. Milan and Naples: R. Ricciardi.
———. 1969. *Settecento Riformatore: Da Muratori a Beccaria, 1730–1764*. Vol. 1. Turin: Einaudi.
Villari, Lucio. 1958. *Il pensiero economico di Antonio Genovesi*. Florence: Le Monnier.
Wahnbaeck, Till. 2004. *Luxury and Public Happiness: Political Economy in the Italian Enlightenment*. Oxford: Clarendon Press.
Wolf, Hubert, ed. 2011. *Römische Inquisition und Indexkongregation, 1701–1813: Register*. Paderborn: Schöningh.
Zambelli, Paola. 1972. *La formazione filosofica di Antonio Genovesi*. Naples: Morano.
———. 1978. "Antonio Genovesi and Eighteenth-Century Empiricism in Italy." *Journal of the History of Philosophy* 16:195–208.

13

Maria Gaetana Agnesi (1718–1799)

Science and Mysticism

MASSIMO MAZZOTTI

Maria Gaetana Agnesi was born in Milan, then the capital of a Duchy under Austrian rule, on 16 May 1718. She was the daughter of Pietro Agnesi (1690–1752), the scion of a family of wealthy merchants who traded in luxury textiles. At the age of five, Maria Gaetana was already known in her native city as a prodigy, well versed in languages, memorizing lengthy Latin speeches, and performing effortlessly in front of an audience in her family palazzo. Available descriptions of her skills may contain symbolic elements—for example, her alleged ability to speak seven languages fluently—but it is clear that the young girl was highly talented, and most intriguingly for her contemporaries, she would soon excel in the typically masculine art of philosophical disputation. A booklet dated 1727 celebrated Agnesi's wit and the female intellect through a collection of poetry composed within a circle of family friends, and included a Latin oration in defense of the right of women to pursue any kind of knowledge (Agnesi

1727). That oration had been written in Italian by one of Agnesi's tutors, and she had translated and memorized it as part of her studies. In the following years she studied natural philosophy and mathematics with prominent local scholars. Her studies were interrupted in the early 1730s by a mysterious and persistent malady, coincident with a period of repeated performances, the departure of her favorite tutor, and the death of her mother. Her "convulsions" eluded any diagnosis or treatment until about 1733, when she apparently recovered and returned to her studies. Her healing was attributed to the direct intervention of Saint Cajetan (*San Gaetano*), for whom the family had a particular devotion, as evidenced by her name, Maria Gaetana. Saint Cajetan was the founder of the Theatine order, to which Maria Gaetana kept a lifelong, profound spiritual connection.

In 1738, aged twenty, Agnesi concluded her studies with the publication of her thesis, under the title *Philosophical Propositions* (*Propositiones philosophicae*), thus mimicking the academic path of male students in contemporary colleges (Agnesi 1738). By this time she had achieved the status of a minor celebrity in northern Italy and was the protagonist of the *conversazione* (literally, "conversation") that met regularly at palazzo Agnesi. A year later, at the height of her career as a *filosofessa* (woman philosopher), Agnesi expressed the desire to abandon the very public life imposed on her by her father. She longed for a more secluded life, in which she could dedicate herself entirely to the study of mathematics, as well as to charitable activities and devotional practices. After initial resistance, Pietro eventually accepted his daughter's requests. On her part, she promised that she would still participate in the *conversazione,* although only sporadically (Frisi 1799, 28–30). The following decade of intense mathematical study culminated in the publication of *Analytical Institutions* (*Instituzioni analitiche*; 1748), a remarkable introduction to the new techniques of differential and integral calculus "for the Italian youth," and the first book of mathematics to be authored by a woman. *Institutions* was well received in Italy and was later translated into French and English (Agnesi 1775; Agnesi 1801). In the aftermath of its publication, Agnesi was invited to join various literary and scientific academies, and in 1750 she was offered an honorary lectureship in mathematics at the

University of Bologna, then under the control of the pontifical government. However, she did not accept the position, considering her work in mathematics concluded with the *Institutions*.

Pietro's sudden death in 1752 made it possible for Agnesi to cut her last ties with the world of the *conversazioni*, give up her wealth and inheritance rights, and devote the rest of her life to charitable activities—such as teaching children in parish churches and assisting infirm women at the Ca' Granda, the ancient city hospital. In 1771 the archbishop of Milan, Giuseppe Pozzobonelli (1696–1783), offered Agnesi the directorship of the female section of the Pio Albergo Trivulzio, a new institution created to house invalid and chronically ill patients from the lower urban social strata. She took up the job with her usual determination, steering the Albergo through the jurisdictional conflicts that characterized the reformist age and the turbulent close of the century. Maria Gaetana Agnesi died of pneumonia in the rooms of the Albergo on 9 January 1799. Milan was under French occupation at the time, and she died a citizen of the Repubblica Cisalpina. All forms of public ceremony had been prohibited to avoid confrontations between French troops and the local population. Agnesi was buried hurriedly in an unmarked mass grave outside the city walls, together with fifteen other women from the Albergo (Frisi 1799, 104–8).

The Lives of Agnesi

Reconstructing the life of Agnesi means engaging with a number of important historiographical issues. These include the relationship between science and religion—her understanding of it, as well as ours—and the way scientific practice, mathematics in particular, was gendered in the eighteenth century. In this essay I shall focus on the first issue, although the two questions are closely related. It is precisely this connection, and the extreme form that the tension between science and religion seems to assume in Agnesi's experience, that makes her life especially interesting, and one that can be used to shed new light on the notion of "Catholic Enlightenment."

Agnesi's contemporaries and her eighteenth-century biographers agreed that her unprecedented scientific achievements were far from being the only noteworthy traits of her life. Her religious and existential experience was considered equally extraordinary. While the kinds of devotions and charitable activities favored by Agnesi were familiar to the Milanese, the intensity of her experience was certainly exceptional, as were her radical life choices—her asceticism, the intensity of her devotional practice, the unpublished mystical-devotional writings, the decision to provide material and spiritual assistance to children and infirm women, the abandonment of the family house, and the renunciation of inheritance. To her contemporary admirers Agnesi's life was exemplary, and it was perceived as a whole, with moral and intellectual virtues, wisdom, and piety sustaining each other.

However, by the time of her death, the world of the Catholic Enlightenment—which had sustained her self-understanding and action—had come to an end. One expression of the disintegration of this culture can be found precisely in the transformation of the narratives of Agnesi's life from the 1790s onwards. It is in the revolutionary years that the unity of the early accounts is replaced by the opposing narratives of the heroine of the Catholic reaction versus the daring woman mathematician of the Enlightenment age. Throughout the nineteenth and twentieth centuries, biographers struggled with what they saw as a fundamental interpretive problem: how to reconcile her religious devotion with her aspirations for social and cultural change and her admiration for modern science. Typically, the solution was found in giving preeminence to one dimension over the other; hence the spate of nineteenth-century pamphlets on Agnesi as a protofeminist, an enlightened pedagogue, and a modern mathematician, rather than a devout Catholic, a mystic, and a charitable woman. Faced with such contradictory accounts, a distracted reader might well think it a case of homonymy. Agnesi's persona was split as neatly as the eponymous protagonist of Italo Calvino's *The Cloven Viscount,* whose good and bad halves had been separated by the sword of a Turkish warrior. If splitting up Agnesi's life has been the historiographical strategy most adopted, others have insisted on the dual nature of her own personality. Thus a fin-de-siècle author defined Agnesi as a "psychological enigma"—an elegant way to bypass the problem of the tension between tradition and innovation that pervades her life without really engaging with it (Mazzotti 2007, xi–xii).

These historiographical approaches have been shaped by precise assumptions about the nature of science and its relationship to religion. Thus, the apologetic lives of the revolutionary period incarnated the concerns and values of the reaction against the alleged conspiracy of the *philosophes* and the depravity of modern science, while the positivist renderings of the late nineteenth century are a direct expression of the so-called warfare thesis of science and religion. According to this view, the interaction of science and religion always and necessarily engenders some form of open conflict, because of the essential incompatibility of religious dogma and scientific method. The analytical tools shaped by the warfare thesis have turned the experience of Agnesi into an enigmatic, and ultimately incomprehensible, historical object. The very categories of "science" and "religion" used to refer to two incompatible sets of practices would be meaningless to Agnesi and those who shared her culture. The conceptual dichotomies that have shaped the narratives of her life should not be taken for granted: they are themselves part of the story that we need to reconstruct and interpret.

The warfare thesis and its anachronistic historiographical lenses have been long discredited in the history of science, although they seem to enjoy an undiminished popularity in other discourses. Their dismissal has coincided with a profound revision of our understanding of the dynamics of the scientific revolution and the nature of early modern natural philosophy. The transformation of the scholarship on Isaac Newton (1642–1727) in the last twenty years is emblematic of this broader historiographical reorientation, which has emphasized the way in which religious concerns and the technical-operative dimension are best understood as integrated and shaping each other, rather than separated and opposed. Newton's religious and alchemical texts have begun to be studied systematically and related to his work in mathematics and natural philosophy only in the late twentieth century. It is not that these texts were previously unknown; rather they became historiographically significant only when the rationalist task of devising a demarcation between science and nonscience lost its relevance within the mainstream history of science (Mazzotti 2005).

Agnesi's unfortunate historiographical destiny is thus far from being an isolated case, though accounts of her life and work are extreme versions of that attempt to isolate the "scientific core" from "the rest" that has plagued the study of early modern natural philosophers. This work of putative purification has taken many forms. For example, it was assumed that after the publication of the *Institutions* in 1748, Agnesi must have experienced some kind of a religious crisis, which turned her away from the study of mathematics for the rest of her life. This interpretation shapes most of her nineteenth- and twentieth-century biographies, and it provides a comforting solution to her "enigma" by postulating a clear-cut separation between her scientific experience, culminating in the publication of her most famous book, and her religious experience, which would characterize the rest of her life. To reinforce this alleged rupture, some biographers claimed that she took the habit of the Augustinian nuns, a "fact" that found its way into the *Dictionary of Scientific Biographies*. In reality, Agnesi never became a nun, and her surviving manuscripts show that intense devotional practices, theological concerns, and social commitment were already important parts of her life during her youth. It is also clear that she did not perceive any radical break when she abandoned the study of mathematics for a full commitment to social work, as she saw her scientific studies and the making of her book as components of her broader apologetic mission (Mazzotti 2007, 145–46).

Entering a Conversation

Reconstructing the world of Agnesi and the meaning of her choices is complicated by severe documentary limitations. This is due to various historical contingencies, including the perception that a woman could not be a truly significant protagonist of the philosophical and mathematical debate. And yet, through her surviving manuscripts and the indirect evidence about the management of her family's properties, it is possible to glimpse her world, which for an important part of her life had its center in the *conversazione* of palazzo Agnesi.

The term *conversazione* was used to refer both to the group's most assiduous participants and to the site of the meetings, and was a form of sociability that found expression in many palazzi of the city. The *conversazione* of palazzo Agnesi, however, stood out in many respects. While most *conversazioni* were hosted by the great senatorial families and focused on gambling, the reading of poetry, and informal conversation, what Pietro had built around his talented daughter had a somewhat more severe, academic form. The soirées at palazzo Agnesi were carefully staged spectacles, typically opened and closed by the virtuoso performances of Gaetana's sister, Maria Teresa (1720–1795), who would become a distinguished harpsichord player and composer. Jean-Philippe Rameau was a favorite, but she would also play music and arias she had composed herself. Her music and singing framed the different stages of the soirée, providing rhythm and a recognizable theatrical pattern. Visitors included a circle of friends—mostly clergymen and members of the local administrative and scholarly elites—as well as visitors from across Europe. Typically, Maria Gaetana would converse amiably with the newcomers. Then, under the attentive direction of Count Carlo Belloni, she would engage in a set of formal debates. Inspired by academic disputation, these *accademie domestiche* (*domestic academies*) saw Agnesi defending a set of propositions against an opponent who would try to contradict them. The topics were taken largely from natural philosophy, and Agnesi was keen on defending the positions of Isaac Newton (1642–1727) and of those contemporary philosophers who criticized late scholastic doctrines. Among her favorite subjects were the nature of light and colors, the theory of tides, and the origins of spring waters. Sometimes visitors were invited to step in and debate with Agnesi on topics of their choice, be they philosophical or mathematical. The discussion could thus take less predictable directions, touching metaphysical questions such as the nature of the soul and the relationship between the soul and the body, or the properties of certain geometrical curves. The language of choice would be Latin, so that everyone could understand, although visitors would sometimes ask permission to speak in French. At the end of the spectacle, ice creams and sorbets were served by liveried servants (Brosses 1986, 1:135–52, 162–64).

It is not just the form of the Agnesi *conversazione* that is remarkable, but also its setting. The two sisters performed against a severe background of religious paintings in which the representation of the passion, death, and resurrection of Christ had a preeminent role. The display also included a number of landscapes and seascapes. Patrician families in Milan, by contrast, built their collections around the Renaissance masters, emphasizing the mythological themes that could function as a celebration of the virtues of the house. Ancestral portraits were also particularly relevant in a city like Milan, where local politics depended on connections with distant capitals like Madrid and Vienna. Signs of political affiliation and patronage were proudly exhibited through the clothing and decorations of portrayed family members. One would look in vain, however, for such paintings in the rooms of the palazzo Agnesi. Rather, the taste that shaped the collection was similar to that of high-ranking Milanese ecclesiastics, who were traditionally among the foremost art collectors in the city. Thus the collection of Archbishop Pozzobonelli was characterized by the same thematic dichotomy between sacred subjects and landscapes, expressions of the moral classicism of early eighteenth-century Arcadian culture. Another common trait was the complete absence of minor genres such as pulcinellas, beggars, and macabre scenes that were favored by the local aristocracy (Mazzotti 2007, 8–9).

One cannot but notice that it was Count Belloni, a family friend, who played host. While carefully directing events from behind the scenes, Pietro always maintained a low profile, while there is no evidence that his wives—he married three times—ever played a significant role in the *conversazione*. Belloni, from a family of the provincial aristocracy, aimed at entering the Milanese stage and had ambitions that could not be fulfilled in the provinces. To Pietro, he offered his easy speech and the savoir-faire of a well-groomed and connected patrician. Pietro needed them both, as he was a new man, the first in his family to move away from trade and warehouses and to embrace the lifestyle of the aristocracy. But he had no titles, and those that were attached to some properties he bought were insufficient to allow him to join the patrician elite. Thus his sons could not enter the colleges for the nobility, nor could he access those administrative positions that were reserved for members of the senatorial families. His entire life was devoted to a strategy of social enhancement that eventually proved too expensive to be sustained, and caused the family's economic ruin. When the coat of arms of the Agnesi was recorded in the Heraldic Tribunal of the state of Milan in 1773, Pietro was long dead, and the family had lost most of its properties and wealth (Mazzotti 2007, 9–16).

Understanding this family strategy is essential to contextualize the nurturing and showcasing of Agnesi's talent, and to interpret the distinctive features of the Agnesi *conversazione,* including its distance from contemporary aristocratic models. It is not just that it was a different form of sociability: the kind of knowledge that was being produced, discussed, and promoted within it was also different. Natural philosophy and mathematics as understood within the *conversazione* and as practiced by Agnesi, for example, were markedly different from the hegemonic Jesuit model. It is not a coincidence that Jesuit science was absent from the otherwise well-stocked Agnesi library, and that the *conversazione* did not include any of those prestigious Jesuit scholars who lived in the city at the time and were organic to the great aristocracy—especially to the so-called Spanish party. The cultural and political referents of the Agnesi were to be found elsewhere, along networks that connect the family to Vienna, on the one end, and Rome, on the other. In an effort to bypass the sclerotic social structure of his native city, Pietro indeed looked for distant but powerful patrons. One was the emperor himself, keen on rewarding faithful new men from the provinces of the empire: Pietro received an imperial fief in 1740. The other was the archbishop of Milan, and through him, that part of the Roman Curia that aimed for a renewal of Catholic culture, an engagement with modern philosophy that would go beyond the Jesuit resistance, and the return to a more sober and pure religiosity.

I refer to this reform movement as "Catholic Enlightenment," a term used by historians such as Émile Appolis to describe a "third party" between the conservative front and the varied world of Jansenism, which was active in the early to mid-eighteenth century (Appolis 1960; but see also Plongeron 1969; Rogier 1975; Rosa 1981). It is in this specific and rather narrow meaning that I describe Agnesi's world as the world of the Catholic Enlightenment. The movement found some of its key texts in the writings of Lodovico Antonio Muratori

(1672–1750) and achieved maximum visibility in the 1740s, when it was backed by learned cardinals, literary periodicals, and the pontiff Benedict XIV, who considered Muratori "the light of Italian science" (Pastor 1955, 16:148). Historians have explored the historiographical, liturgical, and theological dimensions of this movement, and its aspiration to return to the experience of an idealized primitive church—hence the relentless critique of Baroque devotions and modern, especially Jesuit, theology. But the battle against the perceived rampages of impiety and heresy needed more than an austere religiosity. Enlightened Catholics believed that religion was not an obstacle to, but rather the means of, transforming society, and that this transformation should necessarily pass through a critique of the traditional ways in which knowledge was produced and legitimated. The transformation of the education system envisaged by these reformers can be described succinctly as a dismantling of the Jesuit curriculum. In particular, scholastic metaphysics had to be expelled from the study of natural philosophy and replaced by the study of Descartes, Malebranche, Newton, and the Dutch experimentalists. The Catholic Church, they argued, could respond effectively to the challenges of the new century only through this alliance of primitive theology and modern science. It is emblematic that the offer of an honorary lectureship in mathematics made to Agnesi by the University of Bologna (1750) was extended by the pontiff himself. While the theological and liturgical reformism of the Catholic Enlightenment have been studied in detail, the role of this movement in shaping contemporary scientific life has attracted less attention, and the very notion of "Catholic Enlightenment" is hardly familiar to historians of science. Agnesi's existential and scientific experience lies precisely at the intersection of the Catholic Enlightenment and the contemporary practices of natural philosophy and mathematics. It is therefore an ideal site for the study of the scientific dimension of the Catholic Enlightenment.

The Enlightenment of Agnesi

The *Propositiones philosophicae* (1738) offer a good insight into the kind of natural philosophy in which Agnesi was trained and gives some indications of her own distinctive take on important philosophical issues. These propositions are a fascinating medley of scholastic, Cartesian, and Newtonian ideas, which was indeed a trait of much early eighteenth-century scientific culture in continental Europe. The organization of the materials seems to follow a rather traditional structure: logic, ontology, pneumatology, general and particular physics—not unlike a course of philosophy in a contemporary Jesuit college. Even the main textbook Agnesi used for her studies was a familiar choice. If one goes beyond the formal structure of her *cursus,* however, and looks at her manuscript notes as well, the differences begin to emerge. For example, while college students would focus on logic, metaphysics, and general physics, Agnesi moved quickly through them, while deepening her study of particular physics and mathematics. Logic and metaphysics simply provided the occasion to reflect on methodological and epistemological issues that she saw as preliminary to her scientific work, which was a complete reversal of priorities with respect to traditional college education. In other words, the materials used are largely the same, but they are used differently.

Propositiones also gives us a good sense of the modern authors that Agnesi managed to integrate into her study. The epistemological framework is Cartesian, as is the emphasis on evidence and the discussion of the conditions of truth of an idea. It is, however, a decidedly apologetic Cartesianism, filtered through the lens of a devout sensibility. A belief in the fundamental harmony of faith and reason shaped Agnesi's understanding of the process of cognition, and made her turn to authors like Nicolas Malebranche (1638–1715), probably the single most influential author in her studies. Agnesi was not interested in Malebranche's problematic metaphysics and theology, but rather in his effort to integrate modern science and the Catholic tradition. Thus Agnesi was interested in the doctrine of occasionalism, and the image of knowledge as the product of the "vision in God." The belief that human reason is an essentially passive faculty, which requires divine illumination in order to "perceive" its objects, returned often in Agnesi's own notes. The framework of general physics was also Cartesian, although this did not prevent Agnesi from enthusiastically embracing many Newtonian "doctrines"—from mechanics to the origin of celestial bodies, to the theory of colors. Agnesi seemed to have an aesthetic appreciation of Newtonian natural philosophy, which she called a "most beautiful and simple theory" (1738, 81). Already at this early stage, it is possible to see that Agnesi was especially fond of mathematics, as a source of both certainty and unparalleled intellectual pleasure.

After the renegotiation of her lifestyle at the end of 1739, Agnesi gave up the study of natural philosophy to concentrate on the study of mathematics and the making of her main book. This was in many ways a mystifying choice. While topics in natural philosophy could make for sparkling conversation, it was much less clear that this was the case with mathematics. In fact, Francesco Algarotti's best-selling *Newtonianism for Ladies* (1737) had explicitly banned mathematics from genteel conversation. Not surprisingly, her tutors tried to dissuade her from this choice, but to no avail. One should not think, however, that after 1739 Agnesi had disengaged completely from the world—quite the contrary. She intensified her charitable activities, mainly through her participation in some of the numerous religious congregations that articulated religious life in Milan. She volunteered at the Ca' Granda hospital and set up a small infirmary in a corner of the palazzo, where, much to the dismay of her father, she would welcome poor and infirm women. Agnesi would also teach children to read and count at Sunday schools in her neighborhood. At the same time, she intensified her theological study and devotional practices, especially those related to Theatine spirituality and the Theatine church of Sant'Antonio Abate, where the priest she had chosen as her spiritual father resided.

Profoundly interested in mathematics but still unclear about the nature of her possible contribution, Agnesi began by planning a commentary on Guillame de l'Hospital's treatise on curves, to make it more accessible to students. Gradually, however, she came to believe she could work on a much more ambitious project: an introduction to calculus that would guide the beginner from the rudiments of algebra to the new differential and integral techniques. This would be a great work of synthesis, aiming at a clear presentation of materials that were mostly written for specialists, in Latin, French, or German, and published in hard-to-find journals. During the making of her book,

Agnesi interacted with leading Italian experts, such as Jacopo Riccati (1676–1754). Her correspondence with Riccati sheds light on some of the distinctive traits of Agnesi's mathematical style (Soppelsa 1985). Thus we learn that she was consciously excluding from her book anything that had to do with empirical states of affairs and with possible applications. This choice was at odds with the practice of most contemporary specialists, including Riccati, which was guided primarily by the physical meaning of formulas. Also in marked disagreement with leading practitioners was Agnesi's geometrical style, which originated in her essentially geometrical understanding of algebra and calculus. This explains, among other things, her interest in Newton's fluxions, and the ease with which her work was translated into English for a British audience (Agnesi 1801). At a time when the practice of calculus on the continent was moving away from its immediate geometrical meaning, Agnesi aimed to rediscover those techniques of Cartesian geometry designed to bridge the gap between the two fields.

The single most striking feature of the book, however, is its lack of examples of applications of calculus to rational mechanics or experimental physics. Agnesi claimed that she wanted to limit her book to "pure analysis" and its geometrical applications. Anything that had to do with physics she would leave out, to preserve the simplicity, rigor, and evidence proper to classical geometry. This inclination explains her interest for the Oratorian tradition in mathematics, and especially for authors like Malebranche and Charles Reyneau (1656–1728). The reference to Reyneau as her main source of inspiration for the *Institutions* has surprised many readers, as he was hardly considered a valuable resource for mid-eighteenth-century continental mathematicians, and was often described as a pedantic and obscure writer. To Agnesi, however, Reyneau offered an example of how to understand recent developments in calculus within an essentially Cartesian framework. Furthermore, he was also uninterested in the empirical applications of calculus, and invested the practice of mathematics with important spiritual meaning. Far from being an odd curiosity, Agnesi's interest in the Oratorian tradition provides a lead to understanding her motivations and otherwise puzzling choices.

Why did Agnesi decide to write a textbook of calculus when there was little or no interest in Milan in these mathematical techniques, and when they were not being taught in any local school or university? And why did she write a textbook that focused on the foundational and purely geometrical dimensions of calculus, ignoring those applications that made it interesting in the eyes of most contemporary specialists? I believe that these questions can be answered only by considering the preeminent role of intellectual exercise within Agnesi's own religious experience. Among her surviving manuscripts is an undated text titled *The Mystic Heaven,* which is especially significant in this respect (Agnesi n.d.). This text is distant from the visionary mystical tradition of the Baroque Age. Rather, it describes a contemplative practice that moved from the meditation on the mysteries of the passion to the gradual elevation of the soul toward God. The style and themes are largely derived from a tradition that exalted personal love for Christ and the contemplation of his death and resurrection— one that held a special position in Theatine spirituality. Key to this practice was the ability of the believer to move from the contemplation of the concrete objects of the passion, or their pictorial representation, to contemplation of profound truths of faith, and ultimately to the contemplation of the Holy Trinity. Agnesi described this process of elevation as built upon the use of two faculties: intellect and will. It is only their cooperation (*cospirazione,* Agnesi would say) that allows the believer to experience the final vision of God. In other words, Agnesi saw no conflict between rational knowledge, contemplation, and mystical experience. A clear and robust intellect is indeed necessary to support the early stages of a spiritual experience such as the one sketched above (Mazzotti 2007, 90–92).

There is one notion that captures nicely the intersection of intellectual ability and spiritual achievement as understood by Agnesi: the "capacity of attention." Many early modern devout authors—most notably Malebranche—used this expression to describe a particular state of mind, a form of intense concentration that was seen as a necessary condition for contemplative practices, and more generally for a fulfilling spiritual life. At the same time, this state of mind is described as a prerequisite for the investigation of nature, and in particular the study of mathematics. Wary of Baroque piety and what Muratori called "disorderly devotions," Agnesi valued highly the capacity for concentration and a well-trained intellect. Superstitious devotions stimulated and relied upon fantasy and imagination, inducing a credulous and fatalistic attitude rather than a clear understanding of one's religious duties. Believers should rather train their intellect and ground their spiritual experience upon it. And which is the best way to exercise the intellect? The study of mathematics, geometry in particular. Agnesi believed that calculus was the most subtle branch of mathematics, and therefore that which required the highest level of concentration and the strongest intellect. Once one realizes that for Agnesi the preeminent role of calculus is precisely that of exercising the intellect, it becomes understandable why she decided to ignore completely its empirical and applicative dimension—a move that puzzled many contemporaries who did not partake in her religious culture as well as later historians of science (Truesdell 1989). This notion of "attention" will find a striking visual representation in the paintings of Giuseppe Petrini (1677–c. 1755). His anti-Baroque style aimed to celebrate and promote a religiosity built upon the values of the Catholic Enlightenment. Petrini had a keen interest in representing states of religious and intellectual absorption. His saints, evangelists, astronomers, and philosophers are captured in that particular state of attention that was a prerequisite for the acquisition of both true knowledge and divine enlightenment (Mazzotti 2007, 85–87).

The World of the *Filosofesse*

Agnesi was not the only *filosofessa* active in northern Italy in the first half of the eighteenth century. A handful of women gained visibility as competent scholars in that period, the most famous and successful being certainly Laura Bassi (1711–1778), who graduated at the University of Bologna in 1732 and taught experimental physics there for much of her life (Findlen 1993; Cavazza 1995). In her pioneering study of the gendering of modern science, Londa Schiebinger detected the unusual presence of learned women philosophers in northern Italy during the first half of the eighteenth century. She described it as an interesting anomaly in search of an explanation: "Italy was an exception in Europe, and little is known about why women professors were acceptable to the Church and university" (Schiebinger 1989, 16). We now know much more about the world of the *filosofesse* and the way they could achieve visibility and legitimation though specific networks of patronage (see, for example, Findlen and Messbarger 2005). The reconstruction of Agnesi's experience can contribute to shedding light on this anomaly by bringing to the surface its relationship to the culture of the Catholic Enlightenment. It was indeed this culture that offered Agnesi a set of resources and possibilities that were absent in other European settings. The reformism that supported her action placed particular significance on the contribution of women to religious and social life, celebrated a new kind of lay sanctity that engaged with the daily problems of the poor, and valued popular education and the role of the intellect in spiritual life. Most importantly, enlightened Catholics were not inclined to believe that the mind was gendered, as maintained by certain recent scientific doctrines, nor to accept that the female mind was unfit for scientific and especially mathematical studies (Conti 1756, 2:lxv–lxxv; Cavazza 2003). The defense of an essentially Cartesian and antimaterialist image of the mind lies indeed at the core of the explicit defenses of the right of women to study the sublime sciences that were produced within this culture (Bandiera 1740). This is not to say that the question of women's education was perceived as equally relevant by all enlightened Catholics—Muratori himself was ambiguous on this point (Mazzotti 2007, 142). However, the Catholic Enlightenment created the conditions for the emergence of an alternative discourse on the female mind and made it possible for a few talented women to use its network of alliances and resources to establish themselves as credible and legitimate scholars. The phenomenon of the *filosofesse* reached its apogee around 1750, with the invitation to Agnesi to join Bassi as a lecturer at the University of Bologna. That gesture was emblematic of Benedict XIV's strategy of bringing back luster to the ancient university and placing the Catholic Church once again at the center of the European philosophical debate. Far from being a curious anomaly, the *filosofesse* should be seen as a meaningful component of the world of the Catholic Enlightenment. In fact, their experience illustrates effectively some of the distinctive traits of this movement and its otherness with respect to other strains of Catholic and enlightened culture.

Bibliography

Agnesi, Maria Gaetana. 1727. *Oratio qua ostenditur: Artium liberalium studia a femineo sexu neutiquam abhorrere*. Milan: Malatesta.

———. 1738. *Propositiones philosophicae*. Milan: Malatesta.

———. 1748. *Instituzioni analitiche ad uso della gioventù italiana*. 2 vols. Milan: Nella Regia-Ducal Corte.

———. 1775. *Traités élémentaires de calcul différentiel et de calcul integral*. Paris: Jombert.

———. 1801. *Analytical Institutions*. London: Taylor & Wilks.

———. N.d. "Il Cielo Mistico, cioè contemplazione delle virtù, de' Misteri e delle Eccellenze di Nostro Signore Gesù Cristo." Published in *Maria Gaetana Agnesi,* by Maria Luisa Anzoletti, 435–72. Milan: Cogliati, 1901.

Algarotti, Francesco. 1737. *Il newtonianesmo per le dame, ovvero dialoghi sopra la luce e i colori*. Naples [but Milan].

Appolis, Émile. 1960. *Entre jansénistes et zelanti: Le "tiers parti" catholique au XVIII siècle*. Paris: Picard.

Bandiera, Giovanni. 1740. *Trattato degli studi delle donne*. 2 vols. Venice: Pitteri.

Brosses, Charles de. 1986. *Lettres d'Italie du Président de Brosses*. 2 vols. Paris: Mercure de France.

Cavazza, Marta. 1995. "Laura Bassi e il suo gabinetto di fisica sperimentale: Realtà e mito." *Nuncius* 10:715–53.

———. 2003. "Women's Dialectics, or The Thinking Uterus: An Eighteenth-Century Controversy on Gender and Education." In *The Faces of Nature in Enlightenment Europe,* edited by Lorraine Daston and Gianna Pomata, 237–57. Berlin: BWV.

Conti, Antonio. 1756. *Prose e poesie*. 2 vols. Venice: Pasquali.

Findlen, Paula. 1993. "Science as a Career in Enlightenment Italy." *Isis* 84:441–69.

Findlen, Paula, and Rebecca Messbarger. 2005. *The Contest for Knowledge: Debates over Women's Learning in Eighteenth-Century Italy*. Chicago: University of Chicago Press.

Frisi, Antonio. 1799. *Elogio storico di Maria Gaetana Agnesi*. Milan: Galeazzi.

Mazzotti, Massimo. 2005. "The Two Newtons and Beyond." *British Journal for the History of Science* 40:105–11.

———. 2007. *The World of Maria Gaetana Agnesi, Mathematician of God*. Baltimore: Johns Hopkins University Press.

Pastor, Ludwig von. 1955. *Storia dei papi*. 16 vols. Rome: Desclée.

Plongeron, Bernard. 1969. "Recherches sur l'Aufklärung catholique en Europe occidentale, 1770–1830." *Revue d'histoire moderne et contemporaine* 16:555–605.

Rogier, Louis. 1975. "L'Aufklärung cattolica." *Nuova storia della Chiesa* 4:151–74.

Rosa, Mario. 1981. *Cattolicesimo e lumi nel Settecento italiano*. Rome: Herder.

Schiebinger, Londa. 1989. *The Mind Has No Sex? Women in the Origins of Modern Science*. Cambridge, MA: Harvard University Press.

Soppelsa, Maria Laura. 1985. "Jacopo Riccati—Maria Gaetana Agnesi: Carteggio, 1745–1751." *Annali dell'Istituto e Museo di Storia della Scienza di Firenze* 10:117–59.

Truesdell, Clifford. 1989. "Maria Gaetana Agnesi." *Archive for the History of the Exact Sciences* 40:113–42.

PART 6
Catholicism, Enlightenment, and the Iberian States

14

Benito Jerónimo Feijoo y Montenegro (1676–1764)

Benedictine and Skeptic Enlightener

FRANCISCO SÁNCHEZ-BLANCO

In the little village of Casdemiro in the northwest of the Iberian Peninsula, far from the royal court and the main universities of Spain, Benito Jerónimo Feijoo y Montenegro was born in 1676 as the son of a family that belonged to the rural gentry. Though the first-born of ten siblings and thus the heir of the family, he left home when he was eight years old to begin his studies at the nearby monastery of San Juan de Samos. At age fourteen, he entered the Benedictine Order, and later graduated in theology from the University of Salamanca. His talent was obvious early on, so it is not surprising that he soon began teaching the adolescents of the surrounding monasteries. In 1709, he accepted a chair of theology in Oviedo, and subsequently rejected all future offers for more prestigious positions or honors. Only for arranging his publications or brief research trips did he leave the city of Oviedo, where he died in 1764 as one of the most important Spanish intellectuals of the century.

Spain's Long Way to Enlightenment

In the last third of the seventeenth century, the decay of Spain's political reputation among the European powers, as well as an increasing decadence in its art and literature, seriously affected its cultural and intellectual life. The last great writer of the *Siglo de Oro,* the Spanish Golden Age, was the dramatist Pedro Calderón de la Barca (1600–1681), who, with his death in 1681, left a distressing literary emptiness behind. At the universities, late scholasticism dominated the curriculum. Different authorities in theology (Holy Scripture, magisterium, church fathers) and in philosophy (Aristotle, Thomas Aquinas) continued to draw the same conclusions, and the same discussions and controversies between rival schools were repeated ad nauseam. Everything not grounded in tradition was viewed as a "novelty" or potential heresy. Nevertheless, signs of an intellectual renewal were also detectable. In ethics, Francisco Gutiérrez de los Ríos (1644–1721) laid the foundation for secular activities in commerce and in the family with his publication *The Practical Man* (*El hombre práctico*; 1686). In Madrid, a small circle of physicians gathered around Juan de Cabriada (1665–1714), who openly embraced empiricism (Cabriada 1686). In philosophy, there were the first cautious attempts to overcome the rigid discipline of the university schools. The Jewish thinker Isaac Cardoso (c. 1603–1683) argued for a renewed "free philosophy" (in his *Philosphia libera*; 1673) with an eclectic method, but without an empiricist agenda (Yerushalmi 1981). The decisive break with traditional university scholarship happened in Seville at the end of the seventeenth century. There, a group of physicians, who had substantial experience in anatomy and pharmacology, engaged in a fierce debate with so-called Latin physicians at the university, who relied on their knowledge of quotations from Hippocrates or Galen. The innovators ultimately won the argument and, in 1734, with the help of the Bourbon dynasty, established an academic society of medicine, the *Real Sociedad Médica*. Empirical research was now officially institutionalized in Spain.

The Spanish Crown also supported the foundation of other academies, for example, the academy of language (1714) and of history (1738). Knowledge now seemed to emerge from social institutions, whereas universities and professors had lost their leadership role, and private *tertulias* (discussion groups) disseminated new concepts of nature, theology, and politics. These meetings were not as pompous as in some French salons, but were nonetheless similarly effective. People with similar interests met in the living quarters of an aristocratic family, the cell of a monk, the office of a jurist or a physician on a regular basis and discussed a variety of themes. These groups did not exclusively discuss new literature, but also and especially new discoveries in the natural sciences, new mechanical inventions and machines, travel stories, and political events. Members were those who felt disenchanted with the cultural life in their immediate vicinity and who wanted to learn about Spanish (as well as foreign) books, pamphlets, and journals. Feijoo was one such member, and not only his writing style but also the form he gave to his thoughts echoes the dialogical style of the Spanish "salons." He never intended to project a new philosophical system or even to recommend one. Rather, he desired to learn about the mistakes of contemporary philosophers in order to refute them successfully. Moreover, he wanted to be in a sincere dialogue with people whose aim it was to advance Spain's culture and intellectual life. Feijoo's philosophy was therefore mostly polemical, but he understood himself to be something of an intellectual warrior, supported by his interlocutors—be they monks, politicians, writers, or physicians.

From Aristotelianism to Skepticism

In 1714, the theologian Francisco Palanco (1657–1720), a Minim friar, had attacked the "innovators" (*novatores*) because their innovations in theology and philosophy were, in his eyes, heresies (Palanco

1714). With the term "innovator" Spanish critics usually meant the physicians of the aforementioned *tertulia* in Seville and theologians who embraced the thought of the Minim friar Emanuel Maignan (1601–1676) and his explanation of the truths of faith (especially creation and the Eucharist), which attempted to combine Catholic thought with modern atomist physics (Whitmore 1967, 163–86). Since the Middle Ages, Catholic theology had been formulated in Aristotelian categories, especially regarding the dogma of the real presence and the teaching of transubstantiation. Every change in the vocabulary of this theology necessarily triggered unease among those for whom tradition was the ultimate criterion of truth.

The accused responded immediately with a number of books and pamphlets by authors such as Juan de Nájera (c. 1700–c. 1737). Nájera most likely also used the pseudonyms Francisco de la Paz and Alejandro de Avendaño to combat his opponents. (Nájera 1716; Paz 1716). The central issue of this polemical debate was the role of Aristotle's authority in questions of Christian theology. The critics of his influence reiterated traditional arguments, for example, that the Greek philosopher had not only been a pagan but also a materialist of questionable moral character. Therefore, a Catholic could not accept such a man as an authority in the quest for truth. Moreover, almost no pagan interpreter of Aristotle had ever accepted the basic teachings of his metaphysics in their entirety without alteration and adaptation. The controversy of 1714 was the first big attack on Aristotelian scholasticism in Spain, and even two important figures of Madrid's cultural life, the historian Juan de Ferreras (1652–1735) and the physician Diego Mateo Zapata (1664–1745), engaged in it, but the innovators soon gained the upper hand. In 1723, another physician from Madrid, Martín Martínez (1684–1734), disclosed that he was a "skeptic" and endorsed the ideal of empiricist experimental research in his publication *Skeptical Medicine and Modern Surgery* (Martínez 1722). This caused a scandal among theologians. Thus, the theology professor Bernardo López de Araujo (c. 1690–c. 1760) responded in 1725 with his widely read *Medical-Aristotelian Guard against Skeptics* (*Centinela médico-aristotélica contra scépticos*; 1725). This book did not contain any new ideas but was, like so many others, a piece of polemical literature in an already two-decade-long intellectual war that became fiercer every year. Yet another good example of Feijoo's polemical style occurred in 1725 when the Spanish Inquisition began a process against Diego Mateo Zapata, who had accepted the "new" empirical sciences and attempted to use his influence in Madrid to protect the innovators. That such an important figure of experimental physics as Zapata would be persecuted endangered the whole agenda of cultural renewal that the new Bourbon dynasty was attempting to propagate in Spain (see also McClelland 1991).

Toward a Christian Skeptical Philosophy

Feijoo's intellectual formation can be understood only against the backdrop of the dominant scholastic university system of the Iberian Peninsula. As a Benedictine monk, he had continually defended Jean Mabillon's *Treatise on Monastic Studies* (*Traité des études monastique*; Mabillon 1691). This treatise, quite apart from its historical erudition and critical assessment of the past, had demonstrated the legitimacy of "private" studies among monastics. Mabillon permitted Feijoo to engage with the empirical sciences. Certainly, Feijoo was a lecturer who was well acquainted with the works of Pierre Bayle (1647–1706) and Louis Moréri (1643–1680), but also the proceedings of the different European academies, the French Jesuit *Journal de Trévoux,* and other recent publications in medicine and physics. He had access to the most up-to-date scientific information and philosophical discourses on the continent.

Nevertheless, it must surprise us that as monk and professor of theology, he defended the Spanish physician Martín Martínez against the ferocious criticism of his fellow theologians and leading experts in medicine. In the eighteenth century not only did books need to be approved by state and church authorities (and their decree of approval was usually printed at the beginning of a publication), but famous writers were also asked to contribute notes of approval in order to assure the reader that no questionable or heretical doctrine would be contained on the following pages. For the second edition of *Skeptical*

Medicine Feijoo wrote an apologetic note of approval, with which he wanted to defend the author from rumors being spread by López de Araujo. It is important to note that this was not just a gesture of goodwill, based on a friendship between the provincial monk and the famous Madrid physician. There is no evidence that Feijoo had close private contacts with Martínez or that the monk frequently visited the court in Madrid, where he could have met him. Instead, evidence seems to suggest that Feijoo's intervention was part of a greater plan aimed at securing the much-attacked modernization of Spanish culture, which the Benedictines spearheaded together with politicians associated with the recently appointed minister José Patiño (1666–1736). This plan also intended to restrict the influence of theology on other scientific disciplines, to enlarge the liberties of the sciences, and to decrease the impediments to the kinds of empirical research already so successfully and usefully exercised outside Spain for a century. Feijoo and his friends wanted to abolish the tutelage of theology and to establish autonomy as the principle of every academic discipline.

For this purpose, however, it was necessary to undermine the authority of Aristotle and to separate medicine, as well as all the other empirical sciences, from theology and philosophy. Instead of the widespread dogmatic and deductive method, a new type of preliminary and probable knowledge had to be legitimized and set against the secure knowledge Aristotelians believed they could deduce from the canonical texts of their authorities and the art of syllogisms. The form of skepticism of Robert Boyle (1627–1691) that was used in chemistry came close to the epistemological practice suggested by Feijoo.

In *Apologetic Approval of Medical Skepticism* (*Aprobación apologética del escepticismo medico*; 1727), which he wrote in 1725 but published two years later, Feijoo used a sophisticated strategy of defense. He began by introducing himself as a disciple of Aristotle and stating that the attacks of López de Araujo on Martínez had not helped the cause of scholastic philosophy. The enormous differences in interpreting Aristotle were widely known, so another dispute about the correct understanding of the master would come as no surprise to a contemporary reader. Nevertheless, Feijoo's Aristotelianism was minimalist in that he shared with the great philosopher only an interest in the philosophy of nature and corrected López de Araujo's interpretation of Aristotle's physics. Apart from this, Feijoo denied that Aristotelian "doctrine" was useful to medicine or in the advancement of natural sciences. Even though Aristotle's physics, his metaphysics, and his dialectics were still important to theologians, Feijoo claimed they were stumbling blocks for all other sciences. His suggestions for an improvement of the study of medicine aimed ultimately at banning Aristotle from the lecture halls of this discipline.

In *Apologetic Approval* Feijoo also acknowledged the validity of doubt as a scientific principle of empirical research. He showed, however, that this doubt was not identical with the total distrust of every sensory experience, as taught by Pyrrho (Pyrrhonism is the radical variant of skepticism taught by the Greek philosopher Pyrrho of Elis, c. 365/360 BC–c. 275/270 BC). Neither was it the absolute doubt of Descartes. Instead, Martínez's doubt was something new and not derived from previous philosophical schools. The physician wanted to develop a middle way between dogmatism and skepticism. Feijoo makes this point clear by quoting Aquinas, who viewed doubt as the result of fear or misgiving in the mind. Even if one embraced a thesis, Aquinas explained, the antithesis could still be true. In other words, discussion between scholars had to rest on the premise that the opponent *could* be right. Feijoo connects this question with the science of moral probability, which the Jesuits defended as an orthodox ethical option among the rivaling systems of moral theology (Alonso-Lasheras 2011). In this system, one could hold an opinion about a moral problem even if it were not the most certain one, so long as it remained probable—that is, intelligible. This system of probabilities was considered a science since, like empirical research, it relied upon observation and preliminary findings. Thus, it is hardly surprising that *probabilism,* as it was called at the time, was unacceptable to scholastic authors who believed that true science must be free of "uncertainties," because it derived from eternal truths discovered by previous authorities. Feijoo thus defeated these scholastic writers with their own weapons by quoting a number of recognized authorities in the field of medicine who supported his view, most notably Thomas Sydenham (1624–1689) and Giorgio Baglivi (1668–1707).

Apart from the methodological renewal Feijoo and his fellows advanced, it is important to note that their philosophical discourses were published in the vernacular, in Spanish. As a philosophical language, Spanish had not been used at all until Martín Martínez, Benito Jerónimo Feijoo, and José Berní (1712–1787) began to use it in their writings. However, theirs was still a Spanish that contained many Latinisms because of Latin's role as the universal language of spoken and written academic discourse. Every publication about a problem, whether in moral theology or physics, had to use the established Latin terminology. Feijoo's custom of speaking Spanish, not only to his academic peers but also to a wider public, increased public awareness of scholastic jargon. Nevertheless, his readers certainly knew Latin and were well educated; it would be wrong to presume that he wrote for people who were largely unfamiliar with the general language of academic scholarship. He knew that his readers were predominantly theologians, but hoped for public acceptance beyond the closed doors of university lecture halls. Certainly, some technical terms would be necessary in order to translate the Latin terms into the vernacular, but the Benedictine knew this would make his writing less appealing to his new readers. Therefore, he invigorated his text with numerous allusions, jokes, and often biting polemics in order to persuade readers to agree with his own views and those of Martínez. His style, in short, was no longer that of a professor but of a gung-ho pugilist on the street, who ridiculed the pretentiousness of university teachers, passionately infusing complicated content with a new literary style refreshingly distinct from that of scholastic diction.

The War against Prejudices

Between 1726 and 1739 Feijoo published eight volumes of the *Universal Critical Theater, or Some Discourses about All Kinds of Subjects in Order to Dissolve Common Errors (Teatro crítico universal, o discursos varios en todo género de materias, para desengaño de errores communes)*, in which he discursively addressed a variety of themes (Feijoo 1726–1739). The amiable pressure of his fellow monks became the primary motivation for Feijoo, at the age of fifty, finally to make public this panoptic of hitherto private ideas. One of his main goals was to show that the traditional opinions and prejudices common people held could not withstand a thorough and critical investigation, but were incorrect and irrational. Simultaneously, he also demonstrated that academia was similarly infested by the spirit of prejudice and dogmatism. The first essay of the first volume is therefore entitled "The Voice of the People" (*La voz del pueblo*), and this essay sets the tone for the entire series by casting doubt and uncertainty on numerous propositions of medicine, astrology, and history. Nevertheless, Feijoo was far from being a Pyrrhonian skeptic; he believed that one could approach truth proximately and gain true knowledge. Nor did he share the first principle of Cartesian doubt, even as he consistently upheld a critical stance toward all traditional opinions, and especially the hegemonic and dogmatic certainty promised by scholasticism. Even though Feijoo knew the French libertines of the seventeenth century well (for example, F. La Mothe le Vayer, P. Gassendi, G. Naudé, and B. le Bovier de Fontenelle), his critical stance was inspired by Francis Bacon (1561–1626) and Robert Boyle (1627–1691).

The first volume of *Teatro crítico* also provoked controversies with physicians and astrologers. By invoking the basic human interest in preserving one's own health, he carefully scrutinized both the opinions of contemporary and classic physicians, as well as popular beliefs about medical practices. The skeptical and experimental conviction Feijoo shared with Martín Martínez was also the basis from which he argued against the Salamanca professor of mathematics, Diego de Torres Villarroel (1693–1770). Villarroel predicted the future and increased the popular fear of sun eclipses and comets. He had made a fortune with his pseudoscience. Feijoo's essays, however, treated the controversy with such a fine sense of irony and humor that they became entertaining reading to an educated public. It is not surprising that his writings reached a wide audience that soon adopted the critical and distrustful views of the respected author.

Another idea Feijoo opposed is theological in nature even if, at first glance, this is not obvious, for he did not share the opinion that the physical universe was close to its final demise. Instead, he believed firmly that there would be no physical demise of the fallen world. Only in his second volume did he develop this thesis in relation to the moral universe, where he stated that the people of Israel (despite constant acts of grace and improvements spurred by God) had committed crimes that were at least as bad as those of modernity. To Feijoo, the morality of the Roman Empire was no better than the succeeding centuries of Christian evangelization. Thus, Feijoo is neither an enthusiastic optimist who admired modernity, nor a pessimist who assumed that original sin had fatal effects on the nature of man.

Further essays of the first volume contain a defense of academic studies, a defense of the intelligence of women, and some essays on aesthetics (for example, essays about the beauty of the Spanish language and of sacred music). Ample demonstration of Feijoo's broad range is his inclusion in the first volume of an essay "On Most Subtle Politics" (*Sobre la política más fina*), criticizing the princes whose lust for power had been causing wars and tremendous suffering. A similar variety of themes is present in the other volumes. The emphasis of the second volume is on physical questions, like the weight of air and the nature of fire. Feijoo began by stating that the kind of scholasticism taught at the universities was useless, because students were merely wasting time in heated discussions, leading nowhere. In another essay, he ridiculed those who trusted in magical or supernatural powers or believed in predictions about the future. In natural history, he argued, one should follow modern science because it is based on experiments and on the reports of travelers. The classical writers should no longer be accepted as authorities in this field of research. With such statements, the Benedictine made many enemies, including the humanist Gregorio Mayáns y Siscar (1699–1781).

In the subsequent volumes of the series, Feijoo broadened his criticism of contemporary philosophy by questioning the arguments of the classical authorities, especially Aristotle, and made a case for a "magisterium" of experimental science. Consequently, he also suggested a list of themes from logic and metaphysics that should be banned from any university curriculum. In physics, he dealt with a number of paradoxes and reflected on the nature of light, blood, and the existence of a vacuum. In his essays on natural history, he considered the rationality of animals, conceding grades of sensibility and intelligence among them, as well as discussing the extinction of old and the origin of new species, thereby rejecting the presumed biblical teaching about the uniformity of species since the time of creation. This rejection of the traditional biblical interpretation became especially apparent when Feijoo deliberated on the earthly place of paradise and the origin of the human races (see *Teatro crítico universal*, vol. 7, discourses 3–4). He mentioned the errors of the Latin translation of the Bible (Vulgate), and at the same time proposed many physical and geographical explanations of biblical history. He also argued against religious traditions like pilgrimages, superstitious hagiographical works, and reports about false miracles and invented biographies of saints.

Although Feijoo, by supporting allegedly dangerous opinions only indirectly, avoided direct confrontation with theologians, his writings were nevertheless denounced to the Spanish Inquisition, which demanded the deletion of several passages. Because of strong support by powerful friends in the Spanish government, Feijoo was able to continue his work without further impediments and without being forced to defend his views. Against the first two volumes, Salvador José Mañer (1676–1751) wrote *A Critical Anti-Theater* (Mañer 1729–1731). This attack on Feijoo originated in pseudohumanist circles, which met in the Royal Library in Madrid and whose members attempted to find mistakes in Feijoo's quotations or sources in order to prove the entirety of his theses wrong. The Benedictine refuted the criticism of Mañer in his *Illustration in Defense of the First and Second Volume of the Critical Theater* (*Ilustración apologética al primero, y segundo tomo del Teatro crítico*; 1729) and in *Exact Rejection of Unjustifiable Accusations* (*Justa repulsa de inicuas acusaciones*; 1749).

Between 1742 and 1760, Feijoo published a new series of writings in which he attempted to popularize his main ideas. In this series, *Erudite and Curious Letters in Which Are Continued Most of the Aims of the Universal Critical Theater, Disputing, or Reducing to Doubts, Many Common Opinions* (*Cartas eruditas y curiosas en que, por la mayor parte, se continúa el designio del Teatro Crítico Universal, impugnando, o reduciendo a dudosas, varias opinions communes*; 1742–1760), instead of treating the topics in long essays, he discusses them in 145 letters. These letters present brief and rather casual answers to questions from friends, fellow citizens, and persons from other cities. Often the author of the question was fictitious or remained anonymous, but in a number of cases, this correspondence was real, for example, the letter regarding the earthquake in Lisbon in 1755. Here, Feijoo rejects the opinion of the theologians who tried to explain the event by referring to divine providence rather than geology. Characteristic of Feijoo is his insertion in the first volume of *Cartas* (1742, vol. 1, Carta 15) of a speech defending and honoring his fellow monk Antonio José Rodríguez (1709–1781). As an innovator and skeptic, Rodríguez had problems with the Inquisition, especially because he targeted the prevalent dogmatism and the uncritical belief in authorities in the sciences much more harshly than Feijoo, and much more convincingly presented deist physico-theology (Rodríguez 1736).

Feijoo, however, also saw limits for the acceptance of modern physical theories, such as, for example, the Cartesian conclusion that mere accident influenced the spiral movements characteristic of the formation of atoms, or, as many materialists argued, that intelligence derived from the chaos at the origin of the universe. That complex forms of organic life might come about by mere accident or depend upon unintelligible accidents was, in Feijoo's view, irrational.

An objection against the *Cartas* was raised by the Franciscan Francisco de Soto y Marne (c. 1698–c. 1770/1775) in his 1749 *Apologetic and Critical Reflections of the Works of R.R.P. Master Benito Jerónimo Feijoo* (*Reflexiones crítico apologéticas sobre las obras del R.R.P. Maestro Benito Jerónimo Feijoo*; 1749), which defended the philosophy of Raimundus Lullus (set forth in *Ars magna*), a medieval author (1232–1316) whose writings experienced a renaissance in Germany (e.g., Ivo Salzinger, 1669–1728) and Spain (Marcos Tronchón and Rafael Torre-Blanca). A crucial part of Lullism was its "inventive method," which was based on an a priori system of combinatorial logic in order to find new truths without the need to conduct experiments. Lullus's followers argued that Feijoo defamed the Catholic faith by adhering to the principles of a heretic like Francis Bacon instead of a saint like Lullus. In his answer, Feijoo not only defended his empiricism but also declared that non-Catholics have the obligation to seek the truth and that, therefore, a church cannot exclusively embrace the opinions of its own members. In this controversy, King Ferdinand VI (1712–1759) intervened with a decree in 1750 that prohibited writing *against* Feijoo. The Benedictine monk could trust securely in the support of the royal administration.

Feijoo: A First-Rate Spanish Thinker

An estimated three hundred thousand copies of Feijoo's books were sold over the course of the eighteenth century in Spanish-speaking countries. He was by far the most-read Spanish author. Without a doubt, Feijoo's writings influenced the opinions of his contemporaries, especially by promoting a new understanding of the empirical sciences and preparing society for their acceptance. Moreover, his criticism of popular devotion and superstitious practices that had crept into ecclesiastical culture lent support to religious change. Feijoo's essays instructed his readers, making them more critical and thus more strongly fortified against the manipulations of poorly educated clergymen. Together with Feijoo, the Jesuit José Francisco de Isla (1703–1781) contributed to a more intelligent, less superstitious homily culture in Spain, with his novel *History of the Famous Preacher Friar Gerundio de Campazas* (*Historia del famoso predicador frau Gerundio de Campazas*; 1758), which had ridiculed the average, ignorant homilist.

Juan Luis Roche (1722–1794) imitated Feijoo's work in his 1758 *Curious and Erudite Fragments of Some Modern Inventions, Where a Universal Criticism Is Exposed* (*Fragmentos curiosos y eruditos de algunos ingenios modernos en que se expone una crítica universal*). Likewise, Faustino Muscat y Guzmán (1740–1812) tried, without much success, to continue the *Critical Theater* (1770). Feijoo's reputation spread with remarkable speed, and soon translations of his works were available in French (1731, 1742–1743, 1746, 1755), Portuguese (1737, 1746–1748), English (1739, 1751), Italian (1740, 1744, 1745, 1766, 1777–1782), and even German (1781, 1790).

Although Feijoo emphasized the power and range of natural reason, he never went as far as the more radical English deists. In aesthetics, he trusted intuition, and this allowed him to create new things and to find an individual synthesis, rather than merely following rules or copying models. He was a steadfast defender of the freedom of academic disciplines, which enables the search for truth. As a faithful Catholic, he conceded certain limitations to the freedom of thought, but never engaged in an apologetic campaign against the English and French freethinkers. Instead, he preferred to admonish the church to reflect critically on her own institutional and theological framework. Thus, he gave very practical and concrete advice even in his most polemical writings. Moreover, Feijoo was always very cautious not to get involved in doctrinal disputes. He remarked that such arguments could have harmful effects on one's health and named his fellow Spaniard Miguel Servet (1511–1553), who had been burned at the stake in Calvinist Geneva, as an example.

As a Catholic author, Feijoo preached his faith neither in ignorant credulity nor in militant fanaticism, but distanced himself from the scholastics because in his eyes they demanded an extreme dogmatism that did not allow any leeway for nuances and progress. He demanded greater freedom in university studies and independence for the natural sciences, which, in his view, should be allowed to flourish without the interference of dilettante theologians. Feijoo also encouraged monastic reform. He thought that novices should not be excessively restricted out of fear that they could make mistakes. Instead, he argued, one should show humility and tolerance toward them and forgive mistakes. An open and more forgiving Catholicism should recognize, he thought, that human understanding progresses, and that all must continually strive for internal progress as well. Therefore, he saw the old monastic traditions as not without flaws, but in need of updating according to the needs of the era. Fidelity to tradition could never be absolute, because traditions are always in flux. The Benedictine also criticized the church by shedding light on false miracles or questionable practices, which were rooted in ecclesiastical historiography and popular devotion. In his minimalist view of miracles, he found support in the writings of Prospero Lambertini, the future Pope Benedict XIV (1740–1758). Nevertheless, because critics argued that perennially seeking greater understanding of the world's mysteries in natural philosophy would eliminate divine action from the world, Feijoo frequently indulged an almost religious delight in finding natural explanations for sensory phenomena, all the while insisting that his regard for God was undiminished. Indeed, Feijoo exalted divine transcendence, and saw in God the intelligence and will that governed the universe through natural laws, not through the constant and arbitrary interference of a supernatural power. In his thinking, consequently, natural philosophy gained full independence from theology. In the final analysis, however, it remains an open question just to what extent faith played a vital role in his empirical and somewhat skeptical worldview.

Translated by Ulrich L. Lehner

Bibliography

Aguilar Piñal, Francisco. 1981–2001. *Bibliografía de autores españoles del siglo XVIII.* 10 vols. Madrid: Consejo Superior de Investigaciones Científicas.

Alonso-Lasheras, Diego. 2011. *Luis De Molina's "De iustitiae et iure": Justice as Virtue in an Economic Context.* Leiden: Brill.

Ardao, Arturo. 1962. *La filosofía polémica de Feijoo.* Buenos Aires: Losada.

Cabriada, Juan de. 1686. *Carta philosóphica médico-chymica, en que se demuestra que de los tiempos y experiencias se han aprendido los mejores remedios contra las enfermedades por la novo-antigua medicina.* Madrid.

Cardoso, Isaac. 1673. *Philosophia libera, in septem libros distributa: In quibus omnia quae ad philosophiam naturalem spectant, methodice colliguntur et accurate disputantur.* Venice.

Cerra Suárez, Silverio. 1986. *Las ideas antropológicas de Feijoo.* Vol. 1, *La génesis del hombre.* Oviedo: Seminario Metropolitano.

Coletes Blanco, Agustín. 2003. "La huella de Feijoo en Inglaterra (1739–1818)." In *Feijoo, hoy (semana Marañon 2000),* edited by I. Urzainqui, 287–307. Oviedo: Instituto Feijoo de Estudios del siglo XVIII / Madrid: Fundación Marañón.

Elizalde, Ignacio. 1982. "Feijoo y la influencia de los libertinos eruditos franceses." In *Actas del Séptimo Congreso Internacional de Hispanistas,* 407–18. Rome: Bulzoni Editore.

Feijoo, Benito Jerónimo. 1726–1739. *Teatro crítico universal o discursos varios en todo género de materias, para desengaño de errores comunes.* 8 vols. Madrid.

———. 1727. *Aprobación apologética del escepticismo médico*. In *Medicina scéptica y cirugia moderna con un tratado de operaciones quirúrgicas,* by Martín Martínez. 2nd ed. Vol. 1. Madrid. Previously published 1725.

———. 1729. *Ilustración apologética al primero, y segundo tomo del Teatro crítico*. Madrid.

———. 1739. *An Exposition of the Uncertainties in the Practice of Physic*. London: J. and R. Tonson and S. Drapere.

———. 1742–1760. *Cartas eruditas y curiosas en que, por la mayor parte, se continúa el designio del Teatro Crítico Universal, impugnando, o reduciendo a dudosas, varias opinions communes*. 5 vols. Madrid.

———. 1742–1745. *Nuevo aspecto de la teología médico-moral, y ambos derechos o paradojas phisico-teológico-legales*. 4 vols. Zaragoza.

———. 1749. *Justa repulsa de inicuas acusaciones*. Madrid.

———. 1764. *The Honour and Advantage of Agriculture*. Dublin: William Williamson.

———. 1778. *Three Essays or Discourses on the Following Subjects: A Defence or Vindication of the Women, Church Music, a Comparison between Ancient and Modern Music*. London: T. Becket.

———. 1952. *Obras escogidas del padre fray Benito Jerónimo Feijoo y Montenegro*. With notes on his life and a critique of his works by Don Vicente de la Fuente. Madrid: Ediciones Atlas.

———. 2009. *Cartas eruditas y curiosas*. Edited by Francisco Uzcanga Meinecke. Barcelona.

———. 2010. "A Defense of Women: Equality despite Difference (1726)." In *Other Voices: Readings in Spanish Philosophy,* edited by John R. Welch, 262–84. Notre Dame: University of Notre Dame Press.

Gutiérrez de los Ríos, Francisco. 1686. *El hombre práctico, o discursos varios sobre su conocimiento y enseñanza*. Reprint, Madrid, 1764.

Isla, José Francisco de. 1758. *Historia del famoso predicador frau Gerundio de Campazas*. Vol. 1. Madrid.

López de Araujo, Bernardo. 1725. *Centinela médico-aristotélica contra scépticos: En la cual se declara ser más segura y firme la doctrina que se enseña en las Universidades españolas y los graves inconvenientes que se siguen de la secta scéptica o pyrrhónica*. Madrid.

Mabillon, Jean. 1691. *Traité des études monastique*. Paris.

Mañer, Salvador José. 1729–1731. *Anti-teatro crítico sobre el primero y segundo tomo de Teatro Crítico Universal del Rmo. P.M.Fr. Benito Feyjoo*. Vol. 1, Madrid, 1729. Vol. 2, Madrid, 1731.

Martínez, Martín. 1722. *Medicina scéptica y cirugia moderna con un tratado de operaciones quirúrgicas*. 2 vols. Madrid. 2nd ed., 1725.

McClelland, I. Lillian. 1991. *Ideological Hesitancy in Spain, 1700–1750*. Liverpool: Liverpool University Press.

Muscat y Guzmán, Faustino. 1770. *Años eruditos españoles, o Continuación del Teatro crítico de Feijoo.* Madrid.
Nájera, Juan de [Alejándro de Avendaño]. 1716. *Diálogos filosóficos en defensa del atomismo y respuesta a las impugnaciones aristotélicas del R.P.M.Fr. Francisco Palanco.* Madrid.
Napoleone, Caterina. 1996. "Monastic Caprices: The Monastery of Trinità dei Monti: The Anamorphosis by Emmanuel Maignan." *FMR: The Magazine of Franco Maria Ricci* 71:19–44.
Otero Pedrayo, Ramón. 1972. *El padre Feijoo: Su vida, doctrina e influencias.* Orense: Instituto de Estudios Orensanos Padre Feijoo.
Palanco, Francisco. 1714. *Dialogus physico-theologicus contra philosophiae novatores, sive thomista contra atomistas: Cursus philosophici tomus quartus.* Madrid.
Paz, Francisco de la. 1716. "Carta al Rvmo. P. M. Palanco (1714)." In *Diálogos philosóficos en defensa del atomismo.* Edited by Juan de Nájera. Madrid.
Roche, Juan Luis. 1758. *Fragmentos curiosos y eruditos de algunos ingenios modernos en que se expone una crítica universal.* Puerto de Santa Maria.
Rodríguez, Antonio José. 1736. *Palestra crítico-médica en que se trata introducir la verdadera medicina, y desalojar la tirana del reino de la naturaleza.* Pamplona.
Sánchez-Agesta, Luis. 1945. "Feijoo y la crisis del pensamiento político español del siglo XVIII." In *Revista de Estudios Políticos* 12:22–23, 71–127.
Sánchez-Blanco, Francisco. 2003. "La filosofía de Feijoo." In *Feijoo, hoy (semana Marañon 2000),* edited by I. Urzainqui, 239–56. Oviedo: Instituto Feijoo de Estudios del siglo XVIII / Madrid: Fundación Marañon.
Soto y Marne, Francisco de. 1749. *Reflexiones crítico apologéticas sobre las obras del R.R.P. Maestro Benito Jerónimo Feijoo.* Salamanca.
Universidad Oviedo. 1966. "El P. Feijoo y su siglo: Ponencias y comunicaciones presentadas al simposio celebrado en la universidad de Oviedo del 28 de septiembre al 5 de octubre de 1964." In *Cuadernos de la cátedra de Feijoo,* vol. 18. Oviedo: University Press.
Whitmore, P. J. S. 1967. *The Order of Minims in Seventeenth-Century France.* International Archives of the History of Ideas 20. The Hague: Martinus Nijhoff.
Witthaus, Jan-Henrik. 2011. *Sozialisation der Kritik im Spanien des aufgeklärten Absolutismus: Zur Genese literarischen Engagements im Spanien des aufgeklärten Absolutismus, von Feijoo bis Jovellanos.* Frankfurt am Main: Klostermann.
Yerushalmi, Yosef Hayim. 1981. *From Spanish Court to Italian Ghetto: Isaac Cardoso; A Study in Seventeenth-Century Marranism and Jewish Apologetics.* Seattle: University of Washington Press.

15

Josep Climent i Avinent (1706–1781)

Enlightened Catholic, Civic Humanist, Seditionist

ANDREA J. SMIDT

Born in Castelló de la Plana on 11 March 1706 during the Spanish War of Succession, Josep Climent i Avinent was raised by his mother alone, because his father died of malaria just before he was born. Having begun his education in the grammar schools of Castelló, Climent moved to Valencia at age thirteen to live with his paternal uncle, a Mercedarian priest. There, he continued his studies, matriculating at the University of Valencia in 1722. As sole heir to his father's estate, Climent could have chosen a career as a civil servant. Instead, he opted for a career in the church and earned his doctorate in theology in 1727 (Tort i Mitjans 1978, 3–5).

After receiving his first benefice in 1729, Climent rose through the ranks of the secular clergy while maintaining a teaching position at the University of Valencia. By 1738, he had become an ardent moral rigorist, antiprobabilist, anti-Jesuit, and antiregalist. He had befriended Dominicans who protected him in and outside university walls from Jesuits and regalists with whom he had made enemies. His anti-Jesuit position had left him isolated from the Academy of Valencia, one of the country's most prestigious scientific communities. Yet Climent associated with individuals such as Francisco Pérez Bayer (1711–1794), Andrés Piquer (1711–1772), Felipe Bertrán (1704–1783), and Gregorio Mayáns (1699–1781). One friend, Andrés Mayoral (1685–1769), became bishop of Valencia in 1738 and appointed Climent as an adviser. Yet by 1740, Climent had made known his desire for pastoral work and was appointed parish priest of St. Bartholomew parish in Valencia. As a parish priest from 1740 to 1748, Climent earned a reputation for his austerity, charity, and especially his skill in preaching. His homilies, preached every Sunday afternoon in the parish church, presented a framework of "Jansenism and Enlightenment and at the same time countered the theological currents of laxism and probabilism" (Tort i Mitjans 1978, 8). He gained popularity as a preacher, and eventually was promoted to Magistral Canon of the Cathedral of Valencia's chapter in 1748. For eighteen years, he traveled throughout Valencia as one of the best-known preachers of his day.

Climent's talents in speaking and writing earned him many responsibilities and projects as part of the cathedral chapter. Most notably, he was commissioned in 1756 to plead the chapter's case in Madrid for the return of some tithes and first fruits that the chapter found the central government in Madrid owed them. Climent spent three years in Madrid negotiating for the Valencian church and met with success by 1760. In the process, he made good friends with anti-Jesuits, such as Manuel de Roda (1706–1782), a future minister of grace and justice. He also made a few enemies, such as the ardent regalist Pedro Rodríguez de Campomanes (1723–1802).

By the time of the happy verdict for Climent and Valencia, Charles III (1716–1788) was king, and his ministers were exceptionally eager to bring down the Jesuits. Even though Climent's enemies in Madrid would work against his promotion to bishop a few times in the early 1760s because of his antiregalist, proclerical, and proepiscopal positions, the Esquilache riots of 1766 changed the tune of his enemies so that they were singing any notes that effectively would silence the Jesuits once and for all. The riots were a major embarrassment for Charles III, who was forced to flee for safety to his palace in Aranjuez, outside of Madrid, while a military junta ruled Madrid in his place until order was restored. After returning to Madrid in April, the king became convinced that the Jesuits were directly responsible for stirring up the people against him, using the rising prices of bread, oil, coal, and meat caused by the policies of the royal minister Esquilache (1700–1785) as a pretext to provoke the unrest. In response to the Esquilache riots, the chief end of royal policy became the expulsion of the Jesuits from Spain, galvanizing regalist ministers to achieve this goal even if it meant appointing a known antiregalist such as Climent, who was a strong anti-Jesuit. When the bishopric of Barcelona became vacant in 1766, Climent received word of his nomination to the position. However, since Barcelona was known for its strong Jesuit presence, he did not hesitate to decline the post. Yet Madrid remained insistent that he accept the bishopric, seeing in Climent a subject very capable of subverting a potential pro-Jesuit reaction if the expulsion of the Jesuits occurred, as it eventually did in April 1767. Finally, Climent accepted the appointment after the king's confessor threateningly implied that failing to follow the will of the king and God would endanger his eternal salvation (Tort i Mitjans 1978, 26).

Climent as Bishop of Barcelona (1766–1775): A Key Figure of Catholic Enlightenment in Spain

It is as bishop of Barcelona that Josep Climent made his greatest contributions to the Catholic Enlightenment, both in thought and deed. In Spain, he was exceptional not for his status as a churchman but for his insistence on finding a genuinely Spanish and independently ecclesiastical way to try to enlighten the faith of his parishioners. Unlike other contemporary ideas of religious reform and enlightenment, Climent's vision focused on independent or free provincial and synodal councils as the ideal and mandatory agency of Catholic Enlightenment. He saw such councils as the sole means to purify the faith, as was illustrated in his published pastoral instructions in Barcelona and his letters to the Abbé Augustin-Charles-Jean Clément de Bizon du Tremblay (1717–1804), a French Jansenist canon of Auxerre who corresponded with Jansenists and their friends all over Europe in what has been labeled the "Jansenist International" (Bradley and Van Kley 2001, 69). Climent was extraordinarily lucid about his vision for reform, the obstacles to reform that he faced, and the means by which he would hurdle them (Smidt 2002).

Climent illustrated a different side of the Spanish Enlightenment, one that distinctively overlapped with Catholic Enlightenment. While the Spanish Enlightenment included a physiocratic program for economic progress sponsored by the regalist state, by mid-century it also included at least two strands of Catholic Enlightenment. Given a series of highly charged political events, different Catholic groups in Spain were fragmented "towards the poles of the monarchy or the papacy, or the rejection of either one, creating in the process a mosaic of different Catholic Enlightenments" (Smidt 2010b, 412). Therefore, the practical implementation of Catholic Enlightenment in Spain did not always have the same austere tone as that of Climent. Typically, it coincided with the efforts of regalists, "Jansenists," and other moral rigorists to overpower and eliminate the Jesuit influence, weaken the Inquisition, bolster interior spirituality at the expense of Baroque extravagance, and reform education at the university and elementary levels (Noel 2001). Thus, as Samuel Miller states, "There were no Voltaires in either Spain or Portugal, but there was a minority in both countries, an extraordinarily influential minority it must be said, that eagerly read and adopted, in all fields, ideas of reform which did not threaten the essence of the Catholic religion and did not contradict too sharply [with] native traditions of how to make society better" (1978, 22). Indeed, Climent can be identified with this Spanish movement of Catholic reform affiliated with the regalist government of Charles III. Climent was a key anti-Jesuit player in Barcelona before and after the expulsion of the Jesuits. His sermons and pastoral instructions make clear his desire to bolster interior spirituality in each parishioner's devotional life in contrast to Baroque rituals. His pushes for seminary reform and increased lay literacy in Barcelona make him an exceptional figure of Catholic Enlightenment (Smidt 2011). Yet for

Climent, it did not entirely suffice. He would not stop with these goals and continued to campaign for greater austerity and open deliberative procedures within the Spanish Catholic Church, in a spirit of Christian civic humanism that resonated with other voices of Catholic Enlightenment outside of Spain (Van Kley 2008).

While regalism was not unique to Spain, Spanish regalism under Charles III was uniquely concerned with separating the jurisdictions of church and state. There were three overarching facets of Caroline regalism with relation to the church. The first was the crown's attempt to control the church through the nomination of higher-ranking officials amenable to expanded state authority. The second was a proactive refusal to permit the Roman Curia to intervene in Spanish ecclesiastical affairs. The third was an effort to increase state intervention in ecclesiastical affairs, effectively effacing the demarcation separating temporal from spiritual power (Paquette 2008, 71).

Spanish regalists often were labeled "Jansenists" by contemporaries because of their opposition to excessive papal power and their anti-Jesuit inclination; however, these regalists shared few concerns with Jansenists in France or the Netherlands, for example, on issues of metaphysics, theology, or the church's overall welfare. Spanish regalists were primarily concerned with the political and economic welfare of the Bourbon state by means of a more "nationalized" Catholic Church in Spain. While Climent was much more theologically Jansenist than regalists in Madrid, his major bone of contention with them had to do with the regalist importation of Gallicanism as an ideology and model for transforming the Catholic Church in Spain into something of a royal church independent from Rome (Smidt 2010a, 25–53). Gallicanism in France had been employed by *parlements* to limit monarchical authority. With no *parlements* in Spain, Spanish regalists employed Gallicanism to work toward a church structure similar to Henry VIII's of England, with the king replacing the pope as the head.

While Climent never labeled himself a "Jansenist," he had many Jansenist leanings and sympathized with the cause of Jansenists in France and the Netherlands. These sympathies, as well as his similarities to and departures from Jansenism, are most clearly illustrated in his contacts with the French Jansenist Clément. Climent was fully aware of how Gallicanism had influenced French Jansenists in their efforts at reform, providing clergy and state a common ground for protecting certain liberties as they met with resistance from Rome. French Jansenist clerics naturally appealed, then, to the state to establish more jurisdictional authority, and although their monarchs were not sympathetic to their cause, they were encouraged by the success they had had in appealing to the state authority in the form of the Parlement of Paris. Distinguishing his uniqueness as a reformer, Climent remained at odds with the French position toward secular authority. In addition, elsewhere in non-French Catholic Europe, his enlightened counterparts who wished to reform the Catholic Church and purify the faith, specifically of superstitious practices, tended to appeal to their regalist monarchies for help. Unlike these other eighteenth-century proponents of Catholic reform, Climent was just as suspicious of royal sponsorship of ecclesiastical and religious reform as he was of the expected opposition from the papacy. As he maintained in his letter of October 1768, "The ills . . . are exposed; it is apparent that the undermining of the Discipline, mentioned in the letter of the 6th, comes as much from Regalism as it does from Ultramontanism, the secular authority claiming and acquiring the powers that the Pontiff is losing, leaving the bishops as badly off as, or worse off than, they were before" (Climent, 1768e).

In his letters of correspondence with Abbé Clément, Climent was clear that the institutional means to carry out ecclesiastical reform did not lie within the bounds of the regalist state. Citing particular actions having been taken by Charles III and his Council of Castile that revealed Madrid's tendencies, Climent insisted that their assistance in ecclesiastical reform would only further enserf the Spanish church to the absolutist monarchy. Thus, the power of the regalist state and that of Rome were equally threatening to their cause, and as he repeatedly told Clément, "[The Spanish bishops] are between two fires that beat us down and humiliate us" (Climent, 23 November 1768, 21 October 1769).

Climent saw that the power vacuum left by the Jesuits was being filled by the secular, regalist power of the state in the name of the *pa-*

tronato real: "Many bishops fear that the secular powers will usurp the faculties of Rome that the Jesuits have left" (Climent, 5 April 1768). Dating back to the *Reconquista* of Spain and the founding of the Inquisition by the *Reyes Católicos,* and more currently with the Concordat of 1753, Spanish monarchs had a tradition of establishing themselves as an authority on Catholicism independent from the pope or the Spanish clergy. It was at this particular juncture that Climent saw precisely how the regalist state's manner of proceeding in the name of Spanish Catholicism would lead directly to a national church led by a king and his ministers, rather than by the clergy.

Climent maintained that, if the objective were to be a church similar in structure and moral discipline to that of the early church, then the secular authority of the king must not be instrumental in attaining this goal. The ecclesiastical structure of the early church had developed independently of the state and, furthermore, without the sponsorship of any secular emperor to assist early Christians (*Nouvelles* 1769, 157). According to Climent's reasoning, using the protection of regalist states to realize ecclesiastical reform in the eighteenth century would not succeed in fully achieving the ecclesiastical structure of the early church. Instead, it would only further subject the bishops to the authority of the absolute monarch, in a sense replacing one master with another. This obstacle course forced Climent to navigate between the papacy and the monarchy, and to seek leverage without sacrificing autonomy. All eighteenth-century proponents of reform faced the problem of an institutional means for effecting it. However, Climent stood out by pursuing independent means for reform in the Spanish Catholic church that would lie between the nonreformist defenders of an infallible pope and the secular, yet Catholic, Spanish monarchy. In his opinion, the monarchy tended to expand its own secular power at the expense of the national church. The Spanish clergy, already divided on various political and theological issues especially after the expulsion of the Jesuits in 1767, possessed no institutional means by which to convene, discuss, and potentially form a unified stance on issues that would serve to counter the direction of the regalist state. Hence, Climent took interest in and advanced the idea of independent or free councils as the ideal agency of enlightened Catholic reform.

Most of all, Climent was concerned with an enlightenment of religious behavior among parishioners, but this enlightenment depended on the success of bishops and councils in effecting ecclesiastical reform. For Climent, the convening and success of councils lay solely in the hands of the bishops; by relying on the authority of Scripture, decrees of previous church councils, and the works of the holy fathers, not only were bishops capable of making a rational case for reform of the church hierarchy, but they also were obligated on an individual level to reform their discipline (over self, clergy, and laity) in the spirit of austerity. In this way, the reforms of popular piety and of ecclesiastical structure were intertwined. Climent employed pastoral instructions to communicate this connection to laity and clergy alike. By definition, pastoral instructions were letters written by priests to explain to their parishioners how the collective laws of the church (canon law) should bear fruit in their everyday lives. In Climent's instructions, the heart of the message always went back to the connection between large-scale ecclesiastical reform and moral reform in the lives of both clergy and laity, maintaining that the starting point for each bishop was the spiritual well-being of his flock (while the material well-being of the poor remained another primary concern).

Yet as things stood at that time in Catholic Europe, moral reform would need to be effected within each diocese in order for spiritual well-being to be achieved. Thus, for Climent, councils were key in providing a forum for bishops to convene and share advice with each other in order to find proper solutions for problems and to return Catholics to the virtue of the past. He observed: "Today we must confess that each one of us [bishops] uses to our individual satisfaction whatever jurisdictional powers remain for us; we live isolated in our dioceses: we have very little or no communication with our neighboring bishops; and consequently we lose out on the 'lights' we need and that were historically shared between us congregated in councils" (1788, 1:225). Calling upon the bishops of Spain and, by extension, upon all bishops, to increase communication among themselves, Climent indicated that such communication would serve as the first step toward the assembly of councils in Spain.

Besides uncovering ways to enlighten the faith of their parishioners, councils would also serve as the best institutional means for achieving reform of the individual cleric. With regular assemblies, bishops would ideally hold each other accountable for the proper distribution of alms and oblige themselves to live more modestly, with temperance and charity. For those who did not use their revenues according to church law, "their provincial brothers, assembled in council, will have the duty to reprimand and punish them" (Climent 1788, 2:225) Thus, Climent's letters also focused on the reform of the individual cleric as the key means to large-scale ecclesiastical reform. From the bottom up, bishops must come together for the success of reform.

In his letters to Abbé Clément as well as in his pastoral instructions, Climent promoted the use of open, deliberative procedures for church governance that would emphasize austerity and prevent luxury from creeping in the back door of the church. His proposed forum for Spanish clergy encouraged a greater role for bishops within their dioceses to the extent that, in spiritual affairs, they should be left unhindered by outside forces (Rome or Madrid), with the exception of provincial councils. While Climent did not have seditious intentions, Madrid saw the vision that he preached for the church as an implicit threat to regalist authority. Fully aware of the existing barriers to reform in the papacy and the monarchy, Climent proceeded to minister as bishop of Barcelona without diluting his vision for provincial councils and greater austerity in the church. In practice, however, the obstacle course proved to be a difficult one to maneuver.

The Ecclesiastical Correspondence between Bishop Climent and Abbé Clément of Auxerre (1768–1781)

After the expulsion of the Jesuits from Spain in 1767, the French Jansenist Abbé Clément of Auxerre seized what he considered an opportune moment, calling upon Spanish bishops, such as Climent, to unite across state borders with the "Jansenist International." The French abbé targeted Climent as a cleric whose words could be exploited specifically to improve the political situation of Jansenists in France and initiated a correspondence with him. Despite Climent's pessimism about the papacy and the forces of ultramontanism, the dates of their letters correspond with those of the pontificate of Clement XIV (1769–1774), a pontificate widely perceived as a window of opportunity for significant reform. Yet it became ever more apparent, as the story unfolded, that the window would not be large enough to accommodate Climent's goals.

After a Parisian book publisher and bookseller with Spanish connections put him in contact with Climent, Abbé Clément wrote his initial letter to Climent in December of 1767, introducing himself and addressing their common interests in moral theology and ecclesiology (Clément 1802, 21ff.). Praising the abbé's proposal that the two correspond to share news of each others' churches, Climent responded that in Spain there was "less freedom to write" than in France (Climent, 28 January 1768, 3v). Yet, Abbé Clément countered, "From the moment of the expulsion of the Society . . . you have reached the time in which you have a lot more liberty to defend the Holy Doctrine and the great efforts that you have to make for bringing about the Reform of Studies and of morals that should be the result of the expulsion" (Clément, 18 March 1768, 5v). Climent agreed with him on the necessity for reform and continued writing about his efforts at implementing such changes.

From this point on, the two wrote a series of letters covering topics such as regalism, ultramontanism, and the parameters surrounding popular piety. Abbé Clément was apparently hoping that the Spanish bishop would have the same opinions and seek the same direction as the French. In August of 1768, in an effort to form Jansenist "audiences" in Spain, the abbé traveled from France to Madrid, entering Spain by way of Barcelona, and actually visited Climent for about ten days in order to make his acquaintance in person (Clément 1802, 43). While Climent never went as far as to throw in his lot completely with Abbé Clément and the French Jansenists, he did regard them as allies. In their correspondence, the Frenchman would attempt to use Climent's Jansenist sympathies to build support for the French cause. At the same time, Climent made clear in his letters his ideas regarding the church universal, as well as the church particular.

Climent fought with the secular authority over educating the laity of his diocese, and he recounted these conflicts in his letters. First of all, Climent noted to Abbé Clément exactly why he felt the need to establish his own schools. "They say that a plan of studies is coming out of Madrid; but I fear that it will be directed toward the teaching of Mathematics and experimental Physics rather than Theology, because what comes out of Madrid (given their prerogatives) is greatly inclined toward the profane rather than the sacred sciences" (Climent, 14 June 1768, 20v). In some ways, Madrid's trend toward secularization opposed the moral reform that Climent sought to implement in his jurisdiction of Barcelona. A second area of conflict that Climent described concerned relations with the populace at large. Rather than spending a great deal of time outside of his diocese, as many of his contemporaries tended to do, Climent was convinced of the importance of staying within the confines of his diocese and interacting directly with his people, describing himself as a bishop of, and for, the people. Given his mission to the general public in Barcelona, Climent reacted negatively toward the Spanish secular power: the bureaucrats of Madrid were all nobility "of the highest rank," and the concept of the *pueblo* (the general masses) was beyond their comprehension (Climent, 14 June 1768).

Later that year, Climent continued to write negatively about Madrid. In his letter of 25 June 1768, he noted a disturbing sign of the regalists' pursuit of power when he complained how the king had ordered publication of anti-Jesuit brochures without consulting or even seeking the permission of Spanish clergy. "I wish that these truly extraordinary steps had been taken with the agreement of the Prelates of the Church" (Climent, 25 June 1768, 24v). Although Climent agreed with the contents of the publication, the fact that the king felt no obligation to consult his Spanish clergy on the matter demonstrated that the state, embodied by the king, claimed religious authority independent of the pope and of the Spanish clergy. Giving a different response from Climent's, the French Jansenist publication *Nouvelles ecclésiastiques* positively reported the royal act. Likewise, it viewed similar royal actions in Spain, regarding publications and prohibitions of books found in the king's ordinance of 16 June 1768, as evidence of an enlightened monarch because the anti-Jesuit pamphlets praised not only Pascal but also the school of Port-Royal, both strongly associated with the Jansenist cause (*Nouvelles* 1768, 157–58).

Not an advocate of that kind of Gallicanism, Climent responded to Abbé Clément and the Gallicans of the *Nouvelles* publication later that year. Distinguishing his reformist ideas, he articulated why he objected to the French course in his letter of 23 November 1768. The lucidity of Climent's thoughts is exceptional:

> I am criticizing that all, or almost all, of those that follow Saint Augustine or Jansenius are on the side of the secular power against the ecclesiastical; I attribute it to the disgraceful fact that many of the popes and bishops have been Molinists, and thus such disciples have implored and found protection in the Parliaments.... I see that the discord will only endure between these same clerics over the issue of jurisdiction while the clash regarding doctrine will also endure.... The worst of it is that such jurisdictional disputes that began in France have transcended to all the provinces of the Christian realm, while the secular magistrates there adopt maxims that only subject and impoverish the cleric without bringing any reform in his office. What utility follows from this for the church as a whole? (Climent, 23 November 1768, 83v)

Augustinians and Jansenists placed more emphasis in the redeeming role of efficacious grace over that of free will and had doctrinal disagreements with Molinists, who reversed the order of importance in salvation. That forced Augustinians and Jansenists to seek support for their reforms outside of the Molinist haven of Rome. Even if the state were able to offer protection to clerics within their jurisdiction, the ideological differences between the reformist clerics and Rome would always remain. Rather, as Climent later points out in the same letter, the key to progress in reform lay within the unity of bishops, implemented by convening councils.

Clearly, Climent deemed the secular authority to be an obstacle to the reform of Catholicism. Moreover, he did not even trust Madrid to be sympathetic to his cause. Climent wrote that a royal decree had just made the king the owner and dispenser of all former Jesuit property, and he noted that, even with the absence of the ultramontanist Jesuits, the Spanish church had not gained the opportunity to freely proceed with reform: Regalism is taking what ultramontanism is leaving behind, "leaving the bishops as badly off as, or worse off than, they were before" (Climent, 23 November 1768, 83v). In his next letter, of 4 July 1769, Climent further addressed the implications of the state's redistribution of Jesuit wealth. While he acknowledged that the church could benefit from this great wealth, Climent would not accept any state endowments for his seminary. "Under that condition the king or, better said, his ministers, would name the directors [of my seminary], who would remain independent of the bishops" (Climent, 4 July 1769, 237v). Since the training of candidates for holy orders was important to Climent for widespread moral and ecclesiastical reform, it was imperative for the good of the church that the directors of such seminaries share the common vision for a morally rigorist and conciliar church. Thus, Climent feared that having men appointed by Madrid would not lead to the appointment of directors who would share and work toward this common reformist vision.

Climent's Pastoral Instruction of 26 March 1769

The disagreement between the two clerics over the means of reform came to the surface on the occasion of Abbé Clément's discussion of Climent's pastoral instruction of 26 March 1769, which he had recently received that summer. Given Climent's opinions on ecclesiastical studies and the necessity of councils, the abbé desired to publish a French translation of Climent's instruction. Nowhere is Climent's plan for reform of Catholic society better unfolded than in this controversial work, mentioned later that year in *Nouvelles ecclésiastiques*. It is in this instruction that Climent not only required Claude Fleury's (1640–1723) *Manners of the Ancient Israelites and Christians* (*Mœurs des Israëlites et des Chrétiens*; 1682) as reading for his pastors-in-training but also recommended it to all laity and clergy of his diocese as a sort of catechism (Climent 1788, 1:187–268). Climent's praise of Fleury was seemingly endless. Fleury's treatment of, and implicit argument for, a return to the model of the early church struck a chord with Climent, who saw in it a rational case for a reconceptualization of what Christian life is. Additionally, Fleury's work was valuable not only for its use of reason but also for its natural and concise style, which made it accessible for all classes of readers.

Written by a Gallican in pre-Enlightenment times, the works of Fleury were translated into other languages and widely reprinted throughout the seventeenth and eighteenth centuries. Thus, it was easily available to the literate in Catholic lands. Because *Manners* retold the history of God's people without overtly criticizing the Catholic Church or questioning church doctrine, a variety of parties—including Rome, many Catholics, Gallicans, Jansenists, and to a certain extent *philosophes* such as Voltaire (1694–1778) and Diderot (1713–1784)—appreciated the style and content of Fleury's argument. He lauded the virtues of the Israelites and early Christians as integral models for shaping a reasonable lifestyle. Telling the stories of the humble beginnings of both the Old Testament Israelites and the early church of the Roman Empire, Fleury pictures these two communities as initially characterized by purity, later by corruption, and finally by renewal within the two groups. Thus, Fleury's work was both Catholic and enlightened, given his use of reason to argue that the Israelites were the early model of virtue in classical times, exceeding that of the Greeks and Romans, and that the early church preserved that virtue as a pristine Christian republic. Fleury's book was regarded as a work of Catholic Enlightenment, since it essentially used modern epistemological methods to conclude, first, that the ancient customs of the early church were superior to those of early modern Catholicism, and, second, that they established a model for heavenly life on earth.

Written in response to Claude Fleury's 1682 publication of *Manners,* Climent's pastoral instruction (published during his lifetime in Castilian, Catalan, French, and Italian) developed some of Fleury's points in order to suggest ideas for the welfare of his diocese as well as the church universal. (Since Fleury's work was practically unknown in Spain, Climent's recommendation of it is particularly noteworthy.)

Climent also taught in the instruction that Fleury's works would assist bishops in establishing moral reform in their dioceses, since it discussed interdiocesan communication and the benefits of convening councils. While interdiocesan communication would benefit the priests and parishioners of Spain, Climent maintained that the mutual correspondence and assistance of bishops was also imperative for the good of the church universal. In his pastoral instruction, his case in point was the Catholic Church of Utrecht in the Netherlands. The church of Utrecht remained one of only two strongholds of Catholicism within a Protestant country, even after the pope had officially broken ties with Utrecht during the 1720s. Given its relative isolation, in 1763 the church there held a provincial synod in order to organize itself as independent from the Protestant state. Furthermore, the church of Utrecht had written letters to various bishops across Europe to relate their situation and request whatever assistance was possible, such as a letter of communion. Such conciliar action taken by the Dutch clergy, along with their undying commitment to the Catholic Church while remaining in a Protestant country, moved Climent to single out Utrecht as the model of ecclesiastical reform for particular Catholic churches to follow.

Supported by Fleury's accounts in his *Manners,* Climent wrote that, in the past, when a church had incurred the indignation of the pope, bishops wrote to the pope to inquire about the reasons for his indignation. This was in order to hold the pope accountable, as well as to ensure that he would treat his flock with justice. The episcopal obligation, according to Climent, was to stand united as *one* church and *one* episcopacy to help each other as *one body*. Here was a call for a lateral system of ecclesiastical communication: for the benefit of the church universal, bishops should correspond with each other and with the pope, to guarantee that the pope would deal justly with the church of Utrecht. "From what one sees of churches in distant provinces, we have not received even one notice of their joys and concerns. Not many days ago, we received a letter written to all bishops in which the Church of Holland, while communicating to us their works and afflictions, makes present to us the unity of the church and the episcopacy; wherein the necessary obligation to help her [Utrecht] is born" (1788, 1:225). Not only *should* bishops unite as one body, but they were *obligated* in this duty, as expressed by church fathers such as Cyril (c. 376–444) and Basil (330–379). Climent indicated that this was not merely an appeal to history, but rather a fulfillment of the orthodox definition of the Catholic bishop.

In his letter of 12 August 1769, however, Abbé Clément warned Climent that some elements of his instruction were too critical of the authority of the king. Indeed, the abbé warned that he was unable to publish the instruction without the addition of notes that would mute the inevitable criticism by the French state. Specifically, Climent's instruction had used Bishop Ambrose (c. 337–397) of Milan's refusal of sacraments to the Roman Emperor Theodosius (347–395) in the fourth century as an example, explaining that restoring the authority of bishops to the degree common in the early church was the model for reform. The matter at hand was the threat the church posed to temporal power because of its power of excommunication, through which the episcopacy could exercise indirect authority over the temporal affairs of the kingdom. Given the example of Ambrose and Theodosius, the emperor of an officially Christian empire could be legitimately excommunicated. If this action were permissible, then it would seem to follow that a monarch would no longer be effective, since his Catholic subjects could use his isolation from the church to justify their own disobedience. Given other historical examples, such as the medieval investiture conflict beginning with Pope Gregory VII's excommunication of Henry IV, Climent's words were implicitly threatening to monarchs.

In his letters to Abbé Clément regarding the publication of his pastoral instruction, Climent realized the possibility that his instruction might fall into the wrong hands in Spain. Given his enemies in Madrid, Climent would then be an easy target for an accusation of sedition if his goals did not coincide with those of state authorities. Thus, he begged the abbé not to publish his strong words on the actions of Ambrose, aware that there were Spaniards who would seize the opportunity to attack him. He wrote, "I judge that not all will be happy, and that while there lies a hidden fire under the ashes, if my letter is published with the words regarding those actions, I fear that I would discover that fire. And so I again implore you passionately, not to permit the publication of my letter" (13 August 1769, 252v). After he learned of the publication of his pastoral instructions, he wrote again, demonstrating the gravity of his predicament: "I beg you to buy all of the copies, paying twice the price for them, advising me of their cost, so that I will be satisfied. No money that I will ever spend will be better employed than this. Please assure me that no copy will ever reach Spain . . . as I am convinced that if even one comes here from France it will light a fire that I will have to endure (21 August 1769, 258v). However, as the Abbé Clément regretfully acknowledged in response, it was impossible to prevent the publication, and so he could not make such promises to Climent.

Soon the flames of Climent's dreaded fire were lit. Rome was intending to censor his instruction because of the questionable remarks he had made regarding the pope's treatment of the church of Utrecht. He indicated in his letter of 21 October 1769, "If such a thing were to occur, they would take me for a heretic in Spain, in which the majority think that the Congregation of the Holy Office is an infallible council" (21 October 1769, 26v). Pope Clement XIV wrote to Charles III on 7 September 1769, indicating his desire that the king put the pastoral instruction of the bishop of Barcelona before a council of ecclesiastical judges since the instruction was not befitting a bishop in Spain, a kingdom of purity and piety (Mestre 1979, 623).

Manuel de Roda, as the king's secretary of grace and justice, commissioned both the Council of Castile and another council formed of appointed religious and political authorities to analyze Climent's pastoral instruction. They were to inform the king on the document's tone toward regalism, as well as its religious orthodoxy. While the Council of Castile found nothing but a few phrases that could be interpreted loosely as questioning the authority of the king (or regalist state), the mixed lay and ecclesiastical council focused its concern on Climent's attitude toward the church of Utrecht, supposedly the most controversial topic of his pastoral instruction. As they expressed in their letter to the king, the members of the council judged that Climent had not praised the present state of the church of Utrecht, but rather had paid tribute to "the virtues of the early church." They found that, above all, Climent had insisted that it was the mission of the bishop to intercede before the authorities, in this case Rome, in order to resolve problems justly and with the utmost respect for authority (Letter to the King of Spain, 22 November 1769). Therefore, Climent's words were not interpreted as schismatic for the Catholic Church, and the fire he had dreaded was extinguished for the time being.

Climent's Place within the Catholic Enlightenment

While the state had treated him favorably in this matter, Climent remained, at most, a "moderate regalist" (Appolis 1960, 468). The way the charge against Climent was resolved had precisely demonstrated the validity of Climent's concern, illustrating the twin dangers of ultramontanism and regalism, even though in this case they had acted in complementary fashion rather than as mutually exclusive forces. In other words, the crown had taken up the charge against Climent at papal request and then handed it over for judgment to a mixed lay-ecclesiastical commission that it had appointed and subordinated to the Council of Castile. Nevertheless, Climent avoided censorship in the end, and his honor was henceforth restored as bishop of Barcelona.

To appreciate the significance of Climent's call for reform in his pastoral instruction, Francesc Tort i Mitjans reminds us that, while "Climent defends his convictions in the instruction with extraordinary bravery, even more significant is how well he himself knew that there was no freedom of speech in Spain" (1978, 113). Furthermore, Climent placed the work of ecclesiastical reform solely in the hands of the bishops, even though he knew Spanish bishops had their hands tied by the state. As John Lynch affirms, the cause for reform in Spain was only as successful as the state allowed it to be: "The Church could not present a firm front to the encroachments of the state" (1989, 272–73). The state appointed both the bishops and archbishops of Spain, selecting only those candidates who were considered "regalists." While many were also reformers, their reformism had to conform, pursuing only those projects that would also be useful for the government. Even though, for many years, his projects seemed to conform satisfactorily to the interests of the state, Climent managed to fall out of favor with Madrid and was forced to abdicate his episcopacy and begin an early retirement in 1775.

Before Madrid's displeasure with him caused his resignation, Climent sought to bring about a Catholic Enlightenment in Barcelona. He detailed this not only in his correspondence with the Abbé Clément but also in his many published episcopal edicts and pastoral instructions in the local Catalan language and in the actual reforms he effected as bishop. In 1767, he attempted to convene a diocesan synod, and from the parish priests' response to his call he learned, if nothing else, that their primary concerns centered upon their parishioners' failure to learn doctrine, to observe the Sabbath and holy days, and to abstain from premarital sex. In 1767, Climent also established ten free elementary schools in the city of Barcelona. In 1772, he founded the first public lending library in the region (Smidt 2011). His ideas regarding the "liberty of bishops" and its relation to conciliarism would put Climent on the map of the Catholic Enlightenment. On the other hand, his views on the use of indulgences and the moral rigorism it entailed would establish him as a proponent of austerity, civic humanism, and moral reform in Baroque, post-Tridentine Europe. Alas, despite his efforts to protect the church from the expanding powers of the absolutist state, Climent himself became a "victim of regalism" (Appolis 1960, 473). In the six years following his retirement, while he continued to exchange letters with Abbé Clément covering areas of needed ecclesiastical reform in the Catholic Church, Climent remained in relative obscurity until his death in 1781.

Nevertheless, if one is attempting to understand the Catholic Enlightenment in all of its complexity, Josep Climent's life story arguably could be a microcosm for the larger history of Catholic Enlightenment. Just as Catholic Enlightenment could at times be composed of multiple and diverse programs of reform throughout Europe, Climent encountered and responded to multiple strands of Enlightenment, uniquely Catholic or otherwise, in pursuing his own program of Catholic Enlightenment at the ground level in Barcelona. His reform work enmeshed him in both local and domestic affairs in Spain on the one hand and in Catholic reform in other parts of Europe on the other, all associated with multiple strands of Enlightenment. As a Spanish cleric in the 1750s, Climent's growing anti-Jesuit position illustrated how the Catholic Enlightenment in Spain was fracturing into at least two major versions. The Jesuit version employed a "moral theology that adopted a more optimistic view of human nature and moral capability which best accommodated the *philosophes*' faith in empirical or Lockean 'reason' to achieve civility, progress, and happiness in contemporary society." The philo-Jansenist version, to which Climent adhered, "is correctly associated with Enlightenment because of its tendency to appeal directly to the critical common sense of the individual in his own internal spiritual devotion." Similarly, this version's adherents "refused to allow the Church hierarchy 'to dictate everything they should believe,' making them in some scholars' eyes 'authentic harbingers of the modern world'" (Smidt 2006, 410, quoting Doyle 2000, 89–90). As a strong anti-Jesuit cleric during the reign of Charles III, Climent played a role in the expulsion of the Jesuits, which furthered both the philo-Jansenist Catholic Enlightenment and the state-sponsored Enlightenment based on economic and political progress for the Spanish monarchy. In his advocacy for open, deliberative procedures promoting austerity and transparency within institutions, Climent embodied civic humanism using rhetoric not unlike that of his contemporaries Rousseau and Mably praising the virtues of Ancient Greece or Republican Rome (Baker 2001). Yet this program of Catholic Enlightenment ran counter to the agenda of the predominant mode of Enlightenment in Spain, leading to Climent's early retirement as bishop in 1775. Climent's correspondence with the French Jansenist Clément, leading to the publication of his pastoral instruction of 1769, put him on the "Jansenist International" map. The words of his instruction and his specific initiatives in Barcelona would be remembered by bishops convened in 1780s and 1790s Tuscany and France when they advocated for church reforms promoting social welfare (Smidt 2006, 454–69). Indeed, Climent's story reveals the parameters for Catholic Enlightenment given the political landscape in the last days of Old Regime Europe.

Bibliography

Adell Cueva, Marc A., Agustí Flors, Francisco Marco, and Manuel Rosas, eds. 2011. *Josep Climent i Avinent (Castelló de la Plana, 1706–1781), Bisbe de Barcelona*. Castelló de la Plana: Universitat Jaume I.

Appolis, Émile. 1960. *Le "tiers parti" Catholique au XVIII siècle: Entre Jansénistes et zélanti*. Paris: A. et. J. Picard.

Baker, Keith. 2001. "Classical Republicanism in Eighteenth-Century France." *Journal of Modern History* 73 (1): 32–53.

Bradley, James E., and Dale K. Van Kley, eds. 2001. *Religion and Politics in Enlightenment Europe*. Notre Dame: University of Notre Dame Press.

Clément de Bizon du Tremblay, Abbé Augustin-Charles-Jean. 1768. Letter to Climent, 18 March. MS. 1289. Correspondence Clément. Paris: Archive du Seminaire du Saint Sulpice.

———. 1802. *Journal de correspondances et de voyages pour la paix de l'Église en 1758, 1768 et 1769*. Paris: L. F. Longuet.

Climent i Avinent, Josep. 1768a. Letter to Clément, 28 January. MS. 1289. Correspondance Clément. Paris: Archive du Seminaire du Saint Sulpice.

———. 1768b. Letter to Clément, 5 April. MS. 1289. Correspondance Clément. Paris: Archive du Seminaire du Saint Sulpice.

———. 1768c. Letter to Clément, 14 June. MS. 1289. Correspondance Clément. Paris: Archive du Seminaire du Saint Sulpice.

———. 1768d. Letter to Clément, 25 June. MS. 1289. Correspondance Clément. Paris: Archive du Seminaire du Saint Sulpice.

———. 1768e. Letter to Clément, October. MS. 1289. Correspondance Clément. Paris: Archive du Seminaire du Saint Sulpice.

———. 1768f. Letter to Clément, 23 November. MS. 1289. Correspondance Clément. Paris: Archive du Seminaire du Saint Sulpice.

———. 1769a. Letter to Clément, 4 July. MS. 1289. Correspondance Clément. Paris: Archive du Seminaire du Saint Sulpice.

———. 1769b. Letter to Clément, 13 August. MS. 1289. Correspondence Clément. Paris: Archive du Seminaire du Saint Sulpice.

———. 1769c. Letter to Clément, 21 August. MS. 1289. Correspondence Clément. Paris: Archive du Seminaire du Saint Sulpice.

———. 1769d. Letter to Clément, 21 October. MS. 1290. Correspondence Clément. Paris: Archive du Seminaire du Saint Sulpice.

———. 1769e. Pastoral Instruction, published in the "Suite des nouvelles ecclésiastiques du 4 octobre 1769," in *Nouvelles ecclesiastiques*. Paris: [s.n.], nos. 1768–1771, 157–58.

———. 1788. "Carta a todos sus feligreses de Barcelona." In *Colección de las obras del Ilustrísimo nuestro señor don Josef Climent, Obispo de Barcelona,* 3 vols., esp. 1:187–268. Madrid: Imprenta Real.
Doyle, William. 2000. *Jansenism: Catholic Resistance to Authority from the Reformation to the French Revolution.* Basingstoke, UK, and New York: Palgrave Macmillan.
Fleury, Abbé Claude. 1682. *Mœurs des Israëlites et des Chrétiens.* Paris. Reprint, Paris: Pierre-Jean Mariette, 1735.
"Letter to the king of Spain from the mixed lay and ecclesiastical council." 1769. 22 November. *Inventaires des pièces d'archives françaises se rapportant à l'abbaye de Port-Royal des Champs et à la résistance contre la bulle* Unigenitus *et l'appel.* Utrecht: 215, house 4 Het Utrechts Archief.
Lynch, John. 1989. *Bourbon Spain, 1700–1808.* Oxford: Basil Blackwell.
Mestre Sanchis, Antonio, ed. 1979. *Historia de la Iglesia en España.* Vol. 4, *La Iglesia en la España de los siglos XVII y XVIII.* Madrid: Biblioteca de Autores Cristianos.
Miller, Samuel. 1978. *Portugal and Rome, c. 1748–1830: An Aspect of the Catholic Enlightenment.* Rome: Università Gregoriana.
Noel, Charles C. 2001. "Clerics and Crown in Bourbon Spain, 1700–1808." In *Religion and Politics in Enlightenment Europe,* edited by James E. Bradley and Dale K. Van Kley, 119–53. Notre Dame: University of Notre Dame Press.
Les Nouvelles Ecclésiastiques, ou Mémoires pour servir à l'histoire de la constitution Unigenitus. 1767–1781. Paris: n.p.
Paquette, Gabriel B. 2008. *Enlightenment, Governance, and Reform in Spain and Its Empire, 1759–1808.* Basingstoke, UK, and New York: Palgrave Macmillan.
Sarrailh, Jean. 1954. *L'Espagne éclairée de la seconde moitié du XVIIIe siécle.* Paris: C. Klincksieck.
Smidt, Andrea J. 2002. "Piedad e ilustración en relación armónica: Josep Climent i Avinent, obispo de Barcelona, 1766–1775." Translated by Montserrat Jiménez Sureda. In *Manuscrits. Revista d'Història Moderna* 20:91–109.
———. 2006. "*Fiestas* and Fervor: Religious Life and Catholic Enlightenment in the Diocese of Barcelona, 1766–1775." Ph.D. thesis, Ohio State University. Accessed at http://etd.ohiolink.edu/.
———. 2010a. "Bourbon Regalism and the Importation of Gallicanism: The Political Path for a State Religion in Eighteenth-Century Spain." *Anuario de Historia de la Iglesia* 19:25–53.
———. 2010b. "*Luces por la Fe*: The Cause of Catholic Enlightenment in Eighteenth-Century Spain." In *A Companion to the Catholic Enlightenment in Europe,* edited by Ulrich L. Lehner and Michael Printy, 403–52. Leiden: Brill.

———. 2011. "Catholic Reform and Enlightenment in Barcelona, 1766–1775." In *Josep Climent i Avinent (Castelló de la Plana, 1706–1781), Bisbe de Barcelona,* edited by Marc A. Adell Cueva, Agustí Flors, Francisco Marco, and Manuel Rosas, 251–64. Castelló de la Plana: Universitat Jaume I.

Tort i Mitjans, Francesc. 1978. *El Obispo de Barcelona Josep Climent i Avinent, 1706–1781: Contribución a la Historia de la Teología Pastoral Tarraconense en el Siglo XVIII.* Barcelona: Fundació Mossen Josep Sanabre, Editorial Balmes.

Van Kley, Dale K. 2008. "Civic Humanism in Clerical Garb: Gallican Memories of the Early Church and the Project of Primitivist Reform, 1719–1791." *Past and Present* 200 (1): 77–120.

PART 7

Transnational Trajectories: The Intersection of Irish, French, Italian, and Habsburg Developments

16

Ruggiero Boscovich (1711–1787)

Jesuit Science in an Enlightenment Context

JONATHAN A. WRIGHT

In 1807, a decidedly positive assessment of Ruggiero Boscovich's life and works appeared in the pages of the London-based *Annual Register*. Looking back over the Jesuit's extraordinary scientific career, the author had no qualms about describing Boscovich as "an eminent mathematician and natural philosopher," who had made full use of the previous century's advances: "He was transported by the vast display of new and splendid truths which were unveiled." Furthermore, he had shared his wisdom and "honorably engaged in directing the studies of youth and enlightening the world by his elegant and ingenious writings." These activities, the author concluded, had met with a "general blaze of admiration," which was fitting recompense for someone who "with the torch of geometry . . . traced the secret links of nature's operations, and seemed to penetrate the councils of heaven." The only disappointments, in the author's opinion, were that Boscovich had sometimes exhibited arrogance, and rather more worryingly, had continued in the "unprofitable study of scholastic theology," which was a "dark and thorny path" (*Annual Register* 1807, 742–57).

Such adjudications of Boscovich were not uncommon in the early nineteenth century, especially in Great Britain, though this one was more flowery than most. There was no denying how much Boscovich had accomplished: he had made significant contributions to a dazzling array of scientific disciplines—optics, geometry, physics, geodesy, mathematics, and astronomy—to name only the most conspicuous examples. However, the concern about Boscovich's status as a Jesuit cropped up quite frequently as well. The Society of Jesus had endured a difficult odyssey during the eighteenth century, culminating in the order's worldwide suppression in 1773, and those of self-defined enlightened or advanced intellectual tastes tended to treat members of that order with a measure of suspicion. As the article in the *Annual Register* added, Boscovich had endured his own trials and tribulations because "the name of a priest and a Jesuit did not now command respect" (*Annual Register* 1807, 749).

This tension was writ large in the response to Boscovich, both in life and in posterity, and it is this tension that makes him an especially interesting figure who can tell us a great deal about the nature of both the Catholic Enlightenment (upon which Boscovich had a major impact) and the Enlightenment more broadly construed. This chapter aims to explore some of the resulting interpretative opportunities. If, as is often suggested, anti-Jesuitism was a recurring motif of Catholic Enlightenment thought, how does Boscovich fit into this analysis? Second, what do Boscovich's career and work tell us about the nature of eighteenth-century Jesuit scientific inquiry? Boscovich certainly incurred the displeasure of his superiors in the order at various points during his career, but is it sufficient to conceptualize him as a maverick who was bucking the trend of institutional obscurantism? Or is a more nuanced understanding—one that reflects the multifarious nature of the society's intellectual identity—more appropriate? Finally, Boscovich was a well-traveled and well-connected scholar, so his journey allows us to look a little more closely at the rich international nature of the Enlightenment, especially in its Catholic variant. A key question is why he was admired in some places but disliked in others, and why some of his peers regarded him as a valuable colleague while others thought of him as an enemy. The answers, as we shall see, are not straightforward.

Later in the chapter, we will look more closely at such issues, specifically by placing Boscovich in the longer-term context of Jesuit science and locating him in the broader landscape of eighteenth-century intellectual history. We will also spend a little time examining his legacy. The best way to begin, however, is with a biographical sketch. It is from here that any deeper analyses are obliged to flow. One final point: the Italianate spelling of Boscovich's name is deployed throughout, simply because this is more commonplace in the literature. This is not intended to disguise the fact that he was of Croatian stock and known, in those parts, as Ruđer Bošcović.

The Deeds of Ruggiero Boscovich

The basic facts of Boscovich's life are well established, largely thanks to his considerable epistolary efforts and a recent explosion in Boscovich scholarship, and it seems unlikely that any major surprises are in store for future historians. A straightforward digest of events is therefore sufficient for present purposes (for brief technical explanations of his scientific works and publications, see Marković 1978).

Boscovich was born in Dubrovnik, Croatia, in 1711. After attending the local Jesuit college, he moved to Rome in 1725 and continued his studies at the Sant'Andrea novitiate and subsequently the Collegio Romano, one of the society's most prestigious, if habitually troubled, institutions. By the mid-1730s, Boscovich had begun to read the major works of Newton, and in this period were published Boscovich's first major writings on topics ranging from the 1736 transit of Mercury, the Aurora Borealis, sunspots, and spherical trigonometry. Boscovich proved himself a capable teacher and in 1740 was appointed as professor of mathematics at the Collegio. By coincidence, this year also marked the election of Benedict XIV (1740–1758), who would prove to be both a forward-looking pope and, upon occasion, a supporter of Boscovich.

An early indication of this beneficial relationship came in 1742, when Boscovich was appointed to the committee charged with addressing the problem of cracks that had appeared in the dome of St. Peter's Basilica. Boscovich's solution (the deployment of supporting iron rings) was adopted, and throughout his career Boscovich would tackle similar practical issues, including the drainage of the Pontine Marshes, the failing structure of Maria Theresa's imperial library, and projects concerning the harbors at Rimini and Savona.

Major publications during the 1740s included works on the nature of comets and on optics, in the latter of which he challenged various aspects of Newton's theorizing. It was during the next decade, however, that Boscovich scored two of his most significant triumphs. With the assistance of his fellow Jesuit Christopher Maire (1697–1767), Boscovich attempted to take accurate measurements between the Via Appia and Rimini, surveying two and a half arcs of the meridian. This was an onerous and lengthy undertaking, but the results had a significant impact. They contributed to the first accurate map of the Papal States and played a major role in contemporary (and heated) discussions about the size and shape of the earth: Boscovich's data supported the notion of the earth's true shape as an oblate sphere flattened at the poles, in contradistinction to the competing theory of an elongated sphere. This work signaled a continuing interest in geodesy, and Boscovich encouraged both the Royal Society in London and the empress Maria Theresa to back similar research (Pedley 1993).

In 1758 Boscovich's most famous text appeared: *The Theory of Natural Philosophy* (*Theoria philosophiae naturalis*). While this work met only a lukewarm reception during Boscovich's lifetime (see below), it was later hailed as an innovative step forward in atomic theory. Essentially, Boscovich proposed a universal force law in which atoms were conceptualized as tiny points that lack extension. All physical phenomena arise from interaction, a process of attraction and repulsion, between these points. Boscovich's work has been cited as a major influence on later scientists, including Faraday, Maxwell, and Einstein, and, by dint of its universalist ambitions, as a precursor of "Theories of Everything": those ideas in the realm of theoretical physics that aspire to explain all physical phenomena.

Prolific as he was, some of Boscovich's work incurred the suspicion and resistance of his superiors, and as we shall see, life at the Collegio Romano became increasingly troublesome. This led to an extended sabbatical (and ultimately his being replaced), which allowed Boscovich to travel widely. After serving in a diplomatic capacity for the city of Lucca (there was a local squabble about water rights that required negotiations at the imperial court in Vienna), Boscovich headed to Paris, arriving in October 1759. He had been a corresponding member of the Académie des Sciences since 1748, and he took the opportunity to cement friendships that would serve him well over the coming years, notably with Alexis Clairaut (1713–1765), who described Boscovich as "one of the most amiable men I have ever known" and as one possessed of a winning "combination of knowledge and social qualities" (James 2004, 52). The two men dined frequently together and began a mutually beneficial correspondence. By November 1762, Clairaut was assuring Boscovich that his association with the Académie would always be a source of glory for the institution (Taton 1996), but others were not so sure. As future events would show, not everyone in Paris was destined to be an ally of Boscovich (Hahn 1993), and there were signs of this from early on. Paolo Paciaudi (1710–1785), for one, was unimpressed. He described Boscovich as a "quite well-known mathematician" who acted as though he were the greatest visionary in the world. He spoke enough for ten men, Paciaudi complained, and bored everyone with his constant babbling (Paciaudi 1802–1803, 116).

In 1760, Boscovich crossed the channel to England. Highlights of this memorable trip included visits to the universities of Oxford and Cambridge and meetings with the mathematician Thomas Simpson (1710–1761), Benjamin Franklin (1706–1790), and Samuel Johnson (1709–1784). Johnson's antipathy toward the Society of Jesus was well known. He had once declared his refusal to be seduced by the tenets of Roman Catholicism because "an obstinate rationality prevents me," and he seems likely to have been in agreement with the sentiment of Paolo Sarpi (1552–1623), whom Johnson translated, that "there is nothing more essential than to ruin the reputation of the Jesuits" (Cannon 1994, 22; Greene 1960, 109). Nevertheless, the two men dined together amicably and discussed, rather tellingly, the theories of Newton. Boscovich, who could not speak English fluently, was said to have been impressed by Johnson's ability to converse in Latin.

In January 1761, Boscovich was elected as a member of the Royal Society. His nominators declared that Boscovich was "well qualified by his knowledge in astronomy and other parts of natural philosophy to be a useful member" (Torbarina 1967, 6). This international dimension to Boscovich's scholarship was replicated in his membership of the St. Petersburg Academy, though he would never rise above the status of corresponding member in the Paris Academy, largely because of the resistance of his enemies. It is also interesting to note that, while in London, Boscovich dedicated a lengthy poem on the defects of the sun and moon to the Royal Society. Boscovich, a member (under the pen name of Numenius Anigreus) of the celebrated Accademia degil Arcadi in Rome, often exhibited a keen interest in the writing of didactic poetry (Haskell 2003).

Boscovich planned to observe the transit of Venus from Constantinople in 1761, but arrived too late. It was from the same city, however, that he embarked upon a memorable journey through Eastern Europe in 1762. The published account (which appeared in French in 1772, German in 1779, and Italian in 1784) has been positioned as a truly significant contribution to wider European understanding of places such as Moldova, Bulgaria, and Poland (Wolff 1994), and his nuanced analysis of local Orthodox religion has been singled out as particularly important (Wolff 2006).

Academic life again beckoned, and the next decade saw Boscovich take up positions at the University of Pavia (1764), the Scuola Palatina in Milan (1790), and, perhaps most importantly, at the Brera observatory. Here, Boscovich devoted considerable energy to the improvement of lenses and scientific equipment. Unfortunately, this was also a troubled period for the Jesuits. A series of national expulsions and dissolutions culminated in the worldwide suppression of the order in 1773. Boscovich was not silent on such developments, and his status as a Jesuit, along with local scholarly rivalries, was likely a factor in the termination of his academic positions in Italy. He chose to return to France and took up an assignment as director of optics for the French Navy. The final years of Boscovich's life were marred by declining health and a series of scholarly squabbles, including a major disagreement about the trajectory of comets with Pierre-Simon Laplace (1749–1827). He returned to Italy in 1782 with the aim of collecting and organizing some of his works. He died in 1787.

This was a prolific career, brimful of achievements and setbacks. Many other interests could be added, and an indication of how much we still have to learn about Boscovich's work is reflected in the continuing and regular appearance of his name in both historical and technical scientific journals. The most recent academic conference dedicated to Boscovich (held in Pavia in 2011) is emblematic. Subjects discussed included Boscovich's experiments regarding hydraulics, achromatic lenses, electricity, and water-filled telescopes, and his influence on nineteenth-century studies of magnetism and Einstein's unified field theory research.

With this basic biographical information at hand, we will now attempt to place Boscovich in the broader context of his times. The best place to start is his status as a Jesuit.

Boscovich and Jesuit Science

One of the most exciting areas of recent work on the Jesuits has been the detailed exploration of the society's scientific activities during its first three centuries. A great deal of work is still to be done, but various conclusions already seem secure. First, we have been reminded of the staggering number of Jesuits who made important contributions across a wide range of disciplines. The roll call of names is impressive, and as one random indicator, we might look at a map of the moon, where thirty-five craters are named for Jesuit scientists. They include the mathematician Christopher Clavius (1538–1612); Francesco Grimaldi (1618–1683), who had a major impact on Newton's optics; Athanasius Kircher (1601–1680), the very model of a seventeenth-century polymath; and the astronomer Niccolo Zucchi (1586–1670). The dominance of the Society of Jesus in Catholic education is also noteworthy: at the dawn of the eighteenth century, Jesuits were in charge of some seven hundred higher education institutions and as many as two dozen astronomical observatories. They also made scientific work a key component of their missionary activities in Asia and the Americas (see, for instance, Hsia 2009; Prieto 2011). As a host of books and articles have demonstrated (Brotóns 2006; Caruana 2008; Harris 1993; Heilbron 1982; Hellyer 1999, 2005), Jesuit science counted for a great deal during the seventeenth and eighteenth centuries, and this was the tradition that Boscovich inherited; indeed, he would also have a lunar crater named in his honor.

He also inherited the tensions of that tradition, however, so he serves as a very useful prism through which to observe the conflicted landscape of Jesuit science and the ways in which contemporaries perceived it. Various interpretations compete for our attention. It can be stated with certainty that, in this sphere at least, no single "way of proceeding"—always a prized Jesuit commodity—existed. This is hardly surprising, given the nature of the challenges and changes confronted. The theories of Galileo, Newton, and Descartes, to name only the most obvious, created intellectual turmoil; and Jesuits, although many of them proved to be expert synthesizers of "old" and "new" ideas, routinely found themselves in choppy intellectual waters.

One way of analyzing this situation would be to think in terms of a simmering tension between the Jesuit hierarchy and more adventurous individual Jesuits. We might try to discern an institutional commitment to sustaining an existing scientific paradigm (one that continued to revere Aristotle and insisted upon a holistic approach to the intersection between theology and science). The basis of all Jesuit education, the *Ratio Studiorum,* finalized in 1599, remained regnant, Aristotle still dominated in Jesuit classrooms, and there was deep suspicion of overly zealous intellectual flirtations with novel theorizing. Those who were perceived as pushing the boundaries of inquiry too far could expect censure, demotion, transfer to less glamorous institutions, or (one thinks of Honoré Fabri [1607–1688], for example) even worse.

In many ways, this analysis reflects an aspect of the reality of early modern Jesuit science, although, as I will argue in a moment, it runs the risk of lapsing into caricature. In any event, it seems to fit (at first blush) the stickier moments of Boscovich's own career. There is no doubt that he was something of a star at the Collegio Romano. In 1748, he was given the privilege of organizing an observation of a solar eclipse to which three cardinals, fifty prelates, and a handful of princes were invited. Equally clear is that some of Boscovich's colleagues in Rome were highly dubious about some of his more radical ideas. This suspicion first caused problems for one of Boscovich's protégés, Carlo Benvenuti (1716–1797), whose innovative work was frowned upon by leading figures, including the local superior (and later Superior General) Alessandro Centurione (1686–1757), who demanded Benvenuti's removal. Boscovich appealed to his long-term ally Benedict XIV, who expressed deep misgivings about the "flame of dissention which had erupted between the fathers of the Collegio Romano and their superior" (Feingold 2003, 30–31; Baldini 2006, 417).

Benvenuti ended up with a new position at the Collegio, but Boscovich himself soon faced his own tribulations. In 1760, during his extended absence from Rome, he admitted to his brother, "I turn cold at the thought of having to return [to the Collegio Romano]. I have lost all my love for that house." Anyone who did not abide by Aristotelian rules, he grumbled, was destined for trouble (Feingold 2003, 37). He need not have worried. During his absence, his rivals replaced him with Giuseppe Asclepi (1706–1776), who tellingly never mentioned Boscovich in his works (Baldini 2006, 417). The remainder of Boscovich's academic career would have to unfold elsewhere.

It is therefore very tempting to position Boscovich as a plucky, unfortunate maverick who encapsulates the contemporary conflict between Jesuit conservatism and progressivism. This is not an unreasonable starting point for analysis, not least because Boscovich himself expressed his frustrations. However, there is perhaps room for caution. Talk of a neat and tidy schism between the new and old guards does not do full justice to the complexity of eighteenth-century Jesuit science.

There were, of course, flash points (a good many of them, and they have frequently been reported), and there were, beyond a doubt, Jesuits who took extreme positions, but this should not disguise the fact that many Jesuits sought out some middle ground. This could come from both sides. Aristotle clearly remained a dominant figure, but we should not assume slavish obedience. Long ago, the Jesuit Niccolò Cabeo (1586–1650) had declared that "if you never question Aristotle's doctrines your commentary will not be that of a philosopher but that of a grammarian" (Heilbron 1979, 110), and by the eighteenth century the reins were clearly loosening (even at a corporate level) when it came to abiding by everything Aristotle had written. Contrariwise, we should not assume that everyone at the progressive end of the Jesuit scientific spectrum was determined to overturn every aspect of intellectual tradition. There was a major effort to synthesize new and old theories, and many decided to treat novel ideas as useful intellectual concepts, but not necessarily as reflections of physical reality. It would be a little too easy to suggest that this was always the result of cowardice or institutional pressure. Attempting to square new developments with accepted theological nostrums (and crucially, to sustain an all-embracing hermeneutic) was a widespread Jesuit pursuit.

This was the confusing era through which Boscovich lived: a time that combined an expansion in Jesuit scientific publication with ongoing, but increasingly convoluted, efforts to police the outpourings. Boscovich was, by any standard, a bold thinker, but he always insisted that "a contemplation of all the works of nature is in complete accord with the sanctity of the priesthood" (Hellyer 2005, 178), and it would have been hard to locate a Jesuit who would have disagreed. Some of Boscovich's more adventurous ideas patently offended some within the order, but seeing him as an incorrigible firebrand is probably a mistake. Even Boscovich had his cautious moments, and his approach to Copernicanism serves as a good example.

During the 1750s, there was much talk of a change in the dictates of the *Index of Prohibited Books*. Perhaps it was time to allow the publication of books that tackled the idea of the earth moving in the heavens. This was a mighty step, and the Jesuit Pietro Lazzari (1710–1789) was recruited as a consultant to take the intellectual temperature. He mentions his encounters with Boscovich. Apparently, Boscovich had "tried to reconcile the modern discoveries with the earth's rest" but had ultimately concluded that the resulting cosmology was "most improbable from the point of view of pure natural reason" (Finocchiaro 2005, 143). The first half of this report is the most interesting. Boscovich, a cautious Copernican, had *tried* to reconcile past and present ideas. In fact (Dadic 1987), he had conjured up some ingenious (if muddled) theories involving the difference between a Newtonian "relative space" in which the earth moved and an "absolute space" in which it stood still. This was much more than a subterfuge. Indeed, as has been argued, it was part of the "broad Jesuit effort of exhausting all the potential of a received research program before discarding it" (Caruana 2008, 256).

If we always (perhaps out of habit) conceptualize eighteenth-century Jesuit science as an inevitable conflict between old and new, we do so at our peril, and we certainly run the risk of anachronism. Boscovich was one of the most provocative Jesuit scientists of his era, and many people, including a fair number of fellow Jesuits, loathed him; but he was also part of a very complicated scholarly process, and the resulting muddle is not easily captured by even the most elegant of overarching analyses.

Boscovich in Enlightenment Context

As difficult as it is to locate Boscovich in the context of Jesuit scientific culture, it is even harder to chart his journey through the broader intellectual currents of his time. Moving from the "Catholic Enlightenment" (however construed) to the broader "Enlightenment" is a precarious step. Again, a straightforward and initially satisfying analysis is available, and, once more, Boscovich can easily be recruited. There are many hints that Boscovich met with resistance and hostility precisely because he was a Jesuit. Simply being associated with the Jesuits was, by the second half of the eighteenth century, a common complaint against authors.

On a structural level, there were widespread attempts to demolish Jesuit dominance in higher education, allegedly because the order was perceived as a barrier to self-styled Enlightenment nostrums and a threat to the centralizing schemes of national governments. Even before the suppression era, there were many overt acts of hostility, and those that stung most were presumably those at the scholarly level: when the Bavarian Academy of Science was established in 1759, it excluded Jesuits on principle (Sorkin 1999). Various individual Jesuits also suffered. When Maximilian Hell (1720–1792) was slow in turning in his report on the 1769 transit of Venus, he was accused of scholarly negligence or, so some said, waiting to plagiarize the results of others. His status as a Jesuit may well have played a part in provoking such unfounded allegations (Woolf 1959, 126–33).

It would be absurd to suggest that Boscovich's reception was not influenced by similar factors. Perhaps his most determined adversary was d'Alembert (1717–1783), who had little affection for the Society of Jesus. D'Alembert made major efforts to hamper the spread of Boscovich's ideas in France, as demonstrated by Jérôme de Lalande (1732–1807) writing to Boscovich (a firm friend for a while) about his enemies' machinations, and explaining (1769) that d'Alembert's influence made it impossible to deliver one of Boscovich's papers at the Académie (Hankins 1970, 138).

Again, however, we must be wary of simplistic explanations. Can all of the resistance to Boscovich be put down to his Jesuit identity? Take France, for example. There is good sense in positing obvious reasons why Boscovich the Jesuit would have been treated with suspicion (he was unlikely, or so we might assume, to have been embraced by either *philosophes* or proponents of the Jansenist version of Catholic Enlightenment), but such structural assumptions have their drawbacks. As so much excellent recent scholarship has demonstrated, the notion of an all-guns-blazing conflict between Jesuits and Enlightenment lacks authenticity. Though they were reluctant to admit it, many of the champions of the radical French Enlightenment owed considerable debts to their Jesuit educations (Fumaroli 1999, 100) and the legacy of Jesuit scholarship, notably in the pages of the *Journal de Trévoux*. Furthermore, the French Enlightenment must be understood as a multifaceted phenomenon, and the Jesuit contribution, especially in the early part of the eighteenth century, was crucial (Burson 2010).

This all complicates our understanding of how Boscovich was received. He had supporters as well as adversaries in the Académie, and even some of his most determined foes were motivated by factors that had little to do with his Jesuit status. Laplace quarreled with him about comets because of scientific rivalry and disagreement, and even d'Alembert's antipathy can, at least in part, be put down to personal antagonism and philosophical differences of opinion: Boscovich's assault on mechanistic theorizing was surely crucial.

We must not, therefore, emphasize Boscovich's position as a Jesuit too much when trying to explain his mixed intellectual fortunes. There is no better example of this than the response to his boldest piece of theorizing: his talk of point atoms and a universal attraction-repulsion force, summed up in the 1758 *Theoria* but pursued in a series of publications from as early as 1745. For all its later celebrity, the simple truth is that this theory did not fare well during the eighteenth century. We have Ugo Baldini (Baldini 2006) to thank for explaining the details. This grandest idea of Boscovich was usually either ignored or dismissed during his lifetime. It attracted serious attention from a few professors in German universities, but by and large, it provoked a decidedly muted reaction. The review coverage was minimal (even in Jesuit journals), no major scientists seem to have been particularly interested, and crucially, this neglect transcended confessional and geographical boundaries. Indeed, Boscovich was criticized much by his Jesuit colleagues. Boscovich's Jesuit status did not help his cause, but it was not the clinching factor, a supposition that is bolstered by the fact that, when his theory eventually garnered interest, most of it came from Protestant Britain (Wilson 2009, 259–61).

By any measure, Ruggiero Boscovich was one of the eighteenth century's most prolific and innovative scientists, but he had a rare talent for dividing opinion. This resulted from many different causes. Some of his foes were patently motivated by a general antipathy toward the Society of Jesus, and, to make life even more irksome for Boscovich, some of his fellow Jesuits did not relish the existence of such a daring thinker in their midst. To his great frustration, Boscovich was assaulted from many different angles, and this reflected broad cultural tensions and antagonisms. Boscovich's career can tell us a great deal about them.

Other explanations should not be ignored, however. It seems likely that Boscovich also provoked animosity because of his sometimes prickly and haughty behavior (flaws that are anecdotally attested and that seem to have flourished as he grew older and increasingly ill). Contrariwise, he was more than capable of securing and sustaining long-term intellectual friendships and could be a loyal and supportive correspondent. He had more than his share of both allies and enemies, and this sometimes revealed more about the character of the man than about mighty cultural currents. We should also acknowledge that some of his ideas (chiefly his forays into atomism) received a muted response simply because, for better or worse, they failed to whet contemporary scientific appetites. On the other hand, many of his other ideas and accomplishments were embraced and respected by the pan-European scientific community. This mixed reaction was often as much about the quality and appeal of his musings as it was about his Jesuit identity, although, given the untidy contours of the eighteenth-century European scene, this latter factor should never be underestimated.

When we are interpreting Boscovich's career, an obvious and reliable strategy suggests itself. We are certainly entitled to treat that career as a rich and revealing case study, but we should proceed with caution. Boscovich's journey through the intellectual landscapes of eighteenth-century Europe offers us many interpretive opportunities. It allows us to explore tensions and rivalries within the Jesuit order, it leaves us in no doubt about the Catholic contribution to Enlightenment, and all of these issues are brought into much sharper focus because of the international reach of Boscovich's endeavors and the turbulent times through which he lived. Perhaps most intriguingly of all, he can be utilized as a prime example of the many Jesuits who weathered the suppression and went on to pursue worthwhile careers as ex-Jesuits: a very broad and fascinating category of men that warrants the closest scholarly attention. This all makes Boscovich an enthralling figure, but it is best to remember that he was only one man, and a decidedly idiosyncratic man at that.

Bibliography

Annual Register. 1807. *The Annual Register, or A View of the History, Politics, and Literature for 1805*. London: W. Otridge and Son.

Baldini, Ugo. 2006. "The Reception of a Theory: A Provisional Syllabus of Boscovich Literature, 1746–1800." In *The Jesuits*, vol. 2, *Cultures, Sciences and the Arts, 1540–1773*, edited by John O'Malley et al., 405–50. Toronto: University of Toronto Press.

Brotóns, Victor Navarro. 2006. "Science and Enlightenment in Eighteenth-Century Spain: The Contribution of the Jesuits before and after the Expulsion." In *The Jesuits*, vol. 2, *Cultures, Sciences and the Arts, 1540–1773*, edited by John O'Malley et al., 390–404. Toronto: University of Toronto Press.

Bursill-Hall, Piers, ed. 1993. *R. J. Boscovich: Vita e attività scientifica; His Life and Scientific Work*. Rome: Istituto della Enciclopedia Italiana.

Burson, Jeffrey. 2010. "The Catholic Enlightenment in France from the *Fin de Siècle* Crisis of Consciousness to the Revolution, 1650–1789." In *A Companion to the Catholic Enlightenment in Europe*, edited by Ulrich L. Lehner and Michael Printy, 63–125. Leiden: Brill.

Cannon, John Ashton. 1994. *Samuel Johnson and the Politics of Hanoverian England*. Oxford: Oxford University Press.

Caruana, Louis. 2008. "The Jesuits and the Quiet Side of the Scientific Revolution." In *The Cambridge Companion to the Jesuits*, edited by Thomas Worcester, 243–60. Cambridge: Cambridge University Press.

Dadic, Zarko. 1987. "Boškovic and the Question of the Earth's Motion." In *The Philosophy of Science of Ruder Boščovic*, edited by Ivan Macan and Valentin Pozaic, 131–38. Zagreb: Institute of Philosophy and Theology.

Feingold, Mordechai. 1993. "A Jesuit among Protestants: Boscovich in England." In *R. J. Boscovich: Vita e attività scientifica: His Life and Scientific Work*, edited by Piers Bursill-Hall, 511–26. Rome: Istituto della Enciclopedia Italiana.

———. 2003. *Jesuit Science and the Republic of Letters*. Cambridge, MA: MIT Press.

Finocchiaro, Maurice. 2005. *Retrying Galileo, 1633–1992*. Berkeley: University of California Press.

Fumaroli, Marc. 1999. "The Fertility and Shortcomings of Renaissance Rhetoric: The Jesuit Case." In *The Jesuits: Cultures, Sciences and the Arts, 1540–1773*, edited by John O'Malley et al., 90–106. Toronto: University of Toronto Press.

Greene, Donald J. 1960. *The Politics of Samuel Johnson*. New Haven: Yale University Press.

Grössing, Helmuth, ed. 2009. *Ruder Boscovic und sein Modell der Materie*. Vienna: Verlag der österreichischen Akademie der Wissenschaften.

Hahn, Roger. 1993. "The Ideological and Institutional Difficulties of a Jesuit Scientist in Paris." In *R. J. Boscovich: Vita e attività scientifica: His Life and Scientific Work*, edited by Piers Bursill-Hall, 1–12. Rome: Istituto della Enciclopedia Italiana.

Hankins, Thomas L. 1970. *Jean d'Alembert: Science and the Enlightenment*. Oxford: Clarendon Press.

Harris, Steven J. 1993. "Boscovich, the Boscovich Circle and the Revival of Jesuit Science." In *R. J. Boscovich: Vita e attività scientifica: His Life and Scientific Work*, edited by Piers Bursill-Hall, 527–48. Rome: Istituto della Enciclopedia Italiana.

Haskell, Yasmin A. 2003. *Loyola's Bees: Ideology and Industry in Jesuit Latin Didactic Poetry*. New York: Oxford University Press.

Heilbron, John L. 1979. *Electricity in the Seventeenth and Eighteenth Centuries: A Study of Early Modern Physics*. Berkeley: University of California Press.

———. 1982. *Elements of Early Modern Physics*. Berkeley: University of California Press.

Hellyer, Marcus. 1999. "Jesuit Physics in Eighteenth-Century Germany: Some Important Continuities." In *The Jesuits: Cultures, Sciences and the Arts, 1540–1773*, edited by John O'Malley, 538–54. Toronto: University of Toronto Press.

———. 2005. *Catholic Physics: Jesuit Natural Philosophy in Early Modern Germany*. Notre Dame: University of Notre Dame Press.

Hsia, Florence. 2009. *Sojourners in a Strange Land: Jesuits and the Scientific Missions in Late Imperial China*. Chicago: University of Chicago Press.

Israel, Jonathan. 2002. *Radical Enlightenment: Philosophy and the Making of Modernity, 1650–1750*. Oxford: Oxford University Press.

James, Ion M. 2004. *Remarkable Physicists from Galileo to Yukawa*. Cambridge: Cambridge University Press.

Krajnovic, Davor. 2011. "A Jesuit Anglophile: Rogerius Boscovich in England." *Astronomy and Geophysics* 52:16–20.

Marković, Zeljko. 1978. "Boscovič, R. J." In *Dictionary of Scientific Biography*, 2:326–32. New York: Scribner.

Paciaudi, Paolo. 1802–1803. *Lettres de Paciaudi au comte de Caylus*. Edited by A. Sériey. Paris.

Pappas, John. 1988. "Les relations entre Boscovich et d'Alembert." In *Bicentennial Commemoration of R. G. Boscovich: Proceedings*, edited by Maurizio Bossi and Pasquale Tucci, 121–48. Milan: Edizioni Unicopli.

Pedley, M. 1993. "'I due Valentuomini Indefessi': Christopher Maire and Roger Boscovich and the Mapping of the Papal States (1750–55)." *Imago Mundi* 45:59–76.

Prieto, Andrés. 2011. *Missionary Scientists: Jesuit Science in Spanish South America, 1570–1810*. Nashville: Vanderbilt University Press.
Sorkin, David. 1999. "Reform Catholicism and Religious Enlightenment." *Austrian History Yearbook* 30:187–219.
Taton, Rene. 1996. "Les relations entre R. J. Boscovich et Alexis-Claude Clairaut (1759–1764)." *Revue d'histoire des sciences* 49:415–58.
Torbarina, Josip. 1967. "The Meeting of Boškovič with Dr. Johnson." *Studia Romanica et Anglica Zagrebiensia* 13/14:3–12.
Trousson, Raymond. 1974. "Deux lettres du P. Castel à propos du 'Discours sur les sciences et les arts.'" In *Essays on Diderot and the Enlightenment in Honour of Otis Fellows,* edited by John Pappas, 292–301. Geneva: Droz.
Whyte, Lancelot Law, ed. 1961. *Roger John Boscovich, S.J., F.R.S., 1711–1787: Studies of His Life and Work*. London: Allen and Unwin.
Wilson, David B. 2009. *Seeking Nature's Logic: Natural Philosophy in the Scottish Enlightenment*. University Park: Pennsylvania State University Press.
Wolff, Larry. 1994. *Inventing Eastern Europe: The Map of Civilization on the Mind of the Enlightenment*. Stanford: Stanford University Press.
———. 2006. "Boscovich in the Balkans: A Jesuit Perspective on Orthodox Christianity in the Age of Enlightenment." In *The Jesuits*, vol. 2, *Cultures, Sciences and the Arts, 1540–1773,* edited by John O'Malley, 738–57. Toronto: University of Toronto Press.
Woolf, Harry. 1959. *The Transits of Venus: A Study of Eighteenth-Century Science*. Princeton: Princeton University Press.

17

Luke Joseph Hooke (1714–1796)

Theological Tolerance in an Apologetic Mold

THOMAS O'CONNOR

The European Catholic periphery played a crucial role in the Catholic Enlightenment in at least two ways. First, it was on the fringes—in Ireland, Scotland, and England—that the central Enlightenment value of religious toleration found concrete application in agitation to remove anti-Catholic state legislation. This involved the encouragement of tolerant attitudes and practices within Catholic communities and the public presentation of tolerance as a universal value; Catholicism was both a product and an instrument of such encouragement and presentation. Second, through the intellectual activity of Irish, Scots, and English scholastics, who wrote in the Catholic heartlands, the local Catholic Enlightenments added to the movement's intellectual force and range, facilitating intellectual exchange between core and periphery.

Although some sections of Catholic opinion in the British Isles aspired to replace the intolerant Protestant state with its Catholic equivalent, others, especially among the clergy and better-off laity, subscribed to the core Enlightenment value of tolerance. This was especially so in the second half of the eighteenth century, when inherited Counter-Reformation discourse, both in preaching and print, shed some of its sharpness. British and Irish Catholic communities, with their Continental diasporas, produced pastors and theologians who made lasting contributions to the Catholic Enlightenment at home and internationally. One of the most remarkable was the Dublin-born priest, theologian, and historian Luke Joseph Hooke (O'Connor 1995).

Irish Catholicism in Paris

Born in 1714, he was one of three children of Nathaniel Hooke (d. 1763), the historian of Ancient Rome, and Mary Gore, an Englishwoman. According to Luke's later testimony, his father "lived always a very private life, distinguished by no peculiar or remarkable event." From what we can gather, Nathaniel, a staunch, somewhat quietist, and rather eccentric Catholic, was educated at Twyford school with Alexander Pope. He was the son of John Hooke (1655–1712), Anglican, sergeant-at-law, and closely associated, in 1695, with the foundation of the Society for the Promoting of Christian Knowledge (SPCK). Because of the penal code, introduced progressively by the Protestant Irish parliament after 1695, Catholics like Luke Joseph Hooke were civilly disadvantaged, suffered sporadic state harassment, and, unless they emigrated, had access to limited career prospects. Like many eighteenth-century Irish families, the Hookes cultivated links with both Britain and the Continent and deftly manipulated these to compensate for the limited opportunities at home. Luke Joseph's father traveled frequently between Ireland, England, and France and, in the 1710s and early 1720s, acted as secretary to his uncle, Nathaniel Hooke Sr. (1660–1738), who lived in Paris. He probably brought his young son to France at this time.

Nathaniel Hooke Sr. had been a vigorous opponent of the Stuart kings and a man of independent church views in the 1680s. During the war of the 1690s, he changed sides to become a prominent Jacobite and a Bourbon spy in the Netherlands and elsewhere in Northern Europe. He was in retirement when his nephew, Nathaniel Hooke Jr., came to sort his papers. Nathaniel Jr. was swindled in the South Sea Bubble fiasco and, from 1722, sought the patronage of various English notables, including Edward Harley, third earl of Oxford, to whom he dedicated a translation of Andrew Gordon Ramsay's *Life of Fénelon* (1722). A later patron was Sarah Churchill, the duchess of Marlborough, for whom he ghostwrote a set of memoirs (1742). When Nathaniel Jr. quit Paris for England, he left his young son with his granduncle and his first wife, Lady Eleanor McCarthy Reagh (1683–1731) in the rue St. Jacques du Haut-Pas.

The family appears to have intended Luke Joseph for the church. Although he entered the seminary of Saint Nicolas-du-Chardonnet in 1734 as a student for the archdiocese of Dublin, a return to his native city never seems to have been seriously considered. He acquired his master of arts by 1734 and continued to reside in Saint Nicolas-du-Chardonnet until 1737. In Saint Nicolas, he taught philosophy, thereby fulfilling one of the conditions for admittance to the Sorbonne. He became bachelor of theology of Paris University in 1737 and, probably thanks to his family's French connections, succeeded as prior of Saint-Germain-des-Vaux (Normandy) in 1738. At this time, Irish students were sometimes used by the faculty to test points of doctrine and discipline in the courts and public opinion, presumably because those students had less to lose than their French peers (O'Connor 1999). In 1739 Hooke had his first taste of public controversy when, during the preparation of his license in theology, his thesis was referred to the *parlement* of Paris. The *parlement* objected to Hooke's alleged championing of papal authority, disregard for Gallican privileges, and neglect of individual conscience. These judicial jousts probably enhanced his reputation in the faculty, which jealously guarded its traditional liberties against expansionist incursions by the king and the courts. Shortly after the completion of his degree in 1740, he was appointed professor of theology in succession to the Irish-born James Wogan (d. 1742).

Professor at the Sorbonne

In the Sorbonne, Hooke, like most of the Irish contingent in the university, was aligned with the pro-*Unigenitus* tendency and endured rough treatment in the pages of *Nouvelles ecclésiastiques*. Although no radical when it came to basic doctrine, he adroitly wove Newton and Locke into his theological courses; yet he drew the line at Spinoza. In all this he appears as a practitioner of what has been called the "Jesuit synthesis" and an ally of the so-called pro-*Unigenitus* Catholic Enlightenment (Burson 2010, 1–48). These distinctions should not, perhaps, be too sharply drawn, since, like so many others of his generation and his background, Hooke was also influenced by career concerns, family obligations, and, in his case, the challenges posed and advantages offered by his foreign origins. He was well thought of outside the faculty of theology, a crucial factor in mid-century France as the deputies of the faculty became rather reluctantly aware of the importance and influence of public opinion. In this sense, Hooke was something of a faculty asset. On 5 May 1749, Montesquieu was told, a little condescendingly, by François de Bulkeley (1686–1756): "There is a Sorbonne doctor called Hooke, son of the author of the Roman history, whom you saw in England, who is so taken by your book [*De l'esprit des loix*] that, even though a pious man, he thinks as much of it as of his breviary; he is intelligent and learned."

In 1751 Hooke, following faculty custom, was preparing his lecture notes for publication. Before his book appeared, Hooke agreed to chair the defense of the thesis of Jean-Martin de Prades, a priest of Montauban diocese, an associate of Denis Diderot, and a contributor to the second volume of the *Encyclopédie* (Burson 2010, 239–74). There is no reason to suspect that Hooke, given his own intellectual background and allegiances, could have found much to object to in de Prades's unusually lengthy series of theological questions and answers. Consequently, with Hooke's approbation, the thesis was defended and the degree awarded. De Prades, however, immediately fell victim to internal faculty politics and was subsequently charged with deism. In a bitter controversy, so expressive of the fissiparous character of mid-century faculty politics, Hooke was forced to defend himself against charges of supporting de Prades in an alleged plot to slip deistic heresy into faculty doctrine. De Prades's paraphrasing of Montesquieu on the origins of law was equated by some in the faculty to an espousal of Hobbes, and caused a furor. Hooke moved swiftly to distance himself from the new doctor and his supporters outside the faculty. The damage, however, had been done. His position was now fatally compromised in the eyes of the guardians of orthodoxy, and he was forced to relinquish his chair. Despite this setback, he decided to proceed with his publication plans. In 1752 the first two volumes of his *Principles of Natural and Revealed Religion* (*Religionis naturalis et revelatae principia*) appeared, accompanied by a description of his role in the de Prades affair. The third volume was published in 1754. There were Venetian (1763) and German (1783) editions. Reprinted in Jacques-Paul Migne's *Theologiae Cursus Completus* (1860), it influenced the content of generations of Catholic theological textbooks in the nineteenth and early twentieth centuries.

After the de Prades affair, and thanks to increasing faculty skepticism regarding the motivation of the enterprise of Diderot's and d'Alembert's *Encyclopedia,* a question mark hung over Hooke's orthodoxy. This, however, did not entail his total exclusion from either the faculty or ecclesiastical patronage. In an attempted rehabilitation, he was appointed in 1762 to chair the faculty of theology committee set up to examine Jean-Jacques Rousseau's *Émile*. Sections of French public opinion had been outraged at Rousseau's searing criticism of inherited wisdom on education, and even deists balked at his praise of the noble savage, which effectively replaced the authority of traditional institutions with that of the individual. From Hooke's intellectual perspective, this was probably an individualist bridge too far, but in this case his personal opinion was of little consequence. His primary task was to steer the censorship proceedings to a successful condemnation of Rousseau's work, a feat he eventually accomplished. This was a rare enough achievement at a time when the faculty hesitated to raise its voice for fear of drawing down the disapproval of the king or the courts.

Buoyed by the successful conclusion of this charge, Hooke put his name forward for election to a vacant theology chair. His selection was contested by Christophe de Beaumont (1703–1781), archbishop of Paris, who later ordered seminarians to boycott his lectures. In the ensuing legal wrangle, Hooke published his *Letter of Abbé Hooke to the Archbishop of Paris* (*Lettre de M. l'abbé Hooke, docteur de la maison et société de la Sorbonne, professeur de théologie, à Mgr. l'archevêque de Paris qui avait interdit son cours aux séminaristes*; 1763). Persistent archepiscopal harassment obliged him to quit his chair in 1766. However, he retained the support of some faculty colleagues and, in 1767, was appointed professor of Hebrew and Chaldean. He developed strong links with the English Benedictines resident in Paris. Among these was the English Dominican priest John Bede Brewer who, in 1774, undertook to republish and expand the *Principles*. Brewer, a brilliant Sorbonne graduate of Gallican and rather liberal views, added chapters on papal primacy, conciliar and episcopal authority. He would later support Cuthbert Wilkes (1748–1829) in the controversy over an oath of allegiance for English Catholics.

Historiography, Politics, and University Reforms

The loss of his chair permitted Hooke to indulge his interest in Roman history. This was partly out of filial devotion, as he wanted to popularize his father's historical works in France. However, it was also an opportunity for him to express and develop his own views on a variety of topics. Nathaniel Hooke had been one of the most significant English language historians of Rome in the pre-Gibbon era (Addison 1964). Luke Joseph translated a selection of his father's writings, published as *Discourse and Critical Reflections on the History and Government of Ancient Rome* (*Discours et réflexions critiques sur l'histoire et le gouvernement de l'ancienne Rome*; 1770–1784). This proved controversial, as Nathaniel Hooke's views of Roman history—and, by inference, his son's—were in the Tory populist tradition, reminiscent of Henry Saint John Bolingbroke (1678–1751), whose sympathies lay with the plebeian orders. This translation and publishing of his father's work landed Hooke in the then-raging controversy concerning the role of Roman history in the justification, or condemnation, of contemporary political institutions and practices in France and England. Hooke's father firmly espoused the cause of the common people in the history of Rome and, taking "Cicero worship" as his target, criticized the Roman "aristocratic faction" as corrupt, self-serving, and oppressive. For Nathaniel Hooke, the common cause of liberty was served by tribunarian power, agrarian reform, and the extension of the ballot. These were hardly innocent views in late eighteenth-century France, even in translation. Hooke's paraphrase of his father's democratic view betokened sympathy for reform in France, and perhaps an interest in the contemporary campaigns to remove civil disadvantages against British Catholics. Although these views probably owed as much to Hooke's Jacobite roots as to his immersion in the French Catholic Enlightenment, his championing of his father's Roman history was ideologically significant. It raises the intriguing question of the relationship between, on the one side, continental Jacobitism and, on the other, the intellectual critique of political and ecclesiastical establishments. It can be argued, for instance, that in the eighteenth century, as their political options narrowed, defeated Jacobites found themselves obliged to elaborate arguments of accommodation and compromise. These arguments laid the ground for plural visions of social inclusion and alternative ideas of community. In this sense, Jacobitism, in certain circumstances, could become a rallying point for the disaffected (Livesey 2009, 112). This might help explain contemporary Irish Catholic interest in the new science of political economy, as evidenced by the writings of Charles O'Conor (1710–1791) (McBride 2009). The investigation of Catholic membership in Freemasonic lodges, so many of Jacobite origin, could enrich our knowledge of this complex interplay of ideas and political necessity.

In 1775, Hooke welcomed Samuel Johnson (1709–1784) to St. Cloud, where, according to Johnson's frustratingly brief diary entry, they "walked round the palace and had some talk." In the same year Denis Diderot used Hooke's *Principia* as the model for the university theology program in his *Plan for a University* (*Plan d'une université*), presented to Catherine the Great of Russia. Loyal to his Jacobite roots, Luke Joseph Hooke edited *Memoires of Marshall Berwick* (*Les Mémoires du maréchal de Berwick*), by James Fitzjames, the Duke of Berwick, in 1779. In his numerous annotations to this work, Hooke comes across as a well-informed Jacobite historian who was rather impatient with David Hume (1711–1776). In his history of the British Isles, Hume, he charged, like the "best of historians," often wrote "from imagination." He thought no more of Voltaire's account of the Jacobite wars. Voltaire "copied very imperfect and very faulty memoires." In 1778, Hooke was appointed chief librarian at the Mazarine Library, and under his enlightened rule the library's collection grew considerably. Louis-Sébastien Mercier (1740–1814), author of *Panorama of Paris* (*Tableau de Paris*; 1790), recalled that under Hooke's government, visitors to the library were free to read Lucretius and Rabelais, although, because of Hooke's role in its censorship, he thought badly of those who asked for Rousseau's *Émile*. While librarian, Hooke maintained correspondence with literary colleagues in Britain, including the author and printer John Nichols (1745–1826). He also employed Sylvain Maréchal (1750–1803). He was appreciative of the young man's poetic talents and overlooked his atheistic tendencies, at least until the publication of his *Book Escaped from the Deluge* (*Livre échappé au déluge*) in 1784, copies of which were on sale in the library itself. Hooke was obliged to dismiss him.

For a while, Hooke escaped the attention of the French revolutionaries. From the library's accounts it appears that, even as the revolution got under way, Hooke continued to augment the collection with, among other things, copies of speeches delivered in the National Assembly and, from 1790, issues of *Journal de débats* and *Journal patriotique*. However, in 1791, he refused to take the oath imposed on clerics by the Civil Constitution of the Clergy. This exposed him to a plot mounted by his assistant, L'abbé Le Blond (1738–1809), to remove him from the library. He fought back through a series of published letters and petitions addressed successively to the king, the national assembly, and the provisional executive of the French Republic. In 1791, he published *Principles of the Origin, Nature, Sovereignty, Extent, and Alliances between the Sacred and Secular Powers* (*Principes sur l'origine, la nature, la souveraineté, l'étendue et l'alliance des deux puissances*), an important pamphlet on relations between ecclesiastical and civil authorities (O'Connor 1996). It contained a strong argument for an independent state church. Deprived of his position at the Mazarine, he retired to St. Cloud, where he died in poverty on 12 April 1796.

The Bridge Builder between Traditional Theology and the *Philosophes*

Intellectually, Hooke was something of a bridge builder between traditional theology and the *philosophes*. Like many of his generation, he abandoned the scholastic method of presentation; he also attempted to integrate the schools of Newton, Locke, and even, it might be argued, Rousseau into his theological system. Thanks to his Irish background, his inclusion in English intellectual circles, and his membership in the increasingly amorphous Jacobite diaspora, he enjoyed direct access to the intellectual debates outside France, especially those concerning the French reception of John Locke and, more controversially, Thomas Hobbes. Hooke was more an empiricist than a rationalist in his reliance on the testimony of human faculties. He wrote:

> There is a certain sense of right and wrong placed by nature in the minds of men. . . . We know by conscience that this moral sense is in us, and it would be vain to try to demonstrate it by argument; it is analogous to the intuitive perception of truth which is the basis of all knowledge, or to the sense of taste by which we distinguish foods; and just as we should have no notion of truth or falsehood if this intuitive perception of truth were taken away, nor any notion of flavors without this sense of taste, so, if this sense of right and wrong, of honorable and shameful, were removed, these words would have no force of meaning. This sense is so natural, so constant and uniform, that it can be stifled by no prejudices and extinguished by no passions; its sacred judgment can be corrupted by no bribes; it

lives in the most wicked men, to whom virtue is so pleasing that they voluntarily admire their betters. (Hooke 1752–1754, 1:482–83)

There may be shades of Francis Hutcheson (1694–1746) here. These sentiments, while they sat rather uneasily with the Christian doctrine of original sin and certainly annoyed the Jansenists, were in fact intended to present traditional teaching in a manner accessible to contemporary modernizing clerics and those secular intellectuals, like Diderot, who still bothered to read theology and who might believe that theology had a role in the university, at least in Russia.

In the same vein, Hooke held a remarkably positive assessment of human desire, comparing the perception of right to a sensation, testimony to the influence of the school of Locke. He also put great trust in the power of conscience, betraying a surprising proclivity for the school of Rousseau. For Hooke, love of virtue was a kind of appetite, and the fulfillment of duty a sort of refined pleasure. He believed that there existed no moral duty that was not recommended by both human reason and appetite. Like many of his clerical contemporaries, Hooke held that nature was no longer the pure rationality of the world but the inner possession of human feeling. He had no sympathy for the Jansenists, who held the strict Augustinian notion of nature as the privation of God, and consequently evil. He also distinguished himself from those, like Hobbes, for whom nature was shorn, by a principle of method, of all moral significance. For Hooke, nature was what was right, fitting, and proper; for by "nature" he meant the nature that existed by the reason and justice of God. This was calculated to appeal to enlightened modern readers, but it also tended to externalize and marginalize revelation and rendered the explanation of miracles, for instance, problematic. This aspect of Hooke's thinking helps explain his difficulties with ecclesiastical authorities and particularly with the archbishop of Paris. Hooke, like de Prades and Loménie de Brienne, archbishop of Toulouse, shared some fundamental ideas with the *philosophes,* but there were just as many in the Sorbonne who opposed Locke and Condillac, fearing that the human mind was being reduced to a mechanical play of sensations. For them the soul was resolutely immaterial and immortal.

The central organizing principle in Hooke's theological system was the concept of *religio*. In outlining this idea, Hooke made what was perhaps his most important contribution to the divided household of Catholic Enlightenment in eighteenth-century Europe. His apologetic took the classic mid-eighteenth-century form of an apologetic to defend the essential dogmas of Catholic Christianity against indifferentism, agnosticism, and atheism but, at the same time, remained mindful of the need to demonstrate how Catholicism was not only perfectly compatible with rationality, but in fact its purest form. This enabled him to appeal to intellectual elites and to embrace modern theories of economy, science, and constitutional change.

Presenting his basic notion involved, in the first instance, a rebuttal of objections from Catholic conservatives. In the face of traditionalist critics, Hooke defended *religio* as the necessary foundation of all knowledge, political life, and historical religions. For him it was not the exclusive property of the Christian church, but existed also in a positive way among the Jews and virtuous pagans. As an alternative to the conservatives' world, divided neatly between the sacred and the profane, Hooke proposed a vision of creation as the product of one divine wisdom. Against the deists, Hooke maintained not only the possibility, but also the necessity, of one primordial *religio* in time and space. For him, this was Catholicism. Accordingly, he opposed deist efforts to evacuate the concrete institutions of the church of their political and social content. Against the atheists, he wanted to retain the idea of an organizing principle in the universe, which guaranteed both human understanding of the world and the integrity of man's moral motivation. His critique of Hobbes, to which a surprisingly substantial portion of the *Principia* is devoted, was crucial to this part of his system.

In his work, the concept of *religio* moved from being a controversial to a properly theological device, used to structure theological discourse and dialogue between theologians and *philosophes* (Despland 1979). This was part of a more general movement toward a common public religion or *credo minimum,* which was the fruit of the wars of religion and the intractable grace debates associated with controversial theology and Jansenism in the seventeenth and early eighteenth centuries. This new discourse had the advantage of inclusiveness and avoided the thorny controversies concerning grace. It was thanks to the unifying quality of his concept of *religio* that Hooke hoped to reconcile Newton's physics, Buffon's geology, Locke's sensualism, and Rousseau's sentiment with revealed religion. For him, the passions were part of the natural and the natural was part of the good. The human reason was neither the *tabula rasa* of the materialists nor the *tabula polluta* of the Jansenists, but a *terra ferax* that, with careful cultivation, might bear healthy moral fruit. He agreed with Leibniz concerning the comprehensibility of the natural law but was more realistic about the practical difficulties of coming to know it and learning to live by it. It was from the empirical school that he derived his idea of apprenticeship in knowledge, which provided the possibility of talking about an elementary notion of progress, at least on the level of moral excellence and human knowledge.

The Dissemination and Reception of Hooke's Ideas

This presentation of Catholic doctrine, so apt in the intellectual conditions of mid-eighteenth-century France, was not without echo on the Catholic fringes. Although there is no direct evidence that Hooke participated in the political debates that were the hallmark of the Catholic Enlightenment in the British Isles, this way of thinking proved useful to increasingly confident Catholic apologists active in Dublin, London, and Edinburgh (Glickman 2010). From the 1750s, Catholicism in Ireland, as in England and Scotland, was outgrowing its historical loyalty to the political cause of Jacobitism. In this context, the late eighteenth-century Irish hierarchy, with the Vicars Apostolic in England and Scotland, pragmatically agitated with the Protestant administration for the removal of the penal laws that disadvantaged Catholics. Although expediency was the order of the day, the justifications employed to support Catholic relief had a distinct Enlightenment inflection. Arguments for the toleration of Catholicism within the Protestant establishment, for instance, predictably drew on the natural law tradition, and in the case of the Scots stadialists, stressed toleration as a stage in historical progress and an aspect of social evolution (Goldie 1991). Among liberal Irish Presbyterians there were echoes of the Scottish way of thinking, also reminiscent of Hooke, whereby moderate Presbyterians developed a style of modernized natural and pastoral theology that served both to soften Calvinist dogma and combat violent atheistic skepticism.

The current state of research does not permit a firm conclusion on how significant these intellectual influences were on Irish Catholic Enlightenment discourse in Ireland, but they almost certainly informed the evolution of the political campaign for Catholic and Dissenter relief. This culminated in the Catholic Relief Acts and the foundation of the Royal Catholic College at Maynooth (1795) but fell short of Catholic emancipation, which was not granted until 1829 in a very different intellectual environment. Dublin Catholics had practical political concerns, which were probably poorly understood at the time in the Catholic heartland. In his contribution to the general Catholic Enlightenment, and in the influence his published work exercised on the significant number of Dublin clergy educated at the University of Paris, Hooke brought some of the Catholic periphery's issues to the Catholic core, and can only have positively influenced liberal Protestant opinion on the Catholic periphery. For the Protestant government, educated and increasingly wealthy Dublin Catholics, like their Québécois co-religionists, now had to be included—how, it was not yet clear—in the political life of the kingdom.

In France, Hooke was a member of a significant Jacobite diaspora and one of a number of Irish migrants who contributed in a variety of ways to the Catholic Enlightenment there. Although some of the Irish Catholic diaspora were, by nature and formation, attached to traditionalist dynastic and confessional loyalties, others were more reform-minded and responsive to the intellectual and other challenges of the age. Thomas Gould (1657–1734), *missionaire du roi dans le Poitou*, was an innovative exponent of persuasive conversion tactics toward the Huguenots, and an excellent example of the effectiveness of foreign-born ecclesiastics in fulfilling particular ecclesiastical and state missions. Arthur Richard Dillon (1721–1806), archbishop of Narbonne, also contradicts the conservative Irish diaspora stereotype. Serving as president both of the États de Languedoc and the assembly of the

French clergy, Dillon enabled the Académie des Sciences in Montpellier to acquire the famous Hôtel de Builleminet. He also founded technical colleges in Toulouse and Montpellier.

Of even greater interest in this regard was Hooke's contemporary, the Cork-born David Henegan. He was one of the administrators of the Irish Collège des Lombards and provided a series of entries in the 1759 edition of the influential *Great Historical Dictionary* (*Le grand dictionnaire historique*), first published by Louis Moréri in 1674. His essay on Ireland developed a positive image of his native country. In a critique of the stereotypes hawked by Montesquieu and other *philosophes,* Henegan argued that although Irish scholars once devoted themselves to metaphysics and scholastic philosophy, more recently they had cultivated belles lettres, history, medicine, and positive theology. In making a case for the toleration of Irish Catholics, he reminded his readers that most Irish and English Protestants had long renounced the bigoted zeal of their ancestors. This was a staple of enlightened Catholic political discourse in the British Isles at this time. Somewhat more unusually, Henegan's model for state toleration of different religions was the Dutch Republic, which, after final victory over the Spanish in the mid-seventeenth century, had chosen to tolerate nonconformists, including Catholics. Dutch Protestants, he explained, "contented themselves with excluding [Catholics] from positions of state, while according them all of the other privileges of subjects." Henegan's practical version of Enlightenment values had further concrete expression. When the new Irish College in Paris, under construction in 1772, appealed to Irish Catholics for funding, the language adopted was that of civil society: "As all are not called to the altar it must follow from this state of probation that some will not engage in holy orders. In this case a solid advantage accrues to the nation; such persons having received a virtuous and liberal education, may live to be in the world ornaments to their society and in their own sphere supports to religion." (O'Connor 1999).

As a French theologian, a Jacobite historian, and a member of the eighteenth-century Irish continental diaspora, Hooke contributed significantly to the complex intellectual phenomenon of Catholic Enlightenment. His intellectual hallmark was fair-mindedness. Like so many of his faculty contemporaries, he did indulge in antideist apologetic, but that was not his raison d'être. In his case, it was at least partly a personal defense against the accusations of cryptodeism he endured in the early 1750s at the time of the de Prades controversy. More positively, his esteem for other religions, born of his respect for the natural law, permitted him to ascribe to them an importance that made more old-fashioned apologists uneasy. He was sometimes opportunistic in his use of the new sciences, especially Newton's physics, but he used them as building blocks for a theology of religion, not as an antideist assault battery. Like the work of many Enlightenment theologians, Hooke's work has a utilitarian air about it, but it is a utilitarianism based on the oneness of all creation, the utility of every part of the whole. Religion is politically and morally useful because it reflects nature. His desire to ground theology methodologically should be distinguished from his effort to defend it against deist criticism of revelation. For Hooke, both *religio* and Catholic religion are indissoluble, to the extent that when he speaks of *religio* he speaks of all religious reality: the Scriptures, tradition, the institutional church, and religious experience. They are not distinct stages marked by titles such as "natural religion," "Jewish religion," "Christian religion," and "Catholic religion." All these are already presupposed in the dynamic notion of religion, and here Hooke owes something to a thinker he consistently criticized, Spinoza. Hooke's methodological concerns reappear in his choice of language, particularly that of the school of natural law. The natural law was not limited to the juridical domain but extended, he believed, to the spiritual domain, to the pursuit of truth, and to the good running of society. In learning to read and live the natural law, the human subject learns to know and live with God. Hooke's idea of religion speaks of the relations between God, man, and the universe. The whole theological discipline is one of service to religion, whatever the particular area of operation may be. This is what gives the discipline its unity. It is what unites it with the other sciences and constitutes the rationale for the toleration and appreciation of other cultures and histories.

By the 1760s, aspects of Hooke's irenic theology already looked somewhat old-fashioned. Later, in the tumult of the revolutionary and later imperial wars, his equilibrium-seeking theological outlook was discredited by resurgent theological conservatism and scholastic revival. Politically, as the nineteenth century advanced, the rise of nationalism, particularly in its more romantic incarnations, effectively stifled the influence of his intellectual current on the Catholic fringes, especially Ireland. However, Hooke's contribution to the Catholic Enlightenment stands, essentially as an essay in theological tolerance cast in an apologetic mold. The task of investigating his influence on contemporaries like Benedict Stattler has only begun, while an assessment of the real influence of his Jacobite background on his theological views remains incomplete.

Bibliography

Addison, Ward. 1964. "The Tory View of Roman History." *Studies in English Literature, 1500–1900* 4:413–56.

Burson, Jeffrey D. 2010. *The Rise and Fall of Theological Enlightenment: Jean-Martin de Prades and Ideological Polarization in Eighteenth-Century France.* Notre Dame: University of Notre Dame Press.

Despland, Michel. 1979. *La religion en occident: Évolution des idées et du vécu.* Montreal: Fides.

Glickman, Gabriel. 2010. "Gothic History and Catholic Enlightenment in the Works of Charles Dodd, 1672–1743." *Historical Journal* 54:347–69.

Goldie, Mark. 1991. "The Scottish Catholic Enlightenment." *Journal of British Studies* 30:20–62.

Hooke, Luke Joseph. 1739. *Quaestio theologica: Quis non reliquit semetipsum sine testimonio?* Paris.

———. 1752–1754. *Religionis naturalis et revelatae principia, methodo scholastica digesta.* Paris: H. L. Guerin.

———. 1763. *Lettre de M. l'abbé Hooke, docteur de la maison et société de la Sorbonne, professeur de théologie, à Mgr. l'archevêque de Paris qui avait interdit son cours aux séminaristes.* Paris.

———. 1791a. *Á MM les députés de l'assemblée nationale.* Paris: Nyon.

———. 1791b. *Principes sur l'origine, la nature, la souveraineté, l'étendue et l'alliance des deux puissances, la civile et l'ecclésiastique.* Paris: Nyon.

———. 1791c. *Requête au roi.* Paris: Nyon.

Lehner, Ulrich L. 2010. "The Many Faces of the Catholic Enlightenment." In *A Companion to the Catholic Enlightenment in Europe,* edited by Ulrich L. Lehner and Michael Printy, 1–48. Leiden: Brill.

Livesey, James. 2009. *Civil Society and Empire: Ireland and Scotland in the Eighteenth Century*. New Haven: Yale University Press.

McBride, Ian. 2009. *Eighteenth-Century Ireland: The Isle of Slaves*. London: Gill and Macmillan.

O'Connor, Thomas. 1995. *An Irish Theologian in Enlightenment France: Luke Joseph Hooke, 1714–1796*. Dublin: Four Courts Press.

———. 1996. "Surviving the Civil Constitution of the Clergy: Luke Joseph Hooke's Revolutionary Experiences." *Eighteenth-Century Ireland: Iris an dá Chultúr* 11:129–45.

———. 1999. "The Role of Irish Clerics in Paris University Politics, 1730–40." *History of Universities* 15:193–226.

PART 8

Catholicism in Protestant Territorial-Dynastic States: Scottish and English Enlightenment Variations

18

Andrew Michael Ramsay (1686–1743)

Catholic Freethinking and Enlightened Mysticism

GABRIEL GLICKMAN

Andrew Michael Ramsay worked to strike the discourse of the Catholic Enlightenment into the lives of the international Jacobite diaspora, the libraries of the British recusant communities, and the consciousness of a roll call of European thinkers outside his church. Unstinting in his eclecticism, in his writings he brought together classical and Renaissance political precepts with the tenets of the reformist opposition to Louis XIV and the intuitions of Newtonian science, underpinned by a mystical spirituality drawn out of the monastic cloisters. He raised his standard both as a critic and a defender of his adopted church, harnessing his political and moral reflections to the greater biblical narrative of man's fall and redemption. His central mission was to recast the Catholic faith as the friend of "reason," "liberty," and toleration, and to find a home within its learned institutions for the cause of "true, noble, Christian freethinking" (Ramsay to Carte 1736).

Ramsay was born in Ayr, Scotland, in 1686, into a civic merchant family riven by the fault lines that cut across the Scottish Protestant tradition. He had, by the time he entered adulthood, acquired a dissident's sensibility, springing perhaps from his mother's adherence to the defeated Episcopalian Church, but becoming increasingly individualistic in temper. Ramsay's thirst for scientific inquiry was cultivated by a freethinking tutor at Edinburgh University who bequeathed to him a hatred of the religious obscurantism that placed obstacles in the way of the scholarly quest. Yet he was animated no less by spiritual yearnings that ran against the orthodoxies of the Presbyterian nation. The evidence of poetry composed in 1709 falls together with Ramsay's own recollections of prayers by the ruins of a deserted Catholic chapel to foreshadow the pietistic ideals that he later placed at the center of his published work. Throughout his early career as a tutor in Episcopalian households, and in his travels through France and the Netherlands, Ramsay was caught between the conflicting pulls of scientific deism and a mystic spirituality, developed in encounters with the French Prophets of London and in a growing devotion to the texts of Madame Guyon of Blois (1648–1717). His anxieties finally found resolution in August 1710 when he arrived at Cambrai, where he was ushered into the Catholic faith by Archbishop Francois Fénelon (1651–1715), persuaded that within the fold of the church he could find the space to reconcile the empirical and the devotional search for truth (Henderson 1952, 3–10; Ramsay 1723, 33–34, 76–83, 114).

For thirty years, Ramsay stood as the defender of the Fénelon legacy. Entrusted to produce a posthumous edition of the archbishop's works, he enunciated his mentor's vision of church and state in a published biography, and advanced the same ideas in his own *Essay on Civil Government* (1722 [English translation; published in French 1721]), followed by *The Travels of Cyrus* (1727), a two-volume novel of ideas that served above all to establish his literary reputation. Patronage provided by the aristocratic and political circles linked to the Fénelon family brought Ramsay his foothold in Paris: elevated to the title of chevalier in 1723, in his writings he began to echo influences drawn from the city's Masonic lodge and from the political and intellectual discussions held at the Club de l'Entresol in the company of the Abbé de Saint-Pierre (1658–1743), the Marquis d'Argenson (1694–1757), and the exiled Viscount Bolingbroke (1678–1751) (Henderson 1952, 56–58; Childs 2000). Soon, he was attracting the interest of the English and Scottish clergymen in the city, together with the Jacobite population of merchants, bankers, and displaced patricians: in 1724 these compatriots won him an invitation to Rome for a year's tenure as tutor to the young Charles Edward Stuart (1720–1788). Despite his political and religious affinities, Ramsay began to find an equally admiring audience in the British Isles, where the long period of peace with France had opened up the connections between the London and Paris print markets. In his own country, he acquired a network of correspondents that ranged from Alexander Pope (1688–1744) and Jonathan Swift (1667–1745) to Francis Hutcheson (1694–1746) and David Hume (1711–1776); in France, his writings stirred the enthusiasm of Rousseau (1712–1778) and Voltaire (1694–1778). While he preached, in the words of Hume, "a philosophy peculiar to himself," Ramsay has been recovered in recent secondary studies as a civic and religious reformer pivotal not merely to Anglo-French literary exchanges but also to the ideas, networks, and friendships of a Catholic Enlightenment that was starting to disseminate through the different states and kingdoms of the continent (Ahn 2011; Eckert 2009; Glickman 2007, 310–13).

Ramsay's Political Thought

Throughout his career, Ramsay flirted with the peril of censorship and condemnation. In France, he risked provocation chiefly with the political philosophy behind his writings and with his public association with the cause of Fénelon, who had been subjected to virtual house arrest in the last decade of his life at the direction of the court of Versailles. In the anonymous *Letter to Louis XIV* (*Lettre à Louis XIV*; 1692), followed by the allegorical resolutions of his epic, *Adventures of Telemachus Son of Ulysses* (*Les aventures de Telemaque, fils d'Ulysse*; Fénelon 1699), Fénelon had dramatized the maladies afflicting the

Bourbon kingdom in the wake of the Nine Years' War, identifying the religious persecutions, the emasculation of the realm's representative institutions, and the endless succession of territorial conflicts as corrosive to French civic welfare, ruinous to the virtue of the subject, and fatal to the soul of the man who held the throne (Gable 1993). The death of Louis XIV conferred a greater space for the expression of such sentiments. Although Ramsay would complain, "I live in a country where true, noble Christian freethinking, is not allowed, nor even tolerated," he was able to take advantage of a climate, after the Treaty of Utrecht, in which the militant and absolutist methods of the Sun King became subject to subtle reappraisal, in critiques leveled by fellow members of the Club de l'Entresol (Ramsay to Carte 1736; Rothklug 1965). Though the club itself was to take provocation too far—it was suppressed for its dissentient activities at the decree of Cardinal Fleury in 1731—Ramsay was nonetheless able, shielded by the influence of his patrons, to articulate a call for civic revival, which would have resulted in near-certain incarceration only a decade earlier.

Like Fénelon before him, Ramsay can be located within a late flowering of the tradition of Renaissance civic humanism: among authors suffused with the vocabulary of More, Erasmus, and a long lineage of Florentine thinkers, who looked to recover from the wisdom of the ancients the route to a regeneration of the "whole Man," to the benefit of the public domain (Manuel and Manuel 1979, 381–86; Pocock 1975, 423–505). The "taste of TRUE LIBERTY," he believed, would be restored to Europe when its citizens could invigorate within themselves the genius of "the Philosopher, the Painter and the Lover," return "decay'd Faculties to their primitive Vigour," and so rediscover the Ciceronian bonds of virtue and friendship that had taken the classical republics to the threshold of greatness (Ramsay 1732, 1, 19). To this endeavor, the greatest enemy was identified as monarchical tyranny and absolutism, and Ramsay threw anathemas upon the autocrats, emperors, and would-be universal monarchs who had, he perceived, set Europe on the pathway to decline. He claimed to see all around him "the fatal Circle," of regal lust leading to conquest, and thereafter to luxury, "always the Fore-runner of the Fall of Empires."

He perceived in the recourse to religious persecution not merely an erosion of the moral character of the realm but a body blow to its prosperity, when intolerant kings turned citizens against each other and brought their people to the "dreadful precipice" over which Christian charity and public virtue would descend (Ramsay 1727, 1:6; 2:21, 153–57). Moreover, the corruption in the kingdoms he surveyed turned not merely upon the errant *practice* of kingship but upon an entirely flawed conception as to the origins, privileges, and duties of monarchy. For Ramsay, the fact that the *existence* of temporal power was ordained by God did not render a king himself divine—his title could rest only upon civil laws, when "No Man is born a King by Inherent and Natural Right," in the same way that no individual possessed vast reserves of wealth by heavenly decree. He delivered a withering verdict upon "the parasitical principles of unbounded Passive Obedience" that had convinced too many sovereigns to "usurp the Rights of the Divinity and invade the Privileges of the human Fraternity" (Ramsay 1722, 68–69, 77, 92–94; 1732, 19–20).

Ramsay held that European moral revival hinged upon the extension of civic liberty, because it was through learning to love their country that subjects could learn to love heaven. The power of monarchs could become glorious only when exerted through "the universal, free un-bribed consent of the States of a Kingdom." Explicit in his admiration for the ancient constitution of England, despairing of the long slumber of the French Estates-General, he considered it "not reasonable" that "the Royal Authority should be the only power of the state," unfeasible for "laws and taxes to depend entirely upon his absolute will," and "wicked" above all for a prince to interfere with "the Liberty of the Mind." In the "Body Politick, as in the Natural, all the Members contribute something to the Common Life," Ramsay had opined when he first published his *Essay on Civil Government* in 1721; eleven years later, he proclaimed it a "civil right" for subjects to "enter into conference with their Prince" (Ramsay 1722, 23, 92–94, 176–78; 1732, 18–19). Yet Ramsay was no utopian: haunted by the civil tumults in the British Isles within the previous century, he had his eyes no less open to the dangers of democracy, demagoguery, and "leveling Anarchical principles." No system of government could prove immune from corruption, he concluded, "because human Nature is weak and imperfect"; indeed, the greatest dangers to liberty could arise from the schemes of those who would "destroy nature, under pretence of improving it." The melancholy paradox underpinning the political world arose when, "for the Preservation of Order, it is necessary that Men should be subject to Men that are weak, fallible and overcome with innumerable Passions." The only release lay in a campaign fixed as much upon the moral virtue as the constitutional framework behind a polity. Important as it remained to preserve the representative institutions of the public domain, the history of Europe affirmed that the "safety and Happiness of a Kingdom does not depend so much upon the Wisdom of Laws as upon that of the Kings" (Ramsay 1722, 62–66, 107–8; 1727, 2:51; 1732, 18–21).

Ramsay's favored political framework lay in "Monarchical Authority, moderated by a Senate," which he believed to be "the primitive Form of Government in all Wise Nations" (Ramsay 1723, 315; 1727, 1:267). Yet in the slippery, fallible domain of worldly politics, no legal title would be enough to make a prince secure on his throne—virtuous ability provided the only "true right to Crowns" and the safest determinant of success. Venturing through the Grecian world, the eponymous hero of *The Travels of Cyrus* saw "nothing but sad Examples of the Weakness and Misfortunes of Princes": dethroned, usurped, corrupted, or driven to madness. In the composition of *Cyrus,* followed by his 1732 *Plan of Education for a Young Prince,* Ramsay engaged with the tragedy of a mortal man who must "resemble the Immortals, who have no Passion." Choosing the mythic Persian ruler, the liberator of the Jews, as his template, he turned to the materials of the Renaissance "mirror for princes" tradition, to craft and weld the picture of a sovereign who would prove to contemporary Europe that the "Glory of a King consists in reigning over Men whom he renders happy by his Beneficence and good by his Virtues" (Ramsay 1727, 1:146, 307; 2:136–37). If he took direct inspiration from Fénelon, Ramsay also looked further back, to Erasmus's *Institutio principis Christiani* and the reflections of the Jansenist Pierre Nicole, whose *Education of a Prince* (*Education d'un prince*; 1679) had attacked tyranny as the product of sinful self-delusion, and Ramsay saw the extension of civic liberty as the safest means for a king to keep his own temptation in check (Glickman 2009, 117, 179, 240). Ramsay argued that it was the pedagogical experience that conferred virtue on a king: immersion in history and the arts, reverence of God, familiarity with the laws of nations, science, and commerce would provide the most secure apparatus for benevolent rule. Behind the layers of myth and fable, *The Travels of Cyrus* was setting down a counterblast to the confessional and absolutist model of monarchy exemplified in the kingdom of Louis XIV. Animated by "the great love of the Publick Weal," Ramsay's prince would rule through councils, promote fiscal retrenchment at home and peace abroad, set his subjects free in their religion and their trade, and so attain within himself "an Empire over [the] Passions, more glorious than the false lustre of Royalty" (Ramsay 1723, 315; 1727, 1:86; 1732, 7, 14–15).

Toleration, Mysticism, and Spiritual Revival

Ramsay was not born into the Catholic Church; he chose it, as the storehouse of divine wisdom and the living rebuttal to the godless false reasoning of deists and atheists. To the Benedictine monk Thomas Southcott, who befriended him in Paris, the Chevalier (as Ramsay is commonly called) could prove "yet a greater man" even than Fénelon, as an advocate for the Catholic religion (Glickman 2009, 229–30). Yet the avant-garde spiritual and intellectual impulses running through Ramsay's works pushed him into a troubled relationship with the orthodox structures of his church. Ramsay was an unquestioning Christian, but he was also a civic humanist who sought the Renaissance of man upon earth and a self-conscious cosmopolitan who relished the diffusion of new scientific knowledge and celebrated the commonality of individuals across national and religious divides, in a world arranged as "one great Republick, of which God is the common Father" (Ramsay 1732, 17). As his devotion to Freemasonry showed, he believed that the human fraternity could be affirmed in ways other than membership in a single church, and he was haunted by the ease with which Christian authority could be manipulated by "deceitful and cunning men" into seeking its dominion over the soul. From the harrying of Fénelon by Louis XIV's bishops, to the Presbyterian onslaught against Scotland's own dissidents, to the pressure placed upon the Masonic brotherhood by papal decree, Ramsay was confronted throughout his lifetime with instances of religious oppression. *The Travels of Cyrus* repeatedly condemned those who had grounded the principles of faith upon obedience and submission in order "to degrade Religion, and [so] made it monstrous...," so eclipsing "all the sweet Hopes which the Idea of Immortality inspires." Ramsay's 1738 *Apology for the Free and Accepted Masons* denounced "the furious and horrible Inquisition" and bewailed that "Rome has often used barbarities to her best children." In the "corruption and avarice of priests," his hero Cyrus comes to understand, lies a "source of mischief" that pushes the universe ever further from the reach of heaven (Ramsay 1722, 86; 1727, 1:310; Ramsey 1738, 86–87, 126).

From his belief in liberty of conscience and his excitement at the glimmers of new learning, Ramsay sketched out a vision of Christian faith made "conformable to reason." He saw a flourishing church anchored neither upon an unchanging "system of Philosophical Opinions," nor upon simply "a History of Miracles or Supernatural Events," but as promoting the search for sacred wisdom in the manner of "an Experimental Science," centered on the discovery of "the great and noble truths" (1727, 2:184). Yet Ramsay did not place limitless trust in human or scientific wisdom. In religion as in politics, he was gripped by a sense of the frailty of temporal reason, the limits of intellectual endeavor, and the ultimate dependence of man upon the divine agency, given that "in the present state of human Nature all our Faculties are weakened and obscur'd . . . our Imagination clogg'd with gross and grovelling Ideas, our Will bias'd by strong and Turbulent passions." The intellectual darkness that had engulfed human life was captured as the product of the Fall of Man: as "dispersed, deluded souls" groped towards the truth, their nascent philosophical inquiries sprang from the same fragile yearning that made man strain towards the heavenly estate "from which he has fallen." Reaching into Platonic imagery, Ramsay identified scientific inquiry as a pious enterprise, since "the Creation is but an Image or Picture of the Divine Perfection, and therefore bears a Character of his Infinity and Immensity"; from Newton he took the picture of the devout mind teetering on the brink of eternal truths, like "a Child upon the Borders of the Sea, who has only crack'd some Pebbles and open'd some shells . . . while there lies beyond him a boundless Ocean." To seek the truth of the universe without understanding of the higher purpose behind God's creation was an ambition that would be destined to failure (1727, 1:194; 1732, 1–2).

Ramsay believed that the search for civic and intellectual renewal was part of the greater drama of man's struggle for redemption. The classical motifs within *The Travels of Cyrus* are streaked with a Judeo-Christian consciousness of the providential plan, made explicit in the words of the exiled Hebrew sages, who comfort the hero with the assurance that, for all the weaknesses and imperfections his adventures have revealed, "these degenerate Beings will be restored to their Primitive Perfection and Happiness" when "The Great Emanuel, God-Man, will descend upon the Earth" (Ramsay 1727, 2:153–81). Within this providential schema, the Catholic Church occupied a privileged, but not an exclusive, position. In *The Travels of Cyrus,* Ramsay adumbrated an argument that he developed in full in his final published work, *The Philosophical Principles of Natural and Revealed Religion* (1748), where he began to contend that all the religions of the world were touched with a thwarted consciousness of the same universal truths and bound by the common threads of a shared, if distorted, revelation. Prizing out conclusions from the Jesuit observation of sophisticated religious and moral systems in the non-Christian civilizations of the East and familiarizing himself with the writings of Ralph Cudworth and the Cambridge Platonists, he claimed in his own studies to catch the flickers of Trinitarian belief within ancient Jewish thought (Cudworth 1678; Spence 1984; Ramsay to Carte 1736). In his *Universal Prayer* (1738), Ramsay's correspondent and contemporary Alexander Pope would find God's "Temple" in the "earth, sea, skies" of the world, with "saint," "savage," and "sage" turning to the heavens in "one chorus" to venerate the common "Father of all." Like Pope, Ramsay believed that a true understanding of the grand scheme of human life mocked the urge to persecute: the variety of religious faith was not a cause for lamentation, but a perfect insight into the will of God, who had allowed "different Societies" and "different systems" to come into being, and who "overlooks all these imperfections and demands only the heart." When divine blessing was scattered so unfathomably through different countries and cultures, religious men of all stripes had a duty to exchange their wisdom, not to confront one another. Every individual "should be left to the perfect Liberty to examine, every one for himself, the Authority and Motives of the Credibility of the Revelation" (Ramsay 1727, 1:100–101, 106, 194–98; 2:14; 1732, 15–17; Spence 1984). While churches, for Ramsay, supplied vital "salvatory aids" to worship, the deeper truths of the universe could be disinterred only when man was able to distinguish between "the Religion of Means and that of the End, the Forms and the Essence, the Substance and the Ceremonies." The promise of the Christian life was therefore unlocked through private prayer, an experience that probed beyond the limits of human reason and allowed the worshiper to "consult the idea of infinity" to attain a fleeting reunion "with our Source and Centre" (Ramsay 1732, 10, 14–15). His attraction to the Catholic Church developed through a reading of its contemplative traditions: the movements of spiritual perfectionism that stood poised on the shifting line separating orthodox doctrine from heresy.

At the cost of papal condemnation, Fénelon had championed the quietist vision of "Pure Love" enunciated by Madame Guyon, arguing that it reflected teachings embedded within the lives of the saints (Butler 1810, 82–83; Fénelon 1697; De la Bedoyere 1956, 83–86). Ramsay's associates among the English Benedictines traced the lineage of the "mystic way" back to the medieval meditations of Walter Hilton and Mother Julian of Norwich (Scott 1992, 127–29; Brueckmann 1994). Ramsay himself saw the quietist experience of stillness and self-examination as the spur for a renewed civic life, purging the human interior of delusion and prejudice and enlightening the individual on "the Moral and Social Duties both of private and publick," so that the prayerful soul could "bring forth, as Plato says, not the Shadows of Virtue, but the Virtues themselves." He identified pure love as the mental spring behind the model of active Christian charity preached by Saint Francis de Sales, and he seized upon parallels between

Guyon's creed and Aristotelian philosophical contemplation. Through the agency of prayer, "we will become true, just and good, from a Desire of imitating the Sovereign Truth, Justice and Goodness" (Ramsay 1723, 136; 1732, 14–15). As the civic domain would be cleansed through the return of virtue, so Ramsay envisaged Christian life rejuvenated through the Fénelonian conception that "Pure Love and Humble of Faith are the whole of Catholick Religion" and through the practice of the priest as shepherd, gently coaxing his flock into virtue. By emancipating "the pure, genuine original Doctrines" of the church, he could admonish at once "the present contempt" to which Catholicism had been subjected by its deistic enemies, but confute no less "the vain speculations and Glosses" that had pockmarked the traditions of scholastic learning. Above all, a pious hope that the unfettered human mind could leap toward the divine mysteries delivered an impassioned rebuke to those authorities who made their religion known only through the sword, the dungeon, and the inquisition (Ramsay 1723, 94, 182, 241; 1732, 11).

Ramsay in the Catholic World

In December 1722, the Jacobite Lord Lansdowne wrote to the exiled Stuart Pretender, recommending the *Life* of Fénelon and the new editions of the archbishop's works being published in Paris by Andrew Michael Ramsay: "The Situation & adventures of Telemachus in search of his native kingdom [afford] so near a resemblance with your own ... that one would imagine the Author ... had no other Prince in his View but your self, when he wrote it." He concluded: "In all Events of Life, your Majesty may have recourse to these Books as to an Oracle, either for consolation, or advice" (Lansdowne to James Edward Stuart 1720). The first world to absorb Ramsay's ideas was therefore to be found within the scattered fellowship of exiled Stuart loyalists, and his appointment as tutor to the Young Pretender reflected a deepening Jacobite engagement with the experiences of Fénelon and his disciples. The irenic temper of quietist political and religious ideas had strongly attracted those courtiers who rejected revanchist solutions, as they sought rapprochement with the British kingdoms: James Edward Stuart himself frequently invoked the memory of his 1709 venture to Cambrai (Glickman 2009, 117–18). The political affinities behind Ramsay's works were declared in his *Essay on Civil Government,* which condemned the 1688 Revolution for breaking "the fundamental and primitive constitution of the English Monarchy" and contaminating the body politic with "Cabals, Hatreds, Division and Deceit." More suggestively, he plucked at the strings of the Jacobite imagination by filling the text of *Cyrus* with examples of kings who had learned from periods of exile to recover lost moral and political truths, gained courage and virtue through a time of trial, and so discovered the way home. "Happy," he believed, is "the Nation that is govern'd by a Prince who travels over the Earth and Seas, to carry back to his Country all the treasures of Wisdom" (Ramsay 1722, 164–69; 1727, 1:298–99, 306–7). To James Edward, Ramsay claimed he had extracted the lessons of Fénelon's works "only to maintain your rights and endeavour to undeceive my countrymen of their errours"; he exhorted the Pretender that when a man had "seen the world in all its shapes," there could be nothing "more useful" to "to forewarn [him] against an ambition of absolute government" and to present therefore "a model to future Princes of moderation in their grandeur" (Ramsay "To the King"). There was a visionary strain to significant strands of Jacobite literature: to the waiting faithful, Ramsay's narrative of spiritual and political deliverance, with a prince-redeemer foreshadowing the restoration of the Golden Age, offered the sweetest ideological consolation.

Against these exalted hopes, Ramsay's term of office exposed the tension that ran between the Stuarts in exile and the states and societies that hosted them, as the Jacobite court struggled to move away from the *dévot* orthodoxies of Catholic Europe. Although the Chevalier was unprepared for the inveterate factionalism of the Stuart retinue and the animosity of some in court toward his Paris patrons, the lords Lansdowne and Mar, the more serious conflict that impinged upon his appointment was the beginning of a series of confrontations between the court and the entourage of Pope Benedict XIII, as the cardinals cast the lens over heterodox tendencies in the education of the Jacobite princes. "He is hated by the great bigots" in the Holy See, affirmed one observer, "who say that such a man is not fit to bring up a Roman Catholic prince." One member of the Curia had already damned Fénelon's *Telemaque* as a work "very dangerous for princes to read," with the Pretender ordered to disown any public affiliation. In later years, Ramsay would cast his vitriol on the clerical personalities he had encountered within the Holy See; his forced return to France within twelve months evidently continued to rankle (Glickman 2009, 244–45).

But if the Stuarts had been prevented in 1724 from publicly advancing the creed, the vocabulary of the Jacobite manifestos and the visual and literary representations of the Stuart princes suggested that Ramsay's ideas were quietly assisting the intellectual evolution of the movement. Jacobite courtiers were delighted by sentiments expressed by the adolescent Charles Edward Stuart in favor of the Paris *Parlement* against the court of Versailles; later, the prince's own propaganda prints captured him as a man of the Enlightenment, a reader of Locke and Voltaire. The Young Pretender's interest in promoting himself as a reforming prince was evinced in his reputed sympathies for the Masonic order and in his support for a late flourishing of radicalism in Jacobite manifestos that offered Britain extended press freedom and triennial parliaments alongside the established Stuart pledge of a widened liberty of conscience (Monod 1989, 300–303; Szechi 1994, 150–51). The influence introduced by Fénelon and Ramsay brought spiritual and patriarchal conceptions of Stuart monarchy into balance with a civic spirit, a spirit voiced when the Paris Benedictine Augustine Walker hailed the 1745 voyage into Scotland as the return of a "patriot" prince "who neglects his own to heal his people's wounds" and who would rock the thrones of "haughty tyrants" with a restoration of liberty. More potently, Fénelon and Ramsay provided a language to justify the possibility of a Catholic prince ruling over subjects of a different faith: the image of a king who nurtured the civic virtues of his subjects without imposing upon their private consciences could become a credible moral alternative to the template of the confessional "nursing father" (Glickman 2009, 245).

Ramsay's connections to the Jacobite court endured for a further two decades through his work as a salaried agent in Paris, and the affinity was sealed in 1732 by his marriage to a daughter of the Pretender's secretary of state, David Nairne. Latterly, he began to develop his association with the Catholic recusant component of the Jacobite world, initiated in France through friendships with the English monks and the tutors of Scots College, Paris, but increasingly marked within the libraries of co-religionists in the British Isles, whose education and travel had left them well versed in the trends of the French print market. Ramsay had first registered on the horizons of recusants in 1722, after a campaign lobbying French ministers to protest against the threat of new anti-Catholic penal laws when they met with their English allies in diplomatic consultation. Five years later, English Catholic notables pushed unsuccessfully for the Chevalier to be reinstated in Rome, when the post of tutor again fell vacant at the exiled court. Ramsay's name became totemic for those British Catholics who sought to create scope within the church for new scientific and philosophical inquiry—Benedictines such as Thomas Southcott, who regretted that "a great deal of pedantry mingles in the schools of piety and divinity," or Thomas Welch, who adjured his fellow monks to study Newton and Diderot, "to take reason for their guide in all things that belong to Nature," and so become "Lights of the Church" (Scott 1992, 158–70; Glickman 2009, 237). Ramsay's thoughts filtered into the vocabulary of priests in England: the historian Charles Dodd, who believed that "there should be nothing in faith contrary to reason," and the theologian Simon Berington, who shared the notion of the moral and spiritual unity of the religions of the world and contended that the clergy must appeal to that "substance in man endow'd with the noble faculties of thinking, judging, chusing, forseeing," to cultivate the "just and natural use of Liberty and Reason" (Dodd 1742, 57; Berington 1750, 24, 209–12). For these thinkers, the content of the European Catholic Enlightenment could be fixed onto the older raw materials of recusant thought: the writings of a community placed at a remove from the militant Counter-Reformation and seeking greater space to participate within a Protestant realm.

Ramsay and British Politics

Grafting the precepts of Fénelon and his predeccesor Grotius onto the political realities of eighteenth-century Europe, Ramsay's *Essay on Civil Government* ruminated implicitly on the qualms of conscience afflicting Catholics and Jacobite supporters forced to live under Hanoverian rule. He challenged them to retain their engagement with civic life even while they resisted moral and intellectual submission, adamant that we cannot "cure the Diseases of the grand Body Politic, by using violent Methods," and convinced that the universal imperative of service toward the public realm did not diminish even after a malady had entered into the constitution. Dissidents should never sign away the independence of mind that conferred true liberty, and "obedience must never go soe far, as to approve the Injustice of the Usurpation, much less to swear that he hath a Right to the Crown, which he hath seized upon his Violence." Yet taxes must be paid, "order and peace" preserved, and the patriotic spirit retained, even while the legitimacy of the reigning power lay in doubt, because "Kingdoms perish more through want of having good Subjects, than because there are bad sovereigns" (Ramsay 1722, 57–58, 90, 94).

Here Ramsay's arguments reached into a broader realm of national life, outside the Jacobite underground and beyond the mansions of the recusant gentry, to engage with a body of opposition literature that called for the revival of patriotic virtue in defense of civic liberty against overmighty Whig governments. The maxim that "The Happiness of the People ... makes the Happiness of the Prince," the conviction that "their true Interests are necessarily united, whatever Pains are taken to separate them," may have been stirred in opposition to Louis XIV, but the same rhetoric could be turned by Bolingbroke and his supporters against a Hanoverian court accused of falling under ministerial despotism, against the growth of the standing army, the swelling levels of taxation, and the alleged corruption of parliament at the hands of the state (Ramsay 1727, 1:144; Gerrard 1994). Beneath the gauze of Persian and Grecian myth, Ramsay's *Cyrus* presented a political manifesto that far exceeded Fénelon in its engagement with commercial modernity, but was conceived to embody a complete antithesis to the militaristic, territorial dreams of European potentates from the court of Versailles to the electorate of Hanover. His idealized depictions of the cities of Athens and Tyre sketched out the model of a polity empowered by free trade, its monopolies broken, its ports opened up to merchants and immigrants, and its commercial fingertips reaching through the world. Embellishing the concept of "blue water" foreign policy cherished by the English opposition, he preached the virtues of a cosmopolitan marine empire founded on the acquisition of free ports in global thoroughfares and avoiding the errors of monarchs who "sap the Foundations of their Authority" in "seeking to extend their Dominions too far." The fruits of this strategy would manifest themselves within the rising wealth of the people, not just the coffers of the crown, and by entrusting merchants with the charge of the navy, rather than simply their own private profit, the nation could reconcile "the publick Good . . . with the Interest of each private Subject," so that "Trade does not in the least diminish military Virtue." Emporium rather than imperium, commerce without luxury, regal *grandezza* without the temptation of tyranny—Ramsay believed he had unlocked the secrets of lasting national greatness. If his vision was plotted in the salons of Paris, its meaning was pitched westward across the English Channel (Ramsay 1727, 1:285–86; 2:64–65, 77–78).

While recent scholarship has highlighted the anti-French instincts built into the identity of the eighteenth-century nation, the transformation in European politics following the Treaty of Utrecht and the death of Louis XIV reawakened British interest in the intellectual life of her continental rivals (Colley 1992; Wilson 1995). For a generation appalled, as both Bolingbroke and Walpole professed to be, by the conflicts and bloodshed of recent decades, the reformist proposition presented in *The Travels of Cyrus,* of kingdoms abjuring dreams of universal monarchy, united through trade and friendship across cultural and religious borders, could hold resonant appeal. Even before the emergence of Ramsay's works, Fénelon's anatomy of virtue and corruption in a kingdom had conferred a set of references to unite the disparate strands of English opposition politics: the archbishop was cited, translated, and admired by the Whig radicals Isaac Littlebury, John Trenchard, and Thomas Gordon, no less than by the high Tory clergymen George Hickes and William King. *Telemaque* would be rendered in English twelve times over the century before crossing other seas to transplant a vision of civic virtue in the minds of American authors. Yet Ramsay had stamped a mark upon the English mind as more than just the champion of the archbishop. Searching for amity with sections of the French church, Archbishop William Wake of Canterbury declared his attraction toward *The Travels of Cyrus*; translated by the Irish Catholic scholar and historian Nathaniel Hooke, the Chevalier's works drew sufficient attention for him to be inducted into the fellowship of the Royal Society and raised to an honorary Oxford degree in 1730 (Gordon 1724, 16; Manuel and Manuel 1979, 391; Glickman 2009, 248–49). Soon, the Jacobite court would be unable to claim a monopoly over the political doctrines of the Paris reformers. In 1729, Frederick, Prince of Wales, received the dedication of an edition of *Telemaque* that exhorted him to make his stand against ministerial tyranny and corruption. A decade later, the same ideas began to circulate within the mercurial blueprint of Bolingbroke's *Idea of a Patriot King,* notorious as a fabled influence on the future George III. Ramsay, the Jacobite tutor, had helped to shape the refashioning of the house of Hanover (Henderson 1952, 135–46; Armitage 1997). Observing Ramsay in Rome in 1724, an agent for the British government had reported that "although he is of the Pretender's party . . . he hates slavery as well as the greatest Whig in England. . . . [H]e hates bigotry and rather loves freethinking" (Glickman 2007, 311). If the Chevalier's prince never did sit upon the throne of the three kingdoms, and if the manifesto of a Catholic Jacobite mystic and naturalized Frenchman failed to shift the religious and political orthodoxies of Hanoverian Britain, the applause he received was all the more remarkable for that.

Once located at the solitary, radical limits of European intellectual life, the career of Andrew Michael Ramsay took shape in reality within the domain of the Catholic Enlightenment, in a literary and ideological realm created by Jacobite exiles, Benedictine monks, and mystical French dissidents. A civic and intellectual reformer, he was, no less, a champion of religious revival, who dwelt upon the Hebrews as much as the Greeks, and who brought the humanist political mind into contact with the contemplative traditions stored within Anglo-French Catholicism. In his eyes, the search for Enlightenment within the temporal world was intertwined with the cosmic narrative of Christian deliverance, and for all his spiritual individualism, one of his principal aims was to promote, protect, and purify the church that he had chosen.

Ramsay's works were shot through with implications for the British Catholic and Jacobite worlds through which he moved—milieus that have been all too readily damned as somnolent intellectual backwaters. Half a century after his death, his works left literary footprints over the writings of a later generation of readers—John Courtenay Throckmorton, Joseph Berington, Charles Butler—who sought to chart a pathway for their co-religionists between the extremes of moral submission and dyspeptic isolation in a Protestant kingdom, and who implanted the language of "reason," "virtue," "liberty," and "toleration" within the dawning campaign for Catholic Emancipation (Chinnici 1980). The realm of British Catholicism may have been smaller and more precarious than that of its continental co-religionists, but in its mental landscape it was no less wide ranging. In the encounters that took place inside the churches, salons, and coffeehouses of the continent, recusants could start to drink in the full variety and complexity of the greater religious world of which they were a part.

Bibliography

Ahn, Doohwan. 2011. "From Greece to Babylon: The Political Thought of Andrew Michael Ramsay (1686–1743)." *History of European Ideas* 37:421–37.

Armitage, David. 1997. "A Patriot for Whom? The Afterlives of Bolingbroke's Patriot King." *Journal of British Studies* 36:397–418.

Berington, Simon. 1750. *Dissertations on the Mosaical Creation, Deluge, Building of Babel, and Confusion of Tongues*. London.

Brueckmann, Patricia. 1994. "Paradice it selfe: Hugh Cressy and Church Unity." In *1650–1850: Ideas, Aesthetics and Inquiries in the Early Modern Era,* edited by Kevin L. Cope, 1:84–102. New York: AMS Press.

Butler, Charles. 1810. *The Life of Fénelon, Archbishop of Cambray.* London: Longman, Hunt, Rees and Orme.

Childs, Nick. 2000. *A Political Academy in Paris, 1724–1731: The Entresol and Its Members.* Oxford: Oxford University Press.

Chinnici, Joseph. 1980. *The English Catholic Enlightenment: John Lingard and the Cisalpine Movement, 1780–1850.* Shepherdstown, WV: Patmos Press.

Colley, Linda. 1992. *Britons: Forging the Nation, 1707–1837.* New Haven: Yale University Press.

Cudworth, Ralph. 1678. *The True Intellectual System of the Universe.* London: Richard Royston.

De la Bedoyere, Michael. 1956. *The Archbishop and the Lady: The Story of Fénelon and Madame Guyon.* London: Collins.

Dodd, Charles. 1742. *An Apology for the Church History of England.* Brussels.

Eckert, Georg. 2009. *"True, Noble, Christian Freethinking": Leben und Werk Andrew Michael Ramsays (1686–1743).* Munster: Aschendorff.

Fénelon, Francois de Salignac de la Mothe. 1697. *Explication des Maximes des Saints sur la vie intérieure.* Paris: Pierre Aubouin, Pierre Emery and Charles Clousier.

———. 1699. *Les aventures de Telemaque, fils d'Ulysse.* Translated by Tobias Smollett.

———. 1776. *The Adventures of Telemachus, the Son of Ulysses.* Reprint, edited by Leslie A. Chilton and O. M. Brack. Athens: University of Georgia Press, 1997.

Gable, A. T. 1993. "The Prince and the Mirror: Louis XIV, Fénelon, Royal Narcissism and the Legacy of Machiavelli." *Seventeenth-Century French Studies* 15 (1): 243–68.

Gerrard, Christine. 1994. *The Patriot Opposition to Walpole: Politics, Poetry and National Myth, 1725–1742.* Oxford: Oxford University Press.

Glickman, Gabriel. 2007. "Andrew Michael Ramsay (1686–1743), the Jacobite Court and the English Catholic Enlightenment." *Eighteenth-Century Thought* 3:293–329.

———. 2009. *The English Catholic Community, 1688–1745: Politics, Culture and Ideology.* Woodbridge: Boydell and Brewer.

Gordon, Thomas. 1724. *An Essay on the Practice of Stockjobbing.* London: J. Peele.

Henderson, G. D. 1952. *Chevalier Ramsay.* London and New York: Nelson.

Manuel, Frank, and Fritzie Manuel. 1979. *Utopian Thought in the Western World.* Oxford: Blackwell.

Monod, Paul. 1989. *Jacobitism and the English People, 1688–1788*. Cambridge: Cambridge University Press.

Pocock, J. G. A. 1975. *The Machiavellian Moment*. Princeton: Princeton University Press.

Ramsay, Andrew Michael. 1722. *Essay on Civil Government . . . according to the Principles of the Late Archbishop of Cambray. Translated from the French*. London: Randal Minshull. Published in French 1721.

———. 1723. *Life of François de Salignac de la Motte Fénelon, Archbishop and Duke of Cambray*. London: Paul Vaillant.

———. 1727. *The Travels of Cyrus*. 2 vols. London: T. Woodward and J. Peele.

———. 1732. *A Plan of Education for a Young Prince*. London: J. Roberts / A. Dodd.

———. 1738. *An Apology for the Free and Accepted Masons*. Reprinted in *The Golden Remains of the Early Masonic Writers*, edited by George Oliver, vol. 3. London: R. Spencer, 1847.

Rothklug, Lionel. 1965. *Opposition to Louis XIV: The Political and Social Origins of the French Enlightenment*. Princeton: Princeton University Press.

Scott, Geoffrey. 1992. *Gothic Rage Undone: English Monks in the Age of Enlightenment*. Bath: Downside Abbey.

Spence, Jonathan. 1984. *The Memory Palace of Matteo Ricci*. New York: Penguin.

Szechi, Daniel. 1994. *The Jacobites: Britain and Europe, 1688–1788*. Manchester: Manchester University Press.

Wilson, Kathleen. 1995. *The Sense of the People: Politics, Culture and Imperialism in England, 1715–1785*. Cambridge: Cambridge University Press.

Unpublished Letters

Andrew Michael Ramsay, "To the King of Great Britain." N.d., Rawlinson MSS, D1198/247. Bodleian Library, Oxford.

Andrew Michael Ramsay to Thomas Carte, 22 November 1736. Carte MSS. 226 fol. 419. Bodleian Library, Oxford.

George Granville, Lord Lansdowne, to James Edward Stuart, 16 December 1720. Stuart Papers (cited by kind permission of Her Majesty the Queen), 59/100. Royal Archives, Windsor.

19

Alexander Geddes (1737–1802)

Biblical Criticism, Ecclesiastical Democracy, and Jacobinism

MARK GOLDIE

Alexander Geddes pressed the Catholic Enlightenment to its limits, and beyond. He appalled conservative contemporaries in three domains: scriptural, ecclesiastical, and political. Yet although he took his positions to extremes, he reflected several characteristic strands of late eighteenth-century Catholicism, which would be obliterated in the ultramontane revanche of the following century. From the wider culture he absorbed German hermeneutics, French Gallicanism and Jacobinism, English Protestant "Rational Dissent," and European literary Romanticism. He was arguably the most wayward, unorthodox, iconoclastic, and intellectually daring priest to emerge from the British Catholic community of his time. Virulent and doctrinaire, Geddes broke the boundaries. The Catholic community sought a vernacular Bible: he embarked on one, but ended by deconstructing the text and doubting its divine inspiration. The Catholic laity sought ecclesiastical autonomy from the hierarchy: Geddes savaged the papacy and leveled the episcopate. Catholics aimed for civil emancipation: Geddes turned republican.

Geddes was a native of Scotland, but one who established his reputation—and notoriety—in England. Born on 4 September 1737 in Rathven, Aberdeenshire, he was the son of tenant farmers and belonged to Scotland's small and fearful Catholic community. After elementary schooling, he trained for the priesthood at the clandestine seminary of Scalan before migrating to the Scots College in Paris in 1751, where as a student of the Sorbonne he excelled in ancient languages. Returning to Scotland in 1764, he became chaplain at Traquair House, Peebleshire, but was sacked in 1768 for falling in love and for crossing the authority of his bishop, George Hay (1729–1811). From 1769 to 1781, he was priest at Auchinhalrig in Aberdeenshire. Remarkably for a Catholic, he was awarded the degree of LLD by Aberdeen University, for his *Select Satires of Horace*. However, his attendance at a Protestant act of worship cost him his cure, and he escaped his antagonist Bishop Hay by withdrawing to England, where he secured the patronage of a leading liberal Catholic layman, Robert Lord Petre of Thorndon (1741–1801), Essex, and settled in London. He took with him the wary friendship of his cousin, Bishop John Geddes (1735–1799), Hay's colleague.

Geddes abandoned priestly duties and turned to scholarship, interspersed with journalism, polemic, and feuding. He pursued his ambition to produce a new translation of the Bible for British Catholics (a *Prospectus* appeared in 1786), soon superseded by an impossibly ambitious (and never completed) plan for a full variorum edition of the Old Testament, for which he had support from the Anglican scholars Robert Lowth (1710–1787) and Benjamin Kennicott (1718–1783). This in turn led to increasingly skeptical exegeses, grounded in accenting the moral over the literal truth of biblical mythologies. Shortly after publication of the first volume of his *Holy Bible* (1792), Geddes was condemned by the Vicars Apostolic and suspended from the priesthood. His biblical work influenced William Blake (1757–1827) and Samuel Taylor Coleridge (1772–1834). Geddes was himself a poet, whose anonymous work has been confused with that of Robert Burns and has recently been celebrated as evidence of the vibrancy of Scottish national and radical literary culture. He applied his philological expertise to the Scots poetic tradition, his analysis being published by the Edinburgh Society of Antiquaries in a paper still used by dialectologists (Geddes 1792b).

In Petre's circle, Geddes became a leading voice of the "Cisalpine" movement, which sought for Catholics within the Protestant British state both civil emancipation and ecclesiastical emancipation from the papacy. He and his colleagues declared British Catholics to be "Protesting Catholic Dissenters." In politics, he was a radical Whig and espoused such causes as antislavery, civil liberties for Dissenters, and the American and French revolutions, pursuing his republicanism long after Edmund Burke rendered such enthusiasm hazardous. He belonged to the network of "Rational Dissenters," gathered around the publisher Joseph Johnson (1738–1809), for whom (alongside the feminist Mary Wollstonecraft [1759–1797]) he wrote extensively in the *Analytical Review*. Punishing days at his desk were rewarded with beguiling literary dinner parties laced with iconoclasm, satire, and gossip. Geddes was coruscating and made enemies, but the animus was not only personal, for his themes were emblematic of the values and fragilities of the Catholic Enlightenment. We shall examine in turn scriptural scholarship, ecclesiology, and secular politics.

Biblical Hermeneutics

In Marylebone, London, daily for twenty years, Geddes examined multiple editions and manuscripts of the Old Testament, poring over polyglots, collating, and teasing out textual variations, corruptions, and redactions. His linguistic command was formidable: Greek, Latin, Hebrew, French, Spanish, German, Dutch. The initial ambition was modest: to translate the Bible into modern English. Contrary to Protestant mythology, British Catholics were not denied access to the vernacular Bible. In Geddes's own childhood he had learned the English Bible by heart. But the long-established Douai version was outdated, and Bishop Richard Challoner (1691–1781) had made a start on a new one. Geddes quickly rejected Douai as a model, because it derived from Jerome's Latin Vulgate and not the Hebrew and Greek originals. His new project was intended to be, as it were, a literary iceberg: a polished translation for ordinary readers visible above the waterline of vast textual research lying below. The project, or at least its explicatory apparatus, rapidly got out of hand, and only two of eight volumes were completed (Geddes 1792a; 1797). A scholar who could devote eleven pages of footnote commentary to verse 1 of the Bible was never likely to finish.

Though his mind turned increasingly to fundamental questions about the authenticity of the received biblical texts, he remained interested in the etiquette of vernacular translation. Faithfulness to the original should not yield to slavish literalness. But anxious to avoid archaism, he leaned too far to contemporary usage, and was thought colloquial and anachronistic. The effect was to bring Hebrew tribesmen into Hanoverian drawing rooms. Thus, "candlestick" became "chandelier," and seeking to avoid ancient fables, he replaced "unicorn" with "rhinoceros." He could be bland: "Shiloh" became "peaceful prosperity."

The orthodox readily allowed that there were ambiguities in translating the sacred text into the vernacular. However, the broaching of deeper levels of hermeneutic difficulty soon aroused anxiety. The comparison of different manuscripts revealed thousands of variations: plainly the ancient copyists had made mistakes. Only by painstaking collation and redaction analysis could the urtext be established. Worse, ancient written Hebrew was "unpointed": it lacked diacritical marks indicating vowel sounds. Where ambiguity arose, establishing the intended word entailed minute philological exploration of the contextual meanings of Hebrew vocabulary.

Even the urtext seemed to lack coherence. Johann Eichhorn (1753–1827) in Germany and Jean Astruc (1684–1766) in France had suggested that the book of Genesis was a compilation of two earlier sources: the "documentary hypothesis." Geddes thought the sources even more heterogeneous than that: the "fragment hypothesis." This notion was developed in turn by Johann Severin Vater (1771–1826), who translated Geddes's *Critical Remarks on the Hebrew Scriptures*

(1800a) into German: the "Geddes-Vater" hypothesis. Geddes was a voracious reader of the new German "higher criticism," and he bewailed the fact that "sacred criticism" and "sacred philology" were shunned in Britain. He doubted the conventional view that Moses had written the Pentateuch: the probable author of Genesis was Ezra. This alone was enough to damn him, for the Ezra hypothesis had been the leitmotif of scriptural freethinkers ever since it was bruited by the "atheists" Thomas Hobbes and Baruch Spinoza.

Geddes's greatest claim to originality—though chiefly in propagating Eichhorn's ideas in Britain—lay in an exegetical method that marks a watershed between Enlightenment and modern criticism. This was the rejection of naturalism in favor of a mythological reading of the Genesis narratives. Eighteenth-century natural theology deployed vast ingenuity in proposing scientific explanations for the miracles and wonders of the Old Testament. How far Geddes broke with naturalism is unclear. He still, in the style of Casaubon (1559–1614), devoted energy to naturalistic explanations for supposedly miraculous occurrences. Thus, of Lot's wife being turned into a pillar of salt, he wrote that "she was probably struck by lightning, and crusted over with nitre" (Geddes 1792a, 31). However, whereas the natural theologians explained the seven days of creation in terms of ancient calendric conventions and provided a course in geography to locate the garden of Eden, Geddes pronounced the creation narrative a "myth," a symbol-laden heuristic of the natural and human condition. He thus decisively shifted the temper of biblical understanding from science to poetry. The mythological hypothesis detached the Bible from natural philosophy and forged a new connection with literature. The Pentateuch was, in his view, the effort of an ancient scholar-editor to bring order to a patchwork of bardic cosmogonies, perhaps still orally transmitted; it was a compilation of "popular traditions, old songs and public registers" (Geddes 1792a, iv).

It was in making known in Britain the work of German higher criticism and in his mythological theory that Geddes made his most significant impact, for Anglican scholarship was conspicuously slow to absorb these developments. He had an unexpectedly fruitful influence upon Coleridge, who likewise urged the bardic and mythopoeic character of the Pentateuch. Geddes knew Coleridge in the 1790s, providing him with a letter of introduction to Heinrich Paulus (1761–1851) in Germany. Geddes probably also knew William Blake, and here the influence is striking. In 1794 Blake published the *Book of Urizen,* a daring skit, which has the format of the English Bible, with numbered verses, but whose every surviving copy is at textual variance and contains self-contradictory narratives. It is a parody of the book of Genesis and mimics its textual instability. "Urizen" is the god of boundaries, a god of tyrannizing priests and moralists who requisition folkloric tales and transform them into oppressive legal codes. In Blake's hands, Geddes's proof that the Bible is mythic poetry was converted into a critique of priestcraft.

To suggest that Scripture was in need of textual reconstruction implied that there was corruption or impurity in divine revelation. Geddes was rightly accused of treating the Bible like any other ancient and problematic text. The restoring of classical texts was, he said, the glory of the age of rational humanism inaugurated by Erasmus. In recovering the texts of Virgil, Horace, and Cicero, "no pains have been spared; libraries have been ransacked, manuscripts collated, parallel places compared, history, geography, and criticism alternately called into assistance." That was the achievement of the Renaissance; the transcendent scholarly task of modern times was the application of the same techniques to the Bible. The medievals had failed: they built a rubbish heap of glosses and paraphrases without attending to the text itself (Geddes 1786, 2–3).

Inevitably, Geddes was accused of doubting divine inspiration. He certainly rejected the principle that every iota was irrefragable. God did not guarantee the punctuation, or even the word order. It was not only textual fragility that led him thither, but also the fastidiousness of Enlightenment ethical sensibility, in the face of the wrathful and arbitrary Jehovah of the Old Testament. God's command to massacre the Canaanite males while sparing female virgins simply could not, he held, be countenanced as an authentic divine injunction. Like so many in his century, Geddes was apt to collapse Christian ethics into natural morality. He remarked that what he admired in the Bible was what he admired in Plato, Cicero, and Marcus Aurelius. He verged on the deistical: while "the gospel of Jesus Christ is my religious code," "that gospel I would not make my law, if Reason, pure Reason, were not my prompter and preceptress" (Geddes 1800a, vi).

Geddes believed that anthropology and archaeology held vital keys to biblical understanding. He assumed that the contemporary Near East preserved biblical society in aspic, Bedouin chiefs being latter-day Hebrew patriarchs. In the 1760s, Johann David Michaelis (1717–1791) proposed an expedition to the Near East to examine local customs and languages, and Carsten Niebuhr (1733–1815) took up the challenge. Anthropological understanding of nomadic pastoralists was thought to be a means to access the ancient Hebrew mind. Geddes thought biblical cultures fundamentally "Oriental." The credulity of "eastern nations" explained much. His anthropological distancing of Western modernity from the "Oriental" allowed him to extract a congenial essence from the dross of Asiatic barbarism that he found in the biblical narrative. In turn, Geddes applied to biblical society the theory of stages of human development enunciated by Adam Smith and other Scottish social theorists. The ancient Hebrews belonged to the nomadic pastoral phase of civilization. God revealed himself to humanity progressively, in ways appropriate to the understandings and cultures of particular times. Over time, human understanding of the deity became more refined and spiritualized; the ancients were gross "anthropomorphites." The biblical Jehovah was a deity adapted to the mind-set of a "stupid, carnal people" (Geddes 1800a, 25–26). Geddes here approached the religious anthropologies of Lessing (1729–1781) and Herder (1744–1803).

Geddes hoped he had found the secret of a new defense of Christianity. Once we grasp that the Bible was "written in a rude age, by rude and unpolished writers," once we strip away the absurdities attributable to "the genius of the eastern nations" and recover what was pure from its tawdry and "exotic" distortion, once we look for the pure ethics, rational legislation, rustic simplicity, and sublime poetry, then modern men of science and philosophy will no longer be deterred by biblical Christianity. Geddes insisted he was putting the defense of Christianity on a new plane. If we give up the hopeless task of defending the "absolute and plenary inspiration" of Scripture and adopt new critical principles, then we can destroy the weaponry of Christianity's enemies, who ridicule revelation. Geddes proclaimed that his new edition would defeat the "wit of Voltaire, the scurrility of Boulanger, the declamations of Diderot . . . the sarcasms of Paine" (Geddes 1797, xii–xiii). Though hermeneutically daring, he regarded himself as a misunderstood defender of orthodoxy. Not a little tinged by paranoia, Geddes's resentment at his critics grew. How could the ambition to produce the definitive edition of mankind's definitive book meet with such suspicion and finally condemnation?

Cisalpine Ecclesiology

Geddes was violently anti-episcopal and antipapal. When the Vicars Apostolic condemned him in 1789, he denounced their "clerical despotism," and Bishop James Talbot of London he called a "strutting . . . little pontifex" (Geddes 1787b; Geddes 1790a, 1). Yet for all his virulence, his ecclesiological positions were typical of "Cisalpine" Catholicism. Geddes was a spokesman for the English Catholic Committee, which renamed itself the Cisalpine Club in 1792. A movement predominantly of lay gentry, the club espoused a kind of Congregationalist Catholicism. Its ideology mirrored the sociological character of English "seigneurial Catholicism," wherein the lay gentry were patrons, guardians, and domestic household heads of their chaplain-clergy. The episcopate was weak (if voluble), and there would be no English diocesan hierarchy until the mid-nineteenth century. Geddes wrote on behalf of the autonomy of the English Catholic community, alongside other Cisalpine priests—Joseph Berington, John Throckmorton, and Charles Butler—whose stance was not only directed against Rome, but was also designed to render Catholicism amenable to its Protestant host nation.

Geddes played a role in smoothing the path of Prime Minister William Pitt's Catholic Relief Act of 1791, which finally permitted Catholics to worship openly. When the ministry raised the conventional objection that Catholics were suspect citizens because the papacy claimed temporal power, Geddes drew up a memorandum refuting the doctrine that popes could depose heretical rulers. Liberal Catholicism sought to suppress the taint of the "papal deposing power" which had haunted the Protestant imagination since the Reformation. The Relief Bill involved a new oath of allegiance, the draft terms of which brought the Catholic gentry to the brink of schism from the Vicars Apostolic, who objected to undue concessions to the Protestant state and also to the phrase "Protesting Catholic Dissenters." The Cisalpines responded by asserting that the Vicars Apostolic should be elected by the clergy and laity and not imposed by Rome.

These positions were a variant of a Europe-wide phenomenon, the profoundly antipapal (and sometimes anti-episcopal) tendency of the Catholic Enlightenment. A bewildering variety of terms describes this movement: "jurisdictionalism," "Gallicanism," "Richerism," "Febronianism," "Josephism." They took their root in late medieval conciliarism, which asserted the authority of church councils, national churches, and secular rulers against the papacy. Another term must be added—"Jansenism"—which, by the eighteenth century, had lost much of its Augustinian theological character and had become a loose name for lay and clerical resistance to impositions by the hierarchy. These tendencies reached their apogee in the Synod of Pistoia in 1787, presided over by Bishop Scipio Ricci and the Emperor Joseph II's brother Leopold, and in the Civil Constitution of the Clergy proclaimed by the French Revolution in 1790. Geddes admired what he saw on the Continent. In the opening page of his attack on Bishop Talbot (1726–1790) in 1790 he applauded the Synod of Pistoia. The English bishops' dependence on the papacy was a "spiritual vassalage, which your brethren on the Continent begin to be ashamed of. . . . The good bishop of Pistoia . . . has set the example, even in Italy" (Geddes 1790a, 1). He remarked that British Catholics should follow the Emperor Joseph, who refused to hold the pope's stirrup. "I cannot . . . but approve of all that Joseph has hitherto done," in reforming the monasteries, curtailing papal authority, and granting religious toleration (Geddes 1784).

Geddes reprinted the French Gallican decrees of 1682 (Geddes 1800b). He was thoroughly familiar with the writings of the Gallican ecclesiologists of the previous two centuries: Richer, De Marca, Fleury,

Dupin, and Launoy. English Catholicism subsisted, or ought to subsist, he wrote, under "Gallican maxims" and not Bellarminian, in reference to the Counter-Reformation papalist Cardinal Robert Bellarmine. Like all jurisdictionalists, Geddes relished the suppression of the Jesuit order. He was also familiar with the conciliarist tradition (Gerson, Almain, d'Ailly, Mair), admiring the great Council of Constance of 1415, which had deposed three popes, armed with "irrefragable arguments against papal despotism." The false doctrine of the primacy of Rome made "the kingdom of Christ into an absolute autocracy." In his anger at the Vicars Apostolic, Geddes turned his guns also on episcopal despotism (Geddes 1800b, 95, 98, 126). The authority of the church was not uniquely inherent in the persons of bishops. It is scarcely surprising that the future bishop John Milner accused the Cisalpines of "ecclesiastical democracy" (Milner 1793).

In Geddes's mind, his denial of papal temporal power unavoidably implicated also the spiritual power—the doctrine of papal infallibility—for if the pope were infallible it must follow, he thought, that he could dispense with oaths, including the oath of allegiance. Speaking of a hostile Catholic colleague, Geddes professed himself amazed that "towards the close of the eighteenth century" anyone could defend "the infallibility of the Roman See, like a true disciple of Bellarmine" (*Analytical Review* 1791, 524). Papal infallibility was "absurd ... pernicious ... the spurious child of arrogance and ignorance." The pope was merely the first pastor of the church in honor and dignity, and Geddes noted that such Protestants as James I, Grotius, and Leibniz had recognized as much. He believed that the papacy's "usurped empire" was falling away and that Catholicism was liberating itself from the papacy's "spiritual subjugation of the western world" (Geddes 1800b, 59, 76). In hindsight, there is a grand irony in Geddes's position: he thought himself a spearhead for the future, yet at the moment he was making these pronouncements, Chateaubriand and Barruel were beginning to give ideological shape to the dramatic refurbishment of the ideal of papal supremacy that would dominate the nineteenth and much of the twentieth centuries.

Gallicans tended to be Erastian, deferential to civil authority, echoing Protestant notions of the "godly prince," as a counterbalance to ecclesiastical authority. Joseph II governed the Austrian Catholic Church as Henry VIII had the English. The English Cisalpines were ambiguous about the role of the state. As a penalized minority in an Anglican state, they tended to borrow the attitudes of Protestant Dissenters, condemning church establishments and state interference in the lives and consciences of religious minorities. They voiced the Lockean doctrine that a church was merely a voluntary association unconnected with civil magistracy. Geddes chimed with Locke in attacking established churches as mere "favorite sects," which became servile flatterers of states, which in requital supported their incomes and jurisdictions. "Why at all join state and church?" he asked (Geddes 1795, 7–9, 14). Yet it could seem equally natural that even a minority religion should allow some measure of ecclesiastical authority to the civil power—much as the French Huguenots had for so long clung to the coattails of French Catholic absolute monarchy as their protector. Some English Catholics argued that the British Protestant crown should have a veto over Catholic episcopal appointments, again as a counterbalance to Rome. Geddes looked forward to a time when British Catholics would "form a small, but still a national church," and he noted, with Vienna and Pistoia in mind, that the Continental churches were reformed "under the protection of the civil power" (Geddes 1794, 32, 38). He also constantly asserted the Englishness of native Catholics. The "Catholic" was distinct from the "papist."

In turn, Geddes followed a distinctive tradition of melioration of Catholic spiritual practice, seeking to present Catholicism with a quasi-Protestant face. This was the spirituality of the European margins, where minority Catholicism sought to camouflage itself and meld with the religious culture of the host community. Every modern Catholic, he wrote, "must blush" at the excrescences and corruptions of the popish centuries. There had indeed been "idle pilgrimages, the base traffic in indulgences, the propagation of lying legends, feigned miracles, apocryphal revelations," and ferocious inquisitions. Geddes thought pilgrimages were "useless, obsolete things"; "beads, rosaries, medals, agnus deis, scapulas, etc." were but "pious play-things, for old women and children." He was ready to abolish them all (Geddes 1800b, 6–7, 93, 221–22).

For Geddes, the Catholic Church should not be immune from the progressive development of humanity that seemed manifest in the enlightened age. Catholicism was not static, but had a capacity for progressive evolution and intellectual maturation. Again, as in his biblical hermeneutics, he adopted a historicist progressivism. The church's antique barbarisms had no place in our own time. When a Protestant remarked that a returning apostle would be horrified at the sight of modern Catholic worship, Geddes blithely retorted that that should be no surprise: modern peoples worship in modern ways, primitive peoples in primitive ways. And, he added, the apostle would be just as puzzled by the Methodist chapel in Tottenham Court Road as by High Mass in St. Peter's (Geddes 1783, 23).

Geddes, then, rejoiced that he lived "in a more enlightened and less superstitious age" and that "a considerable revolution" in the minds of Catholics had occurred. During the previous three centuries, Catholicism had been overhauled; the "cloud of superstition, which gathered during the ages of ignorance . . . [had] been continually dissipating," so that the church could soon bask in "the gentle sunshine of a rational philosophy." Across Europe, for example, idle festivals had been removed from the calendar, and "frugal industry" had taken their place: here Geddes echoed Protestant deprecation of the unproductive religious holidays that rendered Catholic nations economically stagnant. Yet the task of reform was far from complete: the liturgy must be put into the vernacular, clerical celibacy abolished, and religious orders curtailed (Geddes 1783, 27–28; 1800b, 8, 13–14).

Geddes was by no means entirely deferential to the liberal Protestant mind-set. Like a good Humean, he thought religion should find a middle way between superstition and "enthusiasm," and that if Catholicism had erred too far in its "ceremonious" appeals to the senses, so Protestantism was apt to slide perniciously toward the fanatical "enthusiasm" of the misguided spirit. Furthermore, British Protestants were woeful citizens if they did not concede full toleration to Catholics and Dissenters. He was scathing about Scottish Presbyterian bigotry revealed in the anti-Catholic riots of 1779, as also about English bigotry in the Gordon Riots the following year—London's most violent mayhem for a century and directed against Catholics. In the face of these manifestations, he could suggest that much of contemporary Catholic Europe was more civilized, and that even Spain might better claim to be among the "most enlightened and liberal nations in Europe." When a British Protestant published a tract against Catholics, Geddes spoke of its "disgusting illiberality of sentiment unworthy of this enlightened and tolerant age" (Geddes 1783, 6, 22; 1787a, 29; 1800b, 142–44).

Jacobin Catholicism

Down to the mid-eighteenth century British Catholics were almost all Jacobites, supporters of the fallen Catholic House of Stuart, deposed in the Revolution of 1688. The crushing of the last Jacobite rebellion in 1746 forced the final dissolution of the cause. Remarkably, within a generation many Catholics had moved over, not to Toryism, but to Whiggism, and some even to republicanism and Jacobinism. Whiggery was the party of Protestant Dissent and of the campaign to remove the remaining civil disabilities upon non-Anglicans. The Cisalpines' use of the phrase "Protesting Catholic Dissenters" was a deliberate attempt to align the cause of Catholic emancipation with that of Dissent. In 1792, when the Vicars Apostolic issued a pastoral letter condemning the Cisalpines, one pro-episcopal commentator expressed himself pleased that their "diabolical ... republican and leveling principles" had been proscribed (Duffy 1970, 323–24). Biblical criticism, ecclesiastical collegialism, and Whig politics now came collectively to be tarred with the brush of philosophical and political anarchism. By this point, Edmund Burke's (1729–1797) thundering condemnation of radical politics and speculative theology, in his *Reflections on the Revolution in France* (1790), carried all before it. Nevertheless, Geddes could scarcely complain that it was a false aspersion to connect biblical scholarship with republican politics, for his politics were explicit in the 1792 preface to his *Holy Bible*. There he turned the Hebrew commonwealth into a republic and Moses into a Jacobin. "The scheme of government which Moses presents to them [the Jews], is a pure republic.... Although he makes no formal declaration of the

Rights of Man, all his decrees . . . are evidently founded on that principle." In Israel "all magistrates [were] chosen by the people." Land was shared, and poverty relieved by public authority. Monarchy was later established only because the Jews, in their folly, asked God for a king, and God, in his wrath, granted one (Geddes 1792a, xiii–xv). Critics accordingly ranked Geddes's Bible alongside Thomas Paine's (1737–1809) incendiary *Age of Reason* (1794). Hermeneutics were now subversive, an association which retarded the scholarly reception of German higher criticism.

Geddes applauded the French Revolution. The constitution of 1790 was "one of the greatest efforts of political genius" (Geddes 1790b). His ode, *Carmen Saeculare* (1790), was intended to be read to the French National Assembly. Here he rejoiced at the liberation of the French from "Egyptian servitude." The peoples of Europe should "at the patriot altar swear, / Eternal war with tyranny." He used Thomas Paine's clarion cry of the "Rights of Man," and argued that the "rights of man" extended to the emancipation of African slaves. Geddes swung ambiguously between conventional acceptance of the British constitutional trinity of king, lords, and commons, for it putatively embodied the classical balance of monarchy, aristocracy, and democracy, and a more downright democratic impulse. Like his friends in the Society for Constitutional Information, he called for "a more equal representation of the people," and regretted that the word "republican" was anathema in Britain, whereas it was the acme of political virtue in ancient Rome and the modern United States. He was present at the society's discussion of the American revolutionary Joel Barlow's (1754–1812) *Address to the French National Convention*. Like others in radical circles, he attacked corrupt aristocracies, called hereditary nobility an "absurd institution," and hoped for an "elective senate" (Geddes 1793, 12–18; 1794, 10; 1795, 10).

Geddes remained a friend of France long after most British enthusiasts for the Revolution had reneged: after the Terror, the mass exodus of Catholic priests to England, and the British declaration of war. During the sedition trials in the mid-1790s he was at risk. He abhorred the repression of "shoemakers and tailors talking about mending the constitution," and savaged the new British "holy league . . . to save the sacred rights of kings." His friends begged him to cease making public political utterances, for his own safety. He spat venom against the Burkean scribblers, the self-appointed "loyal and orthodox," the reactionary rants filling High Church pulpits, and was aghast at the betrayal of revolution principles by those free spirits who at first celebrated them. Geddes knew Burke personally, as did others involved in politicking for Catholic emancipation, for Burke was a protoleration Whig. Geddes now thought him a Judas. Like a number of modern commentators, he could not reconcile the earlier "liberal" and later "conservative" Burke. The *Reflections,* he thought, was a work of "glorious bombast," "flimsy [and] unphilosophical," which had "ruined [Burke's] reputation as a friend of freedom" (Geddes 1798, 15, 21, 29–31, 34; Scottish Catholic Archives, Edinburgh, MS P-AG 5; Geddes 1790c, 1791).

At the hub of British radical circles in the 1780s and 1790s was the publisher Joseph Johnson. To his house in St. Paul's Churchyard came Richard Price and Joseph Priestley, William Godwin, Joel Barlow, Thomas Paine, Horne Tooke, Anna Barbauld, Mary Wollstonecraft, and Maria Edgeworth. Johnson published Wollstonecraft's *Vindication of the Rights of Woman* and Godwin's *Political Justice,* though he was frightened off by Paine's *Rights of Man*. Geddes mingled with these people, for example, visiting the leader of the "Rational Dissenters," Priestley (1733–1804), in Birmingham. He was close to the authors Barbauld and Mary Hays, author of *Appeal to the Men of Great Britain in Behalf of Women,* and also to leading Unitarians, such as Gilbert Wakefield, Theophilus Lindsay, and Crabb Robinson. Wollstonecraft and Geddes were (anonymous) workhorse reviewers of recent publications for Johnson's *Analytical Review,* launched in 1788. She covered chiefly education and fiction, and he biblical criticism and ecclesiastical history. The *Analytical* allowed Geddes to disseminate Cisalpine Catholic ideas to a Protestant readership, although this involved alerting his audience to the savage intramural quarrels among the English Catholics. Johnson, a Dissenter, published many Cisalpine tracts; the episcopal party, meanwhile, took theirs to James Peter Coghlan, the principal Catholic publisher of the time, about whose bookshop and its clientele Geddes was predictably splenetic.

Johnson was jailed for sedition in 1798, and the *Analytical* closed. It was the future Catholic bishop John Milner who publicly suggested that Geddes was linked to the Edinburgh Catholic Jacobins, and that he should, like them, be transported to Australia for treason. In 1794 David Downie was condemned to death, a sentence commuted to transportation. His codefendant, William Maxwell, had been present at the guillotining of Louis XVI and was the target of Burke's notorious "daggers speech" in the House of Commons, in which Burke insinuated a British terrorist conspiracy. How far Geddes was in fact involved with Downie and Maxwell remains uncertain. An unpublished poem of his, "The Irish *Ca ira*," suggested that the French Revolution should inspire the Irish to revolt against British rule—which indeed they did in 1798. Geddes seems never to have abandoned his Francophilia, and his alienation from British politics culminated, the following year, in his (again unpublished) ode to Napoleon Bonaparte as mankind's liberator from despotism (Scottish Catholic Archives, Edinburgh, MS P-AG 5).

By the mid-1790s, the English and Scottish Catholic bishops were at war with the Cisalpines, and everything in the ambient culture and politics of the British nations now conspired their way. Geddes's old adversary in Edinburgh, Bishop Hay, drafted a pastoral letter in 1793 hymning the praises of Britain's gracious monarchy and constitution and reviling the philosophical atheism of the French Enlightenment—naming Holbach and Rousseau—and its consequence, the leveling anarchism of the French and British Jacobins (Scottish Catholic Archives, Edinburgh, SM 15/2/8). He sent a complimentary copy to Burke. Meanwhile in London, Bishop Talbot condemned the Cisalpines and biblical criticism. The British Catholic Enlightenment had reached its limits and would now meet its nemesis. In the wake of Edmund Burke, a Protestant who contributed more to the remodeling of Catholicism than Catholics might care to admit, Geddes could only belong with the damned. Though intellectually and temperamentally an extremist, Geddes had done no more than extrapolate and pursue a reductio of the intellectual tendencies of the European Catholic Enlightenment. His fate was tied up with that Enlightenment, the collapse of which now ensued.

After a prodigious publishing career, Geddes died in London on 26 February 1802 and was buried in St. Mary's churchyard, Paddington. Since his death, his reputation has depended on the tectonic shifts in Catholic opinion. A contemporary obituarist in the *Gentleman's Magazine* in 1802 pronounced that many Catholics detested him. Milner called him an infidel and anarchist: Christianity and civil order would be destroyed by him as surely as by Robespierre's guillotine. As late as 1911, Geddes was still styled a "heterodox, bad priest" (Ward 1911, 247). However, after the *aggiornamento* of the 1960s, the odium has been dispelled, and his reputation has been remarkably rehabilitated. Recent commentators praise him as ecumenical, social democratic, an advocate of vernacular liturgy, and spokesman for clerical collegiality (Aspinwall 1977). In the 1990s he was celebrated from a cathedral pulpit. These dramatically divergent reputations are, as it were, iterations of the contrasting spirits of the First and Second Vatican Councils, but neither captures the distinctive idiom of the eighteenth-century Catholic Enlightenment.

Note

This work is an abridged and revised version of Mark Goldie, "Alexander Geddes at the Limits of the Catholic Enlightenment," *Historical Journal* 53, no. 1 (2010): 61–86. © Cambridge University Press, reproduced with permission.

Bibliography

Analytical Review. 1791. London: J. Johnson.
Aspinwall, Bernard. 1977. "The Last Laugh of a Humane Faith: Dr. Alexander Geddes, 1737–1801." *New Blackfriars* 58:333–40.
Carruthers, Gerard. 1999. "Alexander Geddes and the Burns 'Lost Poems' Controversy." *Studies in Scottish Literature* 31:81–85.
Chinnici, John. 1980. *The English Catholic Enlightenment: John Lingard and the Cisalpine Movement, 1780–1850*. Shepherdstown, WV: Patmos Press.
Ditchfield, Grayson M. 2000. "English Catholics and Unitarians in the Age of Milner." *Recusant History* 25:52–73.
Duffy, Eamon. 1970. "Ecclesiastical Democracy Detected." *Recusant History* 10:193–209, 309–31.

Fuller, Reginald C. 1984. *Alexander Geddes, 1737–1802: Pioneer of Biblical Criticism.* Sheffield: Sheffield Academic Press.

Geddes, Alexander. 1775. Letter to George Hay, 27 February. Blairs Letters 3/271/7. Scottish Catholic Archives, Edinburgh.

———. 1783. *Cursory Remarks on a Late Fanatical Publication.* London: R. Faulder.

———. 1784. Letter to John Geddes, 27 February. Blairs Letters 3/404/4. Scottish Catholic Archives, Edinburgh.

———. 1786. *Prospectus of a New Translation of the Holy Bible.* London: J. Johnson.

———. 1787a. *Letter to a Member of Parliament.* London: R. Faulder.

———. 1787b. Letter to John Geddes, 13 November. Blairs Letters 4/4/14. Scottish Catholic Archives, Edinburgh.

———. 1790a. *An Answer to the Bishop of Comana.* London: R. Faulder.

———. 1790b. Letter to John Geddes, 18 January. Blairs Letters 4/23/9. Scottish Catholic Archives, Edinburgh.

———. 1790c. Letter to John Geddes, 29 November. Blairs Letters 4/23/10. Scottish Catholic Archives, Edinburgh.

———. 1791. 15 February. Blairs Letters 4/42/8. Scottish Catholic Archives, Edinburgh.

———. 1792a. *The Holy Bible.* Vol. 1. London: R. Faulder.

———. 1792b. "Three Scottish Poems, with a Previous Dissertation on the Scoto-Saxon Dialect." *Transactions of the Society of Antiquaries of Scotland* 1:402–68.

———. 1793. *Dr. Geddes's Address to the Public.* London: J. Johnson.

———. 1794. *Letter from the Rev. Alexander Geddes.* London: J. Johnson.

———. 1795. *Ode to the Hon. Thomas Pelham.* London: R. Faulder.

———. 1797. *The Holy Bible.* Vol. 2. London: R. Faulder.

———. 1798. *A New Year's Gift to the Good People of England.* [London?]

———. 1800a. *Critical Remarks on the Hebrew Scriptures.* London: R. Faulder.

———. 1800b. *A Modest Apology for the Roman Catholics.* London: R. Faulder.

Goldie, Mark. 1991. "The Scottish Catholic Enlightenment." *Journal of British Studies* 30:20–62.

———. 2010. "Alexander Geddes at the Limits of the Catholic Enlightenment." *Historical Journal* 53:61–86.

Good, John M. 1803. *Memoirs of the Life and Writings of the Revd. Alexander Geddes.* London: G. Kearsley.

Gordon, James F. S. 1875. *Ecclesiastical Chronicle for Scotland.* Glasgow.

Johnstone, William, ed. 2004. *The Bible and the Enlightenment: A Case Study; Dr. Alexander Geddes.* London: T&T Clark.

McGann, Jerome J. 1986. "The Idea of an Indeterminate Text: Blake's Bible of Hell and Dr. Alexander Geddes." *Studies in Romanticism* 25:303–24.

Milner, John. 1793. *Ecclesiastical Democracy Detected*. London: J. P. Coghlan.

Shaffer, E. S. 1975. *"Kubla Khan" and the Fall of Jerusalem: The Mythological School in Biblical Criticism and Secular Literature, 1770–1880*. Cambridge: Cambridge University Press.

Ward, Bernard. 1911. *The Eve of Catholic Emancipation*. London: Longman.

PART 9
The Polish Catholic Enlightenment

20

Stanisław Konarski
(1700–1772)

A Polish Machiavelli?

JERZY LUKOWSKI

Hieronim Konarski was known invariably by the first name of Stanisław, which he received when he entered the Order of Poor Clerics Regular of the Mother of God of the Pious Schools (commonly known as the Piarists). He was born on 30 September 1700, at Żarczyce in what is now central Poland. His little village was situated toward the southwest corner of the largest state in Europe after Russia, sprawling eastward from the German lands, taking in what is now most of Poland, all of Lithuania, and much of Belarus and Ukraine, a gigantic patchwork which had been united under the Lithuanian Jagiellon dynasty after 1386.

The Commonwealth of Poland-Lithuania in the Eighteenth Century

The impressive extent of Konarski's Poland, officially known as the Commonwealth of the Two Nations (*Rzeczpospolita*), comprising both Poles and Lithuanians, masked uncomfortable realities. Between 1648 and 1667, it had been crippled by rebellions and wars with its neighbors, which had cumulatively inflicted at least as much damage as the Thirty Years' War had on Germany. In 1700, it was about to be dragged into the Great Northern War, that prolonged duel between Charles XII of Sweden and Peter the Great of Russia, which was to come to an end only in 1721, ultimately inflicting at least as much damage again. Underlying so many economic and demographic losses were the strains of a dysfunctional governance. The commonwealth belonged to its nobility or *szlachta,* some 6 percent of a population of perhaps ten million. Some twenty aristocratic clans dominated, but half the nobility were little more than landless and often illiterate paupers. Konarski himself, the youngest of eleven children, came from an impoverished family. One thing united the szlachta: they alone constituted the free citizens of their commonwealth.

The szlachta alone had the right to participate in public life and to legislate, through their parliament, the Sejm. They could not be arrested unless caught in flagrante and could be sentenced only after due process. Taxation required their assent. They largely elected their own judiciary. They held a near-monopoly on landownership and complete jurisdiction, including powers of life and death, over the serfs who worked their private estates. Their local parliamentary assemblies, the *sejmiki,* elected envoys (*posłowie*) to the Sejm and furnished them with binding (in theory) instructions. The properties they owned in towns were largely exempt from municipal jurisdiction. The szlachta constantly feared the loss of their freedoms, a fear they identified with, and directed principally against, their own monarchs, for much the same reasons as monarchs throughout Europe were so often identified by privileged nobilities, corporations, and traditional estates as the greatest threat to liberty. So history was their guide, and in particular the history of ancient Rome, whose stories, thought, and rhetoric constituted the major plank of their education. Only unceasing vigilance and corrections during interregna kept the threat in check. Their monarchy was elective; all adult male nobles could vote in the election, which, moreover, had to be unanimous; monarchs were forbidden to work for the election of a successor during their lifetimes—a formal interregnum followed the death of each monarch, not only to elect a successor but to review the reign of the deceased incumbent, to put right any illegalities, and to lay down conditions under which the new king would rule.

The political bonds that kept the commonwealth together were loose. Since the Union of Lublin of 1569, it had possessed in its Sejm a single national parliament, but that parliament was always weak: shackled by mandatory instructions and hobbled by powerful regionalisms, the Sejm had never developed into a dynamic, dominating forum in the manner of the parliament of England. It was more concerned with the preservation of noble freedoms than with the sculpting of the state and the framing of legislation. It had always mistrusted majority voting, for majorities could all too easily be corrupted by the king's extensive powers of patronage. Therefore, the Sejm had always sought to reach decisions by consensus, and preferably always by an overwhelmingly large consensus. In 1652 this collective preference had reached the point where a single parliamentary envoy could succeed in bringing proceedings to a halt. Poland's *liberum veto* had emerged, a device which not only blocked an individual law but wrecked the entire parliamentary session. Increasingly, it paralyzed politics, spreading even to the local assemblies, the sejmiki. During the reign of Augustus III (1733–1763), who was to occupy the throne for the central part of Stanisław Konarski's life span, only one Sejm, that of 1736, succeeded in enacting any legislation.

The wars of the late seventeenth and early eighteenth centuries had drastic cultural and intellectual consequences. Educational establishments suffered badly. The poor quality of teaching on offer in the largest scholarly network in the commonwealth, the Jesuit colleges (around fifty in 1700, over seventy in 1772), was a source of concern to the order's authorities in Rome. Piarist schools were no better. The University of Kraków and the Jesuit Academy of Wilno (Vilnius) were Aristotelian backwaters. The wars drove the nobility to cling to their privileges all the more strongly. To them, deficiencies lay in the failings of human beings, not in a polity dedicated to such undeniable goods as liberty and harmony. In a predominantly Catholic state, trust in Divine Providence counted for more than trust in a powerful army, which could all too easily become an instrument of monarchic absolutism. After 1717, the army counted barely twelve thousand men. The commonwealth gained nothing at the Peace of Nystad, which brought the Great Northern War to an end in 1721. Instead, during the war, Russia managed to make itself the de facto protector of Polish liberties, liberties which kept Poland-Lithuania conveniently weak. Such was Stanisław Konarski's *ojczyzna,* his country.

Educational Background and Reform of the Piarist School System

In 1709, Stanisław was enrolled at the Piarist college at Piotrków. The order, dedicated to the teaching of poor children, was founded in Rome in 1597, but in time cast its social net more widely. In the early eighteenth century, it had twenty schools in Poland and eight in its Lithuanian province. By 1772, the total had grown to thirty-five. It was the commonwealth's second-largest educational organization after the incomparably better-endowed system of the Jesuits. The curriculum was a standard Christian humanist one—prayers and the classics. In 1715, Stanisław entered the Piarist novitiate, and he became a full-fledged priest and teacher in 1717. It was a conventional career choice for the younger son of an indigent noble family.

Whatever the failings of religious orders in Poland, these were international enterprises. Their counterparts elsewhere, notably in France and Italy, were often of an altogether higher caliber. In 1725, the clearly talented Stanisław was sent to Rome, to the Piarists' principal school, the Collegium Nazarenum, run by one of Europe's leading mathematicians, Paolino Chelucci (1681–1754). It was here that he was introduced to a much more progressive educational philosophy, reinforced by a move to Paris in 1729–1730. He was much taken by the views of men like Muratori, Fénelon, Locke, and Rollin on the education of the ruling classes. These experiences persuaded Konarski of one of his great aims in life: to bring Piarist schooling in Poland up to the level of the best of what Europe could offer. His ambitions were delayed. In 1733, following the death of King Augustus II, he found himself, like the majority of Polish nobles, supporting the candidacy of Stanisław Leszczyński (1677–1766) to the Polish throne. However, Leszczyński's rival, Augustus II's son, elector Frederick Augustus III of Saxony, had the support of Austria and Russia—and it was Russian military intervention which secured him the throne. It was at this time that Konarski produced his first major political treatise, *Epistolae ad familiares sub tempus interregni* (*Letters to Friends during the Interregnum*). An elegant plea to respect Polish sovereignty as well as an exercise in persuading the Poles that, without true independence, their liberties meant nothing, it earned him a place on a diplomatic mission to seek French support (Fabre 1952, 55–66, 114–16). Instead, France, nominally engaged on behalf of Leszczyński, King Louis XV's father-in-law, cut its own deal with the Austrians. A disillusioned Konarski, fast rising in his order's hierarchy, returned to educational reform.

His main achievement was the opening in Warsaw of a new educational establishment in 1740, the Collegium Nobilium, aimed consciously at the sons of magnates and wealthier nobles. Its curriculum, toning down traditional Latin, but emphasizing modern languages, mathematics, and the natural sciences, was modeled on that of the progressive knightly academies Konarski had gotten to know in Italy and France. With the backing of senior Polish clergy and of Pope Benedict XIV, Konarski was able to bring about analogous reforms in most of the Piarist establishments of the Polish province, even if traditionalist opposition remained strong. Among his achievements was the cleaning up of Polish rhetoric, hitherto a Baroque hodgepodge of Polish and Latin, into a more straightforwardly classical Polish style—one can trace the changes in the evolution of Konarski's own language. The changes which he and his Piarist collaborators effected even obliged an initially suspicious rival Jesuit order to follow suit. These educational reforms were to produce a new, thinking and patriotic noble elite, which would guide Poland to a better future (Butterwick 1998, 69–73). Konarski's main concern was to fit the szlachta with the skills, principally oratorical and analytical, to conduct the affairs of state. With this in mind, he introduced Polish rhetoric and history, but the bedrock curriculum remained unashamedly classical and Latin based. More modish subjects, principally foreign languages and instruction in the natural sciences, were mainly the preserve of the Collegium Nobilium in Warsaw. It was largely thanks to Konarski that the sort of public scientific demonstrations and experiments which were increasingly common across Europe began to seep gradually into Polish life.

Konarski's educational achievement must be kept in perspective. He was always cautious, particularly in regard to schooling in the provinces. Plays and debates open to a wider public were standard fare in school life, as much in Poland as elsewhere in Europe, but the provincial schools were under firm instructions to avoid controversial issues, such as the *liberum veto* or serfdom. Such topics were, however, aired in the exclusive Warsaw college. Konarski did not question the fundamental structures of the commonwealth, but his writings made clear his disapproval of serfdom and serf exploitation. And even his *School Ordinances* of 1753–1754, regulating education within the Polish province of his order, cursorily made the point that "all men" enjoyed "natural equality; [it is by] fortune and blind chance that one may be born into a noble family. True nobility depends solely on virtue and is an encouragement to it" (Konarski 1955, 2:279). The *Ordinances* applied only to the Polish Province—the separate and more conservative Lithuanian Province actually rejected them. Historians skeptical of the miracle-working powers of a rational education, in which so many enlightened enthusiasts across Europe placed their faith, will not be surprised to learn that the pupils of the Piarist schools remained a mixed bunch, better educated than their predecessors, but by no means uniformly the paragons of patriotic virtue that Konarski hoped to produce.

A Catholic Machiavelli? Konarski's Political Philosophy

Konarski also engaged himself more directly in politics. He may have been of obscure origins, but he had distant connections to some powerful noble families—connections which had been instrumental in his rise to something approaching national prominence. Between 1732 and 1739, under the patronage of a distant relative, Bishop Józef Załuski, Konarski was responsible for producing a six-volume compilation of Polish law, the so-called *Volumina Legum*. Knowledge of that law was to serve him well. Around 1746, he began work on his masterpiece, the four volumes of his *On the Means to Successful Counsels* (*O Skutecznym Rad Sposobie*), which came out in printed form between January 1761 and June 1763.

Where, in all this, does Niccolò Machiavelli come in? Such a comparison would have horrified Konarski, who shared the conventional distaste for the Florentine, as indeed did most Poles (Fabre 1952, 67). Contemplating the annexationist designs of Poland's neighbors, he characterized them as "ever laden with fine words, but in truth, adapted from and brimming with the canons of Machiavelli." Machiavelli was "the evil Machiavelli maliciously [maintaining] that all men are bereft of virtue and bad." Shorn of such sensationalism, Machiavelli was understood by many contemporaries in Europe at the time to have jettisoned the traditionally classical and Christian way of thinking about politics in order to make of politics a theory and practice conducted under its own rationale, according to autonomous rules and guidelines. In both *The Prince* and, to a lesser extent, *The Discourses on Livy,* the old Christian and classical virtues simply formed part of a repertoire of techniques of statesmanship, on a par with mendacity, cruelty, hypocrisy, and other conventional vices (Skinner 1978, 121–38, 156–68).

Konarski did not, of course, advocate the same range of political techniques as did Machiavelli. However, there is a fundamental similarity. Machiavelli wanted to ground politics in the world of practical, concrete, daily realities, taking men as they are, not as how men might wish themselves to be, or how Scripture or classical and conventional writers might say they should be. Konarski wished to do exactly the same for the way in which he thought about politics. Above all, that meant getting rid of that idealized figment of unreality, the *liberum veto*. In the eyes of its defenders, the veto formed the last line of defense against the loss of liberty, a final barrier against attempts to overthrow noble rights and privileges; strictly speaking, then, before Konarski, everyone writing on this subject was the veto's defender. There was criticism, but it was not public. If all else failed, the one indomitable man of virtue could halt despotism in its tracks. Konarski saw things differently: the veto was a pernicious instrument of fiction. To proclaim its utility was to treat as realistic a society in which the full agreement of all was possible. It symbolized a utopian world which did not exist. As *On the Means to Successful Counsels* acidly observed:

> So, there is no man of malice in our nation? Is there no nobleman of ill intent among us? Among 102 parliamentary envoys not a single bad one is to be found? It is ridiculous to consider the human race one way and Poland another, to think otherwise of Poles alone, that they are all, without a single exception, worthy and pious citizens. Let us send such blessed congresses and parliaments to Plato's Republic, to More's Utopia, to Voltaire's kingdom of Eldorado, to the Commonwealth of the Troglodytes described in the wise Montesquieu's Letters, to islands situated on the frontiers of the human race, or hanging in the air—away from here, on earth, where among twelve most excellent men, one Judas was to be found. (Konarski 1761–1763, 1:50–51)

Konarski set out to persuade his readers that the Poles were simply ordinary human beings, bearing the virtues and shortcomings of mankind. Polish political literature constantly demanded moral improvement, lamenting the loss of old Polish virtues and seeing the correction of morality as the way to reform the commonwealth. This amounted to shouting into a void, a pretext for doing nothing, a confirmation of stagnation and the status quo in a world which was changing faster than ever. Konarski admired Montesquieu, but not the Montesquieu of *The Spirit of the Laws* (it hardly behooved a good son of the church to honor a work on the *Index of Prohibited Books* since 1751); he preferred the *Considerations of the Causes of the Greatness of the Romans* (Fabre 1952, 65). Both works stressed the importance and influence of institutions in shaping the political life of a nation, and this was the message that Konarski sought to convey.

> It is the form of our counsels which we need to correct, not people; for people always are, have been, and will be of one and the same nature, some good, some bad; as for their reformation, which exceeds earthly powers, we must leave it not to the commonwealth or to human reason, but to God alone and religion. . . . But it is the form of counsel, or rather, our lack of counsel and our anarchy which, with God's help, we can wholly improve, whenever we choose to do so. (Konarski 1761–1763, 1:96)

It was pointless to bewail human inadequacies or to pin hopes on the person of virtue. There was never an age when complaints did not abound over human failings. It was failing institutions, starting with parliament, which required reform. Only thus could there ever be any reform of morals. For to Konarski, the veto was more than a harmful fiction; it was the instrument of the moral devastation of all noble society. Amid anarchy the very worst elements came to the surface. People could not even distinguish between good and bad. Decent people, demoralized, lost faith in themselves and began to doubt the very possibility of reform. If free republican states such as Venice, the United Provinces, Switzerland, Genoa, or England (whose people he described as "great republicans," which doubtless would have come as something of a surprise to most of them) could govern themselves in an orderly fashion, preserve their freedom, and conduct their counsels by majority voting, then why should not Poland be able to do the same?

Konarski wanted to change the szlachta's political psychology. There had to be an end to the simplistic division of a few persons of virtue and the masses of the corrupt and the venal. For human beings and politics were not the black-and-white contraries that the szlachta's imagination was wont to picture. Politics were driven by ambition; people had different goals and different views. By their very nature they were far too different to attain that unanimity which was the dream of those who believed in it. "Egregious . . . and heroic virtue" was "rare." Human beings were a mixture of constantly opposing and ever-shifting qualities and emotions. "We are men and that is enough. . . . All men in general are more inclined to seek our own private (rather than public) benefits and well-being." In chapter 2 of book 3, where he reviewed the history of broken *Sejmy,* Konarski put an end to the notion of a person of virtue rescuing the commonwealth by adamantine opposition. He could only conclude: "All parliaments were always disrupted out of private motives and to the great harm of the commonwealth."

True, some parliaments and local assemblies did seemingly end in unanimous agreement. But it was always a fictitious unanimity: "Am I some American aboriginal in Poland, that I cannot see how parliaments and assemblies stagger along—if some of them actually reach a successful conclusion? Has even one of them ever [truly] attained such an agreement? Have not objections been suppressed and shouted down? Have not weaker objections been less apprehended, have not protests been disregarded or overcome by some kind of oversight? When have there not been many malcontents, who, had they been strong enough, would never have allowed a successful conclusion?" (Konarski 1761–1763, 2:101–2). Konarski's approach to Poland's politics was something truly new. He treated politics on the basis of hard, empirical facts, as true events. As such, the subject was far removed from the misty-eyed, idealized imaginings with which it was commonly portrayed. In inviting his readers to enter the world of harsh realities, Konarski had to take on not only the sacred cow of unanimity but also that of numerous noble ancestors. Those ancestors, virtuous, willing to lay down their lives and fortunes in defense of their liberties, were everywhere, infecting and paralyzing the szlachta's present. To the inhabitants of the Rzeczpospolita, they were the highest court of appeal. Konarski had to be careful in taking them on. He even tried to mobilize more remote (and therefore more hallowed) ancestors as his allies, trying to demonstrate that the principle of majority voting, *pluralitas,* held sway at the early parliaments which met under the Jagiellonian dynasty, when Poland was at its supposedly most flourishing. He sought to demonstrate that the veto possessed no legal foundations—in fact, as he was well aware, it was enshrined in Polish law. He maintained that the veto was "only some kind of adopted custom . . . a kind of customary law." Konarski's assertion that a custom which is "contrary to the truth, right, and internal justice" was without validity was not very convincing to readers for whom custom—that is, the way in which their forebears behaved and thought—was sacrosanct. This led Konarski to take a remarkably daring step: he declared his readiness to break with those sacred ancestors.

If the commonwealth had clearly enacted such a law, bringing the *liberum veto* into being was a severe mistake. "You would say, at the very least, that such lawgivers had lost their minds and that nothing could be more unworthy, more incomprehensible, more destructive to the commonwealth than such a law" (Konarski 1761–1763, 2:50–51). This was, of course, a purely hypothetical situation (since, according to Konarski, no such law introducing the veto existed). In general, he was very cautious. He praised the forebears whenever he could. But he fully appreciated that the constant, universal, obligatory invocation of the ancestors only reinforced the vicious spiral of those convictions which made any kind of reform of the state impossible.

Konarski's pleas for realism met with limited success. In their polemics, his opponents remained fixated on the *liberum veto*. They ignored virtually all other aspects of his work (Lukowski 2010, 88–95). They were incapable of seeing the destructive complexities underpinning the veto. This may of course have been more than just some pathological attachment. The new world which Konarski invited them to enter was something terrifying, threatening, inconceivable—a world not only of effective counsels, but of an effective state. Konarski wanted not only to get rid of the *veto,* but also to change the entire approach of the szlachta to parliamentary life. Without such a transformation, his whole endeavor made no sense. In 1765, in a polemic with the reformist periodical the *Monitor,* Felix Czacki, among the most diehard defenders of the old order, observed: "It is true, that during the last thirty-year-long reign [of Augustus III], no parliament, save that of 1736, ended successfully. No significant harm has resulted from this . . . ." In a sense he was right. From his point of view, the main role of parliament was not to make laws but to preserve szlachta liberties. But Konarski was putting forth a Sejm which was not a fortress protecting ancient privileges, but a modernized ruling and legislative machine, conducting an effective politics. Hence his praise of Britain's parliament as a model for Poland. In the process, Konarski endowed the Polish parliament with unprecedented powers.

> What monarchs are in absolute kingdoms, which cannot be ruled as limbs without a head, that is what the Sejm, made up of the king and the other two estates [of noble envoys and senators], is with us. A supreme entity must rule over everything. None but the Sejm has supreme rule over us . . . so that we should allow ourselves to be ruled by it . . . —and, if I may so put it, by ourselves, for by envoys elected by ourselves—and be obedient to them. The Sejm, our Parliament, is thus our monarch and absolute ruler. The Sejm is our supreme governor. (Konarski 1761–1763, 1:173)

Poland's parliament had never been described in such terms.

The very thought of such an institution terrified many. Konarski, demanding that the commonwealth's "parliament should be in permanent session" (it normally met every two years for a six-week term), felt himself obliged to add, "As to this permanent session, let it alarm no-one." The mere fact of utilizing the example of Britain, that heretic isle, was something of a novelty in Poland. Konarski made no effort to gloss over the corruption of English public life and did not pretend that English kings did not possess significant powers. However, he was anxious to show that in practice, the power of England's kings had always been limited, and that the system functioned effectively despite the shortcomings of the English themselves. England, despite the all-too-human venality and corruption that prevailed, despite the lack of personal responsibility of its kings for their actions, was nevertheless a state in which freedom existed, flourished, and was, above all, secure. It was so because the political system, the form of English governmental counsels, had this positive effect. These paradoxes were readily resolved. Oaths, instructions to members of parliament, other more or less complex constitutional mechanisms were unnecessary. "It is, in England, the greatest *Arcanum Status* for the restraining of royal power, that although the king wields in full almost all the *jura majestatis* of other monarchs, even those of declaring war and peace, and can do everything, yet this king does not dispose of public monies, that is, taxation contributions" (Konarski 1761–1763, 4:38n). And without the taxes agreed to by the representatives of the nation, the king, for all his powers, was helpless.

The key to the Westminster parliament's success lay in its use of simple majorities. In the face of the nobility's attachment to extreme consensualism, *On the Means to Successful Counsels* is not without its share of hesitations over whether simple or qualified parliamentary majorities should be introduced. Konarski seriously considered recommending decision making by a qualified 75 percent majority before he made his final decision. "I can honestly say that after hearing many reasons pro and contra, the view of those who urged us to content ourselves with a majority in our deliberations of one voice above the half of envoys appeared weightier and more prudent"—in other words, simple majorities. Qualified majorities were too complex; there would inevitably arise many disputes in calculating them. "So it is best to discard these newfangled elaborations, in the manner of the English, Swedish, and other ancient and present commonwealths," and go for simple majorities. "It is best not to wish to be particular and something above other people but to rule ourselves as others do: for these ancient and present commonwealths had and continue to have great wisdom and through experience have come to see that the safest majority in debate is that of one above the half. So let us not pretend that we Poles are wiser and more prudent than others" (Konarski 1761–1763, 3:4, 212). To those who feared that small minorities would introduce dangerous divisions, Konarski observed, "So, it seems harsh to us . . . that 151 envoys should triumph over 149 envoys? Does it not seem harsh to us that for a good century one venal envoy should triumph over almost two hundred . . . that is, over all the envoys over all the senate, over the king and the entire commonwealth?" (Konarski 1761–1763, 4:217).

In one other crucial respect, simple majorities demanded a new type of parliamentarianism. Konarski insisted on bringing out the hypocrisy surrounding the drafting of mandatory instructions to envoys at the local assemblies. He wanted them truly to reflect the views of the electorate; hence his demand that they be drawn up before the election of the envoys. But at the same time he demanded that they be stripped of their binding nature—they would become desirable postulates and not injunctions. "It is but a beautiful act of the imagination," he said, that the sejmiki could direct the affairs of state. "If *pluralitas* is to be salutary for our country, let it be as in England, the *pluralitas* of the envoys, not the artificial *pluralitas* of our constituencies." Policy was to be decided by the commonwealth's new, modernized, absolute ruler—its sovereign parliament—not by provincial backwoodsmen (Lukowski 2010, 77–88).

To summarize Konarski's demands of the szlachta: discard the idealized, heroic, utopian view of humanity. Instead, see human beings as complex, made up of many, even contradictory elements. The world was for ordinary people, not for moral mannequins. A politics based on virtuous perfection was no politics at all, but a delusory chimera—a world as dangerous for Konarski as a politics based on Christian ideals or classical Roman republican virtues for Machiavelli. It followed that politics was not some inevitable clash between good (that is, in the Polish context, noble liberties) and evil (that is, in the Polish context, the monarchy), but was an arduous, complicated game conducted between different elements within the state, whose ultimate purpose ought to be the general good. The *liberum veto* completely vitiated all prospects of such a politics, permitting only the politics of sterility and anarchy. The veto had to be replaced by simple majority rule. Such rule was far from perfect, but it was the best possible in the real earthly republic. Perfection was for God. Majority rule should be introduced into Poland if only because it could not make matters any worse than they already were. But majority rule demanded a new, more active politics conducted by a new, active parliament of the British type. The old pile made up of noble liberties which was the Commonwealth of the Two Nations had to be transformed into a modernized, effective state machine—with Protestant, commercial England as its model.

For some politicians, most notably the anglophile Czartoryski family, this was a clarion call which had been too long in coming. For others, it was a horrifying prospect. "I will not hide," proclaimed Felix Czacki (1723–1790) in the Sejm on 22 November 1766, speaking in support of a motion for the full reinstitution of the veto (partly circumscribed in 1764), "that I have opposed for over twenty years . . . majority voting . . . [as] harmful to the true faith, to national liberty, to the dignity of good kings, to the virtues of great men, degrading and oppressive to the virtuous and excellent mind." Such were the well-worn, self-contradictory platitudes of an oration which made any kind of sense only if one ignored the anarchy, harm, degradation, and foreign interference which the commonwealth had suffered for over half a century.

There were those who grumbled that Konarski, as a cleric, should not be opining on politics. Given the close intertwining of religion and politics among the predominantly Roman Catholic nobility, such complaints had little value. Indeed, it was individual Catholic clergy who were in the vanguard of the cultural revival which began to gather pace in Poland from the mid-1730s. Konarski was hardly unique in rising above the intellectual shortcomings of his age and place. The clergy in general were, in the early stages of the Commonwealth's Enlightenment, more open to new ideas than their lay counterparts. Of 235 Polish-Lithuanian writers with any credible claim to being "enlightened," born between 1689 and 1749, 147 (63.4 percent) were clergymen; and if their proportion subsequently declined, their contribution remained significant. It would have been odd had it not been a clergyman who composed the first major treatise attacking the veto.

The Problem of Foreign Policy

In one key respect, it is possible to accuse Konarski of, at best, naïveté; at worst, of a total lack of realism. He thought that foreign powers would be ready to accept the reforms in Poland if only they could be persuaded of the innocuousness of a reformed commonwealth. The matter is rather more complicated than it might at first appear. Konarski's *Epistolae familiares sub tempus Interregni,* of 1733, had done nothing to prevent foreign intervention in either that year's interregnum or that of 1763–1764 (Konarski 1955). Poland's position remained one of despairing subordination to Russia. It was utterly unrealistic to expect that "protection" to be shaken off, particularly given the deep-rooted internal opposition to constitutional reform. The alternatives for Konarski were brutally simple: either the "optimistic" (or "naïve") vision, with the permissibility of reform—or the pessimistic view, leading to resignation of all thought of reform and surrender to the bucolic, provincial quietism in which Poland had for so long festered.

This was a problem that affected all those who sought to introduce any kind of reform in the Rzeczpospolita. No one could provide a solution; most preferred not to notice it. Among later politicians, only King Stanisław August Poniatowski (reigned 1763–1795) had to wrestle with it, if only because he had no choice.

For his part, Konarski had no intention of resigning his hopes of reform or allowing himself to be diverted from his path by the lurking external dangers. For him, "it never behooves one to despair of the commonwealth." The feeble flickers of hope that still burned should not be extinguished, even at the price of conscious naïveté. After all, no one could foresee how the power relations of Europe were to evolve. And Konarski had at his disposal a weapon which Machiavelli preferred not to use: faith in Divine Providence. "Let us only begin to think seriously about saving our country, about repairing our counsels and parliaments, about finding a sure and lasting way to maintain our Sejmy, that form of counsel so natural to our realm, and, with the help of God, all will be easily restored from the ruination which we threaten to bring on ourselves."

Impact of Konarski

Whether Konarski should really be regarded as a Polish Machiavelli depends on our appraisal of Machiavelli. Both sought to bring a sense of realism to their times and to their contemporaries, hoping to free them from the pietistic maxims holding them in thrall, and so very much at odds with the world in which they actually found themselves. They wanted their contemporaries to look at the world coldly, honestly, without illusions.

Konarski convinced those who were ready to be convinced and who were ready to engage with the politics of the brave new world that he revealed. For others, his call to condemn as a traitor any who might demand the restoration of the veto after its hoped-for abolition must have been appalling and incomprehensible. Publication of *On the Means to Successful Counsels* caused uproar that was soon swamped amid the bitter disputes of the 1763–1764 interregnum which followed. The Czartoryski family demonstrated that there were Poles who took Konarski's lessons seriously; but, held back by the Russian protectorate, they remained unable to enact everything Konarski's supporters wanted. Russian meddling in old sectarian divisions was to bring about near civil war in the commonwealth, and disputes over reform only exacerbated the tensions which wracked it in the late 1760s and 1770s. In his politics, Konarski had always striven to keep a balance between various competing parties and had always sought to play the honest broker. With the publication of *On the Means to Successful Counsels,* that was increasingly difficult, if not impossible. He was drawn ever more to the new king, Stanisław August Poniatowski, and his obviously reformist agenda. Poniatowski, in his turn, reposed great trust in the utilization of Piarist and Jesuit educational reforms in his ambitious plans for the reform of the commonwealth. In 1765, the king set up a noble academy, the Cadet Corps, under his direct patronage, a school which boasted a more sophisticated, wide-ranging, and unashamedly secular version of the Noble Academy's curriculum. Beyond that, however, Poniatowski's and Konarski's hopes for wider reform were stymied largely by Russian opposition.

Later Life and Troubles

Konarski was a conventionally enlightened Catholic clergyman. He held to the basic religious toleration of Poland's political class. State magistracies should not pry into people's consciences. The state had a duty to suppress antireligious literature. Religious minorities should keep to the limits of what the law allowed them but should not expect to enjoy parity of rights with adherents of the dominant Catholic faith. He shared the widespread distaste displayed in Poland (and evinced by such enlightened luminaries as Voltaire and Frederick the Great) for the Jews. Paradoxically, a defense of Catholicism which he wrote against deism led to a spectacular falling-out with the papal nuncio, Angelo Maria Durini (1725–1796), in 1769. In February 1768, a *frondeur* league, the Confederacy of Bar, had erupted in a widespread reaction among the szlachta to royalist reform efforts and to Russian efforts to secure parity of rights for the tiny minority of Protestant nobles (which would have assured Russia of a reliable instrument in Polish politics). "Republican" nobles convinced Durini that King Stanisław August Poniatowski was an irreligious Russian cat's paw, determined to undermine the Catholic Church. Early in 1769, Konarski published his last major work, *On the Religion of Honest Men* (*O Religii Poczciwych Ludzi*). At one level, this was an impeccable, if vituperative, affirmation of Catholicism against skeptical opponents. Pagan philosophers and scoffing moderns alike were dismissed as being in some way or other debauched or depraved—Konarski did not spare even his beloved Cicero. Other targets included Machiavelli, whom he placed on a level with Spinoza, Hobbes, and Voltaire. True virtue required the bedrock of the Christian belief. Those "honest persons" who claimed to adhere to a faith which dispensed with revelation were, at best, superficial utilitarians. Crucially, the work culminated in a clear attack on the leaders of the Barist Confederacy, men whose egotistical shortcomings were wrecking hopes of reviving Poland under a true philosopher-king (Konarski 1771, 94–96, 106). By implication, Durini's Barist friends were the very kinds of anti-Catholic libertines denounced in the tract. Konarski's reward for supporting the king and reform was for his last years to be envenomed by Durini's harassment and denunciations. If he could have, the nuncio would have closed down the Collegium Nobilium. That exceeded his powers.

In August 1772, Russia, Prussia, and Austria had partitioned a hapless Poland-Lithuania, depriving it of around one-third of its territory and inhabitants. Konarski's worst fears had begun to come true. His hopes of persuading his countrymen to adopt a more realist course in politics remained unrealized. He died in his beloved Collegium Nobilium on 3 August 1773, his hopes for his country in ruins.

Life after Konarski

Konarski remained sadly ignored. When, amid the fortunate circumstances of 1788–1792, noble society was able to embark on a degree of genuine reform, enlightened republican activists pursued what Konarski would have called the "chimera" of the will of the nation, expressed in binding local instructions, heedless of his warnings against this. The constitution of 3 May 1791 abolished the *liberum veto* but, in the supplementary legislation, disregarded Konarski's strictures on qualified majorities (Lukowski 2010, 223–50). Those who called for reform preferred not to invoke Konarski's authority—his appeals for realism and majority voting remained too radical in a szlachta society unable to shake off the deadweight of a centuries-old embrace of extreme consensualism. It might have been some consolation, had he lived long enough to see it develop, that the Commission for National Education, set up as one of Europe's first secular education ministries shortly before his death, owed much to his inspiration. A cadre of Piarist writers, schooled by Konarski and writing largely for the new educational institutions, helped keep hopes of reform alive during the sterile 1780s, but even they did not invoke him directly. On the other hand, no one put up a credible case for the veto's defense after 1763; nor did its opponents feel the need to rehearse at length any arguments against it—after Konarski, there was little more left to say. The greatest backhanded compliment that Konarski received came from Catherine the Great in December 1794, when she identified Piarist schools as one of the chief sources of disquiet for Russia in the commonwealth's territories (Jobert 1941, 461–62).

That a monarch who ultimately represented mainstream Russian autocracy (whatever her protestations to the contrary) found the

Piarist reform program unpalatable is hardly to be wondered at. Ultimately, the ideals of European Enlightenment and those of Muscovite centralism were quite incompatible. Konarski had opened the doors to mainstream European thought in Poland: the Jesuits followed, as did those aristocrats who wanted real change, and even, in the end, so too did their opponents—they, too, had to use the language of the European Enlightenment to justify their positions. Konarski could and did draw on the ideals of a specifically Catholic Enlightenment, both as his own inspiration and as a means to energize others. His stay in Italy in the late 1720s and his continued contacts with Italian reformers left an indelible mark. This, too, is unsurprising. If Poland was widely seen as one of the most backward states of Europe, it was not far removed from how many Italian reformers saw themselves; indeed, the latter consciously compared the condition of their Italian homelands to that of Poland (Venturi 1969, 23, 537, 609). Pope Benedict XIV was sympathetic to limited "enlightened" reform (Venturi 1969, 109–13) of the sort that Konarski wanted, and Konarski, like so many Catholic ecclesiastical reformers, was always cautious about what he was prepared to take from the moderns. He was hardly alone among Catholic reformers in advocating the censoring of literary impieties (Konarski 1771, 107; Aston 2002, 94–97). Educational reform was widely seen as a means of revitalizing failing states—it could be Poland, it could be Venice (Venturi 1969, 150–55; Aston 2002, 57–60). Konarski was part of such reform movements, and what he achieved went beyond what was achieved in the Italy which had provided the seedbed for his ideas. He too, in turn, exerted his own influence on Catholic reform elsewhere: his *De Viro honesto et bono cive ab ineunte aetate formando* (*On Making a Good Man and a Good Citizen from an Early Age*), of 1754, originally a moralizing tract for his Collegium Nobilium, was widely used in Piarist establishments outside Poland (Konarski 1955, 2:107–8n).

In the course of the nineteenth century, Konarski became a national icon for a dismembered Poland. His attack on the veto came to be seen as a national turning point. Yet he remains a curiously neglected figure. That he should be neglected abroad is no surprise—the Rzeczpospolita's problems were so sui generis that his ideas had no impact outside its borders. Konarski is routinely, even ritually, invoked in Polish historical literature, but the last substantial biography appeared in 1951, at a time of intensifying ideological pressure on historians. The standard life remains that published by Władysław Konopczyński in 1926. There is still no scholarly edition of *On the Means to Successful Counsels*—the only full edition available, apart from the original, remains a photographic reprint published in 1923. One of Poland's most daringly original thinkers surely deserves better.

Bibliography

Aston, Nigel. 2002. *Christianity and Revolutionary Europe, c. 1750–1830*. Cambridge: Cambridge University Press.
Butterwick, Richard. 1998. *Poland's Last King and English Culture: Stanisław August Poniatowski, 1732–1798*. Oxford: Clarendon Press.
Fabre, Jean. 1952. *Stanislas-Auguste Poniatowski et l'Europe des Lumières*. Paris: Belles Lettres.
Jobert, Ambroise. 1941. *La Commission d'Éducation Nationale en Pologne (1773–1794)*. Paris: Droz.
Konarski, Stanisław, ed. 1771. *O Religii Poczciwych Ludzi*. Kraków: Żupański. Translated into Latin as *De Religione Honestorum Hominum* (Warsaw): Typis Regiis & Reip. apud Sch. Pias.
———. 1761–1763. *O Skutecznym Rad Sposobie*. 4 vols. Warsaw: Piarists. Photographic reprint, Warsaw: Wilder, 1923. Translated into German as *Von einem Nützlichen Mittel zum Bestande der ordentlichen Reichstäge in Pohlen*. 2 vols. Warsaw, 1762.
———. 1955. *Pisma Wybrane*. Edited by Juliusz Nowak-Dłużewski. 2 vols. Warsaw: Państwo i Wiedza.
Konopczyński, Władysław. 1926. *Stanisław Konarski*. Warsaw: Mianowski.
Lukowski, Jerzy. 2010. *Disorderly Liberty: The Political Culture of the Polish-Lithuanian Commonwealth in the Eighteenth Century*. London: Continuum.
Nowak-Dłużewski, Juliusz. 1951. *Stanisław Konarski*. Warsaw: Pax.
Rose, William John. 1929. *Stanislas Konarski: Reformer of Education in XVIIIth Century Poland*. London: Cape.
Sarg, Adolph. 1864. *Die Piaristenschulen im ehemaligen Polen und ihre Reform durch Konarski*. Marburg.
Skinner, Quentin. 1978. *The Foundations of Modern Political Thought*. Vol. 1. Cambridge: Cambridge University Press.
Venturi, Franco. 1969. *Settecento Riformatore*. Vol. 1, *Da Muratori a Beccaria, 1730–1764*. Turin: Einaudi.

21

Hugo Kołłątaj (1750–1812)

The Revolutionary Priest

ANNA ŁYSIAK-ŁĄTKOWSKA

Hugo Kołłątaj was born in 1750 in Dederkały Wielkie, Volhynia, into a semiprosperous noble family. He had a particularly close relationship with his mother, Marianna Mierzyńska. Kołłątaj began his school education at the age of seven in a Jesuit school in Pińczów. Between 1761 and 1768, he lived in Kraków, where he established close connections with the Kraków Academy. While none of the sources confirm with complete clarity just whether he received a doctoral degree in philosophy at that time, it is known that he decided to become a priest. During subsequent years, he traveled and studied abroad, thanks to the financial support of his family. In 1771, he went to Vienna, where he learned about the regalist Austrian model of organizing the Roman Catholic Church (Josephinism), a model according to which the church was largely independent from direct papal interventions but was governed by the state. Then, Kołłątaj departed for Italy to study there. During his two-year sojourn in Rome

(1772–1774), Kołłątaj was able to study more closely the legal, political, and ecclesiastical identity of the papacy, the Roman curia, and the Italian clergy—observations that influenced his views about the Roman Catholic Church as a political institution.

Another important factor influencing Kołłątaj's view of the Curia was the papacy's response to Poland's crises in the last decades of its existence between the Bar Confederation and the third partition (1768–1795). Pope Clement XIV (1769–1774) had protested the first partition of Poland, but his protestations were ignored. Kołłątaj claimed these actions were not in the interests of Poland and showed the weakness of the church's political position with respect to Polish affairs. In response to the weak and inconclusive papal response, Kołłątaj suggested that the Roman Catholic Church in Poland be reorganized similarly to that of the Austrian Empire.

Following his time in Rome, Kołłątaj spent months in Naples, where he was introduced to Ferdinando Galiani (1728–1787). Galiani was a clergyman who, during his stay in Paris, had become acquainted with many encyclopedists and philosophers in person, later adapting their views for his own Catholic Enlightenment writings. From Galiani, Kołłątaj learned about Enlightenment ideas, which presented nature, political systems, society, the human being, and various spheres of life differently from the traditional Christian paradigm.

After returning to Poland in 1775, Kołłątaj was ordained a priest. It must be stressed that for someone like Kołłątaj—a person of semi-prosperous noble lineage now increasingly impoverished—the priesthood was an opportunity to improve his social status. Opinions have differed concerning Kołłątaj's attitude as a parish priest. The authors of his biographies have stressed that the young Kołłątaj was not very zealous in his ministrations, not characterized by piety, prone to absenteeism from his parish, and too keen on financial gain in the form of benefices, stipends and other church possessions (Schulz 1963, 2:660–62), never missing a chance to acquire them. However, Kołłątaj became a good organizer and parish administrator, a fact proven during his tenure as parish priest in Krzyżanowice. Having free time was conducive to furthering his career, continuing intellectual development, and following passions and interests.

In 1776, Kołłątaj moved to Warsaw, where he joined the Society for Elementary Books, in part because of contacts he had made in Rome, including his association with the bishop of Płock, Michał Jerzy Poniatowski (1736–1794), the brother of none other than King Stanisław August Poniatowski (1732–1798). Kołłątaj thus found himself appointed to design and execute a reform of the Kraków Academy. He criticized the level of teaching, the education and qualifications of the staff, and the management of the academy. According to him, the source of these problems was "monastic" education, especially the kind carried out by the Jesuits. He blamed them for inhibiting scientific advancement and for the low level of education. Neither was his opinion about their other activities positive. Kołłątaj criticized the Jesuits' attitude during the Reformation and Counter-Reformation; their influence on kings, princes, and the richest social classes; and their activities during Saxon rule in Poland (Kołłątaj 1953, 24–33, 55). Recent research views the Jesuits' achievements in a somewhat different light; indeed, some Jesuits were well educated and aware of the challenges of their time. Accordingly, Kołłątaj and other critics' negative assessment of this order seems exaggerated and to be quite at variance from the actual state of affairs (Kadulska 1997). Concerning the importance of other religious orders, according to Kołłątaj the most useful were those that dealt with such social problems as taking care of the sick and homeless, running shelters, and providing public education. His view differed regarding the contemplative orders and those based on the principle of begging, which he claimed were of little benefit to public and social life (Kołłątaj 1953, 296). Kołłątaj judged religious communities according to a pragmatist norm that showed traits of Enlightenment utilitarianism.

Because of Kołłątaj's opinions, his draft of the Kraków Academy reform included secularization, modernization of the methods and level of teaching and management, control of the state over the education system, and the secularization of all church possessions to be used as material support for the Kraków Academy (Chamcówna 1957). He particularly strove to remove scholasticism and metaphysics from the philosophy and theology curriculum. Because he did not perceive these subjects as legitimate fields of science, but as "speculative assumptions," he was convinced that they had a pernicious impact on the minds of the students. Kołłątaj believed there should be a uniform moral doctrine based on the concepts of physical and moral laws, human rights and obligations, and the principles of social and political coexistence. He additionally aimed at creating his own code of ethics, the draft of which can be found in one of his last works (Kołłątaj 1955). Because of his views, Kołłątaj fell into disfavor with the Kraków-based academics and clergy. Despite difficulties, thanks to support from Jan Śniadecki (1756–1830) and Ignacy Potocki (1750–1809), he remained the president of the Kraków Academy between 1783 and 1786, executing his plan of reforms where possible.

After 1786, he moved to Warsaw, where he started another chapter of his life involving writing, journalistic, and sociopolitical activities. The 1780s and 1790s were a turbulent period in Polish history—the second and third partitions (1792, 1795) occurred, followed by further efforts to introduce reforms (the Great Sejm of 1788–1792, the Constitution of 3 May 1791 and the war in its defense in 1792, and finally, the Kościuszko Uprising in 1794). Kołłątaj took part in all of these events, although his attitude toward them has been interpreted variously. He had gathered a number of followers, including Antoni Trębicki (1764?–1834), Franciszek Dmochowski (1762–1808), and Franciszek S. Jezierski (1740–1791). They did not form any political grouping or organization, but instead constituted a rather informal association of people, later referred to as Kołłątaj's Forge, brought together by their political views and concern for Poland. Their goal was to carry out a series of reforms in a republican/democratic spirit. As leader of the Forge, Kołłątaj shared in the endeavors of the Reformist faction of Stanisław Małachowski (1736–1809) and Ignacy Potocki (1750–1809) at the time of the Grand Diet (1788–1792), joining them in preparing a draft of the constitution that became the basis for the final text of the Constitution of May 3.

In 1792, during the war to defend the new constitution, Kołłątaj's attitude was ambiguous. He organized military troops against the Russian armies, while expressing his support for the Targowica Confederation, which backed the Russian empress. In the end, fleeing the czarist authorities, he left for Leipzig in Germany, where he focused on preparing the Kościuszko Uprising in Poland. After a while, he became an advocate of the unfolding ideologies characteristic of the French Revolution since 1789. Kołłątaj soon became quite active in soliciting support for the movement in France. Although he did not accept all methods of the revolutionaries, he noticed similarities in the French and Polish situations. Kołłątaj believed they shared the struggle for freedom and republican ideas, and he considered this an opportunity to find agreement and establish closer cooperation (Kołłątaj 2006, lx–lxiv).

During the Kościuszko Uprising against Russian and Prussian rule (1794), he coauthored the Proclamation of Połaniec, which limited serfdom and established principles of limited individual liberty and civil rights for Polish peasants. His other actions resulted in accusations of theft and embezzlement of revolutionary money, although these were never proven. He was also accused of favoring Jacobin ideas. In fact, he was later referred to as the "Polish Jacobin" or even the "Polish Robespierre" (Leśnodorski 1960). When the uprising failed, Kołłątaj did not manage to flee, and was imprisoned. He spent the years 1794–1802 as a prisoner in the Austrian fortresses in Olomouc and Josephstadt. There he began corresponding with the Association of Polish Republicans. After receiving authorization to use the press and books, he was able to begin writing his works, which synthesized his views on social/political relations, historical processes, human nature, and the genesis and development of religion as well as morality (Tokarz 1905, 1:136–215).

Because of Napoleon's rapid rise to power and his military victories against the czarist authorities, Kołłątaj, who was seen by the Russian government as a radical activist, was interned in Moscow, where he lived between 1807 and 1808. After making peace with France at Tilsit, Czar Alexander I recognized that Kołłątaj was no longer any danger, and he released him in 1808. Once released from prison, he went to Volhynia, where he helped organize the Kremenets High School, whose main creator and founder was Tadeusz Czacki. He devoted his final years to planning and drafting an education reform, both in the Duchy of Warsaw (established in 1807) and in Kraków.

He was again put in charge of reforming the Kraków Academy, but never again played a significant societal role, except as a member of the Society of Friends of Science. He died in 1812.

The Genesis and Development of Religion

Kołłątaj's philosophy presupposed the physiocratic principle, a concept advanced by François Quesnay (1694–1774) that asserted the existence of immutable physical and moral laws. This eternal order conserved and guaranteed the prosperity of the nations. Kołłątaj expanded the meaning of this principle, however, by going beyond the views of Quesnay and his followers. Kołłątaj also adapted the newest theories of epistemology for his own philosophical endeavors, be it the thought of Isaac Newton, or Étienne Bonnot de Condillac's sensualism. A first impression might be that Kołłątaj was a deist. For him, however, doubt—or even agnosticism—was the sign of a sound methodological skepticism, which every researcher had to feel if he wanted to remain conscious of his own fallibility and the possible mistakes of his colleagues or whole academic disciplines. Skepticism was for him only a starting point for the analysis of different concepts, hypotheses, and theories. After scientific verification, such skepticism could be transformed into secure knowledge (Kołłątaj 2006, xii–xiv, xl).

Such skeptical tendencies are detectable in Kołłątaj's description of the genesis and development of religion. His notion of hypothesis, or "first reason," assumed the acknowledgment of the first cause and world order, cosmogony—that is, physical order, moral order, philosophy, theology, and natural religion. Natural religion could not simply have its origin in revelation alone, but must also have an anthropological origin, namely, among the first primitive people, who had substantial cognitive skills and were capable of rational thinking (Hinz 1973, 193–95). These early humans learned that the cosmological and moral orders were based on constant, immutable, and rational laws. Upon finding that the physical order cannot be coincidental, such early humans concluded that there was a force that created the world and its principles of operation, and they began worshiping it as their god.

Natural religion nevertheless underwent a gradual process of transformation because of Noah's flood, which proved a decisive moment in the history of humanity. Kołłątaj relied for his thesis, and for the importance of the flood, on a number of sources of contemporary philosophy and natural history, including Giambattista Vico (1668–1744), Georges Leclerc de Buffon (1707–1788), Denis Diderot (1713–1784), Jean-Jacques Rousseau (1712–1778), Voltaire (1694–1778), and, above all, Nicolas Boulanger (1722–1759). While referring to Boulanger and his theory of global disasters, Kołłątaj violated the stability of the physiocratic physical and moral order by advocating a theory of chaos at the commencement of the world, a place for the role of catastrophes (such as the Noahide flood) in shaping natural history. For Kołłątaj, natural laws governing the world were fixed and immutable, but not necessarily opposed to catastrophes, which he considered periods of tension and crisis built into the natural order itself. The occurrence of a disaster such as the flood indicates that neither nature nor the social world is constant. Instead, both are characterized by changeability, which includes periods of stability as well as periods full of anxiety and crisis. Kołłątaj also took from Boulanger his conviction that the flood was a natural phenomenon, which should not be interpreted as divine punishment for sins or a miraculous event. However, the image of the disaster was one of human drama—a narrative about the tragedy of human existence, seeing it as full of sadness, terror, helplessness, despair, uncertainty, and fear about the future (Kołłątaj 1972, 295–353, 361–69, 856–57, 866; Kołłątaj 2006, xxxi–xxxviii; Hinz 1973, 196–99, 272–82).

The human and natural catastrophe of the deluge notwithstanding, Kołłątaj referred to Vico's concept of the primitive era as a golden age, a perfect state of order and harmony. Kołłątaj further stated that in the immediate aftermath of the flood natural religion had not been entirely forgotten. It was only the prolonged uncertainty about humanity's fate after the flood that had resulted in the creation of new articles of faith. Those who had survived the flood and experienced a great shock could be soothed only by a superhuman voice that promised them safety and care. Priests used this intense cultural trauma to justify speaking "in the name of God" and to create the dogma of a new religion about the beginning and the end of the world.

The aftermath of the Noahide deluge, then, resulted in the creation of the only historical religion, namely Christianity (or actually, Catholicism), which Kołłątaj referred to as the religion revealed by God. According to him, it soon was infected with numerous errors—although at the same time, it was a historical and psychological necessity. The basic function of Christianity was to relieve the growing anxiety that originated from such an extraordinary emotional shock. Its goal was to make sure the social balance remained in place and that there would be no chaotic or abnormal human behavior. However, Kołłątaj claimed that the excessive use of the "voice from the heavens" as a trick to calm down flood survivors was a long-term mistake. For in this way the laws of natural religion were violated, and its original purity gradually lost. The survivors lost the key to understanding them, because the new truths became a mystery that should not be explored through rational research. Those who had survived the flood were incapable, therefore, of restoring the original, historic religion of nature revealed by God. The revelation of Jesus was ultimately necessary because of the degeneration of the historic religion (Kołłątaj 1972, 370, 398–419; Łysiak-Łątkowska 2001, 32–36).

Kołłątaj recognized religion as a historical and social fact and therefore treated it as a subject of scientific research, not necessarily as the object of theological or metaphysical discussion. Religion was for him a combination of moral values and social thought focused on the human being as an individual in historical perspective. This perspective seems to anticipate the later rise of "religious studies" as a descriptive, academic discipline. Primitive religion, which according to Kołłątaj was a complex subject because of missing sources and difficulties in defining its historical periodization, was a specific part of human history. The universality of ethical principles and laws of nature determined its value, and, above all, it was for this reason that the rites of the surviving natural religion were used for observing and analyzing the development of religious beliefs, their dissimilarity, and their diversity (Skrzypek 1989, 108–30). In some works on the place of Kołłątaj's thought in European intellectual history, his opinion about the origins of religion has been considered ahistorical. However, it seems more accurate to say his stance was a methodological assumption in order to take a critical look at Christianity, not for the purpose of rejecting it or religion as a whole. Kołłątaj repeatedly criticized revealed religion and indulged in polemical remarks about it; but nearly always, this was in the context of beliefs and practices he considered artifacts of fanaticism, fallacy, and superstition. Thus, his criticism should be seen as part of his agenda to renew the foundations of religion, rather than to reject them. After all, according to Kołłątaj Christianity did play a very important social function: it was a guarantee of maintaining moral norms that integrated society thanks to symbols and fixed forms of worship. Regarding Polish territory, he claimed that the Catholic creed must be dominant, even if this Catholic preeminence rested upon tradition, history, and respect for (as well as recognition by) the law, rather than from the conviction that it was superior to other religions (Kołłątaj 1954, 2:297–98). Kołłątaj spoke of Jesus largely as the principal lawmaker for humanity, while understanding Jesus' redemptive role largely in terms of his moral principles centered on the rightful dignity and liberty of humanity. Like many Enlightenment writers, Kołłątaj celebrated Jesus' devotion to the principles of sound morality even unto death, his concern for ameliorating the condition of the poor, and his willingness tirelessly to instruct humanity on self-improvement, regardless of the unpopularity of his message.

The Concept of First Cause

In his work, Kołłątaj wrote about the creation of the universe out of nothingness and primordial chaos, thus again violating the physiocratic principle of stability and immutability. The order that resulted from the act of creation could not be disturbed through supernatural intervention, but only modified through natural processes.

The creation of the world was brought about by a force for which Kołłątaj used different names: First Cause, Superior Being, Providence, and God. The names used could be taken as evidence for a deistic attitude or even pantheistic beliefs. However, if one takes into account that in his discussion on the creation of the world he emphasized a theory of cognition similar to those of Newton and Condillac, one may conclude that the names themselves were not important to him, but that, rather, he was concerned to establish the First Cause as the source of efficient causality in the creation of the world, as the explanation for the beginning of the world, and as the genesis of its rightful governance by moral and natural laws. However, it is also possible to analyze Kołłątaj's view of the issue of the beginning of the world in the context of "Catholic Enlightenment" and other Enlightenment trends. Interpreted in this way, his words describing the world's prime mover may be an attempt to make the faith intelligible, a kind of compromise between the world of reason and that of religion. His explanation could then also be seen as intellectual admiration for the order of the world and as a rational explanation of the Creator's existence. Moreover, Kołłątaj proposed extreme caution in making propositional statements about the ontological nature of the Supreme Being, because for him it was absolutely impossible to understand fully the world's prime mover. However, he did not refer to mystics as his sources, but instead cited texts conceived by ancient materialists/atomists, although he did not agree wholly with their claims. One could gain only a partial and insufficient insight into the existence of this Supreme Being through the physical and moral laws *as* properties of the universal natural order (Kołłątaj 2006, 14). Was this an argument that could be understood as a sign of his deism or materialism/atheism? On the contrary, Kołłątaj argued against materialism/atheism by stressing that rational cognition was limited by the existence of an unspeakable, inconceivable, yet supernatural ontological foundation. Kołłątaj referred to the biblical book of Genesis and ancient theological systems. He presented them from the point of view of books written by church's fathers, thus attempting to find a connection and continuity of thoughts between them (Kołłątaj 2006, xli–xlviii; Hinz 1973, 236–41; Kostkiewiczowa 2002, 344–45, 358–463; Deszczyńska 2003, 46–48). Specifically, Kołłątaj used Eusebius of Caesarea to suggest that moral principles predated Christianity and were not themselves intrinsically derived from Christian teachings alone; he additionally argued that Christianity is a continuation of natural religion, but in a new form that answered to the present needs of humanity.

Despite his methodological skepticism, he continued to believe in the theoretical possibility of miracles (Kołłątaj 1972, 307–8, 743–46; Hinz 1973, 230–35). To him, although such extraordinary events may have clashed with the physical order and natural laws, hesitation and doubts concerning the nature of miracles was warranted because it was possible for phenomena to occur whose causes would be difficult to define explicitly because of insufficient understanding of natural law or chronic human uncertainty. A miracle, in other words, need not be an event in violation of natural law to be a miracle. God could still theoretically use unknown, as well as unknowable but still natural, causes to achieve his ends.

Thoughts on Morality

Based on the physiocratic assumption concerning a fixed physical order, Kołłątaj acknowledged that moral laws governing the human being were derived from natural order (Kołłątaj 1955, 27). These natural laws are also contained in the gospel (Kołłątaj 1954, 2:297; Hinz 1973, 119, 215–18), as well as in the traditions of other religious systems. Thus he conceived morality (just like physics) as independent of religion. The ethical system that Kołłątaj tried to create comprised what he referred to as "the rights and duties" or obligations of a human being. These rights and duties included the right to have, and the duty to ensure for others, safety, freedom, ownership, mutual help, the guarantee of such recognized rights, and the fulfillment of needs. In citing Helvétius's views and referring to Rousseau's tradition along with Thomas Paine's thought, Kołłątaj included human rights, civil rights, and the need for a patriotic upbringing in the system of moral principles. These human rights and citizenship rights echoed the convictions about the universality of moral norms common to all humankind embodied within the Declaration of the Rights of Man and Citizen promulgated by the French Revolutionary National Assembly in 1789. Kołłątaj assumed that human rights were inherent within the moral foundation of the natural order, and he expected their eventual sociopolitical realization because of the late eighteenth-century Atlantic revolutions. Nevertheless, while he did not specify the content of these rights and duties, it was certain for him that freedom would ultimately win over despotism, truth over immorality, and justice over lawlessness and impudence. While acknowledging the universality of a new world order based on natural rights and duties, Kołłątaj accepted different ways of realizing it. The English model of parliamentary monarchy, the American Republic, and the aforementioned new French Republic were viable ways in his eyes (Kołłątaj 2006, lxxi–lxxviii). The need for a patriotic education according to moral principles was obviously connected with the situation in Poland and the demands aimed at shaping a citizenry aware of its country's needs.

Remarks about the Roman Catholic Church and Clergy

In his opinion about the historical role of the Roman Catholic Church, Kołłątaj, despite his criticism, often remained relatively evenhanded insofar as he emphasized the contributions of the pope and clergy to the development of various spheres of life. When describing the Middle Ages, Kołłątaj focused primarily on their input into the development of education and culture (Kołłątaj 1844, 3:250–51).

As far as Polish history is concerned, the baptism of Mieszko I in 966 was particularly important. According to Kołłątaj, his conversion to Christianity was the first step of the Polish people toward Enlightenment (Kołłątaj 1953, 271–72). The political strengthening of Poland and its increased international significance were two side effects of this conversion. Kołłątaj appreciated what successive Polish rulers had done to promote education (Kołłątaj 1844, 3:251–54).

In addition to the great achievements of the church during the Middle Ages, Kołłątaj pointed to the political, religious, and cultural universalism of that period (Kołłątaj 1844, 1:21–23), which he believed could threaten the sense of individuality and identity among the residents of European countries. However, in general, he did not agree with the opinion expressed during the Enlightenment that the Middle Ages were a "benighted, dark" period that stopped the progress of philosophy and science and halted development in various fields. He believed it was the Reformation and Counter-Reformation that inhibited the process of development (Kołłątaj 1844, 3:254–57). According to him, the 1500s and 1600s were a time in which the Roman Catholic Church focused on defending its theology, dogmas of faith, and religious principles. This negatively influenced the level and methods of education in schools controlled by the clergy, and it fossilized and strengthened scholastic teaching methods.

When discussing the structural organization of the Roman Catholic Church in Poland, Kołłątaj suggested the establishment of a national synod. Importantly, however, he believed this Polish Synod should be governed by state authorities, and its decisions be in accordance with national law, and he envisioned the chairperson of the Synod, the papal nuncio, only as a representative figure. The tasks of the synod should include appointments and promotions of clergy, the control of church funds, the codification of national canon law, doctrinal oversight, and the settling of church disputes. Kołłątaj's ecclesiological vision also entailed a detailed plan for ecclesiastical courts at a local, diocesan level, below a court of appeals under the jurisdiction of the archbishop who sat in the national synod. Ties with the Holy See, he believed, should be maintained through a concordat, which should be drafted on the initiative of the state and not the church authorities. In addition, Kołłątaj also defended the old regalist idea that all papal promulgations (bulls, briefs, and encyclicals) had to be approved by the state authorities before publication. Kołłątaj reserved for the clergy the right to handle matters of conscience and faith, as well as issues concerning religious principles—for example, marital and other dispensations. He allowed the right of freedom of religion and conscience, but he also insisted that Protestants, Orthodox, and non-Christian religions must all carefully keep the laws of the country in which they live. Thus, especially because foreign non-Catholic countries (here he specifically meant Russia) had intervened regularly in Poland's internal affairs under the pretext of assisting Orthodox minorities, Kołłątaj argued that leaders of churches other than the Roman Catholic Church should be subject only to state authorities and law (Kołłątaj 1953, 2:310–17). He also discussed the clerical estate, of which he was himself a representative. Kołłątaj believed that the state should take care of the education and financial security of the clergy because of their importance for the society. On the other hand, Kołłątaj opposed the imposition of additional financial burdens on the clergy, especially on the curés, even when such additional financial exactions had been recommended by the reformers of the Grand Diet (1788–1792) (Kołłątaj 1954, 1:226–31). Additionally, he called for a revival of morals and manners among the priests, ever mindful of the fate of his fellow priests in France during the revolution there. Overall, Kołłątaj did not take a closer look at the sacramental vocation of priests, but instead focused upon their social role, primarily as educators and teachers. That is why he treated them—along with teachers—as "serving the Republic of Poland" and controlled by the state authorities (Kołłątaj 1953, 1:226–31; 2:219–20).

The ambitious and hardworking Kołłątaj continues to be considered a supporter of radical views and methods, but is still a relatively unknown figure outside Poland, which he served in so many ways. His legacy includes journalistic, sociopolitical, and philosophical works. Despite an extremely rich and vast bibliography concerning Kołłątaj and a number of papers devoted to him, much scholarship has yet to analyze his long career and his place within the Polish Enlightenment. Regarding sociopolitical issues, Kołłątaj's participation in the Kościuszko Uprising has triggered numerous disputes and discussions, which may be the subject of further scientific inquiry. Equally noteworthy is Kołłątaj's approach to the French Revolution, which has been analyzed only in the context of its relationship to events in Poland; much of his wider significance as a commentator on the French Revolution remains marginalized or overlooked. New light needs to be cast upon the radicalism of Kołłątaj's views, whose importance should be emphasized without forgetting their historical context and significance. Concerning his philosophical musings, researchers usually stress the elements of deism—or even materialism—and indicate his critical assessment of the importance of religion and the Roman Catholic Church. Some treat Kołłątaj's philosophical radicalism unfavorably. For still others, Kołłątaj's philosophical radicalism shows his awareness of modernity and his devotion to the process of secularization and rationalization (Foucault 2000, 277–94), while yet another group claims that Kołłątaj was a reformer and a modern thinker in the spirit of Enlightened Catholicism. What must be considered in future research are the diverse trains of physiocratic thought that he developed and deepened: he broke the principle of stability and immutability by introducing the theories of chaos and global disasters (for example, the flood); historicized mankind's past, as well as prevailing concepts of morality; and further developed remarkable views on agricultural issues, ethnography, and the value of work (Kołłątaj 2006, lxiii–lxiv, lxvii–lxviii). Clearly, Kołłątaj's legacy and the contours of his worldview invite more detailed analysis and updating. The first step in accomplishing this task would be the publication of a critical edition of Kołłątaj's works, especially including hitherto unpublished material.

A Catholic Enlightener?

Kołłątaj's work contributed to the Catholic Enlightenment in several ways. First, he urged improvement of the educational system and the quality of teaching. To that end he tried to modernize lecturing and modify what was being presented in the fields of metaphysics, theology, and philosophy. Above all, he called for abandoning traditional scholasticism. Second, Kołłątaj strove to revive church life and was interested in improving the role of a parish priest. Parish priests acted not only as intermediaries between God and his people and as stewards of the holy sacraments, but they were also supposed to be teachers in social and moral matters. He was one of the few people who noticed the importance of parishes and parochial schools for the social life of a community.

His organizing efforts to reform education and the functioning of parishes were pioneering and innovative. These efforts stemmed from his reforming zeal and critical approach to the Roman Catholic Church as an institution, and they aimed at restoring its pastoral and cultural importance.

In Kołłątaj's writing, the influence of Enlightenment ideals about the role of Catholicism cannot be overlooked. He discussed many religious issues, criticized superstitious behavior, and even used the concept of "natural religion" and, thus, utilized more descriptive than theological/dogmatic language. Kołłątaj took a critical approach in discussing the importance and presence of Christian/Catholic thought. On the one hand, he used the achievements of philosophy and science to point toward areas that required modernization. On the other hand, he was within the limits of Catholic doctrine, although not always in its traditional sense. He stood out because of the originality and independence of his thoughts and actions. As a supporter of open-mindedness and freedom of scientific research, he helped redefine the role of Catholicism and revive discussion about it.

Bibliography

Butterwick, Richard. 2012. *The Polish Revolution and the Catholic Church, 1788–1792*. Oxford: Oxford University Press.

Chamcówna, Mirosława. 1957. *Uniwersytet Jagielloński w dobie Komisji Edukacji Narodowej. Szkoła Główna Koronna w okresie wizyty i rektoratu H. Kołłątaja (1777–1786)*. Wrocław: Zakład Narodowy im. Ossolińskich (Ossolineum).

Deszczyńska, Martyna. 2003. *"Historia sacra" i dzieje narodowe: Refleksja historyczna z lat 1795–1830 nad rolą religii i Kościoła w przeszłości Polski*. Warsaw: Semper.

Foucault, Michel. 2000. *Filozofia, historia, polityka: Wybór pism*. Warsaw: Państwowe Wydawnictwo Naukowe (PWN).

Hinz, Henryk. 1973. *Filozofia Hugona Kołłątaja: Zarys monografii*. Warsaw: Książka i Wiedza.

Kadulska, Irena. 1997. *Teatr jezuicki w Polsce w XVIII i XIX wieku*. Gdańsk: Wydawnictwo Uniwersytetu Gdańskiego.

Kołłątaj, Hugo. 1844. *Listy w przedmiotach naukowych*. Vols. 1–3. Kraków: Wydawnictwo Uniwersytetu.

———. 1953. *Stan oświecenia w Polsce w ostatnich latach panowania Augusta III (1750–1764)*. Wrocław: Zakład Narodowy im. Ossolińskich (Ossolineum).

———. 1954. *Listy Anonima i Prawo polityczne narodu polskiego*. Vols. 1–2. Warsaw: Państwowe Wydawnictwo Naukowe (PWN).

———. 1955. *Porządek fizyczno-moralny oraz Pomysły do dzieła Porządek fizyczno moralny*. Warsaw: Państwowe Wydawnictwo Naukowe (PWN).

———. 1972. *Rozbiór krytyczny zasad historii początkowej wszystkich ludów*. Warsaw: Państwowe Wydawnictwo Naukowe (PWN).

———. 2006. *Prawa i obowiązki naturalne człowieka oraz O konstytucji w ogólności*. Warsaw: Wydawnictwo IFiS PAN.

Kostkiewiczowa, Teresa. 2002. *Polski wiek świateł: obszary swoistości*. Wrocław: Wydawnictwo Uniwersytetu Wrocławskiego.

Leśnodorski, Bogusław. 1960. *Polscy jakobini Karta z dziejów insurekcji 1794 roku*. Warsaw: Książka i Wiedza.

Łysiak, Anna (Łysiak-Łątkowska, Anna). 2001. "Między religią a moralnością: Zagadnienie aksjologii w poglądach Hugona Kołłątaja." *Słupskie Studia Historyczne* 9:27–49.

Schulz, Friedrich. 1963. "Podróże informatyka z Rygi do Warszawy po Polsce w latach 1791–1793." *Polska Stanisławowska w oczach cudzoziemców*. Vol. 2. Warsaw: Państwowy Instytut Wydawniczy.

Skrzypek, Marian. 1989. *Oświecenie francuskie a początki religioznawstwa*. Warsaw, Wrocław, and Kraków: Zakład Narodowy im. Ossolińskich (Ossolineum).

Tokarz, Wacław. 1905. *Ostatnie lata Hugo Kołłątaja, 1794–1812*. Vol. 1. Kraków: Nakł. Akademii Umiejętności.

Contributors

Carolina Armenteros, Santo Domingo, Dominican Republic

Jeffrey D. Burson, Georgia Southern University, USA

Caroline Chopelin-Blanc, Université Jean Moulin-Lyon, France

Gabriel Glickman, University of Warwick, United Kingdom

Mark Goldie, University of Cambridge, United Kingdom

Niccolò Guasti, Università degli Studi di Foggia, Italy

Ulrich L. Lehner, Marquette University, USA

Jerzy Lukowski, University of Birmingham, United Kingdom

Anna Łysiak-Łątkowska, University of Gdańsk, Poland

Massimo Mazzotti, University of California, Berkeley, USA

Thomas O'Connor, National University of Ireland, Maynooth, Ireland

Ritchie Robertson, University of Oxford, United Kingdom

Mario Rosa, Scuola Normale Superiore, Italy

Francisco Sánchez-Blanco, Ruhr-Universität Bochum, Germany

Andrea J. Smidt, Geneva College, USA

Dries Vanysacker, KU Leuven, Belgium

Paola Vismara, Università degli Studi di Milano, Italy

Thomas Wallnig, Universität Wien, Austria

Jonathan A. Wright, University of Durham, United Kingdom

Index

Abraham a Sancta Clara, 234
Adalbert, St., 210
Agnesi, Gaetana Maria, 30, 289–306
Agnesi, Pietro, 289–91
Albani, Giovanni Francesco, 92
Aldrovrandi, Pompeo, 46
Alembert, Jean le Rond d', 75–76, 364–65, 375
Algarotti, Francesco, 52, 300, 305
Andreas of Rinn, 54
Antonelli, Leonardo, 92, 94
Appolis, Émile, 297
Aquinas, Thomas, St., 15–16, 95, 97, 200, 217, 233, 239, 310, 315
Aretin, Karl Otmar von, 6
Argenson, René-Louis de Voyer de Paulmy, Marquis d', 17, 393
Argenvilliers, Clemente, 51
Aristotle, 94, 272, 283, 310–15, 318, 360, 362, 401, 435
Armenteros, Carolina, 29
Arnauld, Antoine, 272
Artico, Giovanni (Count of Porcia), 250
Asclepi, Giuseppe, 361
Astruc, Jean, 414
Augustine, St., 20–21, 24–27, 29–30, 78, 80, 83–84, 89, 95, 131–32, 139, 141, 158, 180, 217, 239, 272, 338, 380, 419

Augustus II, king of Poland, 437
Augustus III, king of Poland, 435, 443

Bacchini, Benedetto, 251, 253, 258
Bacon, Francis, 20, 130, 136–37, 270, 272, 317, 320
Baglivi, Georgio, 315
Bahrdt, Karl Friedrich, 176, 197
Balbo, Cesare, 57
Ballanche, Pierre-Simon, 154–56, 159
Barbauld, Anna, 425
Barbeyrac, Jean, 271
Barlow, Joel, 424–25
Barruel, Augustin, 420
Bassi, Laura, 303–4
Bayle, Pierre, 23, 64, 75, 270, 272, 313
Beales, Derek, 6, 234
Beaumont, Christophe de, 22–23, 50, 68, 73, 79, 110, 376
Beccaria, Cesare, 271, 283
Bell, David, 8
Bellarmine, Robert, 135, 420
Belloni, Girolamo, 51
Benedict XIII (Pietro Francesco Orsini), pope, 402
Benedict XIV (Prospero Lambertini), pope, 41–60, 91, 95–96, 250, 257, 273, 298, 304, 322–23, 355, 361, 437
Benvenuti, Carlo, 361

Bergier, Nicolas-Sylvestre, 16, 29, 63–88, 194
Berington, Joseph, 408, 418
Berington, Simon, 404
Bertrán, Felipe, 328
Bielfeld, Jacob Friedrich, 271
Blake, William, 412, 416
Boisguilbert, Pierre Le Pesant de, 275
Bolingbroke, Henry Saint John, 17, 376, 393, 405–6
Bonaparte, Napoleon, 25, 28–29, 101, 128, 146–47, 161, 426, 459
Borromeo, Charles, 44, 263
Boscovich, Ruggiero (Roger Joseph), 15, 42, 52, 101, 353–69
Boulanger, Nicolas Antoine, 418, 461
Boyle, Robert, 314, 317
Brewer, John Bede, 376
Brichieri Colombi, Domenico, 260
Brienne, Loménie de, 76, 380
Broedersen, Nicolas, 49
Brucker, Jacob, 258
Budde, Johann Franz, 271
Buffier, Claude G., 65, 69, 77, 86, 171
Buffon, Georges Leclerc de, 136, 382, 461
Burigny, Lévêque de, 69
Burke, Edmund, 18, 413, 423, 425–26
Burlamaqui, Jean Jacques, 271
Burnet, Gilbert, 271
Butler, Charles, 408–9, 418
Butterwick, Richard, 27

Cabeo, Niccolo, 362
Cabriada, Juan de, 310
Campanella, Tommaso, 272
Campanelli, Filippo, 92
Campbell, Peter, 8
Campomanes, Pedro Rodríguez de, 328
Cano, Melchior, 270
Caraccioli, Louis-Antoine, 57
Cardano, Girolamo, 272
Cardoso, Isaac, 310

Carducci, Giosuè, 252
Carlo Emanuele IV, Duke of Savoy, 90–91
Cary, John, 275–76
Catherine II "the Great," empress of Russia, 378, 451
Centurione, Alessandro, 361
Challoner, Richard, bishop, 413
Charles of Bourbon, king of Naples and Sicily, 274
Charles III, king of Spain, 24–27, 328–32, 343, 346
Charles XII, king of Sweden, 434
Chateaubriand, François-René, 156, 420
Chatellier, Louis, 6
Chelucci, Paolino, 436
Child, Josiah, 275
Cicero, 377, 394, 416, 450
Cigna, Giovanfrancesco, 90
Clairaut, Alexis, 357
Clarke, Samuel, 170
Clavius, Christopher, 359
Clément of Auxerre, abbé, 51, 330, 335–39
Clement XII (Lorenzo Corsini), pope, 45, 50, 54
Clement XIII (Carlo della Torre Rezzonico), pope, 56, 73, 250
Clement XIV (Lorenzo Ganganelli), pope, 24, 54–56, 91, 336, 343, 456
Climent i Avinent, Josep, 327–49
Cocceius, Johannes, 271
Cochem, Martin, 234
Coghlan, James Peter, 425
Coleridge, Samuel T., 412, 415–16
Collins, Anthony, 193, 271
Comte, Auguste, 29
Condillac, Étienne Bonnot de, 65, 77, 171, 380, 460, 463
Conti, Antonio, 273
Cottret, Monique, 8
Coyer, Gabriel-François, 275

Cudworth, Ralph, 399
Cumberland, Richard, 271
Czacki, Felix, 443, 447
Czacki, Tadeusz, 459
Czartoryski, family of, 447, 449

Dante, Alighieri, 269
Davenant, Charles, 275
Delpiano, Patrizia, 53
Descartes, René, 15–16, 20, 22, 94, 148, 169, 171, 269–72, 298–301, 304, 315, 360
Desing, Anselm, 211
Diderot, Denis, 23–24, 74, 76, 78, 80, 168, 282, 340, 374–75, 377, 380, 404, 418, 461
Dietrichstein, Andreas Jakob von, 261
Dmochowski, Franciszek, 458
Dodd, Charles, 404
Downie, David, 426
Duhamel du Monceau, Henri-Louis, 277
Duns Scotus, John, 217
Durini, Angelo Maria, 91, 450
Dutot, Nicholas, 275

Edling, Anselm, 235
Eichhorn, Johann, 194, 197, 414–15
Engel, Ludwig, 212, 214
Enríquez, Enrique, 262
Erasmus, Desiderius, 20, 394, 396, 416
Everdell, William, 30, 72, 85
Eybel, Joseph Valentin, 98

Fabri, Honoré, 360
Faraday, Michael, 356
Febronius. *See* Hontheim, Johannes Nikolaus von
Feijoo y Montenegro, Benito Gerónimo, 20, 309–26
Fénelon, François de Salignac de la Mothe, 373, 392–98, 400–403, 405–6, 436

Ferreras, Juan de, 312
Fessler, Ignaz-Aurelius (Ignatius), 137, 243
Fitz-James, François de, 47
Fontenelle, Bernard le Bovier de, 42, 52, 197, 317
Forster, Mark, 6
Fraggianni, Niccolo, 273
Franklin, Benjamin, 357
Frederick II "the Great," king of Prussia, 42, 46–47, 52, 236, 407, 437, 450
Frisi, Paolo, 101
Frölich, Wolfgang, 171, 203

Galanti, Giuseppe Maria, 283
Galiani, Celestino, 101, 270, 273, 283
Galiani, Ferdinando, 57, 456
Galilei, Galileo, 94, 251
Garampi, Giuseppe, 92
Gassendi, Pierre, 317
Gay, Peter, 5, 12, 24
Geddes, Alexander, 411–29
Gee, Joshua, 275
Genovesi, Antonio, 19, 187, 269–88
Gerbet, Philippe, 152, 155–56
Gerdil, Giacinto Sigismondo, 89–105
Giannone, Pietro, 278
Glickman, Gabriel, 15
Godwin, William, 425
Goethe, Johann Wolfgang, 229, 232–33
Goguet, Antoine-Yves, 279
Goldie, Mark, 12, 15
Gottsched, Johann Christoph, 221
Grandi, Guido, 101
Grégoire, Henri, 108, 111, 113, 122
Gregory XVI (Bartolomeo Alberto Cappellari), pope, 153, 157
Grimaldi, Francesco, 359
Grotius, Hugo, 212, 271, 405
Gutiérrez de los Ríos, Francisco, 310
Guyon, Madame Jeanne Marie, 392, 400–401

Hanzal, Josef, 221
Hay, George, bishop, 412, 426
Hays, Mary, 425
Heinecke, Johann Gottlieb, 271
Hell, Maximilian, 364
Helvétius, Claude Adrien d', 75, 80, 112, 243, 271, 282, 465
Henegan, David, 384
Hersche, Peter, 6
Hobbes, Thomas, 76, 271, 282, 375, 379–81, 415, 450
Holbach, Baron d', 29, 69–74, 76–80, 83–85, 426
Hontheim, Johannes Nikolaus von (Febronius), 7, 17, 18–19, 24–25, 92–93, 102, 110, 234, 419
Hooke, John, 372
Hooke, Luke Joseph, 187, 371–87
Hooke, Nathaniel, Sr., 372–73
Hooke, Nathaniel, Jr., 372–73, 376–77, 407
Houtteville, Claude-François Alexandre d', abbé, 69
Hsia, R. Po-Chia, 6
Huet, Pierre-Daniel, 16, 69, 197
Hume, David, 80, 169–71, 195–96, 271, 275, 279, 378, 393, 422

Intieri, Bartolomeo, 273–74
Isla, José Francisco de, 321
Israel, Jonathan I., 13, 24, 85

Jezierski, Franciszek S., 458
John Paul II (Karol Józef Wojtyła), pope, 45
Johnson, Joseph, 413, 425
Johnson, Samuel, 357
Joseph I of Portugal, 55
Joseph II, emperor of the Holy Roman Empire, 9, 24–27, 92, 177, 213–23, 228–29, 235–39, 243–44, 261, 419, 421

Kaunitz, Wenzel, 228, 235
Kennicott, Benjamin, 412
Kinsky, Joseph Philipp, 211
Kircher, Athanasius, 359
Klueting, Harm, 6
Kołłątaj, Hugo, 455–71
Konarski, Stanisław (Hieronim), 433–53
Konopczyński, Władysław, 453
Kors, Alan Charles, 85
Kreiser, Robert, 8
Kressel, Franz Karl, von Qualtenberg, 212

Lagrange, Giuseppe Luigi, 90
Lalande, Jérôme de, 364
Lamberg, Johann Philip von, 261
Lambertini. *See* Benedict XIV
Lamennais, Hugues-Félicité Robert de, 145–64
Lamourette, Adrien, 107–23
Lamy, François, 270
Lanze, Carlo Vittorio Amedeo delle, 90, 95
Laplace, Pierre-Simon, 359, 365
Laurens, Henri-Joseph du, 233
Lazzari, Pietro, 362
Le Clerc, Jean, 271
Legipont, Oliver, 211
Lehner, Ulrich L., 19
Leibniz, Gottfried Wilhelm, 94, 135, 157, 169, 251, 271–72, 382, 420
Lemene, Francesco de, 251
Leopold, emperor of Austria (former Grand Duke of Tuscany), 24, 92, 419
Lessing, Gotthold Ephraim, 193–96, 238, 243, 417
Leszczyński, Stanisław, titular king of Poland, 437
Löbl, Benno, 210
Lochstein, Veremund (Peter von Osterwald), 234

Locke, John 10, 15, 16, 22–23, 26, 64, 67, 69, 94–95, 146, 169–71, 200, 236, 270, 271, 272, 283, 346, 374, 379–80, 382, 403, 421, 436
Loisy, Alfred, 57
López de Araujo, Bernardo, 312–15
Louis XIV, king of France, 21–22, 391, 393–94, 397–98, 405–6
Louis XV, king of France, 22, 26, 47, 75, 109, 437
Louis XVI, king of France, 26–28, 426
Louis XVIII, king of France, 109, 130, 147, 150
Lowth, Robert, 412

Mabillon, Jean, 222, 313
Macaulay, Thomas Babington, 57
Machiavelli, Niccolò, 439, 446, 448
Maffei, Scipione, 42, 49, 52
Maggi, Carlo Maria, 251
Magli, Pasquale Arcangelo, 281
Magliabechi, Antonio, 251
Maignan, Emanuel, 312
Maire, Catherine-Laurence, 8
Maire, Christopher, 356
Maistre, Joseph de, 29, 125–43, 149, 157, 187
Małachowski, Stanisław, 458
Malebranche, Nicolas, 19, 22, 94–95, 97–98, 136, 148, 171, 270, 299, 301–2
Malpighi, Marcello, 251
Mandeville, Bernard, 271
Mañer, Salvador José, 319
Manuel de Roda, 328, 343
Maria Theresa, empress of the Holy Roman Empire, 215, 228, 235
Martínez, Martín, 312–17
Masseau, Didier, 30
Mateo Zapata, Diego, 312–13
Maupertuis, Pierre-Louis Moreau de, 52, 271, 282

Maxwell, James Clerk, 356
Maxwell, William, 426
Mayáns y Siscar, Gregorio, 261–62, 318, 328
Mayoral, Andrés, 328
Mayr, Beda, 191–205
McMahon, Darrin, 12, 29, 78
Melon, Jean François, 275
Mendelssohn, Moses, 177–79, 182–83
Menzel, Beda, 214, 220
Mercier, Louis-Sébastien, 240, 378
Merkle, Sebastian, 2–3, 5, 9
Michaelis, Johann David, 194, 417
Milner, John, 420, 426
Mirabeau, Victor Riqueti de, 112, 114–15, 120
Montealegre, José Joaquín, 273
Montelatici, Ubaldo, 274
Montesquieu, Charles-Louis de Secondat, Baron de, 17, 43, 54, 95, 131, 197, 237, 239, 260, 271, 279, 374–75, 384, 440
Morelly, Étienne-Gabriel, 271
Moréri, Louis, 313, 384
Morgan, Thomas, 170, 197, 272
Mosheim, Johann Lorenz, 218
Mothe le Vayer, François, 317
Mozart, Wolfgang Amadeus, 228
Mun, Thomas, 275–76
Muratori, Lodovico (Ludovico) Antonio, 19, 41–42, 48, 52, 211, 214, 223, 249–68, 273, 279, 297–98, 303–4, 436
Muscat y Guzmán, Faustino, 321
Muschenbroek, Peter van, 271–72
Mutschelle, Sebastian, 186

Nájera, Juan de, 312
Naudé, Gabriel, 317
Newton, Isaac, 15–16, 20, 22–23, 94, 100, 102, 171, 270–72, 282–83, 293, 295, 298–301, 355, 374, 379, 382, 385, 391, 399, 404, 460, 463

Nicolai, Friedrich, 233, 241
Nicole, Pierre, 272, 396
Niebuhr, Carsten, 417

O'Connor, Thomas, 10, 15
O'Conor, Charles, 377
Odazi, Troiano, 278
Opstraet, Jean, 216
Orlandi, Giuseppe, 272
Orsi, Giovan Gioseffo, 251

Paciaudi, Paolo, 357
Palanco, Francisco, 311
Paleotti, Gabriele, 44
Palmer, R. R., 10, 82
Paquette, Gabriel, 19
Pascal, Blaise, 146, 148, 195, 338
Pastor, Ludwig von, 57
Patiño, José, 314
Paul VI (Giovanni Battista Montini), pope, 45
Paz, Francisco, 312
Pérez Bayer, Francisco, 328
Peter I "the Great," Czar of Russia, 434
Petrak, Ulrich, 235
Petrasch, Josef, 211
Petre of Thorndon, Robert, 412–13
Petrini, Guiseppe, 303
Petty, William, 275
Pez, Bernhard, 211
Pezzl, Johann, 227–45
Philip V, king of Spain, 20, 25
Piquer, Andrés, 328
Piter, Bonaventura, 211
Pitt, William, 418
Pius VI (Giovanni Angelo Braschi), pope, 28, 56, 91–94, 100, 228, 250
Pius VII (Niccolò Maria Luigi Chiaramonti), pope, 94
Plato, 70, 94, 130–31, 270, 272, 398–400, 416, 440
Platon, Mircea, 29

Plongeron, Bernard, 7–8, 72, 81–82
Plumard, Louis-Joseph, de Dangeul, 275
Poniatowski, Stanisław August, king of Poland, 448–53, 457
Pope, Alexander, 372
Potocki, Ignacy, 458
Prades, Jean-Martin de, 16, 23–24, 55, 69, 374–75, 380, 385
Price, Richard, 425
Priestley, Joseph, 425
Printy, Michael, 28
Pufendorf, Samuel, 212, 271

Querini, Angelo Maria, 258
Quesnay, François, 460

Radicati, Alberto, 238, 243
Ramaggini, Giovanni Giuseppe, 259
Ramsay, Andrew Michael, 373, 391–410
Ranke, Leopold von, 57
Rautenstrauch, Franz Stephan, 209–25
Raynal, Guillaume-Thomas François, abbé, 79, 99, 236
Rey, Marc-Michel, 69
Riccati, Jacopo, 301
Ricci, Scipione de', 92, 261, 419
Riesbeck, Johann Kaspar, 227
Robertson, John, 12, 14
Roche, Juan Luis, 321
Rodríguez, Antonio José, 320
Rollin, Charles, 436
Rosa, Mario, 28, 255, 262
Rosenblatt, Helena, 9
Rotigni, Costantino, 261
Rousseau, Jean-Jacques, 30, 66–71, 75, 81, 83, 97, 99, 128–29, 133, 135–36, 138, 140, 146, 148, 170, 197, 241, 271, 279, 346, 375, 378–80, 382, 393, 426, 461, 465

Sailer, Johann Michael, 170, 186, 191
Saluzzo, Giuseppe Angelo, 90

Sarpi, Paolo, 357
Schiebinger, Londa, 303–4
Schindling, Anton, 6
Schmidt, James, 29
Schneider, Bernhard, 6
Schnürer, Gustav, 5
Segneri, Paolo, the Younger, 257
Seibt, Karl Heinrich, 212, 215, 216
Shaftesbury, Anthony Ashley Cooper, 236, 271, 282
Simpson, Thomas, 357
Sinzendorf, Philipp Ludwig von, 47
Sismondi, Jean-Charles-Léonard Sismonde de, 57
Smidt, Andrea, 19
Smith, Adam, 97, 417
Soli Muratori, Gianfrancesco, 249
Sonnenfels, Joseph von, 242
Sorkin, David, 9, 11
Soto y Marne, Francisco de, 320
Southcott, Thomas, 397, 404
Spallanzani, Lazzaro, 101
Spedalieri, Nicola, 29
Speransky, Mikhail, 136–37, 139
Spinelli di Fuscaldo, Giuseppe, 273
Spinoza, Benedict (Baruch), 13, 17, 22, 76, 80, 243, 271, 374, 385, 415, 450
Stattler, Benedict, 167–89, 194, 195, 198–200, 203, 386
Strayer, Brian, 8
Stuart, Charles Edward ("The Young Pretender"), 393, 403, 423
Stuart, James Frances Edward ("The Old Pretender"), 401–3
Suárez, Francisco, 212
Sydenham, Thomas, 315
Sykes, Arthur Ashley, 271

Talbot, James, 418–19, 426
Tamburini, Fortunato, 51, 256
Tamburini, Pietro, 98
Tanucci, Bernardo, 277

Tencin, Pierre Guérin de, 55
Thomasius, Christian, 181, 271
Throckmorton, John Courtenay, 408
Tillotson, John, 259
Tindal, Matthew, 16, 170
Toland, John, 271–72
Torres Villarroel, Diego de, 317
Trinci, Cosimo, 277
Tronchón, Marcos, 320
Trouillet, Joseph de, abbé, 63–64, 74, 79, 82–85
Troyer, Ferdinand Julius von, 259, 261

Ulloa, Bernardo de, 275–76
Uztáriz, Gerónimo, 275–76

Van Kley, Dale, 7, 8, 28, 131
Vater, Johann Severin, 414–15
Vauban, Sébastien Le Preste de, 275
Vico, Giambattista, 270, 279, 461
Vincent de Gournay, Jacques-Claude-Marie, 275–76
Vittorio Amedeo III, 91, 93–94, 96, 101
Vittorio Emanuele I, 90
Voltaire, 24, 42–43, 54–55, 64, 66, 75, 83, 196, 197, 221, 235–36, 238, 243, 250, 271, 330, 340, 378, 393, 403, 418, 450, 461

Wake, William, 407
Walker, Augustine, 403
Walpole, Horace, 52, 406
Wangermann, Ernst, 238
Weiß, Ulrich, 211
Welch, Thomas, 404
Whiston, William, 271
Wieland, Christoph Martin, 232–33
Wolff, Christian, 15–16, 19, 167–74, 185–86, 198, 200, 211, 219, 221, 227, 271, 272
Wollstonecraft, Mary, 413, 425
Woolston, Thomas, 271

Zaccaria, Antonio, 92, 99
Zelada, Francesco Saverio de, 92
Ziegelbauer, Magnoald, 211
Zinke, Othmar, 210

Zippe, Augustin, 219–20
Zola, Giuseppe, 98
Zucchi, Niccolo, 359

www.ingramcontent.com/pod-product-compliance
Lightning Source LLC
Chambersburg PA
CBHW071135300426
44113CB00009B/980